Comparative Economic Systems

PREINDUSTRIAL AND MODERN CASE STUDIES

Comparative Economic Systems

Preindustrial and Modern Case Studies

MANUEL GOTTLIEB

PROFESSOR OF ECONOMICS EMERITUS
UNIVERSITY OF WISCONSIN-MILWAUKEE

IOWA STATE UNIVERSITY PRESS / AMES

© 1988 Iowa State University Press, Ames, Iowa 50010

Composed by Iowa State University Press
Printed in the United States of America

First edition, 1988

Library of Congress Cataloging-in-Publication Data

Gottlieb, Manuel.
    Comparative economic systems.

    Bibliography: p.
    Includes index.
        1. Comparative economics—Case studies.
I. Title.
HB90.G665   1988   330   88-2764
ISBN 0-8138-0297-0

Contents

Preface, **vii**

1. The Concept of an Economic System, **3**
   Introduction, 3
   Modes of Production, 3
   Hybrid and Multiple Modes, 17
   Role of State and Public Economy, 20
   Institution of Money, 22
   Institution of Property, 27
   Conclusion, 29

2. The Imperial Redistributive Systems:
   T'ang China and the Late Roman Empire, **30**
   Introduction, 30
   Modes of Production Compared, 35
   Institution of Property, 39
   Institution of Money, 40
   Cultural System Components, 42
   State Regulation and Taxation, 47
   Income Redistributive Patterns, 51

3. The European Medieval Economies, **54**
   Bounds of the Medieval, 54
   The Roman Catholic Church, 55
   Economic Foundations of the Church, 57
   Institution of Money, 61
   Modes of Production, 64
   Innovation in Agriculture, 68
   Mining and Transportation Invigorated, 71
   The Bourgeois Town, 72
   Public Economy, 75
   Feudal Property, 81
   Bourgeois Property, 85
   Medieval Economic Systems, 87

4. The Mercantilist Economic System, **89**

Introduction, 89
Expansion of Europe, 89
Productive Forces Flourishing, 93
Cyclical Instability, 95
Agricultural Depressions, 96
Agricultural or General Depressions, 99
French Agriculture, 101
Economic Stagnation, 101
Modal Complex of the Mercantilist Economy, 106
Industrial Revolution, 108
Inflation Problem, 117
State Leadership in Economic Growth, 119

5. The Capitalist Economic System:
United Kingdom, Mid–Nineteenth Century, **122**

Introduction, 122
Bounds of British Economy, 123
Modal Complex, 126
Hybrid Modes, 133
Allocation of Labor to Modes, 136
Functional Priorities, 139
Property, Money, and Regulation, 140
Public Debt and Taxation, 145
Agrarian Protection, 146
The Poor House, 148
Slavery and Sugar, 152
Irish Famine, 155
British Capitalist Economy and Multinational Capitalism, 160

6. The Mixed Economy, **166**

Introduction, 166
Decolonization, 169
Modal Complex, 172
Dichotomization, 181
Democratization of Work, 186
Progressive Taxation, 195
Regulation, 206
Agriculture Control, 208
Stability and Full Employment, 214
Mixed Economy and Friedmanism, 224

7. The Socialist Economy, **226**

Commanding Heights, 226
Communist Party Dictatorship, 229
A Socialist Regime? 235
Growth Planning, 237
The Socialist Ruling Class, 248
Mass Education and Class Structure, 251
The Chinese Cultural Revolution, 253
Yugoslav Breakaway, 255
Agricultural Modes of Production, 259
Drive for Collectivization, 264
Collectivization in China, 266
Collectivization in Eastern Europe, 269
Rationing and Markets, 273
The "Documentary" Economy, 276

Notes, **281**

Bibliography, **351**

Index, **379**

Preface

This book provides the reader with a set of case studies of comparative economic systems. Nearly equal space is allotted to preindustrial as to modern systems. Preindustrial selections commence with a study of early empires possessing an extended state structure and embracing a diversity of societies, peoples, and modes of production. The particular imperial systems chosen for review were narrowed down to two: the Late Roman Empire in the fourth to sixth centuries A.D. and the T'ang phase of the classical Chinese Empire.

The general characteristics of the medieval family of systems prevailing in Western and Central Europe between the sixth and fifteenth centuries A.D. is examined next. Most of these systems involve a loosely articulated state structure; a predominant feudal mode of production in agriculture; a predominant simple commodity mode of production in urban trade and crafts; an increasingly powerful guild organization of town government led by merchants; and a powerful priestly network, hierarchically organized, charged with the vital functions of education, ministry to the poor and sick, and conduct of religious services. Preindustrial systems are analyzed in a chapter on mercantilist systems involving a much later historical period in Western and Central Europe, the sixteenth through eighteenth centuries. These systems embody a well-defined state power; a developed capitalist mode of production in wholesale trade, finance, mining and woolen textiles; overseas expansion; technological virtuosity; and an energetic state regulatory and guiding policy.

This book also deals with more contemporary systems. It contains a detailed case study of the mid–nineteenth century British capitalist system. That chapter is followed by one bearing the opaque label "Mixed Economy," denoting systems that have evolved in the many advanced capitalist economies and have taken shape around the middle decades of this century. That evolution, it is argued, has produced a pattern of systems quite different from those exhibited by the capitalist economies a century or so earlier. Differences are found in the patterns of modes of production, the role of the state and of the public economy, priorities in resource allocation, patterns of income distribution, and in the institutions of money and property. The last chapter deals with the socialist economies, which run quite a range of variation in different phases of their evolution.

These case studies draw upon a notion of an economic system spelled out by the author in *A Theory of Economic Systems* (1984). Economic systems were there presented in terms of three main ingredients:

1. A set of modes of production or forms of production organization
2. The regulatory and redistributive role of the state and of its tax system and public economy
3. Some form of the two major economic institutions: money and property

Certain subjects treated at length in the earlier work are not repeated. Thus the general characteristics of modes of production spelled out in the earlier work without regard to any particular historical setting are here presupposed. The various stages assumed by the evolution of money were traced in *A Theory of Economic Systems.* In this work the general forms of money are presupposed, and we treat only the way money was used or shaped in a particular system or family of systems under review. The 1984 study also provided a general review of the assets touched by the institution of property, the balance effectuated by control and beneficial use, patterns of inheritance, and how the institution of property was shaped by law and moulded by class interest. This work will treat only the specific forms of property salient in a particular economic system.

Though a diverse range of economic systems deployed over a wide field of history and cultural diversity are dealt with here, I by no means deal with all economic systems. The two imperial preindustrial systems reviewed – the Late Roman and T'ang Empires – are merely examples of a broad class with quite divergent makeup. The reader might think differently about these imperial systems had the selection for treatment been the Mogul Empire in the subcontinent of India of the seventeenth century contrasted with either the Ottoman Empire of the same century or the much earlier Carolingian Empire of Charlemagne. The British capitalist economy of the mid–nineteenth century was no duplicate of the politically and socially unstable French capitalist economy that matured in the same century.

Likewise, I have not made a presentation of the Third World economies that by number and population prevail in the contemporary world, dominating the continents of Africa, Southeast Asia, and South and Central America. Generalization about the Third World is especially perilous because its societies are extremely diverse. At one pole are the petro-states of the Persian Gulf and elsewhere that have taken control of gas and oil resources, shaping a working partnership with the great Western oil multinationals and achieving a degree of monopoly control of petroleum world markets bringing great riches to petro-state rulers. At the other pole are impoverished societies practicing subsistence agriculture with hoe culture and in rural areas with food and water often carried on the woman's head. Social and economic conditions in Latin America diverge from those found in southeast Asia or in the Near East. Newly independent island societies with a few hundred thousand persons and with little or no mechanical industry have a potential for development quite different from settled societies with ancient cultural traditions and a differentiated class structure. My interest in Third World societies and economies is keen ever since I spent two years (1971–1973) in East Africa as research professor at the University of Dar Es Salaam, and I have expressed my views on critical Third World issues growing out of my African experience (see Gottlieb 1984, 422). But the experience and problems of East Africa are hardly typical. Hence I defer treatment of Third World economies until it is feasible to undertake the required extended research and study.

Economic systems are reviewed in this book in a stable state, generally that of full maturity. No attempt is made to trace system beginnings or demise or gradual transformation. What is delineated is a cross section of a historically matured system in a delimited time frame, some by decades, others by half-centuries. It is presupposed that the older systems portrayed have exhibited their full development and thus have achieved a significant degree of closure. In this crucial respect this work differs profoundly from the typical monograph by an economic historian. These usually attempt a fuller portrayal of historical change often encompassing a succession of economic systems phasing into each other without any suggestion of system closure or maturity. Although a history of economic systems is not contemplated, I have drawn upon economic historians extensively. As principal students of earlier economic systems, their writings make up the main source materials for all except contemporary systems in which source materials such as debates, records, statistics, and government reports are readily available.

The search for a mature system in a steady state is not too difficult when applied to older systems that can be portrayed from the perspective of hindsight. But it becomes complicated when applied to contemporary systems that have not achieved system closure. Thus socialist economic systems are still in a process of development; where this process will end is by no means certain. In the presentation of one socialist economy, Yugoslavia, I have noted that this system is evolving in a direction that has gone beyond the principles and institutions of a socialist economy as set forth in this work (see pp. 255–59). A related process of evolution is at work in the Peoples Republic of China, though the process has not gone as far as in Yugoslavia and the system may stabilize in its present form. In this form it is possible to reconcile central planning of investment growth and socialist industrial organization with emphasis on market process and competition as guiding principles of economic life. But Chinese leaders are clearly contemplating more extensive moves in the market process that would allow enterprises and local institutions fuller use of market surpluses. All this would jeopardize price stability and undermine central control of investment growth planning.

In the treatment of the mixed economy—another contemporary economic system whose roots go back to the early decades of the twentieth century—I had certain problems about setting the terminal period for my portrayal. The decade of the seventies was marked by two structural changes: (1) the demonetization of gold and the breakdown of the Bretton Woods system of fixed exchange parities, and (2) the emergence of OPEC oil monopoly that generated a massive wave of inflation and drastically altered the international distribution of income. I decided to treat the mixed economy only up to and partly through the seventies. This terminal period did not attest to a belief that the mixed economy as a form of economic life was then terminated or was being undermined. At that point in the writing I felt sure that a certain phase of its evolution had been reached and that it was too early to evaluate the structural processes of adjustment and adaptation that could be expected to work their way in the Western world and throughout the entire world economy. (Gottlieb 1984, 338).

In the American scene these processes of adjustment and adaptation were soon joined to the more revolutionary structural change in the American form of mixed economy gradually put in place by the Reagan counterrevolution, as it has been called (Tobin 1981). These structural changes can hardly be so widespread or complete as to erase the social evolution of a century and return to the simpler economic arrangements of the nineteenth century capitalist economy, however fervently desired. But I was mistaken in my expressed doubt that "this conservative tide can long be maintained" (Gottlieb 1984, 410). That tide is now well entrenched in the American political economy. The entire tone of thought about economic policy in ruling circles has shifted markedly to the Right. The industrial base of the American working class and the primary home of its militant trade unionism is being liquidated by the decline of American industry and widespread loss of foreign and domestic markets. Progressive income taxation has been drastically curtailed with the top income tax rate returned near the level reached under Herbert Hoover sixty years ago. The fiscal potential of the American economy for the support of social programs, for essential public works, and for environmental protection has been undermined by the threefold process of tax-reduction, the rearmament boom that has virtually turned the American industrial economy into a socially impoverished war economy, and the accumulated and unexampled budget deficits that are mortgaging an increasing fraction of our diminished tax revenue. The U.S. Congress nearly adopted by the requisite two-thirds majority of each house an amendment to the Constitution that would have inscribed Milton Friedman's conservative macroeconomics as an ironclad guide to fiscal and monetary policy.

All this does not signify the destruction of the mixed economy as a social form but only that for some time to come its vigor in the North American scene (Canada of course excepted) will be impaired. The "stabilizing and interventionist policies of government" of which I spoke so warmly (Gottlieb 1984, 410) will for an extended period be largely a memory. All this will probably accentuate the differentiation between two variant forms of the mixed economy. At one pole is a social-democratic variant with an enlarged public sector, a strong central bank, a moderate armament sector, and a progressive tax and social security system. At the other pole is the U.S. variant with its swollen corporate mode dominating both the economy and key positions in the public sector, perpetually seeking to suppress radical Third World revolts, crippled by its heritage of Reagan debt and by higher interest rates and with little ability or will to direct its own course (see hints on this differentiation in Gottlieb 1984, 168).

The sources used throughout this work are mostly secondary, especially for earlier centuries where few reliable quantitative records with general applicability have survived and have been put in usable form by archivists or historically minded statisticians. Thus my analysis of church tithing had to be content with broad estimates of yields and with uncertain knowledge about rates of levy until the fifteenth century. The precise beginnings of tithing instituted by law are for most European countries shrouded in obscurity. Only for the last two centuries have local time series for tithe collections in certain jurisdictions been worked out chiefly by the extensive tithe research instigated by Emmanuel Le Roy Ladurie. For England our most complete knowledge about tithes comes from the investigations that in the early nineteenth century terminated the traditional institution of the tithe (Chap. 3, Chap. 4, App.).

In the chapter on mercantilist systems I tried to make sense out of an immense amount of poorly organized data drawn from original field records of crop yields collected over several centuries with only broad general conclusions indicated (Chap. 4). I have critically reviewed contentions by certain scholars that the mercantilist period lived through the Kondratieff process of "long waves" or "agrarian depressions." I found those contentions unproven by what statistical data properly interpreted can be adduced (Chap. 4). I have prepared estimates of the distribution of the occupied labor force for the United Kingdom by modes of production and by industrial or service divisions (Chap. 5, Table 1). I regret that I could not use or rely very much upon the unusual cliometric research purporting to show why Ireland starved in the 1846–1850 Great Famine (Chap. 5).

A word to critics expected to cluster in three groups: contemporary (Friedmanite) economic theory, standard Marxism, and Wallerstein world systemitis. Devotees of modern economics will be shocked at my loose methodology—seeking to write economic analysis in literary language rather than with regression coefficients and statistical tables and graphs. They will complain that I still seem to believe in the efficacy of Keynsian stabilization economics, that even price control is not abjured, and that I seem to argue that centrally planned socialist economies can deliver impressive results. Marxists will be shocked at my eccentric notion of modes of production—a sacred Marxist concept I apply pragmatically to different forms of production organization. They will lament that I even consider the postal service in a capitalist state as a "public mode of production," that I don't portray depressions and wage earner's real living standards as getting worse, and that I am foolish enough to argue that most former colonies have become emancipated from colonial controls.

The much smaller cult of Wallerstein disciples believe that any analysis of Western systems since the sixteenth century short of "world economies" misapprehends reality, that the international division of income is and has been governed by vaguely stated exploitation relations between ill-defined "core," "peripheral," and "semi-peripheral" areas. I can only counter that in the economic systems treated in this work the great bulk of the income received, wealth produced, and services rendered arises *within* the systems concerned from productive efforts, entrepreneurial and artisan skills, and capital accumulated and applied *within* those systems. Moreover I have taken account of the way in which system behavior has been affected by trading relationships with other economic systems and so-called "peripheral" areas (for example, my treatment of "overseas expansion," regulatory trade policy, and slavery, Chap. 4; my treatment of West Indies slavery and sugar, of slave trade, of near genocide in Ireland, Chap. 5). International trade is not under ordinary conditions a zero-sum game in which the benefits of one trading party are matched by corresponding losses or disabilities of the other trading party. The benefits or as they are termed in economic theory, the "gains" of trade, are by no means evenly apportioned out even under ideal conditions of competitive process, bargaining power, and market access. But it would be a very special case indeed if one trading party would receive zero benefits of trade or sustained losses for long periods of time when alternative use of resources was available and when production and trading decisions of the trading parties were substantially independent of each other. Yet that special case or something closely approximating it is presupposed by the Wallerstein school.

The reader of this work may be assisted by a preliminary comment about certain peculiarities of my use of language. The reader will soon note that as a general rule I shy away from use of the term "capitalism" as a descriptive label for an economic system. I do append the label "capitalist system" to a certain class of economic system more restrictively defined than is commonly found (Chap. 5). Given those restrictions, use of that label was appropriate in application to the United Kingdom in the decades centering around 1850. And since the political culture, ethos, mentality, and even the social philosophy of the society concerned was fully integrated with and adjusted to the economic system, some use of the larger term "capitalism" was suitable. My primary concern is however the capitalist economy that must be undergirded by behavior and relationships found only in the capitalist mode of production. Hence throughout this work where other thinkers and writers would talk about or point to capitalism at work, I point to or expound upon the working of the "capitalist mode of production."

The trouble with the term capitalism is that it is difficult to define and use in some ordered context. The wider the area and the longer the period of time over which capitalism is alleged to prevail, the looser the definition and the more capitalism is reduced to an attitude of mind, a condition of spiritual blight that can only be subjectively apprehended in Braudel's words as a "shadowy zone hovering above the unlit world of the market economy" (Braudel 1979–1982, 1:24; 3:628). May serious social science be spared such phantoms.

The writing of this book has been influenced by circumstances that have left some traces upon it. The book has been worked upon and written discontinuously and in spurts through much of this decade.

Yet discontinuous writing and research have some advantages. There is more time to correct first impressions, repeated study of the subject from recent publications brings new insights, and old drafts lose their glamour and may be readily purged and tightened. But transitions to new viewpoints are sometimes discontinuous. More hampering is the analysis of that part of our subject matter—the mixed economy and the socialist economy—that in this decade have been subject to dramatic change effecting a transformation with uncertain bounds, depths, or lasting quality. I clearly did not want to attempt from my closeted study any very contemporaneous review and recording of a tumultuous flux of events. Yet the transformations were too significant and awesome in their consequences to be totally excluded. Hence here and there the reader will find anticipations or asides touching on developments falling outside the time-span properly covered by this work. Formally that time-span was precisely delimited for the mixed economy with an upper boundary of the late 1970s. For the socialist economy no formal upper boundary was assigned but there was general exclusion of the Gorbachev regime and in China to the post-Mao regime except its early beginnings. Hence, here and there in the last two chapters of this work in the treatment of contemporary developments the reader will find intimations or, as I have just termed, asides, for which logical or empirical foundations have not been laid but which seemed appropriate in the context and which I hope even the exacting reader may appreciate.

Thanks are owed and are here expressed to those who in ways large and small helped me in writing this book and preparing it for publication: William H. Halloran, Dean, College of Letters and Sciences, University of Wisconsin-Milwaukee, for special arrangements to provide secretarial and typing assistance; Frank P. Zeidler who enthusiastically read and offered helpful comments on the final chapters of this book; Dee Alexander and Arlene Handrich for their careful typing of the manuscripts; the editorial staff of the Iowa State University Press and especially its manuscript editor, Suzanne Lowitt, who discharged their editing duties with great skill and care; the chairman of the Economics Department of the University of Washington who kindly arranged with the college authorities that I be issued a "Visiting Scholar Identification Card" which greatly facilitated use of library resources; my wife, Margaret R. Gottlieb, who displayed endless patience in reading and editing preliminary draft versions, in proofing galleys and page proofs, and who prodded me into recognition of some of the deficiencies which she managed to detect no matter how artfully I had smoothed them over; Elizabeth R. Kohlenberg for her warmhearted encouragement of this effort and her keen critique of its embodiment in manuscript; and three publishers – Academic Press, Orlando Florida; the Editorial Board of African Review, University of Dar Es Salaam, Tanzania; Cambridge University Press, Cambridge England – who granted permission to cite copyrighted passages from their publications.

MANUEL GOTTLIEB

Seattle, Washington
June 1988

Comparative Economic Systems

PREINDUSTRIAL AND MODERN CASE STUDIES

1

The Concept of an Economic System

Introduction

The purpose of this book is to provide sketches of major historical economic systems, illustrating their wide variety and divergent makeup. The conceptual scheme that defines an economic system as presupposed in these sketches is spelled out in an earlier (1984) work entitled *A Theory of Economic Systems*. In this chapter I will summarize the salient features of that conceptual scheme, omitting the extended argument, detailed analysis, and illustrative materials found in the 1984 monograph.

Unlike most works with the same or similar title, I shall treat not only modern and contemporary systems but earlier systems of preindustrial society. I do not, however, seek to analyze or review economic systems of primitive or archaic societies. My reference is rather to historic economic systems involving societies with literacy at least among the elite of the society, a widespread scheme of writing, settled agriculture, use of iron and bronze, and the formal emergence of coined precious metals as money.

Modes of Production

A major ingredient in our concept of an economic system is the mode of production, that is, methods or schemes of production organization including the way production activities are directed and guided, the way producers are motivated to achieve their tasks and are related to each other and to their means of production, and the way these means are assembled, controlled, and utilized by entrepreneurship. For purposes of comparative systems study, these modes are formulated in broad terms to draw under a single class economic organizations sharing the most essential characteristics but differing in many important respects. Thus we include in a single mode all peasant proprietors who own all or the larger part of their farm fields and implements, provisions, and livestock, and who operate their farms primarily by family labor. This groups together modern mechanized New World farmers using highly industrialized techniques on large acreages, small horticultural farms scattered round compactly settled villages using hoe culture and intensive hand labor, and classical scattered strip diversified general farms of Central and Eastern Europe yielding very limited crop surpluses. So also under the capitalist mode of production we include wholesale traders of antiquity moving their goods by animal caravan or sailing ships, operating in competitive-type markets on a profit and loss basis, and depending to a major degree on hired or indentured labor.

Though the term mode of production is Marxian, the term is here used with a narrower compass than in Marx's own work and without implication of historical succession. Hence we have uncovered more distinct modes of production with more historic spread than Marx pointed to or than Marxists generally recognize.[1] Our list of eleven modes is presented here with an abbreviated sketch of defining features. An exposition of these is found in three chapters (2–4) of the previously cited work (Gottlieb 1984).

1. *Domestic Mode of Production.* This is the forerunner of all modes since it is the means of providing food and shelter and otherwise maintaining life among so-called primitive peoples. This mode was organized not only around the household but also the clan or tribal kinship group, which provided by collective labor for many of its needs. Products and services within the domestic mode are designed not for sale but for use within the household or kinship group. Much of this activity survives in historical economic systems intermingled with or supplementing newer modes. Thus even in modern society with its widespread specialization much of the business of life is still conducted in or around the household with little guidance, except in limiting cases, from the money calculus or the intermediation of exchange relationships. Here is where most children are raised and nurtured, where the sick are often cared for, where food is prepared for eating and where most meals are served, and where parties and social gatherings are still accommodated. The home is where clothing is repaired, laundered, and stored for use. The home is where most sexual satisfaction,

a prime need and poorly provided for in the marketplace, is fulfilled. Moreover, a host of supportive activities in the home's natural environment of field, garden, forest, or waters yields the delights of hunting, gardening, and fishing that still furnish food for the table. The woodlot still provides fuel for the wood stove or fireplace and healthy exercise to boot. The domestic mode may even assist in erecting the dwelling. It often provides for interior decoration and finishing, and it commonly provides for simpler kinds of building maintenance and repair. The domestic mode draws much of its equipment from more advanced modes. It may be cramped or undermined by greater density of land settlement and the rise of large cities and enclosures of common lands. The mode is facilitated by improvements in transportation that bring it in touch with fresh waters and wood life. The mode draws strength from the rising standard of living and greater amounts of leisure that industrialization, generated by other modes, has brought.

In my 1984 study, this mode was recognized chiefly as a provider of *services* within the household where it was governed by the form of the family and marriage institutionalized within a given society. I did not then perceive its still continuing role in provisionment of food, shelter, and recreation, and its agency in enabling modern man to live more closely attuned to a natural environment. Hence I propose in this work to make up for the "deficiency," as it was labeled, of leaving untreated the role of household production (Gottlieb 1984, 11–12). The immediate stimulus for correcting this deficiency was reading of a quite remarkable doctoral dissertation (Emmanuel 1981). Drawing on suggestions I had made (Gottlieb 1976), Emmanuel suggested the existence of a "petty building mode" that participates in the work of building a home for household use, provides most of its maintenance and upkeep, and provides the capital and entrepreneurship (Emmanuel 1981, Chap. 2). The mode, however, is not properly speaking a "petty building mode" but the "household mode of production" with a major field of operation in the provision, design, and care for owner-occupied housing. I became aware of Emmanuel's work only after this work was completed. Hence only here and there could some appreciation of the important role of this mode both in early and contemporary economic systems be worked into my text.[2]

2. *Village Community.* This is a close-knit village of farming families usually with garden plots adjoining or close to their homes, yards, and barns, surrounded by large open unfenced fields, usually allocated into small narrow strips owned and worked by individual families but farmed according to a common and jointly arranged scheme of cultivation and harvesting. Outside or interspersed with arable fields will be wastelands, woodlots, pasture plots, and adjoining forest regulated by

the village community. In some societies the community periodically reallocates land among village families according to need and usage. Irrigation facilities will nearly always be organized and managed on a common village basis. The village will have its officers and in some cases village employees for whom special forms of compensation are provided. The village community is a very early form of agriculture whose distinctive features were rubbed out in the more advanced societies, but it has survived in some areas through to the twentieth century (Georgescu-Roegen 1976, Chap. 8).

3. *Direct Commodity Producers.* This mode of production involves ownership of the means of production (land, tools, inventories, and buildings) by merchant, artisan, farmer, or professional practitioner who applies in his or her work a skill or art only gradually learned and directs the work of the enterprise. Family members provide most or much of the labor required. The direct commodity producers sell for money in a commodity market a variable part of the product, more in the case of the merchant or craftsman or professional, and less in the case of the farmer. The character of the direct commodity producer is undermined if over the lifetime of the enterprise he or she becomes dependent for essential work on hired labor and is thus metamorphosed into a capitalist producer. The principle subtypes of this mode are: *farmers, ranchers, and gardeners* whose tilled fields or pastures provide for their main subsistence and yield a surplus for markets; *dealers in moneys or commodities* who own shops, strongboxes, inventories, or transport vehicles, and who both buy and sell or lend and borrow; *service practitioners* who have acquired rare and valuable skills and with the aid of special equipment have learned to render valuable services of instruction, healing, entertainment, notarizing or letter writing, repair, design, litigation, singing, storytelling or dramatic performance; *artisans, builders, and miners* who produce or design useful products. The direct commodity producer was described by Marx as "the economic foundation of society during the best period of classical antiquity" in the Graeco-Roman world. In medieval society the direct commodity producer as artisan, dealer, and professional played a powerful role in the organization of the town economy that was based on the autonomous organization of guilds. The direct commodity producer remains an important subsidiary mode in nineteenth and twentieth century Western economies and in the form of peasant proprietor plays an important role in the socialist economies of our day.

4. *Slave Mode.* The slave mode of production was widely distributed in the ancient, medieval, and modern world. It has held a significant place in economies up through the first decade of this century with widespread geographical appearance in nearly all continents. It

involves an expropriation of autonomous personality and total dependence upon a master who controls jobs and working conditions; domestic arrangements including mating and disposition of children; furnishing of goods or supplies for food, clothing, and other consumption. He may at will administer or direct corporal punishment. By artful use and admixture of negative and positive sanctions – rewarding approved behavior and sharply punishing disapproved behavior – a maximum of exploitation can be achieved with a minimum of consumption by the slave and his family habituated to subsist on simple and utilitarian foods, shelter, clothing. Since the slave mode involves ready access to sexual exploitation, it flourished in many societies in domestic service as household drudgery or concubinage. More commonly it extends to labor in fields, mines, or galleys when boats in open waters needed men to labor at oars when suitable wind power was not available. The slave mode has in many economies been extended to urban craft shops and offices or, as in some periods of Turkish Muslim society, to army barracks and to the state service where the slave tends to be transformed into a state ruling class. Slavery persists best when a clear ethnic line separates master and slave, though sometimes variation of dialect, habitual diet, absence of schooling, and rough clothing can draw a sufficient line so that inferior status will be accepted by master and slave alike. The nemesis of the slave mode is that it discourages reproduction. The complete psychological subjection, the lack of freedom in domestic relations with kith and kin, the disappearance of self-respect, and often the barracks discipline where male slaves are cooped up in guarded enclosures does not encourage mating and child nurture. Reproduction, too, is hampered by a tendency to utilize female slaves in household service and concubinage whereas male slaves are reserved for field, mining, or galley labor where brute strength is at a premium. Often, too, there is a disparity in sexual balance in the slave population, sometimes leaning strongly toward female slaves, as in the day when enemy males, elderly persons, and children were killed and only suitable females were reserved for slavery. At other times male captives were at premium, and it would not pay to enslave females or children because their working capacity would be too limited, especially if quick payoff was required to compensate for high costs of carriage as with slavery in the New World.

5. *Feudal Mode.* The inability of the slave mode to exploit without at the same time hampering reproduction and the ideological resistance of the human spirit to the complete subjection of slavery necessarily leads to intermediate forms of exploitation such as the feudal and peon modes. The feudal mode embodies a set of social relations permitting a high degree of exploitation by methods of coercive control

that widen the laborer's scope for independent decision making. It endows him with possessory rights over a subsistence holding of land and an outfitting of farm and household tools and livestock that he can use for his own benefit or market after paying the necessary dues to his master. It permits him a measure of organization often as village community, and it vests the laborer with responsibility for making a household and arranging for his marriage and upkeep of his children.

This measure of freedom and rights is in turn matched with controls ensuring constant obedience and acceptance of an inferior status. The serf is obligated to give to the master a high fraction of his total product by delivery of surplus produce; enforced labor service on the master's own fields and labor in his manor house or cartage of his produce; payment of money fines and dues collected on various grounds that usually include use of pasturage, use of mills, and other community production facilities; fines assessed for violation of manorial regulations and customs; and the privilege of marriage of his children or family succession. In some arrangements the village fields are interspersed with the master's field allowing him or his agents a ready enforcement of their claim on service. In other forms of the feudal mode little labor is enforced but a huge fraction of the harvest of tilled ground, of standing trees, or of livestock is taken by the master and collected as a tax or rent. This unequal exchange is fortified by a fearful preponderance of force habitually exhibited by masters to intimidate and impose their rule. The master's headquarters is often well barricaded. His armed soldiers, often mounted and closely tied to him by economic and social privileges, are authorized to inflict violence virtually at will. Villagers in turn are denied arms or they are entitled to handle only the simplest weapons without protective shielding. Villagers are unable to gather in large assemblies. They are often sworn to fealty or obedience including the paying of necessary dues and fees and recognition of the master's claim to ownership of his home and fields. Often, too, they may not move away from the village without the master's permission. Feudal modes are found in different cultures and societies — in Western Europe from the seventh to the twelfth or thirteenth centuries, in Eastern Europe up to modern times, in Islam especially in the Ottoman Empire, in India, in Japan and China, and in Latin America under Indian masters and later under Spanish and Portuguese settlers and conquistadors. They vary widely in the features of their makeup, in the harshness with which social subordination is enforced, in the ready use of violence, in habits of consultation to obtain the good will and collaboration of villagers. Yet common to all forms of the feudal mode is control by a master class of the local apparatus of government, appropriation of the village surplus of food and fiber, obtaining a full range of local services with little or no compensatory payment, and claiming ultimate authority over use of land and resources. The serf is generally permitted local organization either as a village community under leadership of his own choosing or by council automatically made up of elders of the leading families, and he has immediate disposition of his household arrangements and of his own immediate work. A tendency to struggle against the master is inherent in feudal modes. Under favorable conditions especially where the will to power of masters is abated, or where absentee ownership is widespread and master interests are delegated to agents, or where brutal forms of violence are avoided, serf pressures and protests and field resistance by ca'canny or sabotage or money purchase may work its way.

6. *Peon Mode.* The slave and feudal mode are undisguised forms of class rule and appropriation. Under some cultural conditions that outward form of inequality is no longer feasible or is no longer consistent with the assumption of personal dignity and freedom worked into the culture and enshrined in principles of law and faith. Under those conditions coercion must be more subtly applied by causing the laborer to become saddled with debt and thus to become bonded to his work in an estate or tenant holding until the debt is redeemed. Debt is made up of advances in working capital to commence farming operations or to sustain life until the harvest is reaped from field or stock. Debt may also be incurred to pay taxes imposed by the state. If a low rate of compensation for estate or other work is paid, or if tenant crop shares are sufficiently low, or if merchandise or supplies advanced on a credit basis are booked at a sufficiently high charge, or if accounts are fraudulently compiled — and usually some combination of these is involved — then a standing burden of debt will be accumulated. Peonage results if the debtor is not permitted to leave the estate without discharge of debt and if masters either directly or through local police and government authorities they control will enforce the right of the master to compel a full quota of labor service to discharge the debt. Usually no hereditary disability is visited on offspring who unlike serfs are not bound to the estate. Unlike slaves, peons are not an alienable form of property. Since the kingpin of the coercion arises out of credit advances, the commercial exchange between master and peon becomes critical and merchants sometimes join with estate owners in drawing profit from peonage. The peon mode presupposes a high degree of social subordination of the peon population and often is accompanied by ready infliction of personal violence. The peon mode was the matured form of organization of agricultural, shop, and mining work for the advanced Indian peoples of both tropical lowlands and highland

plateaus of Latin America. When the slave mode in the New World had to be dissolved, it was replaced in the Black Belt of the American South, in Cuba, and elsewhere with some form of peonage. It is also a social form known in pre-1949 China and possibly in the Danubian provinces.

7. *Landlord Mode.* The dissolution of the village community and of the three unfree labor modes frequently leads under certain conditions to a special relatively stable landlord mode. The landlord mode is better adapted to the general conditions of bourgeois society since the mode allows tenants and landlords freedom to negotiate contracts, it gives tenants full mobility so that they can improve their condition by searching for new opportunities, and it permits very hard working and fortunate tenants to accumulate some wealth and eventually join the landlord class. This mode played a significant role in the Late Roman Empire, in northern Italy since the twelfth century, in Ireland in the eighteenth and nineteenth centuries under British rule, in most of Southeast Asia under colonial dominion, in Japan and China in modern times, and in Russia and the United States after the abolition of serfdom and slavery in 1861–1865.

This mode involves a form of peasant proprietorship on small holdings operated and managed by a tenant farmer and his family using only occasional hired labor. The small holdings in land are owned by landlords who make up an essentially parasitic gentry class able to sustain a higher standard of living by collecting rents from tenant farmers either on a cash rental or a sharecrop basis. Terms of sharecropping are negotiated with each tenancy but tend to become stereotyped over broad areas and are relatively slow to change. Cash rentals are usually more favorable to the tenant farmer if he can bear the risks involved and if he is favored by rising trends of farm prices. Neither landowners nor tenants are able or are motivated as a general rule to carry out entrepreneurial improvements in soil management or husbandry. Landlord and tenant tend to share equally or near equally in farm proceeds. The tenant cannot afford to invest time, effort, and resources in improvements, which if successful will so handsomely reward the landlord. The landlord is not entrepreneurially oriented, does not control farm management, and cannot provide the incentives for tenants to modify their husbandry to suit a newer technology financed by the landlord. Hence the tendency of the landlord mode is to neglect the entrepreneurial function and to keep agriculture at a stagnating level of technology.

8. *Capitalist Mode.* The capitalist mode is the most well known of all since both modern and Marxian economic theory has focussed upon it. At the center of this mode is the capitalist enterprise owned and

managed by capitalists provide some or all of the risk capital and who have established and guide the enterprise to achieve business success and the profit it brings. Other participants in the enterprise are passive capitalists who contribute use of their holdings of land or money in exchange for promise of a contractually set return (either as royalty, rent, or interest); workers recruited and assembled for labor service in jobs set up by the capitalist-entrepreneurs and in facilities usually provided by them in return for wages or compensation generally set by the employer when recruiting his work force and adjusted from time to time as the employer finds it expedient. The capitalist enterprise disposes of its product or services to customers from all modes of production. The capitalist enterprise purchases supplies, materials, and necessary services from other capitalist enterprises which provide for each other in an elaborate division of labor. It also procures from other modes of production located within or without the society: from direct commodity producers, feudal lords, landlords and tenants, and slave masters. Profits earned by capitalist enterprise are essentially a residual quantum left over after contractually fixed costs are paid, after the necessary allowances are made for consumption or replacement of invested facilities, and for possible uninsurable liabilities that may have been incurred by past operations. Profits earned are essentially a composite return both on risk capital invested and on entrepreneurial effort with a handsome allowance for willingness to bear uncertainty.

The capitalist enterprise in one field generates and fosters capitalist enterprises in other fields. And a successful capitalist enterprise inevitably encourages others who compete for markets, for labor, and for materials and equipment. It is this mutual competition that brings into existence a zone of mutually acceptable earning levels for different occupations; a market-induced level of land rents based chiefly on differential advantage; and levels of commodity prices that assure a zone of equalized profit return adapted to differential risk, entrepreneurial capabilities, and innovation.

Though the capitalist mode achieved its greatest success in industry where it became almost predominant in advanced Western countries by the end of the nineteenth century, it by no means commences with industry. Its earliest beginnings are probably found in the field of wholesale trade. Already in antiquity the merchant capitalist invested capital in navigable ships, caravans, supply depots, and warehouses holding his inventories. His principal capital was his merchant skill and knowledge of commodities and marketing opportunities. To operate his means of production he and his partners often hired workers or apprentices or agents or purchased slaves. The capitalist merchant organized the markets that in turn sustained his activity. The great international fairs of the medieval epoch are witness to his industry and enterprise.

The second major field for the capitalist mode emerged later in historic time in agriculture where the starting point was feudal production in overlordship of a village community. When this mode dissolves it can form into the landlord mode or degenerate into peonage or a mixture of the two. But it can also turn into capitalist enterprise by two routes. One route not often traveled is for the once feudal lord to turn himself into a landed proprietor and invest not only his resources but himself in the business of farming his estate with the aid of hired workmen. Many English landed proprietors took seriously to farming ventures on their estates and retained a "home farm" under their direct control. The East Prussian Junker was a landowner (*Grundherr*) with aristocratic pretensions who in the eighteenth and nineteenth centuries converted his tenants with their cottage rights into wage laborers on a rationalized farming estate. Capitalist farming enterprises have been built up in many other countries and dominate American cotton cultivation, fruit gardening, and cattle ranching. When capitalist enterprise predominates and leads in either wholesale trade or farming, we may speak of "mercantile" or "agrarian" capitalism.[3]

But in the main the development of capitalist agriculture depended not so much on landed proprietors for entrepreneurship as on able tenant farmers. In England these gradually became an independent class. They gained control of relatively large farms and hired the labor to operate farms under their direction and control. This form of capitalist enterprise based on rented land and the use of relatively sophisticated lease agreements that converted landlords into a kind of business partner assumed its classical form in Great Britain in the eighteenth and nineteenth centuries.

The capitalist mode of production was slow to develop in industry partly due to the tenacious hold of guild organizations on the skilled trades and the prevalence of handicraft technology. The first form of capitalist industrial enterprise was linked to the need to develop deeper and more intricate mining ventures – to use falling waters to drive blast furnaces; grind or crush ores and other work materials; or to use a new fuel, coal, as boiler fuel for industrial operations calling for sustained high temperatures. Once workmen with craft skills were brought together under capitalist control, specialization developed among them. The subdivision of labor in time led, under favorable conditions, to mechanization of production with machines driven by a new source of power using fossil fuels. Though the industrial revolution drew strength from improvements and technologies developed in many European countries and in China, it was perfected in its early phase in England where there was special interest in the natural sciences and in their application to technology, where the power of guild monopolies had been broken, and where entrepreneurial interests were widely cultivated.

Six basic laws of behavior may be formulated for that completed form of the capitalist mode of production Marx called "machinery and modern industry." First, capitalist industrial production is usually associated with high rates of reinvestment of earned profits, ploughed back to serve the needs of expanded reproduction. Second, this process of expanded reproduction is associated with continuous extension of specialization and refinement of technology so that the level of productivity continually increases in a way unknown to previous modes of production. Third, the combination of increasing scale of investment, of widening markets, and changing technology all harnessed to the goal of profit-making with its speculative uncertainties makes the pace of industrial activity and especially of new industrial investment unstable, giving to economic growth a cyclical character. Fourth, the capitalist mode of production is destructive of the life and health of its industrial operatives coping with its harsh, hurried, and dangerous conditions of work and ready tendency to overwork. Equally, this mode of production is destructive of the environment whose ambient air and groundwaters are poisoned with industrial and sanitary wastes while nonarable soil is stripped of its forest cover. Finally, the capitalist mode of production with its excellence of technique gives its greatest service to knowledgeable and informed buyers who know how to exert market pressure and reward good performance. For the average consumer unschooled in modern technology who has neither time nor ability to conduct market research and who is susceptible to the blandishments and trickery of capitalist marketing, the capitalist mode of production can be damaging because of product adulteration, cheapening of quality, and use of dangerous chemicals or materials.

9. *Corporate Mode.* The matured quasi-public corporation resembles the capitalist enterprise in many respects. They both invest capital, employ wage labor, and dispose of their product for profit. They both arrange their own marketing and regulate their rate of production to what customers decide to buy. They both tend, in the absence of government controls, to pollute their environment, abuse and overstrain the work force, and employ deception and trickery in marketing their product to final consumers. Both modes are unstable.

The differentiating characteristics between the two modes are the giant size and approach to monopoly power permitted the corporation, which can assemble capital contributed by an enormous number of investors. The corporate world is also distinguished by the emergence of a professional class of managers, hierarchically organized, in the main salaried but commonly reimbursed additionally with profit sharing, to whom control over the enterprise and entrepreneurial functions is entrusted. The obverse of this also holds that owners of common stock have in the main divested themselves of effective participation in control of the matured quasi-public corporations by their deliberate preference for a high degree of diversification in their investment portfolio. The securities market enables fixed capital to be attracted by issuance of new corporate securities that appeal to investors. That market evolved with the quasi-public corporation and is an essential support for it. That support comes from the great stock exchanges organized by dealers in securities to make a fair market for the purchase and sale of securities, the nationwide network of security dealers to whom investors may readily turn to arrange sale or purchase, a limited number of investment bankers who have won the confidence of corporate management and of investors and who are able to provide a nationwide or even international market for newly issued securities.

The stock market functions with the aid of a network of publications offering advisory and reporting services to keep investors and corporate management in touch with new developments. The purchase and sale of corporate securities made possible by the securities market establishes a clear and constantly fluctuating level of market value. The stock market serves as a guide to investors and to corporate overlordship, which has ultimate authority over the corporate system. The centralization of capital into huge corporate combines enables corporate giants with established security acceptability among investors to buy up smaller capitalist or corporate enterprises by issuance of new securities. The securities market not only services corporate investors and promotes new corporate security issuance but also serves as a general loan and securities center to equilibrate demand and supply of investable capital serving local and state governments, financial institutions, foreign agencies or governments, and the federal government. Whereas the commercial bank was the financial center of the capitalist mode of production, the investment bank and the stock market are the corresponding center of the corporate mode.

Corporate overlordship is formally embodied in directoral boards approved in elections by common stockholders. These boards are vested with general authority over corporate affairs. That authority chiefly boils down to appointing the chief executive officer heading up corporate management, fixing his salary, disposing of or acquiring new subsidiaries or merger partners, approving new security issuance, and confirming allocation of earnings into retentions and dividends. Commonly these decisions are not initiated by boards but reflect recommendations of management given near automatic approval by overlordship. From a third to a half of all directors are salaried chief executives drawn from upper management levels of corporations. A significant number of directors everywhere represent large stockholding interests. Another large fraction of the directors are prominent corporate executives drawn from other corporations – often large banks, brokerage firms, or investment banks. Many of these directors, especially those serving the largest corporations, will hold numerous other directorships with interlocking patterns suggesting broad communities of interest.

10. *Cooperative Mode.* The cooperative like the corporate mode raises its capital by public subscription from shareholders who in periodic meetings elect a governing board. But the socioeconomic pattern of relations is quite different in the cooperative. Shares are low in value, may be easily acquired on the installment plan, earn only a fixed interest return, have no market value, and entitle each holder only to a single vote. Shareholding in a cooperative is merely a way to raise capital from a group of neighbors who may conveniently patronize cooperative facilities and who are brought together in a more vital and pervasive relationship than shareholders in quasi-public corporations. Since profits of enterprise are distributed to shareholders and sometimes other patrons in proportion to their contribution to production or patronage, providers of capital are encouraged to dedicate their patronage to an institution of their own devising. This provides a constructive outlet for social energies and an emulative spirit. Cooperative shareholders and activists are drawn from quite different social strata than corporate stockholders. Corporations recruit shareholders from well-to-do families and capitalists. Cooperative shareholders are chiefly working farmers or ranchers and urban wage earners, clerical workers, and artisans drawn together in a movement to a considerable degree suffused with ethical intent to make a more democratic form of business organization and egalitarian distribution of benefits. In line with this deeper purpose the cooperative movement has always been associative, not competitive, and by federation it has built up great national societies organized on the same principles as the local cooperative society, its root institution.

The cooperative mode is essentially adjunct to other modes. In rural society where the mode has become well-established and powerful in most Western countries, it is adjunct to peasant proprietors or to small capitalist farmers who join in cooperatives to control their own harvesting and marketing; to carry out cooperatively the necessary grading, processing, and packing or canning; to arrange for long-term loans at favorable terms of credit; and to combat where feasible monopoly buyers of farm produce or monopoly sellers of farm supplies or equipment. Urban cooperation is essentially adjunct to the capitalist and corporate mode and in the main displaces the small inefficient private trader or lender whose commodity and loan shops are replaced by cooperative enterprise. But though adjunct in scope the cooperative mode is powerful in its effects in training broad masses of the population in the art of business management. It establishes at the core of the economy an egalitarian sector dedicated to the principle of producer or consumer democracy. It provides the socialist economy a basis for superseding or checking the role of private traders without involving the state in the difficult problems of retail store management. Producer cooperation gives small farmers an opportunity to employ modern farm machinery in staple crop farming, especially food grains, and thus provides another alternative to the plantation, the capitalist farm, or the state farm.

11. *Public Mode.* The core of the public mode of production is made up of the general services of government providing protection against foreign and domestic enemies; administration of frontiers; provision of standing law and courts to govern social relations and to resolve controversies; regulation of rivers to avoid floods and to provide irrigation water; building of ports and harbors where navigable ships can be safely shielded from rough waters or from enemy craft; construction of a network of roads or canals to assure ready communication and transportation throughout the society; erection of public buildings and facilities for meeting, worship, and celebration; and finally assuming the duty of coinage or provision of other suitable and acceptable moneys to facilitate the ready acceptance and circulation of a general medium of exchange and store of value. City life is especially dependent upon government services to provide networks for circulation for man and beast, for fresh waters, and for disposal of wastes. These services of government because intangible and nonmarketable are no less real though they are more commonly abused and neglected than privately marketed services of teaching, entertainment, healing or nursing, litigation, ministry, barbering and whatnot. Unlike private services, government services generally cannot be financed on a fee for service basis. The core area of governmental service is characterized by relative incommensurability of cost and benefits handicapping rational decision making. Hence the need for financing the core area of public service in the public mode by compulsory levy or taxation, a very strategic part of the core public service inherent in the state itself.

Productive activity in the public mode is carried on under special circumstances. Public employees are usually sworn to special fealty to the state service. They often wear special insignia or are commissioned to function in armed detachments under the command of special officers. In more advanced societies with greater concentration of population and with a developed scheme of taxation, public service is organized in hierarchical fashion with careful provision for layers of supervision and oversight. Hierarchy allows for greater specialization of function and permits supervision to detect abuse of power by local members of the public service. Hence the spelling out of duties and responsibilities in law codes, the frequent retention for decades and even for centuries of public documents and records, the enmeshment of action in red tape and rootedness in tradition. These features are characteristic to varying degrees of public service in different historical economic systems.

The quality of public service has been greatly improved by appointment to office based on competitive standing in open written examinations. These were first used on a large scale in classical China in the seventh and eighth centuries A.D. Compensation for public office is usually in twofold form: a set salary and perquisites of office by way of gifts and gratuities. These are offered or extorted from those who seek the service or favor of government. The salary form of compensation is shared by other modes of production using hired labor. The second form of compensation is more widely prevailing in public than in private modes, especially where a double standard of morality prevails with an official creed clashing with a more indulgent unofficial creed. Where the regulatory work of the state has become vexatious or where standards of honesty and devotion to public service were low, corruption in public service increased. More unique to public service is the tradition of lifetime service, with security of tenure, periodic promotions to higher rank, and termination of career with pension or lifetime annuity.

Hybrid and Multiple Modes

Modes materialize not only in pure form, as delineated, but to a considerable extent in hybrid form embodying a mixture of two or more modes. The leading contemporary instances of such hybrid development in the twentieth century American economy are the crosses between the public and corporate mode embodied in the huge complex of regulated public utilities. There a deliberate effort has been made to allow corporate enterprise to carry out under special regulation and public control what in effect are public services often calling for power of eminent domain and monopoly privilege. Another comparable hybrid development is found in the cluster of quasi-public corporations specializing in the design, manufacturing, and marketing of military, space, and nuclear technology for which the principle customer is the federal government. The defense and space agencies of the latter were the prime spawning ground for what was later called by President Dwight D. Eisenhower the "military-industrial complex," born, he said, of the "conjunction of an immense military establishment and a large arms industry." (Gottlieb 1984, 162–68). Public service and corporate enterprise are deeply entangled with intermeshing staffs and mutually penetrating influences in product design, research effort, actual production, lobbying before Congress, and international marketing of one of America's great fields of commercial export.

Another hybrid cross between the public and corporate modes is the early form of the quasi-public corporations in Europe in the seventeenth and eighteenth centuries, with authority at once mercantile, imperial, and military. The colossal power of empire in India was built up by a chartered profit-seeking corporation effectively nationalized only late in the eighteenth and early in the nineteenth centuries. The English national currency was issued and the public debt was administered by a chartered corporate monopoly controlled by capitalists as stockholders. On a purely local scene the English "turnpike trust" was a private profit-seeking corporation to whom was turned over or farmed out the construction and administration of toll roads. The whole field of tax collecting was in many historical systems in the ancient, medieval, and even modern worlds farmed out to finance capitalists. They offered advance payment, embodying a form of loan to the state, and undertook to administer and collect state revenues with every interest in maximizing their yield for private gain.

The capitalist enterprise is itself readily hybridized as it evolves from or deals extensively with craft producers. The tendency of merchants and manufacturers especially in the textile and finishing trades to provide the craftsman and his family with work materials and then to dispose of the finished product fabricated according to design and specifications set by the merchant results in a hybrid form of enterprise, half-capitalist and half-commodity producer. The craft producer himself as he takes on additional apprentices or "helpers" and concentrates on entrepreneurial functions tends to turn into a capitalist producer, the line between them being fluid and inconstant. Hybridization with the capitalist enterprise is at work also at the other end of the spectrum. In the early stages of the formation of the public corporation, it is still dominated and run by major capitalist founders. This form of "entrepreneurial corporation," so labelled by John Kenneth Galbraith, is reproduced every time a new major public corporation rises into the galaxy with its multimillionaire founders still active in its management. Hybridization is found especially with the unfree labor modes. Historians have often noted that it is difficult to place unfree workers into a slave or serf or feudal category. The characteristics of unfree labor may themselves change over time, stiffening as when in the Late Roman Empire the nominally free tenant became bound to the estate or when the Russian village serf in the eighteenth and later nineteenth centuries declined to a status near slavery. Hybridization is frequently found on the fringes of the cooperative movement where it results from the junction of the cooperative and the capitalist or corporate mode. Capitalist enterprise has actually utilized the cooperative movement as a convenient vehicle. Many American nominally cooperative financial organizations, like the mutual insurance company or the mutual saving and loan association, embody only a disguised compromise between a capitalist enterprise operating for profit to capitalist owners and a true cooperative with profit distributed to patrons or depositors. And the contemporary socialist world virtually without exception has turned the institution of producer cooperative into a hybrid mode, part cooperative and part state plantation with rigorous control of means of production, of farm husbandry, and of product disposal.

Our account of the standard modes of production and of their numerous hybrid forms already clearly indicates that historical economic systems will commonly contain at least two modes of production and frequently many more. This is true generally of the public mode present in all systems, of hybrid modes, and of the cooperative mode characterized as an adjunct or auxiliary to other modes. Though the public mode is predominant in socialist economies where it operates most of industry, commerce, and finance, yet an obstructive peasantry still plays a role on private plots as simple commodity producer and provides the labor force for the hybrid collective-farm sector. The simple commodity producer mode has been present – sometimes dominant, usually auxiliary – in virtually all economic systems from antiquity onwards and has had varying scope in agriculture, petty trade, urban services, and artisan craft work. Usually the simple commodity producer as peasant small holder has had to share the field with slave plantations or feudal manors or landlords and tenants or capitalist farmers. Sometimes he has been nearly crowded out though often he dominates agriculture in historical societies. The capitalist mode has had a similar near universal course in earlier societies in the field of wholesale and overseas trade where it flourished especially in the late medieval and early modern worlds. But even in the nineteenth century – the heyday of the capitalist mode in industry, wholesale trade, and finance – the capitalist enterprise had to share the day with quasi-public corporations in the early vintage form especially in banking, canals and railways, and some large manufacturing ventures. By the time the capitalist mode of production was well-developed in machine industry, the corporate mode was pushing ahead chiefly as a vehicle for monopolistic combinations.

Since economic systems are made up of shifting congeries of competing and complementary modes of production, some agencies must function to coordinate the use of resources within and between the modes. This work of coordination is achieved by (1) operations of *markets* where peaceful voluntary exchange of goods and services occurs using chiefly money; (2) by *rationing* where compulsory allocation of goods and services is made by force of authority within a solidary body as in a social security system, a bureau of taxation, a corporate chain-store network; (3) or finally by *central economic planning,* a combination of government forward budgeting with long-term business capital planning. The balance between these three methods of coordination will vary in different economic systems (Gottlieb 1984, Chap. 5). Central economic planning is the hallmark and principal defining feature of the socialist economies of our time.

Role of State and Public Economy

The economic system is undergirded but is by no means exhausted by its complex of production modes. There is also the pervasive role of the state and public economy to consider, operative in the first instance through its public mode. Of first consideration are the economic functions of the state with primary reference to economic behavior. The more narrowly economic functions of the state treated in this work are *regulation* of modes of production and behavior therein, erection of *public works* with provision for their use and financing, and *redistribution* of income and other beneficial uses to suit the broader social priorities of the society or of its ruling class. Other functions of the nonsocialist state are also carried out by its public mode – that is, education, defense, regulation of the institution of the family, and marriage – but there is a question whether the economic primacy of these other functions is so compelling as to call for thorough treatment here. To treat these functions effectively would extend our field of enquiry from the economic system to the entire sociopolitical system, from economic behavior to all sociocultural behavior, an extension I earlier ruled out. For the socialist state I must add the function of central economic planning by which the entire process of economic growth and industrial development is masterminded and controlled.

The regulatory work of the state is found on a more or less extensive scale in nearly all historic economic systems though the means of regulation vary considerably. Foreign trade is a natural field of concern for promoting national security, for promoting domestic industry, for collecting taxes, and sometimes for injuring rival national states. Domestic production is regulated to provide proper markets, to assure adequate quality, to prevent abuse of the environment or of the workforce, to prevent public nuisances or the spread of contagious diseases, to enable producers to organize into a self-regulating body, to regulate prices of essential foodstuffs in short supply, to prevent lenders from oppressing distressed debtors seeking loans, to reduce fire hazards, and sometimes to maintain orderly economic growth.

Essential public works all provide public benefits and meet real economic needs, but it is impossible for ordinary producers to construct them and operate them as private enterprises. That is especially true of systems of transport and communicative networks that to be optimally effective must have distribution through the entire territory of the economy concerned. These networks cannot be constructed in lands already settled, parcelled out, and put to prior use except by the coercive power of the state that may insist its subjects, with adequate compensation, permit a public interest to be satisfied though some private hurt may be felt. These networks may involve road or rail systems, navigable waterways, pipelines for gas and oil distribution, wires for conduct of electric energy, and harbor facilities or waterway development to regulate water flow, provide irrigation, and generate power. These great works so radically transform the environment and condition of the consequent human settlement that only the state can assure that local, regional, and national interests have been properly consulted. Moreover, these public works frequently call for investment on such a gigantic scale that only an entire people using its resources can raise the necessary capital or labor force to do the work. Yet again, where essential services are provided the state may feel the obligation to protect its subjects against the ability of a service monopoly to extort to the utmost. Even if this obligation is not recognized, the state often seeks to exploit fiscally the monopolized service for its own gain.

Beside these utilitarian works there are others such as the provision of beautiful parks and recreation or wilderness areas; of public beauty laid out in ornamental buildings, shrines, and temples; or great libraries and museums that most peoples through their governments seek to bring into existence or promote and then sustain with public funds or privileged revenues.

The third economic function of government is to modify the pattern of wealth and income distribution generated by the modes of production. This is partly achieved by indirection through pursuit of other objectives as when the state levies protective grain tariffs raising the value of farm fields and landlord incomes. More generally redistribution is achieved by measures such as minimum wages or welfare grants or old-age pensions that directly change the stream of income payments. These measures depend in large part on ability to raise funds in taxes and to use these funds in ways that foster changed patterns of income distribution. The more powerful the tax system, the greater its enmeshment with processes of income disbursement at the source. Direct taxation of large incomes, taxation of inheritance mediated by probate courts supervising the distribution of estates of deceased persons, and the increasing taxation of corporate income partly as a measure of fiscal socialization all have multiplied fiscal potential and make it possible for the modern state to redistribute through fiscal channels a high proportion of the net income of the society, ranging up to a quarter in ordinary times and in wartime to one-half or more.

Varied patterns of redistribution have been exhibited by different economic systems. In few cases have the effects been egalitarian or populist in character. They sometimes have been crudely inegalitarian, favoring already established upper classes in dominant production modes. Sometimes the most favored parties have been the dynastic families occupying the pinnacle state positions. Sometimes the entire armed forces of the society are its main beneficiaries. In a few cases redistribution favors a lumpenproletariat as in the ancient city of Rome, or a stratum of parasitic landlords who have long since ceased being the warrior noblemen that originally justified their privileges.

Institution of Money

The economic role of the state is by no means exhausted by the exercise of these functions, important as they are. For the state plays an essential role in furthering, formalizing, and at times guiding the general process of institutionalization that is at work in the economic system as elsewhere in the sociopolitical order. The concept of institutionalization—and its finished product, institutions—is a fundamental concept of sociological theory that was late in emerging in formal analysis and is now given a broad range of meanings. These meanings relate chiefly to the patterning of authority to be wielded in accordance with socially defined performance in roles by persons holding defined status positions. These roles and positions are defined in terms broadly accepted by the parties involved so that behavior in accord with them has become self-reinforcing. Since the process of institutionalization extends over time, the behavioral patterns projected by the institution become customary and habitual. In historical societies with which we are concerned, institutions are given final form by the state. Through its courts and the powers of law, it can shape and mould behavior by its fines, its sanctions, its formal decrees. The state must at the very least give the institution a seal of approval by tolerating its facilities, its authority, its value standards. Institutions are relatively stable and change slowly since the institutions are worked into the tissue of daily life of the community and involve an ordering of authority valuable to those who enjoy its privileges.

Institutions are clusters of behavior that may be closely pinpointed. In detailed enquiries into particular societies many economic institutions may be singled out. These institutions, however, must be mutually adapted to each other. As they persist over time they will tend to form a gestalt or configuration whereby the needs served by particular institutions are fitted together. Of these institutional gestalts two are focal in all historical economic systems and embrace the most basic needs of all modes of production: money and property. Some form of the institution of money and of property will be found in every economic system and will reflect the pattern of modes of production and public economy found in them. As the economic system evolves, the working of these institutions must become adapted though the process of adaptation may be complex.

The first major form of the institution of money in historical economic systems results from intervention of the state to facilitate the circulation and ready acceptability of precious metals used in exchange by minting precious metals into standard denominations of given weight and fineness. Coined money was the first massive exercise in standardized weights and measures. It stepped up the process of monetization that makes for a more rational use of resources. It also provides a ready fiscal resource for the state and is often abused since the market price of the raw metal and the value of the coined piece may diverge considerably from each other.

As soon as the institution of money begins to rely heavily upon the state for certification of the weight and fineness of its various denominations of money coins, the state begins to wonder whether a certificate might be denominated and issued as money without precious metal accompaniment. That practice is slipped into for small denomination coins because their wear and tear is relatively greater and they more readily pass current by tale rather than by careful weighing and assaying of value. Since copper was a common metal for alloying of silver, mintmasters had a fiscal motive for raising the proportion of copper in the alloy thus causing ostensibly low–denomination silver coins to take on the red copper hue. Thus there gradually emerged a purely token coin, whose mintage was strictly controlled by governments and whose usage was confined to petty payments. Britain then led the way in the eighteenth century by slowly extending the token principle to its silver coins, which were nearly full bodied in value but were made legal tender only for payments of moderate value. The British example was followed by other nations, and now virtually all coins are tokens – usually silver plated – issued by the state for limited payment purposes. In Europe and in America token moneys were metallic, but there was no reason why the material for the token need be so expensive. As the Chinese learned, it could well be printed on fancy paper which was first issued as a kind of token money in the Sung dynasty in the tenth and eleventh centuries A.D. and was given generalized use by the Mongol (Yuan) dynasty. They sought totally to supplant coined precious metals with state–printed paper money. That experiment and other later eighteenth century experiments with state-issued fiat paper money ended in disaster, the fiat money becoming virtually valueless.

The second form of the institution of money, token money, cheapened its relative cost for payments of small value. But where larger volumes of payments were involved – as in wholesale trade, government purchase, church finances, real-estate transfers, and property settlements at probate – the cost of even a well-designed and unabused coinage system using gold or silver was relatively high. There is always wear and tear on coins as they move about. Especially in earlier centuries minting practice was somewhat uneven so that over time coins would lose value at the rate of almost 10 percent a century for gold coins and at a higher rate for the more fully used silver coins. Any commercial center that has developed trading relationships with distant peoples will unavoidably tend to inherit a polyglot supply of coins of varying vintage. Any large transaction would call for careful assaying and weighing. Transfer of such money involves its own hazards. Hence the tendency to develop banking and credit money, the third form of the institution of money.

Banking evolves from the money changer, a form of small business automatically generated by use of coined money. For the money changer to become a banker proper, it is necessary that he deal not only in moneys but in one or more classes of debt. If he functions as borrower (as when the banker accepts deposits), it will be easier for him to act as lender. In the ancient world the money changer rarely carried on both debt functions but he learned to do so in the medieval world, both in Islam and in Western Europe. The precocious Italians developed widespread fractional reserve banking already by the thirteenth and fourteenth centuries. Early banking had not learned to separate itself from other forms of mercantile business and it was constantly hampered by the secrecy of its operations, inviting suspicion that cash funds were short or had been lost in ill-fated loan ventures. Accordingly, deposits would be withdrawn. Moreover, the institution of property had not evolved to the point where money debts could be freely assigned to third parties by written order. Hence there was a bias against ordering bankers to transfer deposit liabilities by written order and banks did not seek to circulate evidence of their own liabilities or debts. It was not until the eighteenth century that the finished form of the commercial bank evolved. In this form of banking, loans were made to cover payments arising out of invoiced shipments. Banks made loans for relatively short term. They issued their own demand liabilities in standardized denominations for payment use and transferred deposits on their books by acceptance of written orders. As thus evolved, the commercial bank carries out three major functions. It creates a flexible and economical easily transferred form of money brought into existence by the action of giving credit in business transactions. Use of this money reduces the need for gold and silver held for monetary purposes and enables the capital resources of the economy to be invested in more productive form. Secondly, the bank can arrange for settlement of indebtedness of its depositors by offset or clearing in the books of a bank or in the exchange market. Third, the bank concentrates the liquid working capital of its depositors where it can be readily loaned out to business users on a revolving basis, subject to the market test of ability to pay interest charges that in turn help to finance the services extended by the bank to lure its depositors.

The commercial bank with its circulating currency notes and deposits exchangeable at will into full–bodied coined money was a powerful institution. Much of the economic success achieved in the early stages of the Industrial Revolution is attributable as much to the commercial bank as to machine industry. But the very success of banking produced its nemesis and thus induced a further process of evolutionary development. The banker's profit depends on obtaining with a given amount of bank reserves held as bullion or coined money a maximum volume of lending or extension of credit that yields the interest earnings that, after deducting bank expenses, constitute the banker's profit. Time and again bankers have overextended credit and have seen their reserves withdrawn to satisfy demand for ready cash for wage payments or to purchase foreign goods and services. At a certain point when reserves dwindle, the bank must close up operations for it cannot satisfy depositors or note holders on demand. Then again, bankers often have extended credit loosely on speculative, sometimes even on swindling, projects that cannot pay off. When report of the swindle or bad loans becomes known, the bank will close. One closed bank brings down others. If the sense of insecurity becomes panicky and a rush for payment occurs, then all banks are in trouble no matter how well managed and even if reserves for normal times are more than adequate. Finally, it is awkward to have different banking establishments in one economy issue their own currency notes. These notes will tend to get into a more general circulation and it becomes difficult for even well-informed credit establishments to keep appraised of financial developments in distant financial centers.

The response to these problems was the further evolution of the commercial bank and of credit money that created a twofold banking world: at the national center a *central bank* established by government as a chartered quasi-public banking corporation endowed with monopoly power and usually closely linked to government in a sort of working partnership. The commercial banks no longer issue currency notes but they are able to create deposit liabilities by extending credit or by receiving cash or bullion deposits. Their ability to extend credit will be governed by the scale on which the central bank is extending credit to member banks or to government on the basis of given gold reserves or their working equivalent in foreign exchange. These credit transactions will meet the credit needs of commercial banks proper and to a certain degree of government itself. In its full evolution the central bank relinquishes private banking business and no longer seeks to maximize profits by intensive use of its monetary reserves. It undertakes broad responsibilities for monetary and credit guidance of the economy, now relaxing, now tightening credit, watchful of broad movements in exports and imports and of the associated balance of payments, of price movements at home and abroad, and of exchange relationships with other national systems.

This form of the institution of money had hardly become perfected before its further evolution continued apace. The basis for the credit activities of the classical central bank was its gold reserves usually held in bullion form or in equivalent foreign exchange with unquestioned gold value. In the immediate post-World War II world that foreign exchange was chiefly dollars whose gold value was guaranteed to all bona fide holders of international monetary reserves at a statutorily set price of $35 per ounce. The American gold reserves were ample and our balance of payments was on the credit side. Our industrial capacity had been enlarged during the war and we were kingpin suppliers of industrial goods, agricultural produce, and energy. For international payment purposes to hold dollars was as good as holding gold and more remunerative. The dollar accounts paid interest whereas gold could only be held with warehousing, safekeeping, and insurance expenses. So the American dollar in the Pax Americana, which opened up after 1946, became the dominant money of the Western world. This was recorded and codified by international agreement that set up the first truly international central bank, the International Monetary Fund (IMF), constituted by governments operating through their central monetary authorities with voting power proportioned to capital subscribed. This fund was endowed with a large working capital of gold and moneys made available for short-term loan to relieve payment balance disturbances and to determine workable exchange rates between the different currencies (Gottlieb 1984, 328–39).

For some thirty years that institution functioned and presided over a modified gold standard with ultimate currency reserves being held in the form of gold bullion and American dollar credit claims. But year by year the dollar claims grew larger and the gold bullion reserves declined. These dollar claims were not created by credit extension or by banking transactions of standard mould. They emerged rather as the unintended by-product of a persistent tendency to spend, give, and transfer abroad on a gradually larger scale by all classes of American society – households as tourists, corporations locating abroad or buying properties abroad, and government building up empire by spending madly on colonial wars and imperial bases. The result was a growing volume of international dollar claims some of which was converted into gold but most of which was kept in monetary reserves, thus tending to inflate the Western world's monetary systems. The disparity between the gold base and dollar claims grew wider and in August 1971 gold convertibility of the dollar was scrapped. By that time by international agreement a new form of international credit money, Special Drawing Rights (SDR) usable for balance of payment purposes, was devised by the Western governments operating through the IMF. With a new international money, the Western world acquiesced to American pressure and agreed to the demonetization of gold gradually made effective between 1975–1978. With the collapse of the gold standard as a form of international money commonly accepted at stable values almost since the time of the Late Roman Empire, a new stage in the institution of money in the Western world has been reached.

Institution of Property

The institution of property arises out of modes of production as a socially acceptable ordering established through the power of the state of recognized interests in economic assets warranting protection. Economic assets around which these interests cluster are of a wide variety. They will normally include alienable goods or lands dealt with in markets, circulating moneys and precious metals, parcels of real estate, ordinary commodities, livestock, and—where humans are bought and sold—humans and their progeny. Beside the main corpus of property objects with this crucial feature of ready alienability, there will be a floating margin of objects saleable under special conditions and hence potentially objects of property such as children in classical China or brides subject to bride price. Beyond alienable things there is property also in valuable and appropriable things that are nonalienable such as state property in the socialist countries or land held by village communities or public roads, bridges, shrines. A whole category of valuable economic assets subject to property rights is made up of intangible "quasi-material objects," which confer rights protected in law relating to such things as patents, copyrights, and business goodwill. Finally there is a vast universe of assets made up of *claims* to income or payment or to a share in a stream of income that may be paid in the future.

These assets are in a scheme of property related to certain *interests* held by certain classes of persons or organizations. These interests relate variously to *control, beneficial use,* and *succession in case of death.* Exercise of control provides access, exclusion, or management. Such exercise is rarely complete and is usually variously restricted by obligations imposed by the state to promote general public interests or collateral interests of neighbors and others. This exercise may be coupled with beneficial use but control may as in the modern corporation be not associated with such use since security holders are generally deprived of any participation in control or management.

State regulation of succession at time of death is needed and has played a potent role in all societies for a number of reasons. Inherited is the deep-lying concern from earlier tribal society and religious faith about appropriate lines of succession. Regulation is needed partly to suit the case of unintended death where no plans for property disposal have been made. It offers a convenient opportunity for the state to replenish its tax coffers by a levy that cannot hurt those who have died or be felt too much by those not yet granted possession. Finally, it enables the state to protect important modes of production by assuring suitable succession.

An interest in an economic asset will not be realizable if it is not reciprocally recognized by other relevant parties and unless facilities are available for compulsory inquiry and adjudication so that if necessary, the interest can be protected by established authority. It is at this point that the institution of property meshes with state power, which controls adjudication facilities and enforcement of rights. As the bounds of the state widen and become national or imperial, effective protection of many property interests requires uniform areawide law and a kind of rational jurisprudence. That jurisprudence makes possible the ordering of protectable property interests to minimize conflict and obtain a wider measure of loyalty. Ordering is achieved by applying old rules in new ways or by promulgation of new rules of law, usually alone and sometimes in the context of a general codification. The role of law in shaping the institution of property is to permit this institution to be reordered over a wide territory with reasonable uniformity of application according to norms or rules that are widely accepted.

Conclusion

In this work economic systems will be regarded as complexes of modes of production functioning in various fields with resource allocation within and between modes coordinated by a combination of market methods, rationing, or planning. Associated with these modes will be an institutional overlay based upon a public mode of production, a scheme of state regulation of economic behavior, a scheme of public finance and income redistribution, and two major economic institutions—money and property. This institutional overlay is not a mere adjunct or outgrowth upon modes of production. The operation of the modes is entirely conditioned and permeated by the institutional overlay changing the beneficial distribution of income and wealth and playing an overall integrating role. In this role, choices will be made that will tend to shape the functional priorities of the society, the relative value placed upon the ultimate purposes or functions to be discharged by an economic system.

The Imperial Redistributive Systems: T'ang China and the Late Roman Empire

Introduction

Imperial redistributive systems involve societies that have expanded considerably beyond a narrow tribal community with shared kinship and language. This involves a state with authority over imperial domains and with high levels of taxation chiefly from agriculture. Modes of production encompassed within the genus include many modes: slavery, feudal, direct commodity producer, capitalist, landlord-tenant, and public. The high tax potential made possible schemes of income redistribution that vary widely in different systems. Many of these imperial redistributive systems, especially in the vast Euro-Asian plains and in the early European medieval period, developed considerable instability. Very early systems in this genus under Persian, Assyrian, or Greek auspices one simply does not know very much about. Hence I am selecting for illustrative purposes two imperial systems that were remarkably well anchored, had major historical impact, and have been well researched. Both developed matured state systems. Both became established as imperial powers almost at the same time in the third century B.C. Both societies were subject repeatedly to assaults from without by warlike peoples at a lower cultural level. The Chinese held off these assaults more tenaciously than the Romans and culturally absorbed subjugators when finally they were successful. Both the Romans and Chinese had great assimilative capacity so that a common sense of nationality became spread over imperial domains.

These systems are compared at somewhat different periods. For the Roman system I take their latest matured imperial society in the so-called Late Empire, roughly between Diocletian and Justinian in the fourth to sixth century A.D. Roman military might had only begun to weaken. Roman society had outgrown its two earlier cultural stages. In the first stage the young Roman Republic, grown out of a confederation of related Latin tribes in central Italy, still rested on a base of free self-managing proprietors of peasant farms and craft shops with a proud role in the assembly and with equal rights under law. Predominant power in the state had shifted to an elite of notables organized as the Roman Senate and supported by wealthy citizens casting a class vote in assembly. In the second configuration of Roman society, conquest had extended Roman domains through the Mediterranean basin with a greatly expanded role of slavery both in the countryside as latifundia and in town crafts, domestic service, mining, and galley labor in ships. The democratic element in the state was nearly extinguished. Rule concentrated in a wealthy class of notables and shifting cliques associated with successive dynasties. Italians are favored as a ruling nationality by way of relative exemption from taxes imposed on the conquered provinces, by the higher status of citizenship, and so far as the Roman poor are concerned a generous food subsidy.[1]

In the third stage of development selected for analysis here the role of slavery had become greatly diminished partly because with the cessation of new territorial conquest the supply of new slaves had fallen off. The emancipation of household favorites and servants was a widespread practice. Freedmen dominated urban crafts and rural small landholding in the Late Empire. The landed estate employing "client" freedmen or letting out farms on a sharecrop basis to tenants or to capitalist farmers who could pay cash rents gained ground over the slave plantation with its gang labor and barracks discipline.[2] The special position of Rome diminished as citizenship, except for slaves, became universal in the empire. Italy lost its special fiscal privileges except for public feeding of the lumpenproletariat in Rome and later in Constantinople.[3] As ethnic lines became blurred class lines became intensified; society was structured according to wealth and social status. The hierarchy was headed by a senatorial order: rich, title bearing, and eligible for high positions. The equestrian order, chiefly officeholders or officials graded by salary with lifetime perquisites, was followed by the curial order of local magistrates.[4]

Like Roman society, Chinese civilization was not unchanged from the time of its first emergence somewhere in the second millennium (B.C.) on the upper stretches of the Yellow River. There can be seen the beginnings of a written language, mastery of bronze, agricultural settlement, and an organized state system known historically as the Shang dynasty 1520–1031 B.C.[5] In time, peripheral peoples are touched and attracted. Soon a new era commences with considerable extension of settlement up and down the basin of the Yellow River. We see systematization of a Bronze-Age feudalism involving a layered scheme of hereditary fiefdoms resting on a base of a village community rendering service and products to a local lord in a pattern somewhat similar to the Western manorial estate. This feudalism jelled in the so-called Chou period with its "warring states" and shifting alliances among princely families with some titular supreme authority. At the heart of the "warring-states" period we enter what Needham describes as "the greatest period of intellectual flowering of ancient China" with academies, wandering philosophers, the earliest Chinese books with author's name attached, and philosophical-literary debates—often of a political character—and the emergence of the central figure of Confucius.[6] This cultural flowering was possibly an expression of great advances in the arts of production in fields, mines, and transportation heralded by the appearance of the animal-drawn plough, a great expansion of irrigation, mastery of the technology of iron production, extension of settlement to the Yangtze Valley, and a good beginning on the erection of stupendous walled fortifications to protect settled agricultural peoples from armed nomadic incursions.[7]

A process of consolidation of feudal states ensued. The strongest of them, more centralized than the others and with priority in the use of iron, conquered its rivals. In 222 B.C. a unified Chinese state was established with a single capital headed by the emperor of China, starting the line of the famous Chin-Han dynasties. Except for a short period of civil war, these lasted until 220 A.D. or for about 440 years.

This unification was not merely titular. The power of the old ruling nobility of the feudal states was greatly weakened. The old literature and learning was temporarily put under ban. A new set of administrative districts superseded the old state lines. A comprehensive civil service manned by commoners was commenced. Various measures of unification for weights, measures, and coinage were introduced. New nationwide schemes for an imperial road network, canals, river-valley control and irrigation were carried out using the resources of a nationwide tax levy on farmland and corvée labor. A break was made with feudal land tenure permitting at least in certain areas and for certain landholdings free purchase and sale of land associated with state support of peasant proprietorships valued for their taxes, corvée labor, and soldiers. A certain élan marked the regime and a number of progressive emperors drew around themselves experts in various scientific fields and able administrators who had a vision of economic development based upon improvements in the arts, innovation, and material abundance. During most of this period population continued to grow and the area of settlement enlarged especially to the south. There was adequate protection against the nomadic invaders from the northwest.

If the Chin-Han regime had continued a bit longer, it would have been suitable for comparison with the Roman imperial redistributive polity. But before its institutions had become settled, an extended period of imperial disunity intervened lasting some 330 years with partition into three and later two major areas. The northern area embracing the whole of the valley of the Yellow River and its major tributaries was taken over by nomadic incursions carrying different peoples — Mongol, Hun, Tungusic — to power. Though sinification was steady and though invading rulers utilized prevailing institutions, the effect must have been similar to Gothic invasions of Italy and Gaul during the fifth century in Europe. The nearly constant fighting and war devastation had a dampening effect on economic and social development during the entire era.[8]

Hence for a comparative regime to match with the Late Roman Empire we have selected the well-known and much-studied Sui-T'ang dynasties prevailing over a unified imperial China from 581–906 A.D., widely regarded as "China's Golden Age." Pressure from northern nomadic peoples diminished and effective imperial suzerainty was established over vast outlying lands in Korea, Tibet, Manchuria, and Sinkiang. The position of the literati was consolidated with the establishment of a network of schools and academies preparing students for the newly established practice of competitive examinations used for recruiting officials. The regime of land tenure and taxation became fixed and there was a noticeable development of inventions, improvements in the arts of cultivation, transportation, animal husbandry, mining, iron and steel making.

Though the Chinese economic system has been selected for comparison with a younger Roman system, the latter was the outcome of a longer course of cultural development drawing upon the crafts, skills, and culture of the Greek, Syriac, and Egyptian societies, which became fully integrated with the Roman world. The Chinese and Roman imperial societies had little direct contact with each other but there was a steady passage via a series of adjoining peoples on land or by water of ideas, disturbances, migrations, devices, materials, plants, animals, and products for trade (Teggart 1939). Much gold and silver moved from the Mediterranean to China in exchange primarily for bales of silk, in Rome worth nearly its weight in gold. The passion, writes Gibbon, for "that rare and elegant luxury" for the purpose of "exposing to the public eye naked draperies and transparent matrons" had finally spread from females to males; and the deficit on the Roman balance of payments eastward amounted to as much as a million pounds sterling annually in precious metals, much of which remained with the middleman traders.[9] Finally the silkworm was smuggled out of China by Western travelers in the sixth century A.D. with enough supplementary information about its nurturing to permit cultivation of the silkworm in Europe and Asia Minor. However important the silk and spice trade was in its own right, the mutual fertilization of these two cultures with devices, inventions, and improved arts had a more lasting impact.

The gross physical area of the two empires was nearly the same, around 1.5 million square miles of land surface (Needham 1954–1978, Book 4, 3:27). Well-informed estimates of the population of the two empires are around 50 to 70 million.[10] Both spanned semitropical to temperate zones; both utilized cereals as their basic food. China probably had the advantage in usable arable land, with her broad interior river valleys and extensive irrigation facilities. But the Roman Empire had the fertile well-irrigated food lands of the Nile Valley exploited to the fullest for empire support. Chinese skills and crafts were probably at a higher level in many fields: mining and metallurgy, harnessing draught animals, utilizing falling water for power, spinning and weaving, wheeled vehicles, water-raising devices, nautical construction principles, and paper-making.[11] The Roman Empire however had the advantage of phonetic writing, of being "less cut up by mountain ranges." It was less susceptible to floods and more accessible to inland seas (Needham 1954–1978, 1:66; Book 3, 4:217). Hence it is not unlikely that the average amount of agricultural surplus was probably of comparable magnitude so that both empires supported massive standing armies and substantial urban populations distributed over the territory in a network ranging from giant metropolises to the ordinary run of small towns.[12] Both empires suffered periodically from civil war associated usually with succession to the emperorship or foreign incursions.

Both empires were highly stratified with wealth and social status concentrated in the hands of a dominant class of landed gentry with political power concentrated in a supreme autocrat, the emperor, heading up an immense bureaucratic establishment and standing army. The combination of periodic wars from foreign incursions or civil war among rival claimants for the throne, widespread suffering growing out of extreme exploitation of lower classes, and a cosmopolitan culture that had advanced beyond the early tribal faiths created a susceptibility to savior faiths—in the West to Christianity, in the East to Buddhism. Both developed a broad appeal to populations bored with inherited creeds and rituals and longing for some form of salvation meaningful in a troubled world with such visible suffering and evil. Both were proselyte faiths with gentle savior figures of universal appeal. Both had commenced missionary efforts in the early decades of the first millennium.[13] Both provided solace for suffering by focusing interest on an afterworld or rebirth. Both provided social services to the poor. The faiths became economically relevant after they achieved popularity and in the West by the end of the fifth century became a state religion and in the East an accepted major faith interwoven with the social structure by the advent of the Sui-T'ang dynasty.

Modes of Production Compared

The modes of production in agriculture will be reviewed first. The slave plantation was probably somewhat more important in the West than in the East, although it had receded greatly from its former importance in the Western world. Slavery was found in the East in estates and wealthy households, especially in the northern part of China touched by pastoral conquest.[14] The use of hired labor is frequently indicated chiefly to meet seasonal peak labor needs; otherwise it was found on a very small scale.[15] The predominant modal types both East and West would appear to be the independent peasant proprietor and various forms of landlord farming shading from a form of feudal bondage arising out of peonage to free rental of farm establishments on either a cash rental or shared-crop basis.

The independent peasant proprietor tended East and West to be victimized by harsher tax assessment than his richer neighbors. Holdings subdivided for son heirs might become too small for effective family farming. A single bad year through drought, floods, or failure of irrigation water, or pestilence man-made or natural could lead to the fatal mortgage of the properties that sooner or later would be foreclosed (Balazs 1964, 112, 118). Nevertheless, the independent peasant proprietor survived in the East and in the West in Egypt, in Asia Minor and the Balkans (or older Illyricum and Thrace), but to a much more limited extent in Western Europe (Jones 1966, 773).

Survival in part was due to official policy that sought to protect and expand the role of peasant proprietors partly with an eye to promoting conscription of soldiers and the tax levy. In both empires but especially in the West this was implemented by a long-standing policy of placing army veterans on an unencumbered farm holding. In China the power of land allocation in areas of limited settlement was used to support establishment of peasant farming.[16]

However supported by state policy, tendencies to class differentiation were strong and landlord-tenant relationships probably were a near predominant rural mode on a mixed pattern of cash rentals or share-crop farming.[17] Differentiation did not, however, go so far as to rub out the strong rural position held by small proprietors anchored to the land by the specific Chinese system of diversified husbandry on small holdings farmed with great skill on a horticultural basis by ingenious use of fertilizer and irrigation.[18] The Chinese institutions of property and marriage specifically encouraged partition of landholdings among small proprietors (see p. 40). Moreover, as steadily as the small proprietor was undermined by drought, disaster, or excessive taxation, he was supported by clan assistance that bound closely together different strata in the countryside.[19] So well-established was the peasant proprietor through to the twentieth century that when all landholdings were worked over in the great agrarian revolution carried out in the 1930s and 1940s under the leadership of Mao Zedong, it was found that the modal type was the peasant proprietor who worked over half of all cultivated land.[20]

In other fields of economic life a similar plural-modal pattern East and West may be found. In the arts and town crafts and in retail trade there was both East and West a substantial place for the direct commodity producer usually aligned in guilds or local associations for fraternal or protective services. These guilds were useful to the authorities as a means of collecting taxes, controlling prices, or providing local public services. The more important practitioners of the skilled crafts were metal workers, silversmiths, potters and glass workers, carpenters with inlay capabilities, fullers, furriers, and purple dyers as well as professionals such as surgeons, doctors, architects, veterinary surgeons, painters, and sculptors. Urban people were serviced for their daily needs by a host of retail dealers, street vendors, and peddlers. Many trades and professions were also organized in local associations that were fiscally exploited by governing officials and tax collectors but nonetheless gave members security of tenure and a means when needed for concerted action.[21]

Supplementing these two dominant modes – landlord-tenant and direct commodity producer in rural and urban areas – there was a third important mode similarly organized in both empires and dominating the more advanced technology and the capital-intensive large-scale undertakings of both empires, namely the public economy. The public economy was staffed and managed by the public service, which constructed vast imperial highway networks and operated a postal and transport service with way stations, lodging and supply facilities, including replacement carriage animals.[22] The public economy through its imperial workshops and arsenals manufactured weapons, artillery, armor, military supplies. The public economy included large-scale mining and smelting enterprises; formidable naval yards; imperial stud farms; networks of warehouses where grain supplies and clothing were warehoused; fleets of road vehicles, barges, and ships for the transportation of bread grains and bulk supplies from surplus producing areas to the imperial capitals and the defense establishments on the vast frontiers. It mined precious metals and minted coins. It included factories, mills, and workhouses where supplies, artifacts, luxury articles, and ceremonial objects were produced. It designed and constructed all major public buildings, court establishments, tax-collecting offices, census-taking bureaus.

The public economy for the most part was a sphere where market processes played little role. Raw materials and supplies were collected by tax levy on agricultural producers as with most bread grains and post station maintenance support. Some labor was hired especially for seasonal peaktime needs or for local building operations where skilled craftsmen were available for hire. The Roman Empire was nearly as self-sufficient in its public economy as the Chinese.[23] In China corvée peasant labor for selected periods – and penal labor year-round – provided a massive public labor force.[24]

In the West the transport for grain supply to the major capital centers was hauled by a carefully controlled transport fleet which was privately owned and managed. In the Eastern empire transport of public grain collected by taxation was nearly everywhere in the hands of a state transport service. The East spawned a greater number of scientific or research establishments including astronomical observatories. It boasted of an Imperial University with an enrollment of 5000 students.[25] The East assumed responsibility for managing a vast network of water-conservancy facilities and man-made waterways for transport service, dams, and dikes that called for continuous monitoring, administration, repair, and maintenance.[26] Under the T'ang a nationwide network of grain depots was established with supplies drawn from a special grain tax levy to provide insurance against crop failure (Twitchett 1953/1970, 32). The Eastern state assumed direct responsibility in cities for building and maintaining mercantile quarters that were leased to users.[27] In China a formal state monopoly was erected early in the Han period for control of salt and iron marketing. In the West these industries belonged mainly to the private sector.[28] The East thus utilized to a lesser degree the services of contractors to obtain needed goods or services by purchase or contract from private producers. In one major area, public feeding and doctoring of its urban population, the Romans exceeded the Chinese in use of rationing methods of resource allocation.[29]

In the Western economy there was after the economic and administrative reforms of Diocletian a less consistent use of taxation-in-kind and a tendency to commute labor services, the grain levy, and even conscription to money payments. In both empires the management of the public economy was delegated to a network of far-flung bureaucracies. The Chinese civil service in the T'ang Period was at least in its upper echelons recruited from all classes on the basis of competitive examinations of scholars who could be supported by their families during the long period of study. Necessarily this biased the selection toward wealthy families with a scholarly tradition.[30] And official positions provided not only salaries or stipends but "gifts" or pilferings that in the full maturity of the bureaucratic system in later centuries came to greatly outweigh the official incomes.[31] Perhaps the Chinese system filtered applicants for high positions to persons with higher intellectual capabilities; it certainly promoted the rise of talent through the ranks; and possibly for that reason the Chinese bureaucratic society, as it has been called, survived longer than the Roman.

The bureaucracies were enormous institutions. In the Roman civil service for a single diocese of an African prefecture, the table of organization called for 98 judicial, 130 financial, and 396 subclerical posts (Jones 1966, 1:590). Though tenure for the higher posts was generally for short terms—from one to two years—yet the competition for the posts was so great that it became common practice to make an appointment only for the receipt of cash. In the middle of the fifth century rules were enacted for "orderly sale" of offices. It was not the salaries of office—though they were sufficient—but the perquisites of office that made them lucrative. There was similar pressure for appointment on the Chinese side though outright sale was generally avoided.

Besides the public economy we need only briefly mention other nonagricultural modes of production that played a very small role. Some wage labor existed in merchant and craft shops especially for younger workers sometimes quasi-apprenticed. Large-scale merchant firms will nearly always need extensive labor supply to stock warehouses, to make deliveries, to sort out inventories, and to man the cargo ships and caravans which carried merchandise or materials. Some of this labor would be indentured, some purchased in slave status, and some would be hired. But by far the largest employer of labor was the public sector and army. Even when soldiers are conscripted they were generally paid with handsome allowances for clothing, food, and housing.

Officers of government in both empires were normally salaried. These salaries became the prototype of the wage or salary relationship.[32]

Institution of Property

These institutions have already been implicated by the forms taken in the two empires of the modal complexes. Private property in land—alienable, mortgageable, and transmissible by succession to chosen heirs—was established very early in the Roman Empire. For a long time lands conquered by the Roman Republic outside of Italy were nominally treated as state property and were allocated either to military settlers or landed gentry. They were distinguished from Italian real estate only by being subject to the imperial land and poll tax, the so-called *tributa*. In the Late Roman Empire that distinction had been eliminated. Free persons in the empire were made citizens and their lands were equally taxable throughout the empire. Nor was it only farmlands that were private property. City real estate was privatized and lease rentals for Roman apartment houses were an established feature of Roman urban life as much as lease property in farms.[33]

The Chinese in the process of establishing a unified empire in the Chin-Han period were moving in the direction of private property in land, but they moved far more slowly and irregularly than the Romans both in the countryside and in the walled cities. For nearly a thousand years there were resolute moves to make farmlands saleable, leaseable, and hereditable, the earliest in the fourth century B.C. Just as frequently there were moves to restrict sale and leasing; to proclaim rural land state property; and through local magistrates to allocate land to peasant, merchant, official, and noble households in standard allotments (Balazs 1964, 112). The T'ang dynasty commenced with formal proclamation of the land-allotment system and apparently in at least many regions it was applied.[34] But as before, the search of people for more flexible forms of land tenure, the desire to retain permanent possession of lands they could seek to improve and the itch for exploitation of others by accumulating landed property overcame all official codes just as in the Roman Empire they converted the doctrine of state ownership of provincial land to an empty form. So it was that in the mid-T'ang regime, with the allocation system broken down and with tax collections geared to it falling away, the doctrine of state ownership of land and the effort to check the rural gentry and estate formation was relinquished. Private property in land alienable and hereditable was de facto recognized. This form of land tenure, so suited to the needs and aspirations of the peasant proprietor and gentry alike, survived until modern times, though near-quixotic efforts were still made in later centuries to revert to older forms of land tenure.[35]

In the old walled cities, official encampments of the imperial magistrates and staff, private urban property in land was slow to develop since the mercantile establishments were built by the state and leased to users. However, outside the walled cities a kind of suburban sprawl grew up that was controlled more by merchants and craftsmen. Doubtless a more congenial form of private property developed there both alienable and transmissible by inheritance.[36]

The form of inheritance among the Chinese – gentry, peasant freeholders, and urban bourgeoisie alike – was strikingly different from its counterpart in the Roman Empire where the dominion of an owner over his property was continued after his death. No document was more deeply respected among the Romans than the testament that disposed of his property according to his choices. Dying intestate, his property after satisfying creditors was divided equally among the surviving spouse (who legally was treated as an unmarried daughter) and sons and unmarried daughters, or if these were lacking, first-degree kinfolk on the father's side. Dying testate his estate could be given to a chosen heir or to outsiders as legacies, cut down by emancipation of slaves as was a common practice, or divided among children and relatives as he preferred. Many properties were in this way partitioned among many heirs.[37]

Under the Chinese system all estates, including peasant holdings, were partitioned equally among male heirs. Since more well-to-do Chinese families had traditionally from the earliest period enjoyed the privilege of de facto plural marriage, the number of male heirs would thus tend to be greater than with Roman and the later Christian monogamic family.[38] The Chinese form of marriage and property thus encouraged a faster partition of landholdings of gentry than of peasant proprietors who without plural marriage had fewer heirs. This is well-supported by empirical evidence and competent authority.[39]

Institution of Money

The institution of money also took on a different form in the two empires. Both started out in the early phase of their economic development with the simplest form of coined money made of copper or bronze. Copper was readily available and easily worked; it was valuable for purposes of industry and adornment. It was relatively abundant as a metal, which means that sources of it were widely scattered. Its working was a common occupation, and copper had relatively low value for its bulk. For that reason the Romans by the third century B.C. turned away from copper as the major monetary metal. It was reduced to a subordinate coin and replaced by coined silver.[40] When at the end of the third century A.D. this had become degraded, they shifted to coined gold.

As established by Constantine at 72 coins per pound (solidus), this coin was minted in its purity throughout the entire Late Empire and persisted until the eleventh century. For payment purposes gold coins were regularly weighed and valued on a poundage basis. New coins were minted at a constant standard of purity. To establish the initial circulation, gold was mobilized from all possible sources including old temples, shrines, and city hoards.

Already during the reign of Constantine a sufficient quantity of gold coins was in circulation to provide a money for trade and commerce, to require payment of taxes in gold, and to pay soldiers and officers of government in gold. Since landlords were able to collect rents in gold, it was in common circulation. It is indicated that from the fourth to the sixth century the purchasing power of gold for labor, bread grains, and standard products was substantially level. In the face of records of the earlier experience with a debased silver coinage, this was an achievement of some consequence as the money was acceptable at a stable value within the country and at all frontiers.[41]

Where the Roman achievement fell short was in devising a satisfactory silver or silver-copper money suitable for petty trade of common people who would need to make payments in small fractions of a solidus. Roman efforts with a silver coinage never succeeded possibly because of the ill repute of the previous silver money or because the market value of silver relative to gold was continually fluctuating. It would have been awkward to issue a money that could not be accepted for taxes or use in making payments except at a stated parity. No parity could maintain itself very long without overvaluing one or the other coined metal and hampering circulation. The imperial government continued to mint copper coins but denominations and sizes were changed frequently and inconsistently, and for extended periods copper coinage was insufficient.[42] A satisfactory copper and silver coinage was not devised during the Late Empire. The Roman institution of money was good for government, for wholesale trade, for rich capitalists and landowners, but it was not so good for ordinary people in their ordinary dealings.

The Chinese institution of money once cowrie shells were outgrown never got far beyond the simple level of copper coin. In the Han period there were various experiments with substitute monies including white deer skin, silk, iron, coined gold and silver; but the experiments did not catch on, and copper coinage was the main form of ordinary money up to and through most of the T'ang period.[43] Gold and silver transferred in bullion or dust and rolls of silk cloth or bundles of silk floss were means of payment for large transactions.[44] By the late T'ang period there were some thirty-six copper mints.[45] A considerable annual output of copper, obtained from state-controlled mines, was dedicated chiefly to coining money. Since copper was widely used in decoration, building, and for household utensils, nonmonetary copper was widely held and traded. A wide gap emerged between the metal value of the coin and its money value. That stimulated counterfeiting by private minters who frequently operated more efficiently than government minters.[46] At one time in the Han period the fight against counterfeiting was relinquished and private minting was legalized only to be stopped a few years later to quench the diversion of industrial activity toward making money rather than making goods.[47]

These perennial difficulties resulted from coining a metal relatively cheap and widely used for other purposes and using a crude technique of coining easy to counterfeit while at the same time seeking to draw a substantial mint profit or seigniorage. This will create a poor money, awkward to handle in large sums, expensive to coin, and undermined by counterfeiting. In the almost desperate struggle to improve monetary circulation in the late T'ang period, the regime thrashed wildly. It issued high denomination copper coins, which elicited more counterfeiting. It forced public markets to use official monies. And finally over an extended period it enforced the use of silk or grain for settlement of large market transactions (Twitchett 1953/1970, 76). The only really helpful development emerged out of the efforts of treasury officers and private merchants to facilitate the transfer of large sums of money between distant financial centers. The tea merchants of the South found they could deposit monies collected in the North from the sale of tea at special treasury offices and obtain payment vouchers, which they called "flying money" (*ch'ao-pi*), directing disbursement to named parties by treasury offices in the South (Yang 1952, 52). The idea caught on and became widely used as the Chinese form of a bill of exchange. Only in the late Sung and Yuan (Mongol) dynasties did bearer credit instruments become generalized, eventually to turn into unconvertible government-issued paper currency. When abused and run to the ground this led the way for eventual development of a usable silver standard.

Cultural System Components

The various cultural components will be dealt with together— functional priorities, patterns of resource coordination, institutions of money and property – because they are interrelated. The Roman functional priorities clearly laid emphasis on rights of private appropriation fully protected under law. The Roman state from its early stages incorporated class rule based on property holdings ascertained by census; and the role of property continued to be uppermost in the Late Empire. Rights of property were held in high regard even after Christianization. Juridical process was central to Roman society even in its late period, which witnessed its near-final codification under Justinian in the sixth century A.D. There was little emphasis in Roman society on system growth or development by promoting science and innovation. Intellectual interests after Christianization took on an other-wordly hue.[48] The obverse of this was a tendency to sensual enjoyment as the cardinal virtue with a passion for public sports and games that came to dominate urban living, at times disruptively.[49] Possibly because of the deep hold of private property with juridical protection of rights to its enjoyment, the Roman society institutionalized a relatively advanced kind of money: minted gold and silver as the main money and lesser use of copper coin for petty trade. Corresponding to this form of money was a greater emphasis on the role of market process in the functioning of the public economy, in the payment of taxes, and in the making of expenditures.

There is a significant degree of contrast of the Chinese cultural patterns with the Roman up and down the line. Chinese functional priorities, drawing on their Confucian-Taoist heritage, gave a much greater emphasis to people's abundance as a cardinal value to be promoted by a paternalistic government anxious to promote the people's welfare and thus to be found deserving of the people's support and obedience (Yu-Tang 1963, 164, 199, 203, 226). Combined with this was a cherished norm of respecting the natural environment seeking to conserve its usefulness to man and where necessary modifying the environment by human intervention and collective effort to make it more serviceable for human society. To achieve this goal, as well as to promote the people's abundance, high priority is assigned to research and investigation which will explore nature's ways and improve the arts and crafts by which nature and its materials may be better mastered. Veering off at times into magical recipes found in psuedo-sciences cultivated widely in China as elsewhere, there runs through the Chinese economy in its formative periods a concern for abundance, for public works as a means of mastering the environment, and for improving craft and engineering skills through research and artisanship.[50] Public works must extend the unity of the empire and permit its resources to be collected together since only a unified empire can defend against external enemies and keep the peace within.

With a greater sense of togetherness and a greater desire to master an unruly environment, it was possible for millennia to maintain a going system of corvée labor which most societies would not have tolerated. The Confucian-Taoist ethic, which pointed at once to a benevolent government and to a loyal people with respect for authority, was suited for a comprehensive public economy without monetary exchange or market processes as in a large family. The freedom of this ethic from an otherworldly orientation gave full sanction to efforts intended to make for a better life on earth for there was little or no interest in a future life in heaven.[51] Nor did the ethic derogate, as did Christianity and Buddhism, the acquisition of wealth, which was accepted as a means of making a better life.[52] The slower development of full private property in agriculture, the delayed development of private property in urban land, and the continued retention of prerogatives of land allocation by government authorities all permitted a less developed form of money and reflected the greater sense of social unity marking the Chinese classical political economy.

Since the modal complexes of the two empires are so similar at a related stage of their cultural development, the vivid contrast of cultural patterns that enter into an economic system in nearly all respects—overall values, functional priorities, patterns of resource coordination, and the institutional complexes of money and property—is a bit surprising. What forces or influences could have accounted for this divergent development of what in Marxian terms is "basis" and "superstructure"? Of course only the most tentative suggestions are in order since our ability to disentangle the ultimate forces at work is so limited. We may discount immediately two suggestions of Marx. One was that the "economical function of providing public works" to build and maintain "artificial irrigation by canals and waterworks as the basis of Oriental agriculture" devolved upon central government in the Orient because the level of "civilization was too low and the territorial extent too vast to call into life voluntary association" as in Flanders and Italy. The second suggestion was that in Asia the peasants were not under landowners but a "state which stands over them as their landlord and simultaneously as sovereign" thus coalescing tax and ground rent and eliminating "private ownership of land."[53]

Artificial irrigation and basinwide waterwork control was called for in the West, mainly in Egypt where basinwide hydraulic controls developed. Yet full private property in rural and urban land existed in Roman Egypt, with rent and taxes separately falling upon the land.[54] The prevailing scheme of Roman agriculture elsewhere was dryland farming except for strictly local use of streams and rivers for diversion to adjoining lands. More extensive waterwork facilities were designed to provide public water for cities. In the Near East private property in alienable and mortgageable land went hand in hand with state control of public works making possible irrigated farming and relatively heavy agricultural taxation.[55]

Marx's suggestion that the hydraulic function devolved upon central government in the Orient because "civilization was too low" is perhaps the converse of the truth. The power of central government in the Yellow River, Yangtze, Nile, Euphrates, and Tigris valleys reflected the higher level of civilization associated with the need to monitor, build, and maintain continuous hydraulic control.[56] Coercive basinwide control in China was needed to provide for irrigated farming under conditions of high concentration of rainfall in a few months of the year (80 percent in three summer months) in highly leachable loess terrain leading to alternating flood and drought. There was continual need for oversight either to dredge silted channels or to build up dikes to prevent disastrous flooding.[57] The scope and character of central government control will vary with the climatic background, the physiography of the basin, crops cultivated, variability in rainfall and its relative concentration, tendencies to silt, and the need to use interior waterways for transportation purposes. Thus the comparison of waterworks control in Italy and Flanders with so-called Asiatic or Oriental regions falls on its face because conditions in the areas compared are differently suited for local or basinwide control. Even in the present mixed economy of the United States, with its ingrained hostility to government control, the need for even local irrigation facilities could not call into life "voluntary association" that Marx posited strangely as characteristic of "high civilization." The intervention of the federal government in the United States was needed to call into being the local associations and capital to construct irrigation facilities and to protect the rights of downstream users.

Our suggestions for the explanation of the divergent cultural character of the economic systems of classical China and the Late Roman Empire are twofold. The Western empire was built up by a virile warrior people who imposed their will by conquest over a wide range of peoples, many with a developed sense of nationality and cultural community still subsisting after Latinization had worked its way. Denizens of the Roman Empire could think of themselves as Romans and perhaps as citizens but never as kinfolk. The Chinese empire on the other hand did not know the category of "citizenship" because its diverse Mongoloid peoples came to think of themselves as clansmen, members of the "hundred clans," with a single historic literature and forming one culture already fully sensed in Confucian times across the confusion of petty principalities and states.[58] This, and the social togetherness marking classical China, allows for greater emphasis on the benevolent role of government to promote the abundance and the welfare of the people.

Perhaps for the same reason there was in the early Chinese empire much resistance to the process of social rural stratification built upon private property in land that was such a settled institution in the Roman world. Hence also a greater willingness to support nationwide labor mobilization for public works and a lesser interest in a more refined form of money that would allow for a fuller monetary use of all the precious metals. While China may not have been as favored with the potential for gold and silver mining as the Roman Empire, yet in the nearby Asian plains and Himalayan plateaus gold and silver were sufficiently available to become widely used both for monetary and decorative purposes (Needham 1954–1978, 1:109, Book 3, 4:519). And any state of higher civilization with developed forms of industry tends to attract gold and silver from adjacent less-developed peoples. Moreover, China attracted Western supplies of gold and silver to pay for Chinese exotic products like silks, tea, and jades.

Nor is it clear that domestic mining capabilities of the Chinese interior were so unfavorable for gold and silver. A "consensus of modern mining opinion" holds that "gold deposits are much more widely disseminated in China than has often been supposed" (Needham 1954–1979, Book 2, 5:50). Though in recent centuries little gold and silver has been mined, earlier Han records indicate that large numbers of workers washed sands for gold in the auriferous regions. In Ming times gold was mined in more than "100 places."[59] Records would understate the number because lucky prospectors would tend to hide their finds from competitors and tax collectors. The Chinese had mastered all the arts of gold and silver metallurgy and their techniques for cupellation and refining met Western standards. In T'ang times Chinese miners were probably able to work deeper shafts than Western miners. Many reports from a variety of sources indicate that gold treasures and ornaments were highly regarded as valuables and that emperors often built up immense gold hoards.[60] This widespread appreciation of gold in decoration and artwork does not explain the failure to mint gold and silver coins but underscores that failure. It is only widespread appreciation of gold and silver for domestic use that can support their use as an instrument of exchange by facilitating their ready acceptance. Failure to go on to monetization of the precious metals, following in the pathway of other major advanced civilizations, can only be due to special factors operative in the Chinese setting: the lesser role for market process, the demeaned status of the merchant, and the relative insulation of the state from market pressures because of collection of taxes in kind (Wittfogel 1931, 101).

Our second suggestion for explanation of the special Chinese cultural-economic pattern relates to the twin hazards of the Chinese civilization launched in the Yellow River valley. It was exposed to violent incursions from nomadic pastoral peoples on the adjoining open plains and to the categorical need to discipline the unruly river with its perennial tendency to flood and its excessive tendency to silt. The hazards could be abated only by massive public works involving walled fortifications to protect the frontiers and elaborate hydraulic facilities to control floods, provide for irrigation, and to protect by ever-rising dikes the valley lands. The dominant strains of the Confucian-Taoist ethic – the social togetherness under a benevolent government fostering a progressive technology – were exigent needs of survival. Imperial unity did not have to be imposed on an unwilling people who were thereby freed from the warring jungle of feudal states. The same ethic derogated the merchant, looked down on the soldier who guarded the frontiers, and held in highest regard the scholar or literati who were the central managers of the public economy and the special custodians of the Confucian-Taoist ethic that was made into a state "religion" with local temples and services in T'ang times.[61]

State Regulation and Taxation

We can deal more briefly with the components of the Roman and Chinese economic systems involving regulation and taxation. Regulatory activities of the imperial state were pervasive in both empires though possibly more meticulously detailed in the East. There an elaborate sumptuary code outlined for the various social classes articles of clothing, their style, and the size of dwellings. To prevent an improper form of funerals, "agents and artisans who provided and manufactured the articles used were generally held responsible and punished." Regulations were publicly posted and enforced. Town life was rigorously controlled and the activities of merchants – their prices, equipment, and transactions were "strictly regulated."[62] Efforts to monitor land allocation in the villages, maintained within the T'ang period, sought to extend the regulatory hand of government over village land allocations. Since currency disorders were endemic and crops were variable, in times of scarcity price control projects would usually multiply though they could hardly be maintained in full rigor over extended periods.

The scope of regulatory control was probably as wide in the West but perhaps less comprehensive. The remarkable exchange of correspondence between a Roman emperor and one of his proconsuls illustrates the wide scope of central government surveillance over local matters.[63] Steadily throughout the fifth and sixth centuries the empire sought to maintain private as well as public services by binding soldiers, officials, state artisans and clerks, tenants and craftsmen to localities of origin, and making the callings hereditary (Jones 1966, 2:1049).

Both empires rationalized agricultural tax administration during the periods under review. The West under Diocletian converted the agricultural tax into a twin levy: one on the value of all farm property (including estates as well as peasant proprietorships) determined by cadastral survey and coded into standardized standard land units; the other based on the number of adult workers, with women counting for a fraction of an adult nonaged male. These coded land and labor units were carried in tax records for a long period of time as a basis for fixing the tax to be collected from a particular property. The land and labor units were then summed to obtain provincial totals. Something approaching a budgetary estimate for the province was worked up for the coming year. After approval by the emperor it was converted into a tax rate (*indiction*) on land and labor units applicable to the province. The land tax was usually collected in kind though as the stable gold currency became better established the tax was often commuted in whole or in part to gold, thus expanding the role for merchant capital and private trade. The labor tax was sometimes payable in kind but more often in gold. The system worked quite well though frequently supplementary levies, which the central authorities usually resisted, had to be imposed (*superindictiones*). A certain number of army recruits had to be provided locally each year. If not forthcoming voluntarily, a recruit was to be valued at 36 solidi (a half-pound of gold) to be assessed the local agricultural community according to their standardized units of land and labor. To these land, labor, and recruit levies were added collection fees, some authorized and some locally imposed, and local duties called *munera sordida* for grinding corn and baking bread for troops, provision of extra animals for the transport post, burning charcoal for public purposes, and the like. The system worked well enough so that army requisitions if needed for grain, fodder, or supplies could be charged against the forthcoming tax. In times of crop failure taxes would be waived, and arrears built up from time to time were remitted (Jones 1966, 1:63, 207, 293–311).

The T'ang fiscal system for agriculture was revolutionized midstream. The first system involved a flat national levy on the standard peasant holding of 2.8 cwt. of grain, 20 feet of silk, 25 feet of hempen plus silk floss and yarns. To this was added 20 days of corvée labor, avoidable by paying an exemption tax or provision of a substitute. This in turn was supplemented by a number of special labor services commutable into a tax locally established. Since the peasant proprietorship was increasingly replaced by private estates operated outside the official land tenure system, an additional set of agricultural levies was later imposed on all household establishments (urban and rural) graded by their wealth or acreage of cultivated land. This yielded about as much grain as the peasant levy proper, though this grain was intended as insurance against crop failure and to a considerable extent it was so used. This dual system was partially based on official land registration of peasant proprietors holding a standard allotment and partially based on actual holdings of land unauthorized in the basic land tenure code. This dual system became increasingly awkward and difficult to administer. Hence the system was replaced by two new levies: one from all households and one a levy on all cultivated lands. Obligation to corvée continued along with responsibility for local service. Of the proceeds a set quota was earmarked for the imperial government; the balance was shared between the provincial and local authorities. Quotas were subject to adjustment based on estimated changes in population. By this system substantial authority over the revenue system devolved upon provincial authorities, expanding the role played by local government and laying the basis for what Max Weber termed the "prebendal" state.[64]

Along with the burden of taxes collected and turned over to central government treasuries and warehouses, there were additional charges, difficult to document, imposed by the collectors for their benefit. In later centuries these came to exceed greatly the tax collections going to government in China.[65] In the West the authorized fees (*remunerationes*) came to 2.5 solidi per standard land unit of assessment (*iugum*) to compensate for "various illicit fees" that were denied, bringing total costs of collections in fees to a third of the tax levy itself.[66]

In both East and West direct agricultural taxation on productive farmlands was the most important revenue source. But this was extensively supplemented with levies on merchants and town craftsmen and shopkeepers. There were also tolls on imports, fairs, and state monopolies. In times of trouble there were always special levies or forced loans by local military authorities. The Chinese state monopoly on salt was a big revenue producer (Twitchett 1953/1970, 56). The Romans drew from a source the Chinese never tapped, namely a 5 percent levy on inheritances made possible, no doubt, because of the higher development of private property, with a wide range of testamentary freedom for property owners. The Romans also had a good-sized collection of crown lands scattered over the empire. Crown rentals thus supplemented standard taxation (Jones 1966, 1:413). Besides annual taxes the Romans developed a set of levies payable in gold by various groups of notables including senators and curiales, on the accession of a new emperor and quinquennially thereafter; and heavy special quinquennial tax was levied on money lenders, merchants, and shopkeepers, including artisan dealers.[67] Custom duties on the frontiers were set at 12.5 percent and there were transit dues at provincial interposts on roads or ports (Jones 1966, 2:825).

To list individual tax revenues and their administrative features is easier than to estimate their overall impact. Jones (1966, 1:469, 2:820) estimates that in the time of Justinian the land tax paid on landed property reached over a third of the gross farm product. Standard assessments were not altered if land quality was impaired or if population declined. One detailed report for a district with some 37,410 acres of mostly arable land showed that the taxes assessed on the district amounted to 166 pounds of gold or the equivalent of 3.6 million liters of wheat, somewhat short of the typical rents running at 50 percent of the yield taken by the landlord (Jones 1966, 2:820). For high-grade land well managed these rates of taxation left a little margin. But for poorer land slapped with a standard assessment, as was frequently the case, the taxation was crippling. There is ample evidence of accumulated arrears periodically written off the books as uncollectible though collection efforts in villages were by repute stringent.[68] The testimony of vacant properties abandoned by their owners and workers all over the empire is indisputable. On good authority the scale of this abandonment is found to be "considerable," up to 20 percent for the empire as a whole (Jones 1966, 2:812–16). Contemporaries attributed this *agri deserti* chiefly to crippling taxation. It is interesting that Marx-Engels shared this judgment.[69]

Next to be considered is the dramatic story of Chinese tax drainage. Though the passion for tax revenues was as great, it does not appear the amount that reached the imperial treasury was up to the Roman level. Throughout the first half of the T'ang regime, agricultural taxation was confined chiefly to peasant freeholders settled on registered lands omitting the growing development of estate holdings and the growing holdings of Buddhist temples and monasteries. In intermediary years of the regime marked by intense and destructive civil war, it appears direct agricultural taxation disintegrated and the imperial treasury relied chiefly on salt excises, crown revenues, and the like (Twitchett 1953/1970, 34). In the latter portion of the T'ang regime effective control over taxation was shifted to provincial governors who were becoming in the end years of the T'ang, virtual hereditary satrapies each with their own tax tables.[70] The labor tax however, via the corvée, supported a vast expansion of public works construction, including the building of the Grand Canal which joined together during the Sui-T'ang period the Yangtze basin with the Yellow River valley.[71]

At the peak years of the tax system, imperial tax collections (for which we have a record for 746 A.D.) appear quite ample: over 2 million strings of copper cash, 7.14 million rolls of mixed-grade silk, about a million tons of grain, 1,800,000 rolls of fine silk, and 1,350,000 pieces of cloth (Fitzgerald 1942, 319). That would appear to contrast favorably with the Roman imperial collection at its peak.

Income Redistributive Patterns

Taxation for economic systems is important not for its own sake but primarily for the way it redistributes income and benefits. Here there were similarities and differences. Taxes in kind needed to be transported to the imperial centers or frontiers where they would support the court, the central government establishments, and the army.

Transportation to support armed forces was the most difficult undertaking because the army tended to be placed where invasion threatened in difficult terrain. Transportation to the Roman capitals in Rome and Constantinople was relatively easy using Mediterranean shipping; but supplying the Diocletian army of 435,266 scattered along the Rhine, the Danube, and in outlying Syria was more difficult (Jones 1966, 1:679). Movement of grain and supplies from the Yangtze to the Yellow River valley was for the most part resolved by the construction in the early T'ang period of the great 660 mile canal, which led to Loyang on the Yellow River. But the further movement of supplies up the Yellow River through rocky gorges to reach the imperial capital at Chhang-an was a formidable and costly undertaking (Needham 1954–1978, Book 3, 4:274, 278).

Net available proceeds of taxation were further reduced to pay salaries or provide grain and cloth for the support of the vast civil service and armed forces mobilized by the two empires. In the early T'ang period expenses for the army were not so great because the backbone of the armed forces was a local militia enrolled for short term (Eberhard 1977, 177). The Imperial Roman legions were always salaried and their cost of maintenance tended to rise over time to encourage recruitment and to win favor of the troops, the backbone of the state (Jones 1966, 2:619, 627).

Apart from the army or its officer cadres and the higher civil service, the main beneficiaries of the tax system were the dynastic courts with the central figure of the emperor and his personal family, his immediate kin, all potential royalty or "princes of the blood." Attached to them were the army of servants who tended royalty's table, managed the wardrobe, provided entertainment, and serviced the many residential establishments for the different seasons of the year. In the Western empire, where monogamic marriage was enshrined and bastardy frowned upon, the numbers of close kin were kept down to children, brothers and sisters, mothers and uncles and aunts of the emperor himself and his consort. In China where concubinage was the fashion, the royal household was enormous in size and palatial establishments of royal minions became very costly.[72] The preliminary investment of heirs or coemperors as ruling caesars or augusti by Diocletian, maintained as the basis of the Roman imperial structure thereafter, led as a matter of course to multiple imperial capitals for up to four segments of the empire each endowed with a set of palatial establishments.[73]

The decision to change capitals, sometimes out of boredom or caprice, could result in enormous expenditure – that for the walls and aqueducts of Constantinople running to 30 tons of gold (Gibbon 1776/ 1932, 1:513, 538). Gold and silver were widely used as decoration to symbolize high social or bureaucratic status. A gold belt was the ensign distinguishing the offices of the 60 provincial generals who were allowed beside their pay an allowance sufficient to provide for 190 servants and 158 horses. Nor were civilian governors treated less extravagantly. In the West the salaries collected had been progressively stepped up from 1 solidus to every 120 taxpayers to 1 solidus to every 60 or even to every 13 taxpayers (Jones 1966, 1:397). Sybaritic tastes were no less developed in the East where work in jade, gold and silver, and use of silk permitted ostentation and luxury of an extreme order.

Beyond the imperial court and its entourage, the provincial and prefectual governorships and military commanders and the staff of tax collectors who pocketed the fees they could extort from smaller taxpayers, who else were the beneficiaries of the tax system? Here must be included the savior faiths and their ecclesiastical organizations which became established in both empires in the reference period: in the West, Christianity; in the East, Buddhism. They acquired enormous economic resources from contributions of followers, from gifts or bequests of the wealthy, and from endowments provided by rulers to atone for their sinful ways.[74] By the sixth century in the Roman world "the bishops and clergy had become far more numerous than the administrative officers and civil servants of the empire and were on the average paid at substantially higher rates" (Jones 1966, 2:1046). Added to these were monasteries frequently nonproductive and sustained by landed endowments or from the alms of the poor. It was the same in the East where the Buddhist temples and monasteries were tax exempt and enjoyed the fruits of revenues from landed estates, commercial business properties, and even substantial slave holdings.[75]

But established churches can only function by rendering sufficient service that believers will be drawn to them and offer support. Precisely that character of reciprocal service was conspicuously absent for the other great beneficiary who profited by the fiscal power mobilized in the imperial states under survey—the landowning gentry. These drew upon the fiscal surplus more steeply in China. The Chinese gentry were for the most part only lightly affected by the heavy burden of agricultural taxation. They were not subject to duties of corvée or to supplying silk and cloth and other special local services. Their influence in local tax and prefectural administration was considerable because of their social standing. The Roman gentry for the most part had little tax exemption on their landed properties; and their properties were taxed for the supply of recruits. The gentry was also liable for an inheritance tax. The highest order of senatorial notables was even subjected to a special levy on the accession of the emperor as a coronarial offering and this was repeated quinquennially thereafter. A small annual special tax on all senators was imposed ranging between 40 and 7 solidi according to wealth.[76] When the empire had to raise a lot of gold to pay off Attila's armies, this was raised by a virtual capital levy on senators, especially those who in the past had received tax remissions or exemptions.[77] And both the senatorial and curial orders were expected on ceremonial occasions to provide games and celebrations to regale the populace. These were often very lavish and costly affairs.[78] These public entertainment programs were undertaken without benefit of the tax-deductibility which lessens the cost of comparable programs of public entertainment by which America's corporations now buy their way into public esteem.

3

The European
Medieval Economies

Bounds of the Medieval

Medieval economies gradually emerged in Western and Central Europe following the breakdown of imperial Roman authority in the later fourth and fifth centuries A.D. and the absorption of successive waves of invasions and folk migrations between the fourth and tenth centuries A.D. The development of these economies extended through the thirteenth to fifteenth centuries.

In this extended period of roughly a thousand years there was of course not a single economic system but what a learned Marxist historian in a brilliant synthetic essay has termed "a variegated typology of social formations."[1]

These social formations were in part shaped by relationships of European peoples at their borders or zonal frontiers. To the south and southeast and across the Mediterranean there was association, contact, and often struggle with the more advanced Byzantine and Muslim civilizations. The boundary lines between Muslim, Byzantine, and European worlds were continually shifting in the Adriatic, the Balkans, the Italian and Iberian peninsulas and their island chains, the Western Mediterranean Sea, and Asia Minor itself. Armed struggle between these clashing civilizations was nearly always somewhere in evidence. The frontier was none the less a nourishing one because important materials and products could be drawn from it: luxury products, gold and silver coins or bullion, rare spices, slaves, dyes, cotton and silk fabrics, medicines, and books. The major center of trade, cultural infiltration, and exchange was at the headwaters of the

Adriatic draining the eastern Cisalpine region of Italy where the mercantile Venetian people built up their great power as an interpost between the three civilizations. Rivalling the Venetian Adriatic as interpost was southern Italy, its island extensions, and the Iberian peninsula where Muslim and European control alternated and where trade was facilitated. The main theater of this interplay of three civilizations was the Mediterranean where sea carriage could permit advanced forms of mercantile urban life to take root on its shores. Advanced Italian economic and cultural life owes much to its exposure to the challenge of other advanced civilizations in the Mediterranean, augmented by its own unique heritage from Roman society.

Relationships at the northern and eastern frontiers were of a different character. From the great Eurasian steppes there came wave after wave of nomadic incursions which twice led to lasting settlement. Their first impact was felt by Slavic peoples who had drifted into Central and Eastern Europe and the Balkans after the Germanic migrations had run their course. To the immediate north were the Northmen or Vikings who for nearly two centuries raided for loot and slaves, infiltrated, and finally settled in both Western and Eastern Europe, achieving mastery of Anglo-Saxons in England and of Kievan Russians.

The Roman Catholic Church

All the medieval social formations were structured by the Roman Catholic church carried over from Romanic society. The power of the Catholic church was rooted in the respect of early man for the supernatural whose presence was everywhere sensed and felt. Pushed on by anxieties for survival in an insecure world, the common fear and reverence for the supernatural needed only to be purified and freed of admixture with magic and divisive forms of worship. The church broke out of the old society in which it functioned and to which it was adapted. The church preserved its autonomy and integrity as an international institution through disaster and defeat. It successfully proselytized its conquerors, building a single cultural world of shared faith and belief. Perry Anderson (1974a, 131) has called it the "frail aqueduct across which the cultural reservoirs of the Classical World now passed"; Talcott Parsons (1971, 38) considered it the "primary institutional bridge between ancient and modern Western society."[2]

Perhaps the principal public service of the Catholic church which stood over medieval society as a great overarching presence was to restrain the strong tendency to internecine warfare among peoples with insecure boundaries and with a taste for aggression. The church with its doctrine of amity rather than enmity, its constant chanting for peace, its unified worship service, and common creed and shared ritual formed a spiritual bond between European Christian peoples. Of course the tendency to internecine warfare could only be restrained and somewhat humanized. At least among fellow Christians, captives would not be murdered or enslaved though they could be held for high ransom. It was easier for rulers to accept the arbitrament of battle and consign away territories knowing they would not be withdrawn from the common faith. Ruling families from the most distant of European nationalities became joined together by systematic intermarriage, which again was facilitated by a common faith. This intermarriage, though it brought into existence a single dynastic ruling class, fissured this class with innumerable dynastic claims that spawned almost as many wars for dynastic succession as offspring.

Another form of public service rendered by the church was to minister to the needs of the poor, the distressed, or the very ill. With its mystique of poverty, its veneration for the principle of sacrifice, its worship of a god born in a manger, giving to the poor was turned into a supremely worthy act. By the end of the fifth century A.D. the principle that one-quarter of ecclesiastical revenues from altar dues and offerings were to be used for the relief of the poor had become established as a custom of the Italian church (Gibbon 1776–1788/1932, 1:665). A century later Pope Gregory noted that it was the "custom of the Apostolic See" to "so instruct all newly consecrated bishops" (Bede 731/1955, 72). Virtually the same requirement was imposed by a Carolingian edict in the early ninth century (Rives 1976, 168). The leading figure in the Carolingian dynasty, Charlemagne, set a notable personal example by tithing his own royal estates and by allocating in his will the bulk of his accumulated treasure to the church and to the poor (Einhard 828–884/1969, 87). The monastic orders especially in the earlier medieval centuries were devoted to the ministry of the poor.[3]

Other public services related to education. The church and especially the monasteries kept alive what survived of the writings of classical antiquity. The monasteries provided formal schooling for their novices and opportunity in later years for study and writing.[4] Churchmen were widely placed in service as officers of the state. The universities of Western Europe took their rise out of schools attached to the great cathedrals. By the twelfth century universities as an organized set of faculties awarding degrees or licenses had clearly emerged (Haskins 1957, 161).

The principle of celibacy—a binding rule for all monastics and high ecclesiastics and after the twelfth century for ordained priests—

opened channels of upward social advance in the medieval world. Since high church position could not generally be inherited by male heirs nor could clerical families be united by intermarriage and thus breed their own successors, opportunity for social advance for able men of low status was available in the ecclesiastical world.[5]

Economic Foundations of the Church

The economic foundations of the church were generously laid out. In the former lands of the Roman Empire the church had extensive properties given by Christian emperors (Gibbon 1776–1788/1932, 1:665). The new Germanic rulers were equally generous with church support. Converted kings and chiefs provided for the building of great cathedrals and monasteries. Bishops and monasteries were endowed with princely grants of manorial estates to provide current revenue. In both Anglo-Saxon England and Merovingian Europe, church properties embraced a good third of cultivated land (Postan 1975, 86). William the Conqueror actually assigned to ecclesiastics 26.3 percent of the manorial revenues available for distribution following the conquest (Bury 1929–1936, 5:508).

Gifts and grants of manorial estates and altar offerings and dues did not suffice to finance the ever-widening work of the church and of its many institutions and provide for the extension of worship service in rural villages. Church leaders sought to tap the current flow of income with a compulsory levy. They inherited no such levy from the Roman world in which the Levitical tithe found no favor.[6] It was gradually perceived that manorial collections from villages did not exhaust village resources. By the eighth century, moreover, the Christian faith in Western Europe was no longer an imported novelty but a settled institution that had sunk roots among the people. One church council as early as A.D. 570 proclaimed that failure to tithe would result in excommunication (Boyd 1952, 28). Various minor fees and charges were made compulsory, sometimes with the sanction of the state.[7] As a moral obligation or pastoral precept tithing was strongly advocated by many rulers and by church councils and probably was here and there instituted on a local basis but was not included in the formal legal codes. The break to overt legality for the tithe was apparently made by a nest of Carolingian rulers centering around Charlemagne and his sons but possibly also including his father, Pepin (Boyd 1952, 37). These rulers were devoted followers of the faith. They sought to strengthen the church, over which they retained strict controls, as a major support for the overall regime (Boussard 1968, 92). In the later decades of the eighth century and early decades of the ninth a universal requirement of tithing with loose guidelines for the use of the proceeds by assigned parties was variously imposed throughout the Carolingian Empire. Only much later in the tenth century A.D. was the requirement to tithe imposed with state sanctions in the Anglo-Saxon kingdom (Roundell 1888, 218).

Since tithe collection must take place in villages, it may be surmised that tithing was introduced in manorial villages under the guidance and with the approval of the manorial lord holding jurisdiction, possibly in association with the building or consecration of a local chapel or parish church for which some sort of local support would be needed. The building could only go ahead with the approval of the lordship who would need to make a grant of land for the edifice including burial grounds and for a plot of arable land (glebe) for the minister. The manorial lord would also need to approve the collection from his woodlot of the requisite building timber and other building materials. He would also contribute at least some of the funds needed for purchase of outside craftwork for cabinetry, bells, images, vessels for holy water, candelabrum, bier for the dead, a font with a lock, and other sacramental objects used in worship. A complex pattern later evolved fixing responsibility on lordship and villagers respectively for upkeep and resupply of various items in the church edifice (Homans 1941/1975, 383). Lordship had—or assumed—control over tithe revenues or collections. He also assumed the right of nominating the parish minister and determining the share to be awarded the appointed priest. This right of so-called *avowson* persisted in Great Britain through the nineteenth century.[8] The same right also was claimed both in Great Britain and on the Continent to apply to nomination of heads of monasteries and convents founded on land or with the aid of grants from manorial lordship.[9]

The tithe on manorial estates converted the village church, as a recent medieval historian has noted, into one of the leading revenue producing assets of the demesne "alongside mills, breweries and bakehouses" (Duby 1968, 56). The same historian noted that monastic properties were often reduced to the status of "satellites, indeed almost annexes of the estates of the great families of the region" (Duby 1968, 177). In northern and central Italy, this pattern of manorial or lordship control and appropriation of tithes and local church administration emerged during the last half of the tenth century. The powerful bishops and some village priests who emerged as local rulers during the period rewarded their military knights and local clan chiefs with grants or leases of local church properties and tithes including the right of avowson and generally with the status of local church patron.

The services, chiefly military, initially required of recipients of such grants later faded away. The property rights acquired were stubbornly retained and became the economic basis of hierarchical feudatories who played an important role in later Italian history and whose property rights over peasant producers were later recognized by the Kingdom of Italy in 1887. These property rights to collect a perpetual rent of farm produce were deemed valid as a kind of "dominical" tithe even though the "ecclesiastical" tithe proper was in principle abolished.[10] Elsewhere in northern and central Europe recent authority has noted that in these areas, "often dominated by the nobility and the state . . . the tithes were often secularized, converted into dues and levied arbitrarily. . . ." (Le Roy Ladurie, Goy 1982, 59).

Feudal control of parish tithes or appropriation of these tithes as one of a set of manorial dues is consistent with a notorious fact about such tithes when comprehensive statistics about them became available. Their wide variation regarding rates and product coverage within a locality is conspicuous (Rives 1976, 31). Rates were diversified "even in adjoining parishes" (McMasters 1985, 148). In Maine, Berry, and Campagne it averaged one-thirteenth, around Orleans only one-thirtieth, and even less in parts of Dauphiné and Provence (McMasters 1985, 147). In England "Hall," "Court," or "Manor" farms were often exempt from payment of tithes, a fact consistent with manorial control of tithing (Ernle 1912/1961, 339). In Brittany the tithing rate in adjoining parishes could vary from 10 percent to 2.7 percent (McMasters 1985, 143). So wide a range of variation is consistent with origin on manorial estates where divergent levies of particular types were readily explicable.

Manorial appropriation and control of tithing revenues continued in France to the very end, when in 1789–1790 tithing was effectively abolished in revolutionary France. At that time some 12 percent of existing tithing revenue was reported owned by lay appropriators (McMasters 1985, 149). In the diocese of Auch in Gascony where full details of the tithing distribution have been published, in 13 percent of parishes 37.3 percent of parish tithes was allotted to a seigneur, count, marquis, or other lay holder (Rives 1976, 64–104).

Manorial control over tithing was never absolute or free from church participation. The older established baptismal churches and major cathedrals retained direct control over tithing in the territories immediately served. Early church tradition and express rulings instructed bishops to retain one-quarter of church collections and offerings "for hospitality and other commitments" (Bede 721/1953, 72). A Carolingian edict expressly reserved a quarter of all tithes for the "episcopis" (bishop) (Rives 1976, 169). Later church canons gave the bishop general authority over tithes collected and retained for church use within the diocese (Boyd 1957, 138). Where feudal pressure on the church had been very potent, as in Italy during the tenth century, bishops had transferred to lay control the larger part of the tithes under their jurisdiction. In France, on the contrary, bishops and their chapters tended to hang on to their share of tithes.[11]

Moreover, lay control of church administration by avowson was also limited. A candidate nominated by the patron to an abbacy or church priesthood or even by a king to a bishopric or abbacy had to be confirmed by the supervisory bishop or directly by the pope and consecrated to the office and invested with the paraphanalia of office. In later medieval years this confirmation by the pope would call for a personal visit and presentation of a rich present or offering. Once invested with the office the priest or high cleric was not generally removable by the lay patron and the meshwork and charisma of the church would tend to draw him away from lay influence. And though a lay patron could found a local church it would need to be consecrated by the bishop and endowed by him with a bounded territory both for purposes of tithe collection and administration of religious services.

Thus up and down the line clerical and secular authority developed an intimate copartnership over church administration. This copartnership extended to the state as a whole. The high officers of the church participated as an organized estate in all national assemblies. When the king summoned his forces for warfare, the bishop and the abbot were called upon, too, for a contingent of fighting men in armor and sometimes the bishop or abbot led them in person.

Such a copartnership inevitably would have its ups and downs with predominance shifting now to one side or another. The power of the church perhaps reached its lowest in the early and late phases of the medieval epoch. In the early period the Germanic peoples were establishing residence and kingdoms in the former Roman provinces newly and loosely converted to the faith. Ties between church institutions were necessarily weak and church councils and conclaves were rare. In the final period of the medieval epoch high clerics allowed their national attachments to break the bond of church unity. For nearly three-quarters of the fourteenth century rival pontiffs quartered in Avignon and in Rome set up opposing papal establishments drawing allegiance from differing national communities. When the breach was healed the papal office was turning into an Italian Renaissance principality and exposed to what that great Renaissance historian, Jacob Burckhardt, called the "strange perils and trials . . . as the political spirit of the nation began to lay hold upon it [the papacy]. . . ." (Burckhardt 1860/1958, 126).

Between these periods of weakness was a period of church strength opened up by the Crusades and reinforced by the rise of towns. The German emperor was defeated in the investiture conflict, while the church reasserted the celibacy principle and proclaimed the right to its revenues and tithes. Request was made and no doubt sounded from most pulpits that all tithes and gifts to the church in lay hands be faithfully returned to the church to avoid excommunication. The response was favorable but artful. Many church-appropriated tithes and patronage rights of ministerial appointment were transferred as a gift to a nearby or favored monastery or monastic institution. The friars and monks assembled would be competent to provide priestly services. Monastic institutions were attractive to benefactors by their ability to offer numerous masses at stated intervals and in celebrated cases indefinitely (Coulton 1923–1950, 3:Chap. 5). Finally, in the eleventh and twelfth centuries the life of monastic institutions was still close to the ideals of the saints who founded the principal monastic orders. These institutions were withdrawn from the secular world and its trials. They disdained the comfort and luxury to which the world aspired and were devoted to an austere life replete with study and prayer. Hence kings joined feudal lordship generally and endowed monastic institutions with manorial estates or at least their endowment of tithes and avowson rights (Coulton 1923–1950, 2:63, 3:158, 179). These monastic accessions when added to the previous gifts that endowed monastic institutions with princely revenues, made monastic institutions the major ecclesiastical beneficiary of tithes in many Western European countries in the later period of the medieval epoch.[12] In Italy restitution was made more commonly of only a quarter of the tithes for use of the local church (Boyd 1952, 126, 131).

Institution of Money

The institution of coined gold and silver money was inherited like the Catholic church from classical antiquity. It was steadily maintained in medieval Europe. In the earliest stages of Germanic settlement old dies were used and old mints were allowed to function. Gold and silver coins were minted usually bearing some kingly inscription but often just the name of the local moneyer given the privilege of minting, doubtless in return for some cash payment.[13] As Germanic settlement developed, mints spread, and wherever breaks in transport networks permitted markets or fairs to take shape, there a mint would be established almost as a market accessory (Duby 1974, 67). Recent authorities on early medieval economic life estimate that in the seventh century between 700 to 1000 mints functioned in former Gaul (Duby 1974, 67). These mints and the gold and silver coins recovered from treasure troves, graves, sunken ships, as well as reference to them in contemporary documents bear their own witness to the reality of the process of monetization that characterized the medieval economy.

Of the two precious metals, silver was favored. Mining of silver continued in France and Spain and was extended into rich silver-bearing lodes in Germany and Bohemia (Bautier 1971, 33). Hence the silver penny or denier (Latin *denarius*) was standardized by the Carolingian monarchs at 240 to the pound and issued later in larger pieces (groats, groschen) more suitable for larger transactions (Clapham 1941–1978, 2:579). But gold continued to serve as a money though no longer mined in Western Europe. The region inherited a supply of gold, most of it worked up as ornaments, gold thread, tableware, and sacramental objects. From this source gold could be recovered easily for minting. Gold coin could be drawn by trade with the Byzantine and Muslim world, which obtained raw gold from Asian and African sources not available to Europeans. Since in the Muslim and Byzantine mercantile centers there was a ready exchange between gold and silver, European merchants tended to seek payment of balances due them in gold or bullion, which was more valuable where it was scarce than where it was abundant (Clapham 1941–1978, 2:88, 161). Commercial transfers of gold on trading account were supplemented by gold paid in tribute by Byzantines to prevent attacks on their Italian frontier.[14] In these ways enough gold flowed to Byzantine Italy, which in the early medieval years had extensive trade relations with the Byzantine and Muslim worlds. At Pisa and Lucca between 1000 and 1129, 64 percent of recorded payments were made in gold (Herlihy 1978, 1:4).

Since gold used in exchange would need to be weighed and often assayed, it could almost as readily be used unminted as money in the form of rings, bracelets, bars, thread, or ornamental objects. The goldsmith in Merovingian times was reported a very active professional (Bloch 1967, 198).

Hence resumption of gold coinage in Western Europe in the thirteenth century chiefly by the major Italian mercantile centers constituted no break in monetary practice but only reinforced tendencies already uppermost for a bimetallic set of moneys. One set was widely used by merchants or princes and church prelates. The other was used universally for making daily payments in local markets or paying dues and fees imposed in manorial or public courts.

The scale on which money was coined and kept in circulation throws light on the relative degree of monetization of economic life. At the outset of the medieval epoch the degree of overt monetization was low. We may readily suppose that town merchants and craftsmen who made up the core of the very small urban population in the early medieval period marketed for payment in money most of their services or products. Products channelled by international or interregional trade such as Asian spices and silks, the main working metals of iron and copper, and the critically essential supplies of salt would also be distributed and marketed via money payments. Market dues and customs were usually payable in money.[15] Papal dues were necessarily in monetary form and contributed substantially to international monetary transfers.[16] The marketed fraction of farm produce must have been very low. Of the total surplus harvested by church, lord, and state, a considerable fraction was retained on the estate and stored in cellars and warehouses for direct consumption by an itinerant monarch or lordship and his good-sized traveling parties or shipped or carted to appropriate warehouses where utilization would be arranged. In the early years of the Angevin Norman monarchy in England all the surplus of the scattered royal domain was collected in kind though for purposes of better accounting it was given a money value.[17] In the earlier rule of Charlemagne, standing instructions to managers of royal manors required an unstated fraction of the net disposable output to be marketed so that every year on Palm Sunday there would be delivered to the royal fisc "the money arising from our profits" (Duby 1968, 362). Only late in the twelfth century did the managers of the English royal demesne arrange for a money commutation rendering distant cartage of the royal take unnecessary and giving the crown its revenue in more flexible form.[18]

Yet even of farm output in the earliest phase of the medieval epoch some fraction of available output must have been marketed by village families. They could not otherwise provide for their needs for iron, copper, or brass used for farm implements and household utensils. Salt was essential both for food flavoring, for animal nourishment, and for food preservation. Most of this marketed farm output of food and fiber was consumed by the small productive urban population who produced goods and services chiefly for the landed proprietors, their attendants, knights, and local managers. But some of the available income belonged to peasant villagers, especially those who held allodially or who worked choice farm holdings with the help of healthy sons or who had good holdings of hardy oxen or other livestock. This income would be used to buy in the market necessary supplies of salt, iron, cooking pots or pans, an occasional piece of cloth, a kitty of essential household goods to make up a dowry for a daughter or a few coins for a younger son leaving the house to make his fortune in the outside world, and a gift to the priest for a christening, a burial, or a marriage. Because many peasant villagers had built up a little treasure trove of coins and liked to attend local fairs and markets to bring to it some bit of extra produce or some crafted handiwork, Charlemagne ordered his estate managers to take care "that our domestics apply themselves well to their work and do not waste their time in running about to markets and fairs" (Power 1924, 36).

As in most coinage systems with much hand-to-hand circulation and handcraft mint technology, the quality of the coinage tended to deteriorate as mint masters and clippers sought to spread the deterioration more uniformly by reducing the precious metal content of the coins. Thus the Carolingian denier or silver coin in many parts of Europe became smaller and thinner and heavily alloyed with copper.[19] The process of deterioration was generally very slow so that at any given time the predominant mass of coins handled by merchants or dealers could be readily handled by applying standard discounts allowing only for marked variations in weight. And in many parts of Europe the integrity of the silver coinage was kept intact by repeated reminting, as in Anglo-Saxon and Norman England, where until the mid-fourteenth century "the silver content of the silver penny remained constant" (Clapham 1941–1978, 3:583).

Late in the medieval epoch the use of coined money was supplemented by the first beginnings of deposit banking and credit exchange to facilitate local, international, and inter-regional transfer. In the thirteenth century the capitalist banking enterprise clearly emerged in the prosperous mercantile republics of northern Italy and with it the practice of fractional reserve deposit banking. Loan finance was chiefly by tolerance of overdrawing of accounts and secondarily through purchase or discount of bills of exchange.[20] The modern commercial bank was not yet born partly because the Italian banking enterprise commonly carried on mixed mercantile-banking business and partly because there was little use made of deposit transfer by check or of circulating bank notes. Since these Italian banking enterprises of the thirteenth century played an important role in organizing European trade and finance, they very much entered into the economic systems of Western, central, southern, and northern Europe, which can hardly be reduced to feudalism, the "mode of production dominated by the land and a natural economy."[21]

Modes of Production
AGRICULTURE

Throughout the entire European medieval period—from the earliest to the latest—three major modes of production and transitional forms of a fourth mode are exhibited in combinations that varied over time and space. The predominant mode is unquestionably manorial serfdom. A village community—evolved from earlier Germanic or Celtic background or carried over in the form of a Roman villa with its mixture of slaves and ascribed or bound and free tenants—is put under constraint to support lordship. This may be a warrior lord, his fighting entourage of armed retainers or later knights, or an ecclesiastical establishment. This mode is premised on appropriation and control of village land by lordship. Village peasant holdings are assigned by lifetime grant to each successive holder, following pledge of allegiance and fealty to the lord, sometimes accompanied by payment of a set fee (Gottlieb 1984, 55). This manorial pattern clearly shows up in surviving records of the Merovingian epoch, Anglo-Saxon English society, the classical empire of Charlemagne, the north and later south Italy following Gothic, Lombard, and later Frankish conquests, and variously elsewhere.

In a later period there is less call on labor services to operate the demesne estate. This may be parcelled out to larger farmers willing to pay a cash rent or distributed to tenant villagers on a sharecrop or cash-rent basis. In place of labor services tenant households working a larger acreage make cash payments or share the crop of field and stock. Taxing villagers for use of village resources (oven, presses, bull, firewood, pasture) or to complete the various stages of the life cycle (family succession, marriage of daughters or sending away of sons) tended to remain as a bitter heritage of feudal oppression. But in some parts of Europe—chiefly in Lombardy and Tuscany—commutation of feudal services was well advanced by the twelfth century. There the feudal mode of production was turning into landlord farming, involving not feudal but bourgeois forms of property in contract, in land tenure, and in rights to alienate and inherit.[22]

Along with manorial serfdom are scattered holdings of peasant proprietors concentrated sometimes in small districts. These proprietors are substantially freed from feudal oppression. Their ownership stake in the land usually was shared in varying degrees with a village community having authority over woodlands and pasturage. Villagers have access to the king's justice and are subject to his call for military service. When they reside in or near a manorial holding, they are subject usually to some bit of service and to participation in manorial courts. Their spatial distribution was widespread.

They are reported as surrounding manors in the Carolingian state and as persisting in Aquitaine, southern France, and northern Italy "to the end."[23] In Spain a unique society of peasant-soldiers took shape holding their land freely especially in the early Reconquest period.[24] In most of Germany peasant freeholders persisted; and in Scandinavian territories after slavery disappeared with Christianization freeholders held from 25 to 40 percent of the arable land.[25] In the Alpine mountain valleys freeholding peasant communities fought valiantly and preserved their freedom (Braudel 1973, 1:38).

In Anglo-Saxon England they were known as sokemen or franklins, which in Anglo-Norman dialect signified "free man." Franklin landholdings tended to be smaller than a manorial demesne but somewhat larger than the middle class of villagers: so their economic base was relatively strong. Anglo-Saxon sokemen tended to have small-size landholdings perhaps because holdings could be sold or partitioned among heirs more readily than on manorial establishments. Freeholding areas were concentrated in the former Danish settlements and the eastern counties including Kent and those parts of England where "woodland settlement" was distinct from "champion" country, which later went through the enclosure process. It has been estimated that men holding freely made up nearly a third of the agricultural population at the time of the Conquest.[26]

Individual freeholders and their village communities had to battle against encroachments of nearby feudal lords within whose court jurisdiction they fell. Many freeholders at times of crisis submitted their properties to manorial estates.[27] Others allegedly sold out to big proprietors.[28] But this process of manor enlargement was offset by counteracting tendencies for increased freeholding by formal enfranchisement of serfs who mostly purchased but sometimes were given their freedom. Freehold village communities tended to encroach upon manorial domains especially in waste or woodlands where their holdings could be slowly but steadily enlarged.[29] Vineyard cultivation was available in areas south of the Rhineland and in nearly all of Italy and Spain to small folk who were too poor to keep plough oxen but who with their strong arms, much spadework, and skill could successfully work vineyards (Duby 1968, 140).

A third class of production mode encountered in the medieval epoch was outright slavery equally at home in late Roman society and among Germanic and Scandinavian peoples who had learned that captives were too useful in labor to needlessly slaughter. Through the Carolingian period slave status was mostly confined to household domestics or field-workers domiciled on or near the demesne and serving it exclusively. When assigned to plots with the duty of self-maintenance and control of their own feeding and domestic arrangements, slaves tended over time to turn into serfs. The supply of slaves was diminished by enfranchisement and inadequate incentives for family reproduction. The supply was continually replenished by captives taken on the Slav, Celtic, and Moorish frontiers. As the medieval period wore on, slavery tended to disappear except in the south Mediterranean areas, though the trade of selling slaves captured on the European frontiers to Islam and Byzantium continued.[30]

CRAFT AND MERCANTILE URBAN PRODUCTION

It is in this field of production with its primarily urban organization that revolutionary changes occurred in the medieval epoch. There is every indication that following the major waves of Germanic migration and settlement the fraction of urban population in the former Western Roman Empire diminished greatly. The economic base for the support of the large proletarian population of Rome—fed by grain tribute collected from high-yielding granaries controlled by the empire—ended when imperial control of the western empire and its granaries was lost. Interregional trade going through wholesale urban or shipping centers declined because of insecure passage on the Mediterranean and unsettled conditions in inland territories. Except for very valuable products with few alternatives available—such as silks and spices—long-distance trade tended to disappear. As this trade disappeared the fraction of urban population supported by such trade also shrank—its transportation activity; the construction of vessels; warehousing of its inventories; and processing of its materials including cleaning, washing, sorting, and packing or baling. The relative share of money income earned from agriculture but spent by landlords and patricians or government establishments in cities declined. In the earlier years of the medieval epoch the lords and masters of the countryside resided largely on the estates. The rural castle or stronghold superseded the walled town as upper class residence. Apparently many craftsmen working with metals, wood, leather, fibers, stone, or clay left the cities for the countryside where their urban character was lost. So apparently the number of nonfood producers living outside farming villages diminished relative to the number of food producers, the circuit of their trading orbit greatly shrank, and the taste spectrum for their products shifted to ruder and simpler styles for customers with simpler tastes.[31]

These conditions appeared to persist through the Carolingian renaissance and became accentuated—some historians believe created—by the repeated Viking, Hungarian, and Muslim raids in the ninth and tenth centuries.[32] Thus the feudal mode of production and the manorial system in agriculture took shape and became deep rooted at a time when urban craft and mercantile activity was at a low ebb. The scraggly little urban settlements that remained were readily subordinated to some royal or episcopal palace or rural market place. Urban producers were encysted in a feudal organism and had little freedom of movement or independence of action or spirit. Markets were primarily local.

Then conditions changed and in the next four centuries the economic system was revolutionized by an amazing growth of mercantile and craft activity carried on in sprouting urban communities. Some were self-governing and often wielded formidable military power with large fleets commanding the oceans. Some mercantile states built up far-flung imperial domains. Italy took the lead in this urban development, which spread more slowly to middle Europe, finally reaching Germanic or Slavic territories that had never known Roman rule. International markets for this urban growth were created by large-scale scheduled international fairs drawing merchants from the Baltic, the Mediterranean, and the North Sea.[33]

The predominant mode of production was unquestionably that of simple commodity producers organized in guildlike associations that played a major regulative role. Leadership in these associations and the urban government they created usually fell into the hands of merchant guilds. In many of these urban communities merchants emerged who assembled raw materials and guided the operations of production of fine cloth by independent craft producers. These merchants and the banking enterprises associated with them later more or less clearly took on the form of capitalist enterprises because of the number of workers assembled, the far-flung character of their mercantile operations, the intensive force of competition characterizing their markets for raw materials and product disposition, and the rational character of their record keeping and search for profits.[34]

Innovation in Agriculture

The economic basis for this amazing urban growth was threefold. First and most important was innovation in farming practices and implements, which on our best available estimates almost doubled or tripled the marketable surpluses of agricultural produce providing the essential subsistence for an expanded urban population.[35] The earliest of these innovations was the development of the heavy-wheeled plough probably of Slav origin, pulled by a yoke of oxen cutting deeply into the soil and turning over a slice of turf. This was brought to England by the Danes in the ninth century and probably came into widespread use during the Carolingian period. This plough saved the need for cross-ploughing. It created a marked furrow ridge running the length of the field facilitating drainage, permitting a crop on the crest in the wet years, and in the intervening depression in the dry seasons.[36]

A later development was the substitution of horses for oxen as plough animals following the emergence and widespread use of the horseshoe. The horseshoe adds to the tractive power of the horse and prevents injury to hoofs. The present weight of archaeological evidence is that the nailed horseshoe appeared in wide, and not merely sporadic, use in the Yenisei region in Siberia in the ninth to tenth centuries and in Byzantium in the last decades of the ninth century. It began to be widely distributed in Western Europe in the tenth century and was in general use by the eleventh century. At about the same time as the horseshoe, the improved horse harness developed by the Chinese was carried to Europe by nomadic Asians. This collar harness enabled the horse to pull a load without choking and increased pulling power four to five times. Modern experiments have shown that while an ox and horse exert roughly the same pulling power, the horse moves more rapidly than the ox and can endure a longer workday. In Slavic lands east of Germany the plough land measurement consisted of as much land as could be worked by a pair of oxen or a single horse, a measure of their relative productivity.[37]

Another significant change in agricultural techniques was the development of the three-field rotation scheme in which one-third of the acreage was kept fallow, one-third planted in September in wheat and rye, one-third planted the next spring in coarse grains including oats and nitrogenous legumes, with the order of land use rotated in successive years. The new rotation scheme increased the area a peasant could cultivate by one-eighth. It pushed up productivity by nearly half by distributing the labor of ploughing and sowing more evenly through the year. It reduced the chance of famine by diversifying crops adapted to different rhythms of germination and harvest. It stepped up the cultivation of legumes that enriched the soil and put more edible proteins in the diet. Finally, it made a place for a prime food for horses, oats. The three-field system is first mentioned in the later eighth century. It was memorialized in the new calendar devised by Charlemagne. It spread gradually in the next two centuries, becoming well established in Western Europe by the eleventh and twelfth centuries.

Road transportation was also improved by redesigning the occidental wagon inherited from the Greeks and Romans.[38] This was hard to turn, easily capsized on rough roads if fully loaded, and hard to brake on down hills. The main innovations were the pivoted front axle, the whippletree equalizing tension on the traces, and adequate brakes.

These were gradually improved so that by the first half of the twelfth century we find large, horse-drawn wheeled wagons hauling heavy loads (White 1962, 66).

There were other improvements. One was a fertilizer that could be dug out of a clay soil, combined with carbonate of lime, and spread on the fields in an operation called marling.[39] Equally important in saving labor was the widespread use of waterpower from moving streams or diverted water courses to turn a waterwheel. Though known to the Romans from the first century, after five centuries its use by Romans was still exceptional. In the following centuries however, its use spread where falling waters were available until by the tenth or eleventh century it was an accepted feature of the manorial village, being usually one of the lucrative sources of feudal cash revenues derived from milling fees.[40] And where waterpower was not available, the windmill—probably borrowed from Iran—came to the West in the early 1200s and we are told made "rapid progress" in the following decades.[41] That seigneurial authority East and West used the mill as a source of enrichment does not gainsay that milling lightened the work of processing cereals and thus spared labor for more constructive work.[42]

In the light of this record of improved technology on European farms it appears that the estimates of boost in net farm output from two to three times between the eighth and twelfth centuries are valid. Boosted farm output enables rural society as a whole to prosper at the same time that it makes available to a growing urban population a more abundant provisionment. The European upper classes doubtless took the lion's share of this rural prosperity. But they would not especially want to take their increased output in the form of more farm provisions. They would want fine raiment, luxury buildings and palaces, spices and condiment, beverages, well-woven coats of mail, tournament facilities, gold and silver ornaments. These products and services made by industry or craftsmen were supported by larger supplies of raw farm produce now available. The peasant population could well prefer to utilize what little share of abundance came their way in ampler nourishment or as a greater cash supply, improved clothing, better tools and implements for field and animal husbandry, and occasionally trinket goods for gifts or amusement. Thus I concur in the general finding of White (1962, 78) that the technical revolution in agriculture "provided the surplus food from the tenth century onward which permitted rapid urbanization." This technical revolution and record of innovation in farm husbandry revolutionized the feudal mode of production and demonstrated that at least in its earlier years in medieval Europe that mode of production harbored progressive capabilities.

Mining and Transportation Invigorated

A supply of rural provisionment – food, fiber, and hides – was one essential for urban development. A second was a greater supply of minerals – the working metals of iron, copper, and lead as well as silver to use as money and for ornaments. Much more iron was needed to make the tools and equipment of artisan craftsmen and to provide the cutting edge of the plowshare and swordlike coulter that slices the sod before the plowshare breaks it up. Iron or its refined form of steel was needed for many uses: for shields, armor and weapons, nails, anchors, keels for shipbuilding, carpenter tools, jacksaws and massive planes with which to smooth out heavy planks, decorative grillwork in public buildings, keys and locks and hinges for doors of all kinds. For kitchens iron was needed for grills, ovens, frying pans, and caldrons. In such trades as tanning and dyeing it makes a useful container. It is indispensable in salt making where salt is evaporated from salty brines. The other minerals were rarer and more expensive and hence their use was more restricted but they were much more easily smelted and could be worked without the repeated heatings and hammerings that iron required. Moreover lead and copper (or the bronze and brass in which copper mostly appeared) are nonrusting and hence are more suited than iron for many outdoor uses (Clapham 1941/1978, 2:432).

Small-scale mining continued all through the medieval period for it was essential for military purposes. In the later centuries – from the 950s onward – the expansion of German settlement eastward crossing the Elbe and penetrating into Silesia and the Carpathian mountains led to major discoveries of new sources of workable iron ore, copper, and silver-bearing ores. A major production find in the middle of the tenth century was opened up in the Harz mountains in Germany and increased production was found all along the eastern Alps. German skills at mining in Alpine country became noteworthy. Miners found ways to drain water out of deeper shafts containing more valuable minerals either by digging drainage tunnels to adjoining hillsides or by using animal power to hoist water out of mine pits. For the first time waterpower was used to wash ores, operate trip-hammers, break up ores, or hammer pig iron. From the discovery of the rich silver-bearing ores of Freiburg in Saxony until 1300 we are told that statistics on output would have shown "few decades" in which the production of minerals and metals "failed substantially to increase."[43]

This development of mining especially in and around Germany was partly an outgrowth of artisan-miners associated in small bands, a typical simple commodity producer mode. Miners obtained concessions from landlords or local princes to work mines in Alpine country. They obtained the right to prospect for ores and used the streams for washing ores and driving their mills. They drew freely on the forests for fuel and building, constructed cottages, roadways, forges, and mills. Miners learned how to tame the impulse of princes and landlords to share unduly in the proceeds of the miner's labor. Throughout the whole medieval period mining was a free profession. Mining communities were like medieval towns, self-governing and developing their own "laws and customs" (Clapham 1941–1978, 2:441, 448). The contrast with authoritarian direction and management of mines under Greek or Roman control, often worked by chained slave labor, is striking and must account for the more abundant flow of mineral output in the later medieval period.

A third economic basis for the renaissance of mercantile activity in Europe in the medieval period was provided by significant improvements in ship construction, navigation, and design that facilitated commerce and permitted bigger ships to move more freely and navigate more accurately in ocean waters. The compass was borrowed from China via the Arabs around the turn of the millenium and quickly put to use.[44] The traditional European square sail with one mast of inherited Egyptian design, used by the Vikings and Normans, was supplemented by triangular fore and later aft sails with separate masts, coming late in the medieval period, making it possible to make headway against an adverse wind. Equally helpful was the replacement of the traditional steering oar by the development of the sternpost or axial rudder that came into use in Western Europe about 1200. This rudder made it possible to stand a course in heavy weather and was an essential prerequisite for ocean navigation by large ships (Needham 1954–1978, Part 3, 4:461, 637, 652).

The Bourgeois Town

If a broad economic basis made room for the greater importance in the European economy of craft and mercantile activities in the later medieval epoch, there are major reasons why these activities had to take on an urban form in relatively compact communities of nonfood growers appropriately sited to receive and distribute their necessary materials and products by water or land transportation. Of course nonfood producers can draw together out of an impulse of sociability and to promote their common interests. But drawing together is also an elementary need. It permits a division of labor or specialization to emerge among the different practitioners of the same craft—whether shoemakers, dyers, weavers, carpenters, or joiners—to gain what advantages may be found in making fewer varieties of the product along more standard lines to which tools and equipment may be adapted. It makes for a more competitive market so that buyers can be confident they are exposed to a wide range of choice to use their resources advantageously. It brings close to hand practitioners in other crafts who may provide tools and equipment or chemicals or later or earlier stages of the product that must pass through the hands of a series of processors before completion. Obviously, needed products and materials not locally produced may be more readily arranged for importation in urban than in rural locations. At the same time the transport facilities – the breakwaters that shield docked ships, the docks themselves, the loading cranes that by counterweight principle were developed in the medieval period, the lighthouses that guide navigation into ports, and the naval ships and fortifications that defend the ports – are for the joint use and benefit of all the trades. Such improvements are only feasible if they are given concentrated use. Each craft and trade though producing separately will utilize the same set of cargo ships or barges for moving its wares. Likewise the roads and bridges entering town which enable goods and passengers to use prepared roadways are feasible only if traffic is not broadly diffused but concentrated at favorable sites to and from particular places. Oftentimes a few wholesale merchants will service the needs of a whole set of producers in a wide variety of trades. This is accomplished more easily when these trades are practiced in the same place. The merchants themselves for their mutual protection will need to travel by land or sea in caravans or fleets that can be more readily assembled and organized if the parties involved live close together (Pirrenne 1936, 94). Much of the work of the Venetian state involved conquering or planting naval bases or negotiating treaties to protect Venetian shipping and programing fleet movements annually accompanied by warships.[45] Living and working together in an industrial-craft-mercantile environment provided a mutual stimulus to the diffusion of methods of building or working or designing patterns and styles since the same principle or device applied in one craft may have wider applications to others. Finally only living in close community enabled burghers of the medieval period to achieve that fascinating kind of investment diversification embodied in the "commenda" contract, enabling investors to take shares in a given trading venture, often a single shipment to a designated mercantile center, managed by one of their group. Upon his return he would share with his partners the profits realized, the whole being recorded by a notary and often detailed in a public record. The commenda enabled an individual merchant or investor to cope with the hazards of distant trade and travel by taking shares in many individual ventures.[46] It also provided an outlet for surplus capital and a means by which ambitious young merchants with little capital could get started.

These towns in their earliest stages were small struggling communities with chiefly local markets falling under the control of kingly power or some local feudal lord or an ecclesiastical authority. As the towns became more solidly established, they became jealous of their free status and won or were accorded the right to bestow freedom upon any who had established a home among them and were accepted into the community for a short calendar period, often set at a year and a day. Kings and ruling authorities commonly granted towns charters that appear in historical records in England chiefly after the Norman Conquest.[47] The towns were generally fortified with sturdy walls and their citizens maintained a kind of standing militia. In their fuller development they asserted and were generally given the right to be self-governing and to elect their own officials, hold courts to settle controversies among their own citizens, develop their own legal code, coin money, make public improvements, establish markets, and organize trade. In England city authority was restricted because the central state under the king regulated coinage and trade but the towns selected their representatives to meet in Parliament with the high nobility, rural gentry, and church to fix jointly the terms on which the king would impose special taxes. In the Great Charter the towns as well as barons and clergy made the king pledge to adhere to and respect their customary rights.

In Germany towns had a wider field of action because the state was more decentralized and towns were able early in their growth to throw off local episcopal authority with the aid of the weak imperial crown. Along the North Sea and Baltic coast the German towns leagued themselves to win trade concessions abroad and to fight a war with Denmark to ensure their free access to the Baltic.[48]

But it was in Italy where urban communities had their earliest start, exhibited their fastest growth, and achieved the greatest independence of action. The Venetians led the way from the safety of their lagoons and salt marshes and successfully resisted Lombard and Carolingian assaults. Nesting under nominal Byzantine suzerainty, the Venetian fisherman, burghers, artisans, and sailors built up a trading community in the Po valley, cleared the Adriatic Sea of opposition, and gradually achieved trading supremacy in Constantinople and the Black and Aegean seas. For centuries they dominated the Levant trade on the European side, bringing together and organizing the commerce of three civilizations: Byzantium, Roman-Germanic Europe, and Islam. The southern Italian towns had their commercial growth stifled by Norman conquest around 1000 A.D. but especially in northern Italy — the basin of the Po and Adige and amidst Tuscan hills and valleys — a remarkable group of city republics emerged. Fighting furiously among themselves, they played off emperor against papacy. They banded together in leagues which over time grew stronger. They wore down the authority and power of the emperor with their constant rebellions and military victories. They dislodged Muslim control of the western Mediterranean by conquering Arab island strongholds. They reaped the main gains from the Crusades. They gradually developed control of their rural hinterland, often driving or drawing rural aristocrats off the estates to seek a wider field of action in the commercial towns. They converted feudal property into ordinary bourgeois landed property.[49] Their early form of government drew many citizens, especially those with standing in guilds or local associations, into positions of responsibility for a short term, subject to frequent large citizen assemblies.[50] Later most of these urbanized republics lost their democratic character and in the fourteenth and fifteenth centuries fell prey to military dictators and dynastic families who established despotic personal rule.[51]

Public Economy

By public economy is meant the complex of institutions governing public revenues, the carrying on of public services in a public mode of production, and the development of a scheme for income redistribution (Gottlieb 1984, Chap. 6). The medieval public economy was comparatively undeveloped before the rise of the burgher towns in the later medieval period. Kings and other Germanic rulers who exercised kingly power depended primarily for support upon surplus produce extracted from royal manors governed by their bailiffs or agents. This was in part stored in kind to be utilized on the spot by traveling court retinues. Some of the surplus was carted to the main palace or to army posts. A small amount was sold in market towns for revenues to be sent to the king.[52] From the same public domain the king would draw cash revenues from the towns or cities expressly chartered by him, from the royal share of silver mines, from mints under his own control, and from toll stations where customs could be imposed on merchant shipments. He had rights to "gifts" proffered on the occasion of administering justice. If he was ever captured in body and held ransom, he could call on his free subjects to collect ransom moneys. Likewise he could call on his free subjects for money aids when his eldest son was knighted or when his eldest daughter married. He also collected "relief" when manorial estates or gainful properties originally granted by the crown passed into succession of a qualified male heir. If this heir was lacking, he enjoyed the gainful administration of the estate by "wardship" of minor heirs and widows and sometimes even control of their marriages. Estates of his vassals without lawful heir "escheated" to him.[53] The more unscrupulous monarchs contrived pretexts for the confiscation of properties of subjects believed rebellious or simply coveted for their wealth like the Jewish moneylenders. Finally, he could call on his vassals – usually only for a limited term of service – for military assistance. To repel invasion of the realm he could summon a mass levy of all adult freemen in arms.[54] Most of these feudal public revenue sources were available also to feudal lords and ecclesiastical authorities.

These revenues and aids all had their expenses. Royal storehouses, courts, and toll stations needed to be manned by suitable agents who also shared in the royal largesse. In England manorial and borough rents were collected by the sheriff who kept a share.[55] The king's own personal entourage in his castle or court was usually sizable and much of the royal treasury would be devoted to its support. He was expected to be generous with benefactions and gifts to those who aroused his interest or favor.

There is no record of erection of medieval public works on any scale – apart from fortified castles – on land or water. Roman roads and bridges were generally neglected; the king's highway was an animal track passable with a wagon only in dry weather.[56] The most elaborate administrative staff was built up during the regime of Charlemagne. With his energy and genius he established a network of traveling justices and a supervisory staff over some 300 counts and seven frontier marches assigned responsibility for the empire (Boussard 1969, 79). His successors could not hold to the same standard of administration for much smaller jurisdictions. The counties on the Continent were gradually appropriated by fief holders and turned into hereditary possessions within a century of the death of Charlemagne (Bloch 1939–1941/1961, 192). In England, however, the energy of Norman rulers held the central state intact.

It was not easy for the Germanic rulers to rise much above the limitations of their recent barbarian traditions and heritage. Kingdoms like estates through the Carolingian period were treated as partible inheritances to be divided equally among male heirs. The criminal code until late in the medieval period called for trial by ordeal by immersion of a hand in boiling water or throwing a miscreant into cold water to see whether his guilt would sink him. The obligations of blood vengeance on kindred were still strong (Herlihy 1970, 111). Even though Carolingian rulers took pains to obtain the oath of allegiance from free subjects, their primary base of control for raising manpower and aid was their directly enfiefed vassals. The principal officers of the

Carolingian court still bore the titles of household or estate attendant: chamberlain, chaplain, chancellor (secretarial services), seneschal, wine steward, and constable. Election of kings was still a respected Germanic custom. Late in the Carolingian period annual general councils were held supplemented by a more general assembly of notables "to hear the decisions and occasionally also to deliberate concerning them" (Herlihy 1970, 206, 222).

Through most of the medieval epoch—until perhaps the thirteenth and fourteenth centuries in Italy and the fourteenth and fifteenth centuries elsewhere—the armed power of the state was not composed of armies equipped, supplied, and officered by the state. In the earliest period the armies were the freemen of the tribe or nationality bringing to the service their armor and arms and leagued together under warrior chiefs following their warrior king. This tradition of a yeoman army was altered sometime in the eighth century by the development of the iron stirrup, horseshoe, and wing spear that radically changed the style of warfare conducted by West Europeans. Greater importance was given to mounted cavalry armed with a long sword and heavy lance held firm under the armpit by a stirruped armored rider. He was capable of delivering a powerful assault that would overwhelm much larger numbers of foot soldiers.[57] The new method of fighting greatly increased the investment and maintenance for the soldier. Military equipment for one mounted armed soldier cost in the mid-700s A.D. about twenty oxen or the plough teams of at least ten peasant families. The maintenance for the horse was as costly as that of the squire, the soldier's attendant. Any troop of cavalry would require spare horses for replacement. Investment in training to conduct warfare on horseback was very great. Schooling commenced generally at puberty and included a long apprenticeship to keep in prime condition with constant practice. That soon developed into the "deadly and completely realistic game of war—tournament" (White 1962, 29). After completing his training a candidate would be admitted by a special investiture into the order of knighthood (Bloch 1939–1941/1961, 312).

It appears that of all Germanic peoples the Franks took most quickly to the new style of warfare. White has assembled evidence for the hypothesis that in the middle of the eighth century the Carolingian rulers—first Charles Martel and then his sons and grandsons—began to substitute for the mass levy of armed freemen upon which they had previously relied a much smaller levy of selected trained cavalry men who became the "knights" of a later period. They arranged for the greater cost of this levy by a massive seizure of church manorial properties distributed to vassals on condition of a knight's service in the Frankish host. The major Frankish feudatories and counts all sooner or later assembled on their manorial domains or around their castles small bands of knights for whom warfare was the sole occupation and on whom the king or emperor when his rule was effective would call for service. The old levy of freemen vanished and a gulf appeared, in White's language (1962, 30), "between a warrior aristocracy and the mass of peasants".[58] It added to the drive for intensified feudal exploitation of manorialized villages or freeholding peasantry. The Norman conquests of southern Italy and England and perhaps the reconquest of Spain are largely attributable to the power of the new method of warfare. This was not however so effective against a well-fortified and supplied city or in upland mountainous terrain or against a coastal settlement such as Venice with effective naval power. The ferocity of the knighted shock attack did not overcome high-grade English archers in the fourteenth century. The warrior knight as well as his stronghold, the castle, was doomed in the end by the development of gunpowder capable of sending pellets and missiles that could batter down castle walls and penetrate knightly armor.[59]

Curiously the military side of European life was pristinely feudal during the final centuries of the medieval epoch precisely when economic development was undermining the feudal mode of production in agriculture and building up a competitive mode of production – the bourgeois town – with its powerful merchant marine and ships of war.

If the public economy of the state in medieval society was poorly developed, that of the bourgeois town was fully developed almost from the outset. The bourgeois town was a "commune," a collective property, built up by closely associated citizens. Its sturdy walls or ramparts to provide for common defense; its streets paved in the twelfth century; its canals (as in Venice) to provide internal circulation; its bridges to cross over its waterways; its civic center where markets, public halls, and cathedrals were generally sited; its quays, harbor facilities; its dikes to hold back flood waters if the town was built on a coursing stream; town wells to provide fresh water supply or aqueducts from the countryside bringing in water; public baths – all of these were collective property undertaken and managed by town officers or assemblies.[60] Where the town extended its control over the surrounding rural countryside, which it did on a large scale in northern Italy, Switzerland, and Germany, the town typically banned or undermined serfdom and constructed improved roads through the countryside permitting ready passage to the town and took over or built outlying fortifications to protect town domains or patrolled adjoining coastal waters.[61]

The town as state took over extensive regulatory functions: appointing market constables; establishing night watchmen to prevent thefts; appointing scavengers to collect town rubbish or sanitary wastes; taking measures to abate nuisances, to regulate taverns, and inns, bakeries, and alehouses. The common trades of the town were regulated by the town either directly or through guilds that were usually drawn into the town governing structure. Building permits were often required and fire-control measures imposed.[62]

One responsibility of town government playing a major role through the entire medieval period concerned provisionment, which was by no means left up to private enterprise and merchants to conduct on their own. Each town built up a systematic policy of provisionment sometimes including public granaries, public control of grain imports, price control and forms of rationing in times of scarcity, inspection of private grain storehouses, and careful regulation of grain markets. In time of extreme food shortage city gates would be closed to prevent ingress of outsiders and nonresidents would be expelled. "A whole book" exclaims Braudel (1973, 1:329) "could be written on the grain policy of Venice or Genoa."[63]

Nor did towns shrink from direct organization of production. Except in England and to a lesser degree France where the central state had appropriated control over money and coinage, the towns operated their own mints. The largest of the free cities—Genoa, Florence, Venice—in the thirteenth century initiated gold coinage for which the florin (Florence) or ducat (Venice) became virtually a trade name.[64] The oldest and greatest of the mercantile towns, Venice, had in 1104 established a city-owned and operated merchant marine of galleys capable of serving mixed purposes as ships of war and carriers of cargo. These ships were built in the publicly owned and managed arsenal that supplied ships for the Fourth Crusade and employed in the fifteenth century some 3200 workers.[65] Variously operated by public servants or leased to private carriage for particular seasons, these ships were the mainstay of Venetian commerce and naval power, which kept the control of the Adriatic, the Aegean, and for extended periods the Bosporus and Black seas and steadily fought off Muslim and Turkish power. To assure high-quality cordage for shipping, the government established in 1303 a rope factory and engaged in complex trading maneuvers to assure itself an adequate supply of high-quality hemp at fair prices (Lane, 1966, 269–85).

Whether ships were publicly or privately owned, their operations in most mercantile towns were carefully regulated and orchestrated by the state. For most of the medieval epoch merchant ships traveled, apart from short movements in coastal waters or up friendly river channels of the home country, in convoys nearly always with some protection by one or more armed vessels and subject to exacting regulation both to assure safety of the crew and cargo and fair dealing to all who wished passage or needed cargo space. Elaborate Venetian regulations illustrate the scope of town control and guidance of the merchant marine. Voyages in what were regarded as locally controlled waters in the Adriatic and Aegean seas were operated by private initiative subject only to general maritime legislation specifying minimum crews for various size ships, safety regulations, and special stipulations for certain voyages or destinations prohibited for a limited period because of political or grain requirements. Particular ship owners or operators could at their option undertake to join the fleets serving the main lines to the Levant and carrying the more valuable kinds of cargo—cloth, cash, bullion, spices. These made only regulated voyages at varying dates and sometimes with freight rates and conditions of shipment prescribed. A considerable fraction of the regulated voyages were licensed in advance, the number of ships traveling was determined by the Senate, and the fleet was placed under an admiral, a *capitano,* instructed to lead the fleet on a specified itinerary and make sure that all ships were adequately manned and armed. To ensure unity of command and fair treatment of individual shippers, especially when the entire convoy waited for certain ships to unload, carriage expenses and freight revenues sometimes were pooled. All galley masters were forced to act as common carriers. They were required to load merchandise presented on available cargo space. Freight rates on private galleys could not exceed those charged on governmental galleys. The most valuable wares could only be carried on the galleys. When state-owned and operated galleys participated in the fleet the galley master was a salaried official chosen by the commune and sworn to its service. He reported directly to the chief executive of state (doge) on the commercial outcome of the voyage.[66] The business of the town was fully coordinated and interwoven with the business of the merchants and the carrying trade. The whole foreign policy of the state was turned to the one purpose of assuring adequate facilities for Venetian trade and access to Venetian ships in peaceful waters.

To this developed state of public economy there corresponded a developed form of public finance. Befitting a fully monetized economy, taxes were raised in money with heavy dependence upon excises and tolls or export taxes on products such as salt, a staple product of the Venetian salt marshes.[67] But dependence upon indirect taxation raised the same kind of objections in the twelfth century that it does in the twentieth, that it puts a disproportionate burden on poorer households. Hence supplementary direct taxes were levied in the earliest period at a uniform rate based on hearths or households. Many of the more advanced urban republics began in the twelfth century to tax wealthier households at a heavier rate in proportion to their ability to pay as indicated chiefly by a survey of their property real and personal. This existed at Pisa by 1162 and in most of the Italian cities before the end of the twelfth century and in some German cities a century later.[68] Financial administration was not unsophisticated. In Florence rents or incomes in kind obtained from rural properties were capitalized at a standard interest rate. The property tax known as *catasto* determined the gross value of the taxpayer's estate on the basis of submitted balance sheets. Against the gross value a taxpayer was allowed deductions (*detrazioni*) for debts, charges (*carichi*), and a per capita allowance for dependent members of households including servants and slaves. For a few years of the 1400s the rates of income taxation were progressive to 22 percent (De Roover 1966, 22, 27).

As in modern society, taxation aroused furious struggles to shift the burden of taxation elsewhere. The wealthier burghers (*magnati*) resisted the *catasto* and for an extended period in the fourteenth century it was dropped. Reliance was then placed upon a direct levy on farm property in the *contado,* excise taxation within the city especially on food and borrowing to meet extraordinary needs of fighting wars by voluntary or forced loans repayable with interest in a funded debt (*monti*). This financial scheme with its emphasis on food taxation especially benefitted the *magnati* but hurt the little people (*popolo minuto*). Fighting wars generated wealth by building up public debt that was interest bearing. This fiscal scheme probably played a role in the Florentine social revolution of 1378–1382.[69] In the following century in Florence emphasis again was given to property taxation tolerated partly because *magnati* had learned to keep double sets of books and partly because the rising expense of wars and the inability to service the swollen public debt made the old fiscal scheme untenable (De Roover 1966, 22).

Feudal Property

The institution of property in the medieval epoch before the rise of the bourgeois towns in the eleventh century was distinctively feudal. Once the migrating peoples had settled down and had lost their national identity in a mixed Germano-Roman society that emerged in the Merovingian and Anglo-Saxon period, an inchoate form of feudal property began to develop. It was adapted to the society it served, embodying certain underlying principles.

The essential theme of this form of property was that landholding and its beneficial use was subject to services rendered to higher authority, giving society and polity a pyramidal form. Holdings of peasant villagers were subject to rendering service and produce to the lord of the manor. A holding of lordship in turn was subject to rendering service and produce to a higher feudatory to whom allegiance was given – a count, a duke, or a baron, the title varying with time and place. Many of these higher feudatories in turn were held subject to some claim of obedience and allegiance to a still higher authority – sometimes nebulous or merely nominal – of emperor, king, or pope.

The nature of the services rendered and their magnitude varied in each case, being more onerous for holders of lower status. A holding was generally subject to services and to "relief" upon succession of a suitable heir, "escheat" if no proper heir was available, "wardship" and beneficial management of estate if the heir was a minor or dependent, and "aids" on designated contingencies. Services were chiefly military for the higher feudatories and generally included attendance at court subject to such fines as the court would impose upon judgment of peers. All holdings were deemed potentially subject to a higher feudatory unless carrying some specific exemption or immunity. The principal exemptions were for certain ecclesiastical properties, mining camps, merchant assemblies for holding markets, smallholders granted or claiming by custom allodial standing. Many such exemptions were generally subject to one-time payment or recurrent quitrent. Those holding offices, lands, or fiefs in the feudal chain were bound to service unless specifically relieved; but of course this obligation was more stringently enforced for lower feudatories living or functioning under the control of a master. Binding children to continuation of service was more or less unique to the lowest level (village serfs and domestic servants), for at other levels it was presumed that a suitable heir would desire to claim the holding and that other children would make their way freely (Herlihy 1970, 177–87).

Feudal property left succession to a holding uncertain. For families once settled and established that was objectionable since the desire for continued succession becomes more intense with time especially when improvements calling for investment of resources and effort are made. Hence up and down the line – from lowly serf to baron – a process commences to make a holding hereditable that at the outset and in its naked logic is discretionary with the grantor.[70] The grants often involved immense territories of which only a small part at the outset was settled and used. As population and as economic life developed this created opportunities for profitable disposal of some of these lands for markets, ports, mining undertakings, new villages, or what not. Would-be purchasers could be churchly, bourgeois, or younger sons of knights and nobility. Even within the manor, serf holdings in early periods could be quite substantial. The average size of a yardland or oxgang, the standard tenements in England in the thirteenth century, was 30 acres. Before the Conquest four yardlands made a hide or plough land (*carucata*) that was thought of as the customary allotment of one family.[71] This would allow half of the arable to lie continuously fallow as called for by two-field rotation and it would leave room for expansion of cultivation by larger families. It would also permit alienation of holdings to neighboring households that needed more land. Although the nominal rule precluded such alienations, they became an established right on newly acquired "assart" lands (newly cleared) or on inherited holdings for a lifetime lease and permanently with the consent of the heir. Some manors were especially tolerant of land dealings among tenants (Homans 1941/1975, Chap. 14).

As the practice of alienation became habitual and tolerated, it tended to turn into a right. It became very difficult for higher feudatories to enforce their rights, and efforts to do so aroused objections. Holders of manorial interests were insistent upon their possessory rights and medieval lore records many a rebellion arising out of possessory interests in manors that were granted to ancestors put under question.[72] The same process of appropriation went on within manors where the claims of tenants originally discretionary became vested by custom of manor into a hereditable "copyhold" interest on payment of set quitrents, evidenced by extracts from manorial court rolls, subject only to the "custom" of the manor. Such copyhold forms of land tenure lingered in British life and were recognized in courts through to the nineteenth century.[73]

Feudal tenants tended to extend their rights of inheritance by seeking to restrict collection of relief upon heirs or "fines" upon alienation or the practice of wardship and guardianship. At the upper end of the feudal spectrum such charges could be lucrative indeed, in some cases encompassing the net revenue of an estate for an entire generation as the price for recognition of an heir.[74] It was on such issues that the British nobility leagued with town commoners to force the king to assent to the startling provisions of the Great Charter that laid out a specific schedule for relief, sought to abate abuses of wardship administration, protected the rights of widows and wards in marriage, and checkmated the crown on requests for aids to what the common realm through Parliament would grant (Herlihy 1970, 258–70). To evade inheritance and estate dues and the travail of wardship, British estate owners — baronial and bourgeois — developed evasive legal devices by which a future interest in their estate would be conveyed to trusted friends while custody of estate was retained by owner with the beneficial rights of property to devolve upon a lawful heir, a manifestly collusive arrangement to defraud the state of relief and wardship. A complex effort by a Tudor monarch to restore his feudal prerogatives encountered strong resistance in Parliament and terminated with a compromise making a fraction of the larger estates subject to inheritance dues.[75] Resistance of village peasants to manorial and clerical exploitation of peasant inheritance was equally intense. Peasant death duties were relatively heavy, making up the best and next-best beast, a money fine often amounting to one-year's rent, and smaller church mortuary levies. Peasant possessions on death were carefully inventoried to assure full collection.[76]

The service connected with feudal holdings at the upper end was chiefly military service by so many armed knights. Field labor, menial services, and delivery of produce were characteristic at the lower end of the feudal spectrum. Here, too, resistance was felt both at extended or repeated calls for military service and for an undue drainage from peasant fields. Military service became limited to a forty-day term except at the king's expense and even then there was scrutiny as to the exigent need for service that became commutable to monetary fines — "scutage" in Norman England (Herlihy 1970, 179). The king often preferred scutage, which made for better control over his fighting forces. Already by the time of Henry II, though the number of knights obligated to service was some 6,500, only some 375 were enrolled in Edward's Welsh Wars. The splintering by alienation and partible inheritance of knightly fiefs made it difficult to assess scutage so that in England by the thirteenth century it was on its way out, as were general kingly aids except insofar as they were absorbed into genuine national tax levies payable independently of feudal tenure (Postan 1975, 190). The same tendencies to commutation of feudal service for money payments or quitrents was encountered within manors as tenants struggled for greater freedom and landed magnates, typically absentee, struggled for greater cash return from their estates. As soon as enough free labor was available for hiring within and without the villages — and population growth in times of peace would bring about this condition sooner or later — it was to the advantage of all parties to commute labor services especially if given unwillingly and difficult to police as compared with labor paid on the spot. Many commuting peasants especially those with smallholdings would themselves offer their labor for hire. English and French villages tended to accumulate an underlayer of "manouvriers," cottagers, "undersettles," "anilepimen" for hire (Homans 1941/1975, 73, 239). Hence commutation, springing out of peasant revolt, prompted by landlords desiring more money income, pushed by peasant villagers to gain more freedom, advanced slowly by individual dealings on particular items of service. It was sometimes realized by wholesale purchase of most existing services, leaving such profitable items as tithes, tallage, and mill fees. Such commutation, already accelerated in much of northern Italy in the eleventh century, made rapid headway in England, France, and Germany in the twelfth and thirteenth centuries.[77]

Usually church tithes and fixed head rents or quitrents lingered on. To a surprising degree, except in countries that went through a period of drastic social revolution, the feudal practice of local court administration on manorial domains chaired by the lordship or his steward and holding court on all petty matters arising within manorial jurisdiction, persisted. This jurisdiction included common pastures and fields, nuisances, roads, waste removal, trespasses, and debts. In their monumental *History of Local Government in England,* Sidney and Beatrice Webb (1903–1929, 3–99, 113) have shown that manorial courts – court leet and baron – continued on a substantial scale in England to hold jurisdiction up to and partly through the eighteenth century. Even in well-populated Manchester, one of the greatest English provincial towns, the "court and leet and baron of Manchester" continued to serve as an active local governing authority down to 1846. Under the authority of this court, chaired by the manorial steward, a good-sized staff administered communal affairs, profiting considerably from revenues from the administration of justice, fines for failure to attend court sessions, collection of market dues and dues for use of mills for grinding corn, ovens for baking bread, and kilns for drying malt. This vestige of feudal property was not overthrown but bought off by purchase of the manor by the town for the enormous sum of £200,000 and the corresponding grant of a municipal charter.

Bourgeois Property

We now turn from feudal to that form of property developed in towns by town burgesses and properly denominated bourgeois property. In its earliest forms it is submerged in feudal property as one of the exempted classes of allodial tenure freed from some of the obligations of feudal process. By the time that municipal charters are granted in the tenth and eleventh centuries it begins to be clear that the town burghers had won considerable rights of self-government including the recognition of distinctive kinds of land tenure, inheritance, freedom from most feudal dues, and autonomous administration of justice. In one of the earliest English charters granted in the early twelfth century to burgesses of Newcastle, the core of the charter was the power of local justice administration "to distrain" both on themselves and on foreigners "within their borough and without." Pleas arising within the town "shall there be held and concluded." Nor can a burgess in a suit by "anyone concerning anything" be forced "to trial by battle" except in a charge of treason. Perhaps the royal charter given to London a few decades later gave a fuller unfolding of the scope for judicial freedom and unique law autonomy. Citizens of London cannot be required "to plead outside the walls of the city of London except respecting holdings outside the city and in respect of my [the king's] moneyers and . . . servants." They were to be exempt from trial by combat or from murder fine "and in respect of pleas of the crown they may make their proof according to the ancient custom of the city." In no plea of the city "shall there be 'miskenning' " [slip of the tongue when repeating legal formulas] nor shall a borough court presided over by a royal officer be held more than once a week. Their rights, pledges, and debts shall be "according to the law of the city." "And if anyone in all England shall take a toll or custom from the men of London and shall refuse them satisfaction, then shall the sheriff of London take a surety respecting it within London." The king's sheriff will not collect from Londoners a number of designated fines and penalties (Mundy and Riesenberg 1958, 137, 141). This judicial autonomy for incorporated boroughs persisted in England through to modern times though eventually abridged in significant ways by the rise of national legislation and by appellate court procedures.[78] This judicial autonomy for towns could not have as wide a sway in England and in later years in France as in Germany and Italy where cities were virtually sovereign powers for most of the medieval period.

Judicial autonomy for towns allowed a distinct form of property to evolve known as "burgage tenure." Holdings of land under this tenure "could be sold and purchased, just as movable property, without the consent of the lord" and such sales could not be revoked by heirs and relatives. Widows had half the sales of this tenure made in their lifetime by their husbands claimable against the husbands' estate. Nor did these holdings give rise to claims for aids or relief (Herlihy 1970, 183). A law merchant evolved, applicable especially to towns and fairs and to international commerce (Tigar and Levy 1977, 49). Here were developed the main principles of the law of contracts and sales, credit instrument negotiability, partnership, sureties, bailments, and bankruptcy. The law merchant, given its first documentary expression in ordinances of Italian towns, was soon applied in international fairs and wherever Italian merchants settled for business purposes and it shaped up an important segment of the bourgeois institution of property, which made possible the development of the capitalist mode of production.[79]

Medieval Economic Systems

By the criteria for analysis of economic systems elsewhere set forth and applied in this work to medieval economic life, it follows that there were at least three broad classes of medieval systems to be distinguished. One class follows the widely accepted and well-known periodization of Bloch distinguishing an "early" from a "later" feudalism with the line drawn approximately towards the middle of the eleventh century, "very different from one another in their essential character" (Bloch 1939–1940/1961, 1:59–71). The feudal mode of production is far more predominant in agriculture in the first than in the second period. The level of productive forces is much lower in the first period. There the simple commodity producers and merchants played a very restrained role and functioned as a suppressed order of feudal society. The feudal institution of property then had broad application. The public economy was as yet undeveloped. The promise of a more centralized polity harbored by the Carolingian regime was premature and stillborn partly because European Romano-Germanic society passed under sharp attack by neighboring peoples.

I differ from Bloch and others who have followed him in supposing that the later period is adequately characterized as merely a later or more complicated development of the same system encountered earlier, feudalism. It appears to me that three distinct though interdependent systems evolved in the later period. One was a richly developed complex of urban trading communities, led by its town bourgeoisie with a powerful merchant marine in a fertile region centered in Tuscany and Lombardy. This region broke out of feudal power in the eleventh and twelfth centuries in northern Italy and Switzerland, and in the Aegean littoral. The modes of production here were primarily simple commodity production, landlord-tenant farming, and small-scale capitalist production with hired labor, combined with a richly developed mercantile and public economy. In its political form this artisan, peasant-landlord, mercantile society never could outgrow its urban chrysalis and build a larger state system capable of suppressing internal divisiveness and defending itself against powerful external enemies. At best these burgeoning republics could league together sufficiently to hold their own in the middle years of the medieval epoch.[80]

And as the medieval epoch came to a close the economic basis of the Italian city-states and their mercantile power was undermined by a twofold shift. Trading territory was lost by Turkish conquests in Asia Minor, the Aegean, the Balkans, and eventually Byzantium itself. Trading supremacy was lost to the superior merchant marine of Atlantic states (Portugal, Holland, and England) and the development of industry in Northern Europe.[81]

Secondly, there emerged quite clearly the outline of the powerful centralized English political economy that developed, along with its classical form of manorial agriculture cast in the feudal mode, a burgeoning town democracy led by merchants and artisans of considerable strength and autonomy within a public economy giving each estate a distinct voice in the realm. The development of both the urban and public economy was accompanied by a commercialization of the feudal mode tending to turn it, with commutation of feudal services and dues, in the direction of landlord-tenant and capitalist forms of agriculture. The public economy was invigorated by a considerable growth of taxing power extended over both the manorial and the urban economy partly due to the fiscal exploitation of wool exports that enriched both the crown and the rising merchant class given a trading monopoly. The quite remarkable freedom in England from internal river and road tolls that impeded commercial development everywhere on the Continent promoted a sense of national unity quite unique in the medieval period. It seems difficult to describe the English economic system of the thirteenth to fourteenth centuries as simply feudal.[82]

The rest of Europe falls into quite different categories. The central state is too poorly developed in France and Spain and has practically disappeared in most of Germany, so the English category does not fit. Yet town development both in the economy and polity is too strong though without quite the independence of Italy to enable the feudal to fit. And the situation varies even more in the adjoining societies— Scandinavia, Poland, Bohemia, Hungary—that have become part of the European community long after the early age of feudalism. Here we can accept the typological suggestions worked out for the most part quite brilliantly by Perry Anderson in his chapters "The Far North," "East of the Elbe," "The Crisis in the East," and "South of the Danube."[83] If that multiplies economic systems unduly, it nonetheless testifies to the complexity of the historic process.

4

The Mercantilist Economic System

Introduction

The mercantilist economy is here portrayed as a model of an economic system broadly reflective of West European economic development of the sixteenth, seventeenth, and the first three quarters of the eighteenth centuries.[1] This model reflects the experience of Holland, France, and England in that epoch. To a lesser degree it reflects developments in the Iberian Peninsula. To a still lesser degree it is applicable to developments in northern and Central Europe – Prussia, Austria, and Sweden. The key feature of this model is a structure of economic policy that was fully applied in French and English experience and saturated the thinking of their policymakers. This structure of economic policy gave rise to the first crystallization of economic theory interpreting mercantilist experience and advocating mercantilist economic policy. It is only in this reflected form that present-day economics, both liberal and Marxist, deals with or recognizes the mercantilist economic system. Since present-day economic theory arose in the aftermath of mercantilist experience by critical evaluation of it, present-day liberal economics tends to view mercantilist theory in competitive terms.[2] Marx recognized mercantilism as a stage of development of economic theory.[3] The real structure of economic life corresponding to this theory is portrayed by Marx as a process of "primitive accumulation."[4]

Expansion of Europe

The mercantilist model of an economic system is suited to a Europe that because of its navigational and military skills has won

89

mastery of the oceans and has brought under European subjection tremendous territories in Asia, Africa, and the New World. The coastal areas and the navigable stretch of riverine basins together with their indigenous population of Africa and the New World passed under European control; and the more settled agricultural population of Africa and the Americas became exposed to expropriation or enslavement. Advanced Amerindian societies chiefly in Mexico and Peru became subjugated. Their ruling classes were wiped out or assimilated and their people peonized. Primitive populations were generally extirpated; entire groups of Africans were hunted, chiefly by local African rulers, and sold to European slavers functioning in African coastal areas. From there slaves were shipped to the New World to mine gold and silver or to plant and cultivate sugar, coffee, tobacco, and other tropical products that became major staples of merchandise in European commodity markets during the mercantilist epoch. The subcontinent of India and the stretch of tropical islands that in historical times have nourished the spice trade were given over to systematic plundering. While the stronger societies of China and Japan could more adequately preserve their integrity, European trading footholds on the periphery of their territory were established permitting a profitable trade to develop enriching European consumption with Asian silks, tea, and fine porcelain. It is odd that this overseas expansion of Western Europe was concurrent with a retreat of East European peoples before the onslaught of Muslim and Turkish power, which consolidated its hold in the Balkans and Aegean and ravaged Mediterranean shipping, penetrated the heart of the European continent on the Danube, and challenged Hungary and Vienna to mortal conflict.

The pioneer people in the overseas expansion were the Portuguese who established control of the West African coast and adjoining islands already in the fifteenth century. The Spaniards and Genoese followed closely in train and early in the sixteenth century were emplaced in most of Latin America and the Caribbean. It was not until the seventeeth century that the Dutch and soon the English and French pushed the Portuguese out of most of their Asian and African coastal vantage points and began the development of colonial settlements in the Caribbean and in North America.

Overseas expansion of Europe was critical in three respects for the development of mercantilist economies. The expansion required an enlargement of the European merchant marine to carry the migrating peoples of Europe and Africa and their products between and among the continents. A merchant ship is a capitalist means of production as the plough is a peasant artifact or knightly armor the equipment of a feudal warrior. Expansion of shipping in turn called for an expansion in the shipbuilding industry, which because of its size and the variety of skills required was one of the first capitalist industries to become emancipated from guild restrictions and subject to entrepreneurial control.[5] The annual output of Dutch ships in the mid–seventeenth century at the height of their maritime supremacy numbered some 500. The total European merchant marine probably tripled between 1500 and 1600, and it went up 4.5 times by 1786.[6] A large labor force became engaged in marine navigation.

The European bourgeoisie was called upon for other services besides constructing, financing, and operating the merchant marine. The migration of peoples at the African end called for merchandising as much as military prowess. Local African chiefs needed to be induced to slave catching or to diversion of the older Trans-Saharan slave trade by barter of suitable goods and supplies.[7] On the American end the newly available slave cargoes needed to be placed for sale where recent auctions indicated market returns were favorable.[8] There was competition both at the buying and selling end.[9] Once the labor supply was deposited the resulting products both of precious metals and staple goods – in the early years chiefly sugar, hides, tobacco, cocoa, and coffee – needed to be transported back to Europe and after necessary processing transported to various inland markets. Processing called for elaborate facilities. Sugar refining or distillation into alcoholic beverages made up a considerable industry. Storage facilities to warehouse supplies were needed for continuous distribution.[10]

The Asian transfer of goods and service called for astute merchandising. Military prowess would at best assure ports or facilities of embarkation and storage and ship servicing. Commodities needed to be purchased, not simply commandeered or confiscated, and dealings with the proud Chinese and Japanese needed to be circumspect and proper. Beneficial use of the aboriginal population of North America also required merchandising skills to induce natives to trap and hunt the fur bearing animals of potential value to Europeans.[11]

The European bourgeoisie was affected in yet another decisive way by the overseas expansion of Europe. It was inevitable that this expansion especially into the New World, where two whole continents lay with their virginal fields of precious metals either untapped or at early stages of collection, should yield a harvest of precious metals where fast-moving mountain waters had broken up ore-bearing rocks and left alluvial deposits of gold and silver. Harvesting was begun first by the Spaniards whose soldiers had conquered the more advanced Amerindian civilizations that in Mexico and in Peru had already begun to work their gold and silver deposits. They had already accumulated precious metals chiefly for artistic and ornamental use. At three later stages the European supply of gold was greatly enriched: in Portuguese Brazil from 1690 to 1750, in the fourth and fifth decades of the nineteenth century when the gold finds on the western slopes of the Sierra Mountains in California were discovered, and fifty years later when similar strikes of lesser magnitude were announced for Alaska.[12]

Of these inundations of precious metals, the first wave from Spanish America chiefly of silver had the greatest relative impact. We will never know the full scale of precious metal inundation because we cannot know the volume of preexisting supplies, or the amount of the newly mined gold and silver marketed without paying the king's share. Then too, some of the newly mined output was carried directly or indirectly to Japan, China, and India to purchase export goods. Minimal estimates run at 50 percent over the preexisting amounts but the magnitude of price rise and expansion in the volume of monetized trade indicates that the scale of increase in effective money supply was several hundred percent, extending over more than a century.[13]

Apart from a tendency to promote a mercantile bourgeoisie, the overseas expansion of Europe caused a significant shift in the balance of military power in Europe. The overseas expansion would be organized and controlled by the state, which could build and operate successful war fleets capable of navigating in ocean waters and destroying fleets of an enemy power or coalition. The strongest maritime state could sink or capture the fleets of its rivals, appropriate their overseas port and commercial facilities, and even take over landed settlements as the British did in Canada and India and as the Dutch sought to do in Brazil. Payouts could be channelled to the winning state by permitting only the merchant marine of the winning power or coalition of states access to the trade and by concentrating receipt of all staple produce in the home country (or metropole), thereby facilitating monopoly earnings by control of supply. Since the stakes of victory were great, rivalry was intense and extended over two centuries not only to state systems as such and their dynastic heads but to the national bourgeoisie that had become bonded to and coalesced with the emerging national states. In the case of Holland this bonding was inherent in the act of state formation, since the Dutch state was an ensemble of provincial mercantile republics leagued together by the exigent needs of national defense. Where the national state as in Italy and in Germany was weak or merely incipient, there the bourgeoisie did not take on a national form or participate directly in overseas European trade and commerce, and to that extent the groundwork for the mercantilist economy was weak in those regions.[14]

Productive Forces Flourishing

The mercantilist model of an economic system is suited not only to a Europe which has mastered the oceans and has expanded overseas but also to a Europe whose domestic productive forces are flourishing and reaching higher levels. Resource burdens imposed by net population growth were still moderate. The net population growth for Western Europe between 1500 and 1700 is estimated at around a third. This net growth was probably somewhat greater in the earlier decades of the period.[15] The natural disasters of plague and pestilence were somewhat abated in the seventeenth century. The plague disappeared in Western Europe after 1720 and was last seen in the great capitals of Paris, London, and Amsterdam in the 1660s. Strictly man-made disasters worked havoc and on a greater scale than in previous centuries because of the improvement in weaponry and the greater size of armies and navies built up by strong states.[16]

Provisionment with food in the mercantilist era was improved by higher crop yields. There are abundant indications that farming yields of food crops improved steadily in the mercantilist era in England, the Low Countries, and small districts with advanced agriculture in Italy, France, and Germany. Higher yields were obtained by enclosure of open fields, improved husbandry, and a general shift to market-oriented agriculture.[17] In northern, central, and eastern Europe, however, agricultural yields remained low and evinced little upward movement. This divergent pattern of crop-yields of European bread-grain cereals is clearly exhibited in Table 4.1 drawn from the research of Slicher van Bath (1978, 78–82), a Dutch agricultural historian.

TABLE 4.1.   Average yield ratios of wheat, rye, and barley together, 1500–1820

Periods	Zone I[a] N[b]	YR	Zone II N	YR	Zone III N	YR	Zone IV N	YR
1500–49	15	7.4			32	4.0	36	3.9
1550–99	17	7.3	. . .	. . .	87	4.4	1531	4.3
1600–49	55	6.7	. . .	. . .	142	4.5	823	4.0
1650–99	25	9.3			120	4.1	1112	3.8
1700–49	. . .	. . .	125	6.3	32	4.1	820	3.5
1750–99	506	10.1	181	7.0	578	5.1	2777	4.7
1800–20	157	11.1	192	6.2	195	5.4	. . .	. . .

[a]Zone I: England, the Low Countries; zone II: France, Spain, Italy; zone III: Germany, Switzerland, Scandinavia; zone IV: Russia, Poland, Czechoslovakia, Hungary. For zone II the value of N was too low before 1700 to include in any measure of yield.

[b]N = number; YR = yield ratio.

Food provisionment in Europe was also improved by growing interest of European farmers and gardeners in two food staples taken over from New World farmers, potato and maize. These plants were high-yielding in seed and acreage, were suited to European temperate climates, and were capable of withstanding weather conditions that would injure staple wheat or rye plantings. These plants were advertised soon in gardening manuals. In the seventeenth century they had a significant penetration of farm fields in Ireland, the Iberian Peninsula, southern France, and Italy, and oddly enough the Danubian basin and the Balkans. Grain consumption in Flanders by the end of the seventeenth century was clearly affected by rising consumption of potatoes as a staple carbohydrate.[18]

Food provisionment of common people and especially of urban populations was considerably improved by the development of deep sea fishing which added to the European staple of Baltic herring the cod and whale fisheries of the North Atlantic.[19] It is estimated that in the fifteenth century the French had a fishing fleet of some 40,000 boats (Woytinsky and Woytinsky 1953, 722). Fish in this era became a staple part of the diet especially of the seafaring peoples facing the Atlantic Ocean.[20] The Dutch pioneered in the development of larger and more efficient fishing boats capable of withstanding Atlantic waters and with sufficient cargo hold to sustain fishing efforts for an entire season. The Dutch learned to eviscerate, cure, and pack on board ship by methods that did not impair quality of the product.[21]

Returns to labor in industry and mining were more abundant also. New sources of readily mined high quality iron ore were discovered noteworthily in Sweden and later in Russia. Iron output boomed in the mercantilist epoch rising from an estimated 40,000 tons in 1500 to over four times that magnitude by 1750.[22] Iron masters learned how to generate enough heat in smelting to make for a continuous blast and to liquefy the metal, making cast-iron products possible for the first time in Europe.[23] Improved methods for milling and fabricating iron were developed in wire-drawing, rolling, and slitting mills.[24] New and powerful sources of energy were made available by more extensive use of mined coal and peat that added significantly to Dutch, English, and French industrial might in the period.[25] Mechanical skills of the kind illustrated by the making of watches and clocks were developed in a wide variety of fields making up a kind of incipient industrial revolution still using animal, coal, water, or wind power for energy.[26] Scientific thought was carried to new levels in the age of Bacon, Galileo, Descartes, and Isaac Newton. This is the age of the first beginnings of chemistry when the most important scientific instruments—the telescope, microscope, barometer, thermometer—take form, and the first scientific societies are established.[27] The printing press multiplied and cheapened writings which became readily available to common people almost for the first time.[28] Altogether a new world is dawning. Is it so surprising that a new economic system takes shape?

Cyclical Instability

This new world and new economic system involved a significant surge and groundwork of capitalist enterprise and mercantile activity. Hence we may presume that economic activity in the mercantile period was susceptible to cyclical instability involving a phase of commercial or financial "crisis" or a process of cumulative and diffused fluctuation in spending and production. Since banking, credit, and stock market speculation were making headway, short periods of bank failure and financial crisis in particular financial centers made their appearance variously in France, England, and Holland where early episodes of crisis can be easily identified.[29] Variable rhythms of fluctuation running their course in wholesale markets, real estate and building, and stock markets may be traced in England in the eighteenth century, and these show up with special clarity in real estate and urban building.[30] The movement of trade and speculation accompanying the South Sea Company Bubble which came to a head in 1720 had all the characteristics of a stock market boom and major depression. A prominent expert on business cycles carefully looked over the evidence of cyclical activity in the eighteenth century in England and noted that the "mania of 1717–1720" was, as were later manias of this kind, "induced by a preceding period of innovation which transformed the economic structure and upset the preexisting state of things." "Even the building boom . . . a regular feature of cyclical situations of this type" and as well the "international character of the crisis and that of the operations that preceded it" all point to the same conclusion (Schumpeter 1939, 1:249).

Can we go farther and make a finding that cyclical instability of the modern type – widely diffused and irregularly periodic fluctuations in business activity – was characteristic of economic activity in the advanced centers of mercantilist Europe in the previous two centuries? Schumpeter was prepared to point to quite a few strands of English and Dutch economic development in the previous century (the seventeenth) which were susceptible to being associated with patterns of cyclical instability. He decided, however, not to try to extend the cyclical process to earlier centuries. Our knowledge of the business life of those centuries was and is fragmentary. There were and are too few consecutive tested time series to sketch out the real behavior patterns. Neither the credit arrangements nor the means of communication between leading business centers permitted the rapid diffusion of ideas and influences that are essential for generating and diffusing business cycle processes. Finally, extensive research strongly suggests that business development was far more likely to be governed by episodic and local forces: fluctuations of weather that could bring bountiful or lean harvests; recurrence of plague; civil conflict; resumption of endemic international conflict that so frequently in those years hampered commerce, destroyed shipping, and upset all normal economic life.[31]

Agricultural Depressions

Though the process of business cycles could not safely be projected through the mercantilist period, did that period experience the ravages of the long-wave movement which three times in the nineteenth and twentieth centuries plagued agriculture? Claims to this effect have been repeatedly made by credit-worthy scholars who trace "long waves" not only through the mercantilist period but back to the late years of the medieval epoch. To evaluate these claims the characteristics of the more recent long-wave agricultural depressions about which we have full information must first be examined.

The first agricultural depression set in after the Napoleonic Wars. The second and third depressions occurred in the last quarter of the nineteenth century and during the third and fourth decades of the twentieth century. The central feature of these depressions was a marked decline in farm prices and in farm incomes. Wherever farmers had fixed obligations to service prior indebtedness or to pay previously fixed rents or taxes, these periods of falling or fallen prices produced rural hardship. Weaker farmers would be forced out of business by foreclosure proceedings, losing all of their previous savings and capital.[32]

Farmer hardship would be intensified to the extent farmers had become dependent upon supporting equipment, services, supplies, or materials produced by capitalist industry. The selling prices of capitalist producers—whether they were railway companies, grain elevators, tractor makers, or truck manufacturers—were not set in the auction-market proceedings by which farm prices are commonly set. Each capitalist producer rather sets his selling price with primary reference to his normal costs of production, the purchase prices of materials used, and the quantity of output that could be sold at profitable prices. Since capitalists adjust the scale of their operations to their sales—by laying off hired labor and reducing purchases of input materials – the pressure of supply on demand which drove down farm prices was felt only slightly by capitalist entrepreneurs. Hence selling prices of capitalist industry would decline only belatedly as materials costs were cheapened or as competition for reduced trade induced wage cuts or price concessions to maintain operations on a more profitable basis.[33]

The selling prices of artisan trade and small local producers rendering special services or making special products used by farmers would tend under pressure to flex more generously than capitalist producer prices. There is only scanty statistical evidence of such selling prices. The products or services to which they refer are rarely identified with precision. But artisans are less likely than capitalist producers to disemploy themselves when their customers are in trouble and have reduced ability to buy. Artisan suppliers are accustomed to negotiating selling prices with individual customers, bearing in mind ability to pay and the artisan's need for continuous work. Very commonly in rural communities artisan suppliers (e.g., millers, cobblers, and smiths) take local produce in trade for goods or services rendered. The selling prices of these rural artisan suppliers are poorly measured by the wage rates of the established urban guilds rendering services chiefly to the local mercantile community, to resident nobility or crown officials, or ecclesiastical establishments. Another misleading statistical measure of village artisan suppliers will be found in manorial accounts of expenses of manorial establishments that hired labor on a large scale.[34]

The decline of farm selling prices during agricultural depressions does not characteristically induce a decline of farmer output. Even if the farmer is foreclosed and loses his farm, the farm does not go out of business. The new owner will either operate it himself or rent it out to a tenant farmer, perhaps the very one that was foreclosed. So long as the farmer is able to work, he will not desert the task of tillage if only to prevent his land from being overrun with weeds, to maintain his animal stock, and to provide subsistence to his family. Many farm households will intensify their tillage even at very low prices to raise sufficient sums to stave off creditors and to purchase essential supplies.[35] Many perennial plants – yielding coffee beans, sisal leaves, tea leaves, olives, or grapes – require much preparatory work and tillage years before they bear fruit. They must be tended if the valuable trees and vines are to be maintained.

Thus lower farm prices fail to elicit reduced farm output. In some instances output may increase. In both of the extended agrarian depressions of the nineteenth century fertile new lands were opening up for settlement and improved means of transportation were opening new markets for outlying farm producers. Low-cost new production in new farming territories could adjust to lower prices which older farmers on older lands found insupportable.[36]

Prolonged periods of price decline or agricultural depression result from changes in supply or demand for staple farm products. Demand can be affected by a fall in urban population, by an increase in the money supply that will boost market demand, by the growth of population in urban centers, or by the rise of new industries that step up demand for food and fiber. Supply can be affected by improved methods of transportation that open up to cultivation fertile outlying lands or by substitution of machinery powered by fossil fuels for draft animals, turning fodder acres into food acres, or by improved husbandry resulting in boosted yields per acre.

Every major war upsets the balance of demand and supply for farm staples. War devastation usually results in food shortage and higher food prices that stimulate food production elsewhere. In each historical period the balance of forces affecting supply and demand for farm staples was poised somewhat differently. In the nineteenth century these forces were predominantly positive in character and keynoted development, mechanization, and new settlement. In earlier centuries and again in the twentieth century negative forces—war devastation, epidemics, or famine—were more prominent. At no time, however, did these forces in earlier centuries include a Malthusian kind of impoverishment because population growth was sufficiently checked by the chronic internecine warfare readily indulged by the ruling classes, by delay of marriage widely practiced by European villagers, by relatively high mortality rates especially among infants and children, and finally by unhealthy and unsanitary conditions in walled cities where communicable diseases could readily spread.[37]

One factor tending to tilt the balance of supply and demand in farm staple markets in the farmer's favor is persistent inflation. This lightens the burden of fixed payments on farmers and gives farm markets an upward tilt. Inflation in the mercantilist period arose partly from a tendency of sovereigns and mint masters to augment their revenues by reducing the quantity of precious metal mixed with alloy in coins of standard denomination.[38] A second cause of inflation is much rarer, namely, discovery of new supplies of precious metals from the opening of new lands to settlement and exploration. Four times in the past half millenium have significant quantities of new gold and silver reached Europe from afar and swept up prices. The most momentous and extended upthrust of inflation thus arising resulted from looting Inca and Aztec treasure chests and mobilizing Indian labor to work the silver mines of the New World. A lesser force for inflation came from the gold discoveries in Brazil around the turn of the eighteenth century. The final episodes followed Californian and Australian gold discoveries in the mid–nineteenth century and near the turn of the century the discovery of South African and Alaskan gold supplies and a new technology for working the ores. The first two rounds of inflation occurred during the mercantilist epoch, the latter two during the capitalist epoch. The tendency to inflation was heightened in the late mercantilist and capitalist epochs by increased intense use of money stock through the development of banking networks that added credit money to coin money and speeded up the velocity of money in circulation. The tendency to inflation from all these forces—augmented supply of precious metals, dilution of coinage, and rise of credit banking— was overwhelming during the mercantilist epoch.

Agricultural or General Depressions

Agricultural depressions must of necessity have some adverse effects on other branches of the economy. Some theorists have contended that agricultural depressions tended to contaminate the entire economy. One version of this contamination process was developed by a French economist who in an extended treatise published in 1932 coined the term for long-wave price movements Curve A (for expansions) and Curve B (for contractions).[39] A better known theorist of the contamination process is the celebrated Russian agricultural economist, N. Kondratieff, who in a series of investigations on what he called "long cycles" made a great stir among Soviet economists in the 1920s. After translation into Western languages his work excited Western students of business cycles.[40]

There is some semblance of support for the contamination thesis in the third agricultural depression beginning in the 1920s and extending through much of the 1930s. The agricultural depression contributed to the disturbed environment which entered into the making of the Great Depression.[41] However, the two earlier agricultural depressions extended over a much longer period during which an entire series of business cycles ran their course while the advance of modern industry made great progress both in the older industrial centers of Europe and among the newly industrializing countries such as the United States, Germany, Canada, Japan, Russia. The level of agricultural output reaching world markets increased at a rapid rate during both of those agricultural depressions and industrial activity more than kept pace. This is strikingly illustrated by the evidence for Great Britain between 1815 and 1847. The average annual percentage rate of growth of iron production was 6.5 percent; of textile output 5.2 percent; of consumption of cotton 6.3 percent; and exports of iron, hardware, and cutlery, 5.6 percent (Gayer et al. 1953, 2:623). The expansion of food and fiber output more than kept pace though agricultural prices were relatively depressed.[42] Hence the Kondratieff hypothesis that "long cycles" involved both agriculture and industry has not been accepted by most students who have scrutinized the statistical evidence especially for the agricultural depressions of the nineteenth century.[43]

The great inflation of the mercantilist epoch almost but not quite eliminated the possibility of persistent agrarian depressions. The bulk of Spanish New World gold and silver reached European markets in the sixteenth and early seventeenth centuries. In Spain and Portugal the climax of precious metal inflation was reached early in the seventeenth century and thereafter was financed chiefly by debasing the coinage. In France, England, and the Low Countries the climax of gold and silver inflation was only reached between the sixth and seventh decades of the seventeenth century and in France thereafter was continued by currency devaluation. Unquestionably, farm prices when converted into their silver equivalent for agricultural staples in major West European markets declined during the last quarter of the seventeenth century and through the first quarter of the eighteenth century. The extent of silver price decline was mild, ranging from 25 to 50 percent, less for livestock and dairy produce than for grains. The extent of silver price decline over the whole of Western Europe was uneven because markets for farm staples were imperfectly united within countries and were subject to major barriers across frontiers (Abel 1935/1980, 158, Fig. 17).

In England and in the Low Countries where financial discipline was most respected and hence where monetary devaluation was entirely secondary, the fall in agricultural prices was to a considerable extent offset by improvements in the arts of cultivation and tillage, made possible in England and Wales by major advances in land enclosures.[44] In England, moreover, the fall in grain prices was cushioned by the adoption in 1688 of a program of agricultural price stabilization that severely taxed grain imports, except when domestic prices were high and allowed a generous bounty on grain exports when domestic prices were low.[45] For short periods in this entire half-century there was evidence of "distress" and especially between 1730 and 1750 some show of cumulative "depression."[46] But throughout the entire half-century or the larger part of it, general agricultural depression was nonexistent. Though the extent of price decline in this half-century was carefully canvassed by Adam Smith, he found "great prosperity in almost every part of the country" since 1690, with rents of "almost all the estates continually rising" (Smith 1776/1937, 781). Contemporary students of British agriculture for that half-century find few if any traces of "depression" comparable to the "distress" readily recognized in the post–Napoleonic period.

French Agriculture

French agriculture experienced little of the modernization and upward tilt of productivity that revolutionized English and Low Country farming in the mercantilist period and made England a great grain exporter in the eighteenth century. Moreover, though current farm prices reckoned in milligrams of silver were falling in France, when measured in the current money of the day prices were generally rising.[47] Finally, French peasant farmers paid rents largely fixed as a share of the crop or as a set quantity of grain or produce per acre (Le Roy Ladurie 1974, 116, 214, 254, 257; Bloch 1913/1966, 146). Feudal dues and quitrents had already been substantially devalued by the earlier round of gold and silver inflation or coinage degradation. Church tithes were mostly based, like most farm rents, on a share in kind. What especially burdened French peasants between 1675 and 1715 was not the level of gold and silver prices but the sharply rising level of national taxation from which the wealthiest classes in France – the landowning nobility, nobility of the robe, and high clergy – were largely exempt. Peasant and bourgeois discontent was given a sharp edge since every parcel of land purchased from taxable holders by exempt holders directly increased the quotas of taxation assigned to remaining taxable holders in the district concerned. Peasant and artisan discontent with the rising level of national taxation in France in the sixteenth and seventeenth centuries flared many times into violent revolt.[48] And this burden of rising national taxation was made more oppressive by the decline in levels of real income which marked the French economy between 1684 and 1715.

Economic Stagnation

This decline, which was not at all especially or uniquely agricultural, has been described at length in monographic investigation and may be summarized as follows:

1. Significant decline from 25 to 75 percent in the level of indus-

trial production and investment in such industries as textile manufacturing (including woolens, silks, and linens), felt hat making, tanning and leather making, salt and glass manufacture, coal mining, shipbuilding, fishing, rug and carpet weaving, and overseas commerce.

2. Depressed levels of money income were dramatically exhibited by depressed levels of tax revenues collected even at higher tax rates. Ordinary government revenues in 1710 and 1714 were 36.2 percent and 40.1 percent of 1685 levels. Taile collections in 1715 were 74 percent of 1683 levels.

3. In desperate search for revenues, the coinage was repeatedly degraded and interest-bearing paper script was issued endowed with partial legal-tender privileges, causing high grade coins to go into hoarding or shipment abroad and substantially disrupting foreign commerce.[49]

4. Economic stagnation between 1685 and 1715 was accompanied and in part caused by a significant decline in residential population – by as much as 10–15 percent – resulting from emigration abroad, from a final surge of bubonic plague (1720–1722), and from sustained warfare.[50] The decline in population felt in rural as well as urban households would cause a decline in agricultural output aggravated somewhat by ecologic adversities causing severe famines and for a number of years after 1709 wiping out French olive groves. The extent of this decline of farm output, however, is in controversy. In view of the universal and well-established reluctance of farm families regularly engaged in farming to voluntarily cut back on their farming operations – a reluctance especially deep rooted in subsistence agriculture – it would be strange if farm output, apart from a decline specifically attributable to abnormal weather conditions or to ecologic disasters, should fall off by much more than the decline in rural adult population. On that supposition the general decline in French farm output between 1685 and 1717 should not exceed 12–17 percent, allowing a 2 percent margin for ecological and weather effects.[51]

A major school of French historiography, headed by the redoubtable French scholar, E. Le Roy Ladurie, contends otherwise on the basis of scattered crop and output returns as measured by collections on French tithes. Le Roy Ladurie alleges in a series of publications from 1966 onward that this decline in French real farm output between 1683 and 1717 ran up to 50 percent in the most adversely affected districts. In the north and south of France output allegedly declined between 25 and 33 percent.[52] Le Roy Ladurie's version of extreme retrogression in French agriculture around the turn of the eighteenth century, based upon records of tithe collections, has been contested by many knowledgeable French scholars who have contended that the low level or the slow growth of real tithe collections during the period of economic stagnation and throughout the entire mercantilist period reflects the declining efficiency of tithe collections and the growing resistance to tithing rather than the trend movement of farm output.[53]

These contentions of the critics of the Le Roy Ladurie version are sustained by four major arguments worthy of brief review. Popular resistance by the common people to compulsory tithing was especially strong in the growing cities where feudal lordship could not so readily coerce submission. The collection of so-called "personal" tithes on earnings of work or from a small business or handicraft was greatly weakened in England and in Italy and by the fifteenth century had disappeared from France.[54]

Peasant resistance to tithing was traditional, it being claimed that "the malice of those who possess lands (in shirking of tithes) is infinite."[55] This malice owed partly to peculiar features of peasant tithing. Harvesting operations in good weather could be delayed by the need to give proper notice to the tithing officer. The tithe effected a perverse kind of income taxation, the effective rate being higher in times of poor harvest. The loss of straw as well as grain was resented for straw was needed for animal bedding and for household use. The tithe gatherer who claimed his share from a more bountiful product benefitted from use of valuable fertilizer but did not contribute to the expense thereof. There were constant disputes about house gardens and fruit trees allegedly exempt. Tithing by pastoralists whose flocks were frequently on the move was difficult to police and monitor. The farmer and landowner resented paying full tithes on the product of land reclaimed from waste by expensive operations of drainage or clearing.[56] Peasant resistance to tithing was sometimes reinforced by Catharistic heresy or Albigensianism which flourished in southern France before the fourteenth century.[57]

Taxpayer support of tithing was undermined in the later medieval period by the excess drainage of tithing revenues to outside appropriators, either (1) nobility or gentry with an inherited claim to patronage of the church or a lay bourgeois to whom tithing rights were sold, or (2) a monastic institution endowed with tithing rights by the crown or papacy or lordship, or (3) commercial intermediaries who contracted out for tithe collection, marketing and distribution and who enjoyed substantial profits,[58] or (4) the diocesal establishment of the bishop or archbishop with their various subagencies and offices. The proportions varied in different parts of Western Europe but nearly everywhere outside appropriators—in France especially monastic institutions—received the great bulk of the major tithes on bread grains, wine, and livestock products or what cash incomes filtered through commercial intermediaries. Local priests received only tidbits of the "minor" tithes. The local church acquired from tithes little or no repair and maintenance funds or support for the poor.[59] Parishioners still had to maintain church edifices and pay onerous fees on christenings, marriages, funeral services, and "altar" dues for special services.[60]

Popular resistance to tithing exploded in the Reformation, itself an opening phase of the mercantilist period. The decline in the moral standing of monastic institutions—mirrored in the widely read *In Praise of Folly* by Erasmus, himself a monk of the Augustinian Order—resulted in their dissolution in Protestant Europe, the confiscation of the properties of the monastic orders, and the dissolution or banning of many of the orders most in disrepute.[61] A Huguenot offensive targeted the expropriation and sale of a quarter of church and monastic landed properties.[62] The peasant struggle in the Rhine valley following Luther's public challenge on indulgences and papal authority spread to France and at the "sound of a tocsin" the collection of tithes was stopped or slowed down.[63] Altogether during the second half of the sixteenth century when repression against Huguenots was intense and when an armed struggle between Catholics and Huguenots emerged, tithing revenues in Mediterranean France declined by nearly 40–50 percent from earlier levels.[64] Most French peasants, quipped Le Roy Ladurie, remained good Catholics but became poor tithe-payers (1977, 189). In this period church leaders negotiated lower tithing rates and sometimes arranged for buy outs of future tithe obligations for a set annual payment or a set rental per acre.[65]

The premise of Le Roy Ladurie is that the civil peace which under the Edict of Nantes (1598) allowed peaceful coexistence permitted the Catholic Counter-Reformation to restore Catholic supremacy in France leading to abatement of the anti-tithing animus. Catholic supremacy was achieved but only with the frightful cost of suppression of the Huguenots and their expulsion from France. The anti-tithing animus was not abated but simply driven underground to achieve its ends by sabotage and withholding of product or by court actions and protests in provincial parliaments. In the South of France a recent historian of the French church has reported "in the last twenty years of the ancien régime a revolt against tithe was smouldering" (McManners 1985, 165). The reality of that revolt was brought home by the celebrated action on 4 May 1789 of the elected National Assembly abolishing tithes, construed by this same historian as an expression of "a vast undeclared conspiracy over the whole of France to evade and outwit the tithe holders" (167). If that interpretation holds, slow growth or decline in tithe collections reflects declining rates of levy and tax evasion or profit taking by commercial intermediaries rather than trends in gross agricultural production.

If the economic stagnation in France between 1685 and 1717 was not a generally applicable European phenomenon, and if it was not at all a special form of "agricultural depression," of what character then was it? This is a topic that has concerned French historians ever since Voltaire sought to take the measure of the reign of Louis XIV in one of his major historical works. Fortunately for our purposes, Warren C. Scoville, a thoughtful student of French economic history in the mercantilist epoch, has devoted extended research and a major volume to this very question.[66] He tried to evaluate the various factors that entered into the making of this period of French economic stagnation. I draw upon his work for the following summary:

1. Some role was played by a concentration of very poor weather resulting in crop famines in 1684–1685, 1692–1694, and a disastrous freeze in the coldest winter that Mediterranean France had seen in a millennium that in 1708–1709 destroyed the olive groves and ruined the wine crop. A 2 percent allowance for output shrinkage on ecologic account has already been suggested (see n.51).

2. Two relatively unsuccessful and costly wars, taking up two out of three years in the period of stagnation, involved extensive fighting on or near French frontiers and French fighting forces up to 500,000 men, enrolled only with the aid of conscription. The wars unbalanced French budgets, damaged her overseas commerce and merchant marine, and were financed in part by debasing the coinage and issuing paper scrip.

3. Oppressive taxation rendered especially onerous by substantial exemption of nobility and clergy from taxation and a regime of tax farming that made the tax collector an object of execration.

4. Persecution on an increasing scale of French Protestants (Huguenots) embracing 10 percent of the French adult population and a larger fraction of the entrepreneurial elite active in agriculture, wholesale trade, industry, and artisanry. This persecution was climaxed in 1685 by a declaration of open war on French Protestantism, revoking the famous Edict of Nantes that a century before had terminated a period of civil strife in France by establishing a scheme of religious tolerance. The revocation of the Edict was a mortal blow at French Protestants and drove about 10 percent of them into exile. Significant capital sums were carried or smuggled abroad by wealthy Huguenot exiles and refugees; and skilled Huguenot industrialists and artisans established abroad many industries that later challenged leading French export specialties.

The relative contribution of each of these factors to the making of the economic stagnation of France from 1685 to 1717 was carefully evaluated. The author found each of them important and altogether a sufficient cause for stagnation (Scoville 1960, 434–43). Scoville made it clear that the stagnation in France of 1685–1717 does not grow out of any tendency to "long-waves" or agricultural depression in the mercantilist economy.[67]

Categorical ruling out of long-term crisis or stagnation in the seventeenth century does not rule out the more general contention advanced by some circles of historians that the century was in some cultural or sociopolitical sense characterized by crisis. Here it is necessary to select which concept of crisis appears more adequate in light of the tendency for nearly every century of European history to be in a state of turmoil and structural transformation.[68]

Modal Complex of the Mercantilist Economy

The modal complex in the field of agriculture rested upon the dissolution of the feudal mode of production with its twin institutions of the seignorial manor and serfdom. This dissolution in central, southern, and western Europe—west of the Elbe River as ordinarily demarcated—was variously in process, in a few areas completed, in others only begun, and elsewhere in an uncertain process of change. The peasant revolts that broke out in the fourteenth century in France and England and in the sixteenth century in Germany and Bohemia brought to light the enormous discontent with manorial oppression and serfdom generated by the feudal mode.[69] The depopulation, the product of scourges of plague and famine that swept Europe in the fourteenth century, stimulated this process of feudal dissolution since movement of plague survivors to new locations with improved status was encouraged. Even when the peasant revolts were brutally suppressed and the revolting peasant leaders weeded out, the old regime could not be completely restored (Cipolla 1972–1976, 2:292). Here and there the new royal power emerging in Western Europe sought to sustain and enlarge peasant yeomanry if only to better carry the burdens of royal taxation and to make a willing and able soldiery.[70] Foot soldiers and sailors had come to supersede the elite mounted armored knight—with his lance, charger, squire, and devotion to chivalry—a figure whom Cervantes so effectively ridiculed.

Hence the thesis is credible that except in the Mediterranean and especially in the Iberian Peninsula where the reconquest of former

Moorish territories left a heritage of large estates and an enserfed agrarian population, outright serfdom had substantially disappeared from Western Europe. But the manorial regime with its demesne estate; its claims to outlying pasture, woodlands, or waste; its appropriation of a share of the church tithes; its control over milling facilities offered by falling waters; its monopoly over ovens, winepresses, and other village facilities and its vague claims to ownership of open fields; its right to levy on peasant succession; its profits from manorial administration of justice – this phase of the manorial regime was slower to go. And even where it had become weakened by disuse, its claims in a society where supreme power was held by landed aristocrats could be reasserted in courts aristocrats would influence. Many of these little by-products of the feudal mode lingered long in Britain adding to the rent toll that took in the seventeenth century an unusually high fraction of agricultural income.[71] In central and north Germany many incidents of serfdom remained through the eighteenth century and even where peasant proprietorship over their main arable fields was achieved, feudal rents had been transformed into coercive dues and taxes owed to landed aristocrats ruling the innumerable principalities that made up the German state (De Vries 1976, 61).

Three basic modes of production issued from the dissolution of the feudal agricultural mode of the medieval period. In England noteworthily and to a lesser extent on the Continent, the demesne was enclosed with what augmentation by purchase from smallholders or by appropriation from the common fields was possible and either put in profitable sheep grazing or subdivided into large farms. These were operated by hired wage labor employed by capitalist farmers who provided their own stock and equipment and usually leased the land on medium to long terms for money rents.[72] A less progressive system widely favored in the Mediterranean was one that continued small peasant holdings but leased from the landlord on a yearly basis with the crop shared usually fifty/fifty with special arrangements for sharing in animal husbandry, vine culture, and dairying.[73] A third possible outcome of the medieval period was the peasant smallholder who either had achieved traditional claims to allodial status or had bought his way clear or had fought for his freedom. This class was well represented in the English countryside still making up in the late seventeenth century a fifth of farm families and often combining some form of cottage industry as a sideline.[74] In many sections of France this class was well represented. In Holland and along the Rhineland and in the uplands of the Mediterranean, the Alps, and the Pyrenees, independent smallholdings were well established.[75]

Industrial Revolution

The entire urban complex of industry and trade became considerably enlarged relative to its supporting agricultural population in the mercantile period because of higher levels of agricultural productivity within the European economy and because substantial raw foodstuffs were now drawn from overseas fisheries, from the Baltic, or from the New World sugar plantations. A veritable industrial revolution within the expanded urban-industrial complex brought about a notable shift from small–scale craft production to various forms of capitalist production. These ranged from the now well-established system of "merchant put-out" undertakings whereby raw materials are assembled, put out to craftsmen for processing and finally assembled for finishing and marketing usually through export channels. More novel were the factories, mills, and workshops owned and operated by capitalists who would bring together large numbers of wage workers.

The textile industry where the "putting-out" system flourished in the woolen trades spawned a whole set of developments that brought about the capitalist workshop with its assembled workers, work instruments and assorted crafts. Merchant clothiers brought together their weavers to practice their trade in a common workroom with looms and equipment provided by the employer, sometimes with an accessory dye-house or waterpowered fulling mill (Dobb 1963, 138, 149). The location of the industry was shifted to upland areas to draw water-power to activate fulling mills.[76] A silk-throwing mill operated by waterpower with hundreds of spindles and spools for silk winding was developed in north Italy and became diffused in the entire Po Valley early in the seventeenth century. The work of one of these machines replaced the labor of several hundred spinners and by the end of the century not only were a hundred such machines with an estimated annual output of a million pounds of silk thread functioning but comparable waterpowered silk reeling mills had been established in southern France and elsewhere in Europe.[77] A knitting frame was invented in 1598 involving a complicated mechanism using hundreds of needles capable of doing between 1000 and 1500 stitches per minute, ten to fifteen times more productive than hand knitting. The machine was slow to gain acceptance because of guild restrictions but found a place for itself by the mid–seventeenth century when some 650 frames were functioning under the guidance of Framework Knitters Company, which controlled the hiring out of frames to domestic craftsmen, thus embodying capitalist control over craft cottage operations (Dobb 1963, 145). A ribbon frame permitting one person to make 12 ribbons at one time was invented in Germany in the sixteenth century and was patented in Holland in 1604. It spread to many parts of Europe though it encountered workman resistance especially in Germany. Marx characterized this machine as a precursor to the mule and powerloom since it enabled an inexperienced boy to set the loom in motion with all its shuttles by simply moving a rod backwards and forwards.[78]

In the fields of metallurgy, mining, and heavy industry there occurred what Nef described as an "industrial revolution" involving nearly everywhere good-sized industrial enterprises.[79] Mining depths increased, raising the pressure for development of effective pumping and water-lifting devices. Some English collieries reached a coal output of 20,000 tons yearly. Already in the seventeenth century coke began to replace coal and charcoal in many industrial processes.[80] Nef (1957, 113) estimated that by 1650 English mineral and heavy industry output increased some six to eight times over the level of a century earlier. The continuous blast furnaces used for preparing cast iron caused capital requirements for iron smelting to surpass that needed for the primitive forge and smithy where iron was worked in previous centuries. The Dutch developed a successful wind-powered lumber mill and in their shipyards heavy cranes helped in handling precut timbers (De Vries 1976, 93). In Saxony and Bohemia shareholding mining companies and great capitalist families like the Fuggers and the Welsers leased and operated copper and silver mines in Saxony, Thuringia, and Tyrol and built impressive refineries (Saigerhütten) for processing the ores. New processes for casting and rolling plate glass were developed in Western Europe in large facilities employing hundreds of workers. The invention of movable type and mass printing led to a new printing industry manufacturing movable type, so large publishing houses emerged employing a host of printers, binders, and book finishers and producing hundreds of titles annually (Cipolla 1972–1976, 2:409, 411, 381).

The development of printing and expansion of literacy stepped up the demand for paper. Waterpower was used to operate shredding and pulping machines that considerably increased the scale of production at the plant level and brought about widespread interregional trade in paper.[81] By the mid-seventeenth and early eighteenth century some 30–40 waterpowered paper mills were functioning in England and some 300 in France.[82] Salt making shifted from hauling buckets of brine to be boiled in pans like washerwoman tubs to large-scale mining undertakings or seawater evaporation projects involving large iron vessels and use of coal for boiling.[83] Understandably the new military technology called for large-scale fabrication facilities for assembly of muskets and small arms, for cannon manufacture, for shipbuilding, and for powder manufacture.[84] These are merely the outstanding developments in a panorama of industrial change.

This development of capitalist production hardly signifies the disappearance of the older guild-craftsman mode. The guild-craftsman mode had legal predominance even in England where the spirit of capitalist development was strongest and where the later development of woolen manufactures took place in rural locations mostly outside of guild controls. This predominance is attested to by the universal scope of the Statute of Artificers enacted in the middle of the sixteenth century. It remained in force until early in the nineteenth century with its regulation of apprenticeship, the decisive means for the implementation of the power of the craft guilds.[85] In France especially the entire mercantilist period and the thrust of policy involved the strengthening and extension of guild-craft control.[86] In Germany the practices of guild organization and the role of artisan lingered long in the nineteenth century.[87]

The guild artisan was probably the predominant workman throughout the entire mercantilist period. Moreover, even the capitalist or corporate workshops rested on a foundation, as Marx emphasized in his analysis of "manufactures," of the skilled artisan. Parts of a machine were fabricated individually and were fitted and assembled by hand as were all finishing, sorting, and packaging operations. Marx's commentary on capitalist manufacture is still arresting: though unable to seize upon the production of society to its full extent or to revolutionize the production to its very core, "it towered up as an economic work of art, on the broad foundation of the town handicrafts and of the rural domestic industries" (Marx 1863–1878/1971, 1:368).

What is remarkable about the mercantilist period is that as capitalist production in manufactures was becoming developed, the corporate business form evolved, played an important role in large-scale wholesale trade and finance, and appeared even in industry. The antecedents of the corporation were the merchant guild associations that were sometimes given corporate form as merchant adventurers or as open associations of merchants authorized to regulate the trade to a particular locality or region and to operate some common facilities but trade on an individual basis. The first strictly joint-stock companies with saleable shares and a formal structure of representative corporate government appeared not in the wholesale trade but in mining. Here the investment of large amounts of capital was a requirement for exploiting certain mineral deposits in Germany and in England.[88] The development and exploitation of trade to distant areas then called for the use of the joint-stock device to coordinate individual trading interests and enable all to share in the common expenses. The joint-stock device also enabled the crown itself, the aristocracy, and the gentry to join with merchants and capitalists in developing the national economy and its imperial interests.[89] The first English joint-stock trading companies were the Eastland and the Russia companies in the mid-sixteenth century. The idea became contagious and the East India trade, which the British and Dutch opened up in the seventeenth century was soon turned by degrees into bona fide joint-stock companies though at first stock investment was allegedly confined to the outfitting of ships for definite voyages that on return were to disburse both profits and capital.[90] The companies and the trade were so successful that much of their needed capital could be raised by issuance of bonds marketed to investors concerned more for safety than for yield.[91] Dividends earned and paid variously in the seventeenth century were unusually high, between 1609–1613 averaging 281 percent; "brilliant returns" were realized between 1687–1736 (Clapham 1941–1978, 4:259). Stock in these and other successful corporations was readily saleable on the stock exchanges gradually developed in the seventeenth century in Amsterdam, London, and later in Paris to provide facilities for sale and purchase of securities by investors.[92] The institutional machinery required by a corporate system—a profession of jobbers and brokers engaged in making a market, newspaper reporting of earnings and stock prices—began to emerge by the turn of the eighteenth century (Cipolla 1972–1976, 2:557). Watching all this, the French royal and bourgeois leadership were inspired to try their luck at corporate creation and as in a hothouse under Colbert's management corporations were launched in the later seventeenth century right and left.[93]

Both in England and in France chartered corporations became an agency for centralizing capital and building giant business enterprises usually granted monopoly privileges in overseas colonial development. As the clear-sighted Hobbes (1651/1914, 122) put it: "The end of their incorporating is to make their gaine greater which is done two wayes; by sole buying and sole selling, both at home and abroad." They became a fiscal salvation to the overindebted state with its crushing military expenditures and its poor ability to raise taxes or sell securities because the corporations received their charters partly in reward for their assumption of blocs of public debt.[94] This became the mechanism of the stock market and corporate-promotion boom of 1717–1720 running a near common course in France, England, and Holland, and involving a nest of colonial corporations and the French central bank; a Banque Royale run by John Law, the Scotch financial adventurer; the South Sea Company, a stock corporation assigned the monopoly of the Spanish *asiento* and trade with Latin America; and a corporate promotion boom involving hundreds of corporations and promising to scale down the entire English public debt in exchange for appreciating

South Sea stock. Involved also was a very real investment and building boom, which collapsed with the stock market much as it did some two centuries later.[95]

This speculative boom and bust did much to dampen enthusiasm for the corporate mode. English law became very restrictive in authorizing corporations previously given a free hand.[96] The colonial corporations did not through the eighteenth century retain their earlier high profitability.[97] For projects calling for extraordinary amounts of capital but that were relatively easy to manage when completed – such as a national bank, an insurance company, road-building projects, a canal-building company – the corporate device proved its worth and with proper safeguards held its ground through the years.[98] The entire British highway (turnpike) system of the eighteenth century and her canals and railways in the nineteenth century were developed as corporate ventures (see n.108). But for the later eighteenth and most of the nineteenth century for mercantile and industrial purposes, the corporation was not the favored instrument. The state increasingly assumed responsibility for management of permanent investments called for by colonial settlements as in North America, Africa, and India, and all British subjects were allowed to participate in the trade involved.

MONEY AND PUBLIC ECONOMY

The mercantilist institution of money was deeply rooted in coined gold and silver whose supply was revolutionized by massive silver imports from Spanish New World conquests and by later Portuguese discoveries of gold in the eighteenth century. These imports produced the expansion of business activity and inflation promoting the economic development of the mercantilist economy. That development in turn would not have been possible without a substantial development of commercial banking to provide centers for financial clearing and a form of credit money for international and wholesale trade. This credit development took on three main forms. Throughout the mercantilist period the forms of indebtedness were becoming released from their personal ties making most credit instruments negotiable or readily transferable to bearer by written order.[99] This in the later mercantilist period led to the transfer of bank claims by written order or check, a move long resisted in the first stages of banking development in the Mediterranean (Gottlieb 1984, 291 n. 62). The ready purchase and sale of credit instruments made headway, so essential for early forms of bank lending. The non-interest-bearing circulating bank note was formally introduced by the Bank of Stockholm in the middle of the seventeenth century and on a much larger scale by the Bank of England in the 1690s. Paper currency combined with conventional commercial banking based primarily upon discount of commercial bills and provision of government short-term credit rapidly spread in England and in Scotland. By the early eighteenth century paper currency in England is estimated to have exceeded the total bullion and coin circulation (Cipolla 1972–1976, 2:552).

The British led in the development of a credit system. Continental experience did not economize on the use of gold and silver or so readily favor the development of fractional reserve banking. The attempt by the French to move in this direction ended in fiasco. Coined gold or silver was not the sole basis for the monetary system on the Continent. Paradoxically, the very country that saturated Europe with precious metals, Spain, proved incapable of managing a dependable precious metal coinage. Mercantilist money in Spain in the seventeenth century was copper or bronze, expensive to maintain, easy to counterfeit, and clumsy for large-scale financial transfers.[100] The Dutch who led the way in the early mercantilist period were content to live with a conservative form of banking ostensibly avoiding all lending though secret lending to the East India Company drained its resources.[101]

Institutional development in banking was slow. Traditional ways of thinking about interest on money loans held on tenaciously. In England for the first three quarters of the sixteenth century the law still prohibited the taking of explicit and identifiable interest on money loans. There was considerable reluctance to authorize banking establishments devoted solely to the handling of moneys and the making of loans. The first relaxation of the interest verbot in England in 1571 set a maximum allowable rate of 10 percent that borrowers could legally protest if they chose. Throughout the seventeenth century lending nearly everywhere in Europe was subject to cramping restrictions as to form of loan and allowable interest, frequently calling for use of subterfuge with questionable standing in law.[102]

The egregious failure of national banking in the John Law fiasco in France destroyed the one continental venture in true national banking that went beyond the municipally controlled institutions built up on the Continent in the seventeenth century. In England the Bank of England concentrated its business in the metropolis. Commercial banking in England was largely in the hands of the most unstable form of proprietorial banking with relatively high failure rates.[103]

The mercantilist public economy was even more poorly developed than its banking. It is true that central state power was strengthened except in Germany and northern Italy. The core of a general taxing power emerged so that every grant of funds no longer needed authorization by the assembled estates or parliaments. The more intensive movement of commodities and the development of a wider range of manufacturing prompted the development of excise and sales taxation that proved extraordinarily fruitful and spread from luxury-type products like tobacco and malt and alcoholic spirits to basic necessities like coal, leather, soap, paper, salt, and bread grains.[104] This was supplemented in France by a truly monstrous growth in direct taxation based upon a cadastral-type survey of occupation or property. Tax administration lagged very much behind taxing authority – outside of England where taxes were generally collected by regular treasury officers. On the Continent generally, except for some heavy direct French taxation administered under the intendants, taxes even in Holland were farmed with expensive and often arbitrary collection.[105] Assessments of ability to pay or yield for land, buildings, and income were generally derived from outdated information and were adjusted arbitrarily. Writing at the end of the mercantilist period, Adam Smith made every effort to compare the effectiveness of tax administration in France, Holland, and England. He found that the French treasury received only one-half as much per capita as was collected and transmitted to the British treasury but that the people of France "are much more oppressed by taxes than the people of Great Britain." Dutch taxes he estimated were nearly 50 percent above the British level. They had in the process appreciably boosted the wage level adversely affecting their principal manufactures, "their fisheries and their trade in shipbuilding" (Smith 1776/1937, 855). That finding has been reaffirmed by present-day research (Wilson 1969, 116). "Increasingly burdensome taxes" are listed among the persistent structural causes for the "decline" or "decadence" of Spain in the seventeenth century.[106] Tax potential was used sparingly for essential public works or supportive public services. The rising expense of standing armies and navies, fortifying key installations and fighting wars, either foreign or domestic, drank up most of this tax potential. What was left over was mortgaged by the heavy expense of lavish court life, an essential feature of the quasi-feudal courts still dominating state power in the mercantilist period, perhaps less in England than on the Continent. Hence despite the windfall of gold and silver discoveries in the New World, which contributed sizable revenues to the Spanish crown, that crown was perpetually on the brink of bankruptcy and repeatedly in the sixteenth and seventeenth century cancelled or scaled down indebtedness.[107] An English highway system was built up in the latter segment of the mercantilist period but entirely by locally arranged turnpike toll trusts, financed by borrowing and paid out of toll receipts.[108] The most sizable public works in the mercantilist economy were probably the 175-mile Orleans canal connecting the Mediterranean and Atlantic oceans, crossing a rocky divide 600 feet above sea level with 65 locks, a French highway network that won the praise of Adam Smith, and a vast church-building program in England financed by a temporary levy on coal in the later seventeenth and early eighteenth centuries.[109] Elaborate French programs for internal improvements (canals, port facilities, and navigable river channels) were presented to the Court but few of these seem to have been as favored with finance as the palatial royal facilities (gardens, chateaux, fountains) altogether costing many times the amount invested in useful public works.[110]

The redistributionist bias of the mercantilist economy was crassly inegalitarian. In France the basic property tax or taile completely exempted sizable landholdings of the clergy and aristocracy. No such exemption was allowed for the comparable English land tax though that tax once set in the late seventeenth century was not increased with the rising value of land or growth in rental income (Smith 1776/ 1937, 801). The direct tax burden on the landed aristocracy of England hence was comparatively light. Everywhere indirect taxation concentrated on necessities of life or industry while government outlays beyond the military network and interest on public debt were channeled largely to the upper elite of the courts and to their edifices and the establishments of church and state. Since wars were financed largely by borrowing and public debts were serviced chiefly by excise taxes raised from the bottom layers of the society, wars imposed a double burden on the poor. They were impressed into service as soldiers or sailors and were sometimes driven from their homes and fields by advancing armies. Yet in the intervals of war they paid much of the taxes servicing war debt.

MERCANTILIST REGULATORY POLICY

Mercantilist regulatory policy is a critical factor in the overall mercantilist economic system.[111] The dominant mercantilist policy objectives were: (1) accelerating economic development by encouraging new industry including export industry like woolen cloth and metallurgical industry needed for weapons manufacture; (2) helping merchants achieve the widest extension of their trading markets bringing a wide variety of desired products and materials to the homeland; (3) learning to make at home wherever feasible what products were imported and to use local materials, where available, for domestic industry; (4) acquiring tropical colonies where African slave labor could be procured and settled to mine gold or silver or to produce tropical plantation products such as sugar, tobacco, cotton; and (5) making the fullest possible use of the domestic labor supply to be kept fully employed at reasonable wages providing incentives for reproduction and skillful labor. These objectives were not carried out everywhere as vigorously as in the classical mercantilist economies, England, France, and Holland. These objectives boiled down in Marx's judgment to calling for an "accelerated development of capital" to carry out the transformation of "feudal agricultural societies into industrial ones" and to achieve victory in the "corresponding industrial struggle of nations on the world market" utilizing for this purpose aggressive national policies and "coercive" state measures.[112]

Industrial development in mercantilist thought was dependent upon expansion of the national money supply to drive the trade and provide it with growing markets. This would require a net importation of gold and silver acquired from abroad by trade or by conquest of territories where surface supplies of precious metals abound.[113] Industrial development called for investment of capital funds convertible on demand to good coined money to hire labor and shipping, buy materials, set up facilities, and carry out expanded production and trading ventures. This expansion of production would displace markets for existing industrial activities unless the supply of money and stream of spending was augmented proportionately. Later mercantilist economists like Petty and Locke discovered the characteristics of income, expenditure habits, and credit arrangements that governed the proportion normally maintained between a country's national income and its money supply.[114] If all prices and wages and related charges and taxes flexed freely, as in many agricultural markets at local fairs or exchanges, then the money supply would not play a role in constraining industrial development. Wages are characteristically "sticky" as all employers of labor know and many rents and taxes and local charges for shipping, innkeeping, hauling, medical care, legal services, and the like are commonly kept unchanged for extended periods. The markups for baking bread and brewing ale from malt were fixed sums that were for price-control purposes in the mercantilist period simply added to the more variable allowances for costs of materials. It is this pervasive tendency toward sticky tradition-set wages, charges, rents, fees, and taxes that makes (1) the introduction of an increased stream of money entering a country stimulating to its economic life, and (2) the withdrawal of money from the national economy a cause of what mercantilist writers called the "decay" of trade. Though the characteristics of pricing causing decay of trade were only discovered as a distinct phenomenon by J. M. Keynes in the 1930s, the fact of decay was a commonplace in mercantilist thought, embodied a constant fear, and was well represented in Hume's effort in the mid–eighteenth century to work out a reconciliation between mercantilist and classical economics.[115] It was this fear of decay of trade and enterprise and the desire to maximize employment opportunities that Keynes in 1936 rediscovered as motivating the mercantilist quest for increased supplies of money.[116]

Inflation Problem

There was of course a solid differential class interest in this mercantilist quest for monetary expansion. This reflected directly the immediate and naive interests of merchants in continually seeking wider and more abundant markets. The first fruits of increased levels of business activity always redound to the benefit of businessmen active in the markets of the economy. Mercantilist theory erred, however, in not facing up to the process of inflation, growing markets, and purchasing power. Enlarging volumes of production and trade cannot proceed without at some point raising prices when supplies of products are unresponsive or when producers are quick to take advantage of favorable market conjunctures. This rise in price will be followed in time by boosts in prices negotiated between parties or set by sellers. Wage levels too must eventually reflect the higher price level of subsistence goods and the more active demand for wage labor. Employers must have some regard for the ability of their employees to maintain themselves and their families in health and raise wages somewhat. The process of inflation first became active in Spain within a few decades of the inflow of American silver. Soon Spanish-made goods became relatively expensive compared to goods available in neighboring European countries.[117] New World silver accordingly filtered out of Spain to European confreres. This outflow of Spanish silver was quickened by Spanish debasement of coinage and by the prolonged wars to maintain imperial control over Spanish possessions in the Low Countries, in Italy, and along the French frontier.

The connection of this widespread European inflation with Spanish silver and gold drawn from the Americas was in time recognized.[118] But this did not cause mercantilist theorists and policy spokesmen to modify the high priority assigned to increased money supply as a binding first principle of economic policy.[119] This rigidity of viewpoint is possibly explained by the differential class interest in inflation similar to that of business expansion. When the increased waves of expenditure work their effects in commodity markets especially for agricultural goods where higher prices tend to result from increased expenditures, it is the mercantile class who are least tied down by fixed price commitments and who are quickest to search out avenues of gain by commercial negotiation. Their market information is usually more complete than local producers, wage earners, or landowners. And to the extent that they hire labor for their workshops, warehouses, and ships, wages stipulated are geared to market conditions prevailing at the time of hiring, which means they are becoming devalued by inflation. Once workmen are employed, they have no easy way to determine current market value for their labor. They are usually grateful for the employment and only under very aggravated conditions will they venture to jeopardize a satisfactory job by expressing dissatisfaction with its terms.[120] Hence mercantile profits from depreciated wages and interest — and appreciating inventories — will have first ranking among beneficiaries of inflation. Second to them will of course be capitalist producers in farms, shops, and mines who benefit with their mercantile brethren from depreciated wages and interest or rent payments fixed often for set sums of money. The principal losers from inflation conversely will be annuitants and pensioners, landlords whose lands were leased for long terms at set money rents, and wage earners, the least skillful of all classes in market dealings and the most loathe to disturb accepted arrangements. State fiscs will be disadvantaged if the proportion of their revenues set at fixed rates — that is, borough rents, specific import duties, or land assessments — is greater than the proportion of their outlays that are set at fixed rates for past annuities and pensions, interest on past indebtedness, and the like. The mercantile and entrepreneurial interest in monetary expansion was by no means naive or illusory. That interest grew out of business experience and was fully expressed, though in rationalized form, in mercantilist theory.

The constant desire for more money was achieved in its earliest setting by the simple verbot on exportation of gold or silver especially of domestic coinage. But these metals easily slipped through all export controls. Smuggling precious metals proved irrepressible. The most fearful punishment did not deter widespread smuggling of gold and silver out of Spain.[121] There was also need in certain branches of trade to permit use of gold or silver to procure essential supplies (as in English trade with the Baltic and East Indies). Thus rather than prohibit export of gold or silver, customs officers could limit or prohibit import of foreign goods while the export of domestically made goods could be promoted by payment of bounties (as on English grain and herring). Importation of goods produced at home or for which the need could be satisfied by a domestic substitute could be impeded by taxes levied on imports alone. If these taxes were high enough, importation could be limited to any extent desired. To discourage their use by competitors, the export of equipment or machines or materials — giving national industry an advantage in foreign markets — could be prohibited. Special subsidies for importation of skilled foreign workmen or producers would assist in establishing at home an industry carried on abroad. Acquisition of colonial territories suitable for growing products or mining and exclusion of foreign shipping from access to domestic ports – or at least exclusion from the carrying trade on coastal traffic or between different parts of the national territory – all would help. The development of policies to increase the favorable balance of trade led to an increased concern for domestic industry as such and especially industry producing merchantable exports or industry displacing imports. This shift of emphasis in Marx's judgement transformed the original monetary system into a derived form of commercial mercantilism.[122]

The objective of a growing money supply could to a degree be satisfied by measures increasing monetization of that portion of a country's bullion stock serving decorative or household tableware purposes and even more by measures promoting banking that collected reserve money hoards into large depositories where funds could be remuneratively invested. These measures would speed up the effective velocity of circulation of money and enable credit instruments of high quality to supplant coined money or bullion.

Concern for economic development passed beyond measures directly intended to improve the balance of trade. For if that balance were properly attended to, the need would remain to assure conditions for profitable employment of labor and to regulate wage rates to prevent the spread of inflation in the labor market. Since wage labor first appears on a major scale in the mercantilist period, the problem of unemployment arises along with it and the need for devising forms of welfare assistance that satisfy the Christian imperative of giving alms to the poor without encouraging idleness. Hence the innumerable projects in the mercantilist period for workhouses or workshops where the able-bodied poor could be housed and employed in some form of productive labor while being supported with subsistence.[123]

State Leadership in Economic Growth

The mercantilist objective of accelerated economic development calls for clearing away obstructions to full use of the nation's resources. Thus new industries cannot be fostered if markets for their products or materials will be obstructed by provincial or regional barriers and taxes. So also the administration of justice and commerce will be hampered by diversity in weights and measures. A renovated economy will call for a *national* economy with full leeway for specialization and division of labor. This task of nation building was more easily taken on in England where groundwork for it was laid since the Conquest in the eleventh century but it made progress in France and in Holland where national unity was an exigent need for national defense and survival. National unification in significant dimensions lagged in Spain and it was totally lacking in Italy and in Germany (Heckscher 1955, Chaps. 1–3).

A supporting objective of the mercantilist state is participation in European overseas expansion permitting open access to African slaves, to an endowment of semitropical or tropical land in the New World for growing tropical products, and to opportunities for colonial settlement in the temperate zones of the Americas. Finally, naval bases and ports suited for hosting protective naval fleets and control of crucial avenues of trade with China and India will be needed.

Mercantilist policy aimed at building strong national states with carefully regulated trade relationships to foster balance of payment surpluses and access to key raw materials and products. This aim promoted the relative isolation of the stronger European national economies from each other. Isolation was intensified by the frequent wars devastating the mainland and by the widespread use of discriminatory trade arrangements practically destroying Anglo-French commerce and distorting all natural trade alignments.[124] The price level for many basic products including bread grains was not even unified within countries like France and Germany where provincial barriers to free traffic in grain persisted through to the eighteenth century. Between countries, prices for basic staples would vary wildly. In bread grains it was not until the mid–eighteenth century that the differentials for various national average wheat prices began to move together.[125] Hence in no sense can it be claimed that an all-embracing European world economy came into existence in the mercantile period. At best in only a few restricted commodity areas involving chiefly tropical or Asiatic products did a true world economy come into existence.

The regulatory and fiscal complex of the mercantilist economy employed the power of the state, the concentrated and organized force of society, "to hasten hothouse fashion" the development of the capitalist mode of production (Marx 1863–1878/1967, 1:751). The coercive measures employed included the colonies, subsidized royal factories, African slavery in the New World, the national debt and systematic indirect taxation, workhouses for the poor, protectionism, privileged corporations, and banks. Marx considered all of these as different driving forces of what he termed "primitive accumulation," which he said "distribute themselves now more or less in chronological order over

Spain, Portugal, Holland, France, England" and at the end of the seventeenth century in England arrive at a "systematical combination." It is to be doubted that the profits of these coercive measures contributed directly to the accumulation of *industrial* capital.[126] Direct beneficiaries of colonial development—the monopolizing corporations, the plantation aristocracy, the Conquistadores—were hardly among the progenitors of capitalist industry. But the whole complex of coercive measures of the mercantilist economy certainly widened the inequality of income distribution, fostered the exchange of products among the continents, and increased the scope for capitalist enterprise, which was moreover given direct stimulation by tariff protection and bounties. In that sense "primitive accumulation" is an essential ingredient in the makeup of the mercantilist economic system.

To sum up: we can define the mercantilist economic system as the principal transition system between the dissolving or decaying medieval economy, still resting upon the feudal landownership in agriculture and the free commercial-craft towns, and the capitalist economies of the nineteenth century.[127] This transition system rests upon shaping the feudal monarchy into a strong national state responsive to an alliance of a landed aristocracy that has outgrown its feudal (manorial) mode of production and is in the process of becoming a landed gentry and a bourgeoisie that is outgrowing its mercantile character and is rapidly developing an industrial base dependent upon artisan skills. In the mercantile system the power of the state is employed (1) to shape a national economy with freer use of resources within the nation, (2) to accelerate the development of capitalist industry in new fields of production especially in metallurgy and coal mining, (3) to give local merchants and producers a monopoly of the home market, (4) to assure wider markets for locally produced goods and services by expanding the national money supply and by creating more efficient forms of utilizing and transferring money especially hoarded treasure, and (5) to conquer distant peoples and territories thus creating new markets and new sources of essential supplies and resources.

It is immaterial what label be placed on this economic system, whether its most dynamic and rapidly growing capitalist mode be regarded as its central feature and hence the basis for its labeling or whether a new and more neutral label be pasted on it. In this work it is called "mercantilist" out of respect for Adam Smith who knew well the spirit and the ideas that went with it, out of respect also for the great merchants who were a driving force behind the system, and finally out of respect for Marx who made it plain that "capitalist accumulation" and [mercantilist] "primitive accumulation" involved quite different processes.

The Capitalist Economic System: United Kingdom, Mid-Nineteenth Century

Introduction

Our study of the mercantilist economy is a generalized portrait with features drawn from the leading mercantilist countries of Western Europe. Our study of the capitalist economy will focus attention not on the composite of countries, which in the nineteenth century took on the capitalist path of development, but a single country, Great Britain, that clearly led the way in capitalist development. Already in midcentury the capitalist economy shows up in the United Kingdom, the technical title for Great Britain and its Irish dependency, in near pristine form.

The mid–century decade of the nineteenth century is selected without any presupposition that the capitalist economy did not exist before that date or that it disappeared soon after. Going back to the earliest decades of the century one finds a structure of government quite unrepresentative of and unresponsive to capitalist interests. Mercantilist policies and practices were still in effect. Only the cotton branch of the textile industry had been mechanized. The classical form of movement of capitalist industry and commerce, the business cycle with its various interwoven periodicities, was only beginning to take shape amid the disorder of the Napoleonic wars. The railway so badly needed for speedy movement of industrial goods and materials was a dream of the future. The steam engine was still too crude and expensive to be harnessed for use on ocean-going vessels still dependent upon wind propulsion.

If we turn to the end of the century we find that the capitalist enterprise was more and more superseded by the quasi-public corporation, which has made great headway in mining and manufacturing. The laissez-faire principles of the capitalist economy had begun to give way to new principles. A new structure of regulation and taxation was being shaped. Hence I have chosen to center our portrait of the British capitalist economy in the mid–nineteenth century, drawing however on developments or illustrations that anticipate or overrun this decade before and after. This period corresponds to what political and cultural historians call the "high noon of Victorianism," which "came piecemeal into existence in the first half of the century, prevailed for a period, and then began to disappear before the century ended" (Clark 1962, 31).

Bounds of British Economy

But what were the bounds of the British economy? Its real homeland has always been England proper. By the thirteenth century the Welsh highlands were brought under a subjection not fully secured until much later. The Scotch were for centuries recalcitrant and independent. They were finally drawn into union with England by sharing in a common dynasty, by the development of related forms of bourgeois property, and by a common submergence in the Protestant Reformation.

The case for including Ireland in the nineteenth century British capitalist economy is more complicated. The subjection of Ireland began with Viking enclaves of settlement following destructive Viking raids in early centuries. These enclaves chiefly at port locations to facilitate trade and fishing were later joined to more extended and massive conquest by Anglo-Norman invaders in the twelfth century. With their greatly superior military technology and armed with a papal bull giving the Norman king of England sovereign authority over Ireland, these invaders had little trouble taking over Viking strongholds, breaking resistance of Irish chieftains and establishing a unified Anglo-Norman state that controlled up to half of the island. Conquest had to be periodically renewed to put down Irish revolts. Economic subjection of the land was achieved both by building merchant and craft towns and by confiscating rebel lands cleared of Irish natives and granted in large estates to English or Scotch plantation operators. These confiscations reached their high point under Elizabeth, Cromwell, and William and Mary, the great rulers of mercantilist England. By 1695 some 80 percent of arable Irish land had been enclosed in estates while some 14 percent was retained by "well-affectioned" and loyal Irish, many of early Anglo-Norman vintage (Costigan 1969, 55, 67, 90).

Insurrections were repressed by measures increasing in ferocity, reaching their climax with the Disability Acts following the rising associated with the attempted restoration of King James II in the 1690s. These penal acts – only gradually withdrawn during the eighteenth century and not completely repealed until 1829 – prescribed banishment for all Catholic bishops and most priests, barred Irish Catholics from owning or making or carrying arms, from jury service or military commissions, from intermarriage with Protestants, from the professions of law and medicine, from voting, from buying or making a long-term lease of Protestant-owned land, from attending or keeping schools, and even from owning a good horse.[1] The blighting effect of the penal acts was not easily undone by their belated repeal.[2] In the aftermath of Cromwellian invasion the psychological effects were never undone of the wholesale dispossession of most Irish Catholics, their eviction to the province of Connought in 1652 declared by statute the proper home in Ireland of Irish Catholics except those able to show they were loyal and well affectioned to Great Britain. English estate managers evaded many eviction notices and arranged to let Irish laborers stay and help out. Eventually they were allowed to put up cabins and to use a few acres for a potato patch and pasture or garden in exchange for a year's labor with little or no cash pay. The experience was humbling (Esson 1971, Chap. 7). A capable English agronomist, Arthur Young (1776–1779/1892, 2:54), who visited and traveled widely over the country in 1776–1779, found Irish labor readily disciplined by use of a "cane horsewhip." At about the same time Edmund Burke, who knew well the Irish lot having been born and raised among them, compared their state to "beasts of burden" whose resistance had been broken.[3] That resistance was not fully broken for Irish hopes were raised again by the French Revolution. The insurrection of 1798 was easily suppressed again with massive penal arrests of thousands and condemnation to virtual slave labor in overseas British plantations or colonies. English rulers became convinced that they could not count on their Anglo-Irish settlers in Ireland, often touched by Irish discontent, for effective local government. Hence the passage in 1801 of the Act of Union that abolished a separate Irish parliament and instead invested the Irish with the general rights of British subjects including the right for qualified electors to elect members of Parliament.

Though poor, Ireland was an important part of the British capitalist economy. The ranks of the British proletariat were enriched by Irish emigration that could, with high birth rates, provide large supplies of wage labor. Seasonal movements of Irish emigrants helped to collect the harvest and carry out the heavy construction labor of building canals, digging for sewer lines, building railroads.[4] Most major British industrial centers had substantial Irish slum quarters whose residents held jobs with lower pay and status, thereby tending to elevate English and Scotch workmen to somewhat higher skill levels. Irish wool in the eighteenth century could only be marketed in England. (Smith 1776/ 1937, 231). Irish cottage industry was a source of cheap linens. Dairy products and live cattle were important provisions for the British food basket. Irish recruits helped man the British armed forces and Irish cottagers were usually shipped in to break British strikes. The land-owning aristocracy of England and Ireland was intermingled by marriage and inheritance. A substantial fraction (up to a quarter) of the Irish net rent roll was for the benefit of absentee proprietors mostly resident in England.[5]

Linen handicraft, spinning and weaving, and seasonal migration were important cash income supplements to rural Ireland, and to some degree stimulated Irish nuptiality and Irish population growth.[6] Irish taxpayers contributed to British customs excise and income tax collections. Hence though it is common in analytic literature on the British capitalist economy of the nineteenth century to deal with this economy as if it covered only Great Britain proper and sometimes with the addition of Northern Ireland (torn away from Ireland when it was released in 1922 from British rule) that procedure seems improper to me. Instead we deal with the whole of the United Kingdom, which went through the capitalist experience.[7] But does the United Kingdom alone encompass the British capitalist economy? British settlement and economic life in the nineteenth century was extended far beyond the British Isles. British settlement in the Caribbean was extensive, produced a key raw material—sugar—for British commerce and industry, and yielded a major interest group in the British body politic.[8] The African coastal settlements and the greatest prize of all, the empire in India, continuously extended and consolidated throughout the nineteenth century, played an important role in the British capitalist economy. The newer colonial settlements in North America and Australasia were in the fullest sense offshoots of British society and closely linked to the economy and encompassed within its body politic at least during the period under present review.

Though this wider British capitalist economy has an undeniable reality, it has been approximated in this work by a full inclusion in the economy of all of Ireland. The movement both of labor and capital and the intermingling of property was on a far greater scale and was more continuous and intimate within the British Isles in the mid–nineteenth century than in the outlying imperial domain. British taxes in the empire were not assessed and pooled in a common treasury as they were in the British Isles. Nor is it as convenient to analyze the total imperial system with all its farflung dependencies as it is the Isles proper where most of the British subjects resided and worked and where statistical information is available at regular intervals. Hence in the sections following, an analysis of the British home economy in the Isles is made as if it were a self-contained body. Later a special analysis is made of West Indies sugar and slavery. When the international aspects of the capitalist economy are dealt with, the extended penumbra of the home economy or metropole (as it is now termed) will be reckoned with.

Modal Complex

In the British capitalist economy, the capitalist mode of production was by all measures predominant in agriculture, industry, and commerce. The largest field of activity of that mode was agricultural and landed property predominantly held by an elite class of several thousand landlords holding about two-thirds of rural and farm real estate plus the unimproved value of most urban land. This property was held free of any legacy duty and much of it was tied up in estate settlements that precluded partition among heirs. A much larger number of smaller landlords collectively held some 22.6 percent of the farmland. Altogether large and small landlords held in 1832 records, according to sampled land tax returns, some 86.6 percent of taxable agricultural land.[9] The income of landlords large and small was by the midcentury still extremely high, being estimated for 1860–1869 (after rental income had begun to fall because of the repeal of grain duties) at 13.7 percent of total national income. At the beginning of the century about two-thirds of this was rental income from farmlands; another 27 percent from improved urban real estate and housing; and some 5 percent still from tithes, manors and fines.[10] This landed property is placed in the capitalist sector despite its remaining feudal perquisites and striking political privileges giving landowners a powerful hold on state power and government administration. The land was used in capitalist production. Landowners managed their estates with an eye to profitability and invested substantial amounts of capital in improvements. The some 325,000 capitalist farmers who actually conducted agricultural operations on leased farms hired a large segment of the British labor force, over 1.5 million wage laborers. Farmer profits and laborer wages had to be competitive with like returns in other fields of industry and landowner rentals emerged out of a market process.[11] Though relations among the capitalist farmers, field laborers, and great landlords were often tense, merciless repression had suppressed field hand rebellions and riotous outbreaks.[12] Landlords and tenants

worked out lease arrangements that permitted a progressive development of agricultural improvement and a tolerable compensation to tenants for their unexhausted investment in improvements.[13]

With all its importance and political predominance, landed capital
in Great Britain was increasingly overshadowed by industrial and commercial capital that since the Reform Act of 1832 had become a major
force in British politics and the dynamic center of economic growth.
The modern factory, powered chiefly by the steam engine, was already
well established around the turn of the century in the successive operations of cotton textiles: carding, spinning, weaving, bleaching, and cyl-
inder printing (Landes 1969, 80–87). The gradual application of this
technology to other fibers, the refinement of the steam engine and its
application to diverse industrial operations and finally to road carriage,
the concurrent transformation in metal working and mining, the development of a new chemical industry and of powerful engineering firms
capable of building modern machinery, the development of the technology of using coke with iron ore in the blast furnace making possible a
major spurt in iron production, the first application of the newly found
force of electricity harnessed before midcentury into the electric telegraph – all this has been recited many times and need not be elaborated
here. Suffice it to say that sometime in the middle three decades of the
nineteenth century a preponderance of Great Britain's industrial output
came from a mechanized capitalist sector fully integrated with the
world market. Textile factories regulated by the Factory Acts employed in 1850 some 596,000 workers (Mitchell 1962, Tables 9, 17, 22,
28). The 1861 Census counted 1.6 million operatives employed in textile factories, mines, and metallurgy. (Marx 1863–1878/1968, 1:446).
The mechanized printing industry, chemical plants, grain and feed
mills, hardware factories, engineering works, paper mills, glassworks
add many hundred thousands to the mechanized labor force.

Though lacking mechanization, a number of branches of industry
by the midcentury were organized in formal business enterprises with
entrepreneurial control of the labor force employed. The great bulk of
the building industry employing some 600,000 in 1851 had been passing since early in the nineteenth century under the control of master
contractors or builders who controlled heavy construction for roads,
public works, industrial and commercial facilities, and most home construction.[14] Wholesale trade, a well-developed field in England that
served as the center of the world market, was nearly all organized in
capitalist enterprises in which an estimated 400,000 persons were active. Some 244,000 seamen were employed in merchant shipping with
net annual shipping earnings estimated at £13 million.[15] Moreover, a
significant white-collar labor force must have been employed in the

offices and counters of the hundreds of banking, insurance, and other financial institutions, functioning in part under the capitalist and in part under the corporate banner.

I turn from the capitalist mode of production to the corporate sector, which was nurtured in the institutions of the stock market, security-jobbing and public investment. This sector included the great trading and banking corporations of the seventeenth and eighteenth centuries. Industrial use of the quasi-public corporation with public issuance of securities commenced on a large scale with the development of public utilities in the late eighteenth and nineteenth centuries. They were commonly organized as public corporations, chartered by special acts of Parliament and given the privilege, frequently under broad restrictions, for service of a given territory. The first utilities to get under way extensively were canals calling for heavy investment of capital and only feasible with the power of eminent domain and the obligation of common carrier service. Canal building was pushed in the last half of the eighteenth century. By the 1790s a canal boom was on and in 1792 as many canals were projected as were built in previous years. Shares were oversubscribed in a massive public subscription. By 1824, at which time interest in canal construction subsided, some sixty-three canal companies had raised and invested capital of £12.2 million. Additional investment to 1834 raised the number of companies to nearly seventy, bringing into operation some 3700 miles of canals which with navigable rivers laid the industrial basis for cheap transport of heavy goods and the basis for the first stage of the Industrial Revolution. Labor force was chiefly used not in operating shipping — handled by independent carriers — but in constructing and maintaining waterways.[16]

The next wave of utility construction set in with massive building of loading docks to facilitate loading and unloading of ships at standing docks, waterworks which were established for the public distribution of water in densely settled areas, gaslight companies for the manufacture and distribution of gas made from coal for illuminating and cooking purposes. By 1824 some 50 gaslight, docking, and waterwork corporations were functioning with a capital invested of £10.8 million (Gayer et al. 1953, 1:414, 421). This branch of investment took on massive proportions in the next two decades so that by 1844 some 224 gas and water corporations were active. The corporations were chartered to function in a given territory with authority to lay distributing pipelines and tear up or utilize public thoroughfares or waterfront areas.

The next wave of utility construction using the corporation device concentrated on railroads. Though by 1750 cast-iron rails were widely employed around collieries and though a limited development of horse-drawn trams on tracks was experienced in the early 1800s, the employment of steam power in locomotives operating on iron tracks was not feasible until 1825 when rail development was launched, reaching a minor peak in 1836 with the authorization of £22 million in rail lines. Rail investment reached its real climax in 1846 with the authorization of £133 million. By 1844 some 108 railway corporations were functioning with 2390 miles of railway authorized by Acts of Parliament. In 1845–1846 some 7238 additional miles were authorized with a capital investment of £192 million of which 21 percent was later abandoned. At the railway construction peak in 1847 more than a quarter-million men were employed in constructing railways while only 47,218 persons were employed in operating them. Between 1843 and 1852 mileage opened for service more than doubled and at the end of 1848 it was reported that more than £200 million had been invested in railways.[17] Investment of capital on this scale was only possible by collecting capital en masse from small and large investors by means of the public joint-stock corporation. And this collection was only feasible because the interest of the investing public had been drawn to the spectacle of high railway earnings and speculative appeal of appreciating equities. Hence the railway boom also exhibited (1) the power of organized corporate investment to block effective regulation of a vital public service, (2) the first frenzied campaign of corporate merger to build massive trunk lines building up monopoly power on a considerable scale, (3) the first industrial speculative security bull market that induced middle-class folk "who hitherto had never known the Stock Exchange" to "hurry to place their small accumulation in securities."[18] Based on the real expansion of railway operations and the speculation that was bound up with it, there gradually arose during this period "a superstructure of fraud reminiscent of the time of Law and of the South Sea Company."[19] Yet with all this Marx found it possible to develop a critical analysis of the capitalist mode of production in which only casual and incidental notice was taken of the railway system and the privileged public corporation that was its indispensable instrument.[20]

Banking and insurance was the other major field for corporative development where large amounts of capital were needed to provide nationwide operations and handling of funds with adequate diversification. Already in 1824, beside the Bank of England and South Sea Company, some 25 insurance corporations and 28 investment companies had been established. The relaxation of restrictions on corporation banking after 1826 opened up a wave of corporate banking investment resulting in the establishment of some 20 banking corporations by

1833 with a nominal capital of £23.8 million. By 1844, 172 insurance corporations were functioning. Total investment in major financial institutions that provided banking and insurance services not only for Great Britain but for the entire mercantile world ran to over £35 million (Gayer et al. 1953, 1:412, 439, 450).

The field of industry and mining proper was not conspicuously favored by corporate development in this early stage. Large numbers of mining, trading, building, steam, and provision companies were projected as corporate ventures in the business boom of 1824–1825 with a total capitalization of £79.4 million. And in the decades immediately following, corporate ventures were launched in newspapers, navigation, iron and ore-working, brick-making, breweries (Gayer et al. 1953, 1:412). Many of the post-1824 mining ventures were for development in South America and elsewhere in the colonies.[21] Many of the industrial corporations registered then and around midcentury and later were entrepreneurial ventures with large numbers of sleeping partners for whom the corporate form was a convenient vehicle for business operations.[22] In part this limited development of the true industrial or commercial corporation as a business form was due to inability until 1855–1856 to obtain the privilege of limited liability for corporate stockholders, withheld except for specially chartered public undertakings such as banks, insurance companies, and railways. Experience with limited liability soon exhibited the hazard of this form of investment since a significant fraction of corporate ventures were abortive or ended up insolvent within a few years.[23] Nevertheless, successful industrial corporations would tend to gain the confidence of the investing public and a small share of industrial and commercial enterprise of the midcentury must be credited to the account of genuine quasi-public corporations.

Next to be considered is the large class of simple commodity producers working either alone or with family members and the assistance of hired labor in farms, shops, and offices. It should be recalled that occupying smallholders in a representative farming area in 1832 worked 13.4 percent of the land according to surviving records of land tax assessments.

Retail trade is another field of enterprise dominated by the small shopkeeper using mostly family labor or the peddler or street seller carrying the goods on his back or more fortunately having a cart and pony or barrow for the purpose. Early in the century the itinerant peddler or packman making the rounds on the highways or towns and villages was still a competitor to the stationary dealer with his shop and front windows.[24] In Clapham's judgment the shop was supplanting the peddler though in London at midcentury the peddler seemed to be holding his own.[25] Some 45,000 costermongers and other street sellers were estimated to work the streets of London: costermongers alone used 1,000 carts, 5,000 barrows, 1,500 donkeys, and 200 ponies; from one-third to one-half of the potted or cut flowers in London; one-half of the dry shellfish; from one-quarter to one-half of most categories of fresh fruit and vegetables; and from one-third of all domestic fowls and one-fifth of the geese were hawked on the streets.[26] If the census undercount of London street sellers was characteristic of the national census count, then the recorded (1841) enumeration of hucksters, peddlers, and hawkers was 380,000 rather than the enumerated 17,270.

It is known that in 1850 the number of taverns licensed for sale or consumption of intoxicating beverages was enormous: 123,396 (Clark 1962, 122). The number of small shopkeepers of all kinds including street sellers was collated from census counts by Charles Booth (1886 App. A) at 730,000 in 1851. That statistic does not allow for certain food handlers and taverns or for hired labor or unpaid family workers, and it includes some kinds of wholesale dealers. If we break down the British totals of manpower employed in trade and commerce by the more precise statistics available in the American census for 1869, the labor force engaged in retail trade including employees and family helpers may be estimated at around 800,000 persons.[27]

Then there is the broad field of traditional handicraft exercised by masters of a trade or skill who own a place of business or tools and equipment who commonly buy materials needed or work on materials provided and who deal directly with customers who use their services. Some of these crafts can be identified from the census enumeration as for example bakers, of which 63,000 were enumerated in Britain in 1851; shoemakers, 274,000; wheelwrights, 30,000; millers, 37,000; and tailors, 153,000 (Clapham 1926–1938, 2:24, 35). Other crafts have however largely functioned as outwork departments of merchants or dealers who procure materials, provide markets, and arrange terms of dealing—nailers, lace makers, weavers. Other craftsmen such as most shipwrights, fishermen, printers, glove makers are commonly hired by employers who provide the equipment and facilities. Since many occupations are mixed and can be practiced by craftsmen working in their own or their customer's premises and with their own equipment on customer work (such as many milliners, dressmakers, and building craftsmen) or alternatively can be employed by commercial go-betweens or entrepreneurs, the total numbers in the field working as simple commodity producers cannot be accurately established.

Another field of genuine handicraft or of the simple commodity producer is found in the free professions drawing income from independent professional practice. The most important practicing professions in midcentury Britain were in medicine, law, dentistry, architecture, surveying, veterinary science. The field includes teachers and ministers though few of these practiced independently. The census registration of "professional" callings is itself subject to question on two counts. First, some professional callings such as surveyor, civil engineer, and architect were included in the building trades.[28] Then the major professional fields were not well demarcated. The professions were in the process of becoming organized (with public registration achieved for practicing physicians only in 1858 and for dentists in 1878). Practice of a profession was not generally limited so that each profession had a wide following of unqualified or semiqualified practitioners sometimes forbidden to attach certain labels to themselves. The apportionment of professional service between free practice and employed service is difficult to determine from existing records. The latter-day American pattern of the twentieth century if applied to midcentury England results in an estimate of free practicing professionals of 127,000.[29] That is certainly excessive for the early nineteenth century but it is likely that somewhat over 100,000 professionals in the United Kingdom were at work in the midcentury. Some 86,900 lawyers and doctors were enumerated under that or comparable titles in the 1851 Census and most of these were in free practice. Probably one-fifth of that number, at least, had a professional calling in the theater, in literature, in education, as opticians, engineers, and surveyors.

One other mode, landlord-tenant farming that had evolved its own pattern in subjugated and victimized Ireland, the first English colony, employed significant quantities of the labor force. In Ireland up to 1846, the Famine Year, some three-quarters of a million tenant families were active in farming and related fields of cottage industry and outside wage labor.[30] As indicated previously, nearly all urban and rural land was held in sizable estates, from a quarter to a third absentee owned. One or more intermediaries usually appeared between the ultimate landowner and the working tenant or cottager supporting himself with a few acres of potato land and the proceeds of cottage industry or outside work. The smaller tenants and cottage laborers with the lowest income and meager assets were the first to leave or be cleared out in the years following the great Famine, partly by emigration to England or overseas and partly by premature death.[31] As cottage laborers with small plots were weeded out, peasant proprietorship became more feasible and under the pressure of widespread agrarian terrorism and field resistance and criticism at home of the frightful results of absentee landlordism, a succession of parliamentary enactments in the latter quarter of the nineteenth century made ejectment of tenants more difficult, supported tenant rights to long-term tenure with rights of sale, restricted landlord rentals, and finally supported purchase programs by which English landlordism in Ireland was rooted out. However, for most of the phase of the matured capitalist economy in the nineteenth century an important though a steadily dwindling mode of landlord-tenant farming prevailed in the United Kingdom.

The final of our standard modes of production is that of public service. The old principles of local government gradually evolved during the medieval and mercantilist period involved avocational organization as the basis of government with an obligation for gratuitous service by local notables or property owners. Persons were selected for service by volunteering or by co-optation according to local custom and the term was often for life. A minimum of paid officers of government functioned at the level of parish and rural county while even the larger towns had comparatively few paid officers. Even road repair and street cleaning were obligations of the abutting householders.[32] The Census returns for 1851 enumerated 63,500 paid civil servants for local and central government (Booth 1886, App. A). Budget estimates submitted to Parliament before the Crimean War indicate the British armed forces numbered 170,000 (Marx-Engels 1841–1870/1974–1986, 13:11, 14:416). The old-fashioned parish or borough constable was a negligible force. But in the nineteenth century a formidable centralized paid uniformed police service was gradually built up enumerated in the 1851 Census as 33,400. This got its start in Ireland during the Napoleonic Wars when scares of invasion and domestic insurrection were frequent. Beside the standing army a special Irish constabulary force from 10,000 to 20,000 was maintained under central control.[33] Coming after the Irish constabulary but in time for the Chartist disorders, a metropolitan police force was established in London with a strength by 1850 of some 5,000 men.[34] The outlying chartered cities and counties were then given blanket authority and some fiscal assistance to establish modern police forces and by 1850 most of the country was under constabulary control though not on the scale of either London or Ireland.[35] A small paid teaching staff employed by local authorities by this time was beginning to become established though primary school education was in England and Wales reserved primarily for church and local voluntary societies and endowments or clubs.[36] Altogether, a total public employment of 280,000 nonmilitary persons is indicated.

Hybrid Modes

Our roster of modes in Great Britain will be completed with two hybrid modes both of unusual importance. The first relates to that complex of cottage and shop industry, still resting on a foundation of craft skills and handiwork, but to varying degrees taken over and exploited commercially by merchants, manufacturers, or large dealers who play an entrepreneurial role, usually soliciting orders and marketing the final product, sometimes designing patterns and styles and commonly procuring materials. This field is a hybrid between the capitalist and commodity producer modes. Lace making was an example of such an industry that employed in 1861 over 100,000 persons of whom only 10,000 were employed in factories regulated by the Factory Acts.[37] In the home or shop branch of this industry, young girls or women either mend lace or put the finishing touches on factory-made lace. The colossal scale of commercialized handiwork is further illustrated by the entire wearing apparel industry, which in 1861 employed over a million persons comprising straw-hat makers, ladies-hat makers, shirtmakers, dressmakers, corset makers, glove makers, and makers of other apparel such as neckties, collars, outerwear. The raw material was supplied chiefly by the mechanized textile factories. The work of cutting, seaming, and sewing items of wearing apparel or head wear was done by nimble fingers working the needle and scissors. On this craft and homework foundation, intermediaries sprang up to provide the work materials and arrange for product sale. Conditions of labor were wretched and compensation was unusually low. Into this industry in the mid–nineteenth century was introduced the decisive means of its mechanization, the sewing machine, invented and commercially developed in 1846. This machine was soon adapted to working on a wide variety of materials from leather to heavy canvas and was soon geared to steam power to accelerate the flow of the work. In the 1850s and 1860s mechanized factories were beginning to replace the small shops and cottage industry that had previously dominated the field.[38] This handicraft, commercialized, small-shop mode of production was found in Great Britain in the middle of the nineteenth century not only in wearing apparel and lace and straw products but in many branches of metal fabrication. Even in the 1870s the nail-making industry centered around warehouses from which rods and orders were distributed to nailers who had no forges of their own. Of the Birmingham metal trades, a contemporary writer noted that in most shops only five or six workers would be employed. In gun making, jewelry, the brass foundry, saddlery and harness trades the 1860s still witnessed "a remarkable coexistence of highly subdivided processes of production with the small production unit of the shop-owner putting out work to domestic craftmen."[39] In Irish cottages through the middle decades of the nineteenth century hand spinning and weaving of woolens and linens remained the predominant source of income outside of agriculture.[40] It is this prevalence of outwork and cottage industry in the United Kingdom which has led so outstanding an authority as J. H. Clapham to declare that outwork in the 1830s was still the predominant form of capitalist industry since what it was losing on the one side to the great factories and mills it was gaining at the other side by crowding out genuine handicraft and household production (Clapham 1926–1938, 1:33, 99, 175).

The other hybrid mode of production playing a large role in the British economy of the nineteenth century was household domestic service that often places the independent craft worker, the indoor household servant, under almost feudal subjection. Handicraft is involved since the work was unmechanized and skills were acquired by learning and habituation to a strict code of deportment. Performance of household duties and much sheer drudgery was blended with practiced training in subservience and observance of good form. Compensation and conditions of work had to be sufficiently attractive to reward the special discipline of will and mind called for by sustained personal abnegation in a vocation that typically precluded marriage and an independent home life with children. The work was however attractive to many because of its clean surroundings and a sense of mutual dependence that precluded sudden layoffs. In societies such as the British with a background of feudal tradition and a deep-flowing source of rural overpopulation with stationary or slowly growing employment in agriculture proper, paid domestic service had become a major occupational calling. In 1851 some 1.3 million persons are enumerated in the census count of indoor personal service, some 11.7 percent male.[41]

Compensation earned seems to compare favorably with other occupations.[42] Marx (1863–1878/1967, 1:446) thought this high employment ratio for personal servants reflected the tremendous productivity of industrial labor that allows considerable "unproductive employment" of labor in personal service. In the United States where industry had a comparable development and where labor was as or more productive than in England, only some 7.3 percent of the labor force was engaged in domestic service in 1870 and 6.0 percent in 1900.[43] In countries with very low development of industry, extensive employment for personal service is indicated.[44] It would seem that the productivity of industrial labor hardly influences employment in domestic service. Industry cannot produce certain services needed in the home and if life-styles call for conspicuous consumption and stigmatize performance of housework as menial, then if a suitable supply of servant labor is available a larger fraction of household income by those who can afford it will be utilized in purchasing servant services.

Allocation of Labor to Modes

A rough estimate of the total manpower employed in the various modes of production around the midcentury year is set forth in Table 5.1. The basis for Table 5.1 was the estimation of labor force as of 1851 allocated to broad divisions of production by Deane and Cole (1962, Table 33). The allocation fractions by which divisional labor force was apportioned to various modes of production in a given division – such as commerce or manufactures – had to be improvised sometimes with a slim statistical basis. The various allocating fractions are set forth in column 2 of Table 5.1 and footnotes indicate the sources principally relied upon to make the allocation. The allocations in Great Britain of agricultural labor force to capitalist and simple commodity production are relatively well founded in farm acreage owned by landlords and smallholders. The distribution of "commerce" between retail and wholesale trade is also believed to be relatively well founded though drawn as previously noted from American experience. The allocation of mining and quarrying between the capitalist and corporate sectors is based largely on the feeling that most of the mining corporations – of the sixty reported to exist in 1844 – were entrepreneurial ventures wearing the corporate form for convenience only. The substantial allocation of "manufacturing" to the hybrid commercialized craft or shop mode is based on the substantial evidence for this mode in the wearing apparel and metal working industry, as previously indicated. The order of magnitude as fractions of the occupied labor force of the six mode classes listed should be within a 10-20 percent range of error but little reliability can be assigned the estimates for individual activities within the modes. Allocation estimates in 1861 or 1871 would yield larger fractions of the labor force for the capitalist and corporate sector, smaller fractions for the hybrid shop and of course reduced fractions for the landlord-tenant mode being liquidated by death or emigration of Irish cottars and laborers and by conversion of Irish agriculture to capitalist farming, landlord-tenant farming or peasant proprietorship with greater emphasis on pasture and livestock.

Utilization of labor force is a crude measure of productive achievement that leaves out of account capital investment, marketing power, and entrepreneurial skills. The first two sectors may only employ some 50 percent of the total employed labor force but they probably contributed well over three-fifths of social product and probably generated more than three-quarters of the income available for distribution. Factory owners of the capitalist and corporate sectors probably received, as we will see, a large share of final income after tax and other redistributive shiftings connected with public debt and taxation.

TABLE 5.1. Estimated distribution of occupied labor force of Great Britain (including all of Ireland, Scotland, Wales, and England) among Modes of Production[a] (in thousands)

Mode and type	Allocating fraction (%)	Labor force Number	Labor force (%)
I Capitalist Production:			
Agriculture and landed property	88[b]	1,850	
Manufacturing	55[c]	2,145	
Wholesale commerce	33[d]	400	
Building and construction	90[e]	540	
Mining and quarrying	80[f]	320	
Transport	60[g]	240	
Personal service	5[n]	75	
Total		5,570	45.8
II Corporate Production:			
Mining and quarrying	20[f]	80	
Manufacturing	5[c]	200	
Transport	40[g]	160	
Subtotal		440	3.6
III Simple Commodity Production:			
Small farm proprietors	12	250	
Retail dealers	67[d]	800	
Building	10[e]	60	
Free professions	[h]	100	
Independent handicrafts	10[c]	390	
Personal service	22[n]	330	
Subtotal		1,930	15.8
IV Hybrid Modes:			
Mercantile or capitalist-controlled shops or cottage industry	30[c]	1,170	
Quasi-feudal household domestic service (wage basis)	73[n]	1,100	
Total		2,270	18.7
V Public Mode:			
Military (including forces stationed abroad)		170[i]	
Civil service (except judiciary, police, constabulary, teachers)		61[j]	
Judiciary, police, teachers, others		219[k]	
Subtotal		450	3.7
VI Landlord Tenant Mode:			
Irish farming as of 1846		1,500[m]	12.3
Total I–VI		12,160	100

[a]Table 33, "Distribution of the Occupied Population of the United Kingdom" except "all other" presumably including unemployed, retired persons, and paupers (Deane and Cole 1962, 147).

[b]Based on land-tax assessment and census returns indicating some 12 percent of the land was farmed by smaller occupying holders (for Great Britain only, less Ireland).

[c]This distribution of "Manufacturing" grows out of the allocation to four modes.

[d]The "commerce" breakdown between wholesale and retail is based upon the corresponding allocation in the U.S. Census for 1869 of "commerce" between "retail" and "wholesale" (Barger 1960, 327).

TABLE 5.1. *(continued)*

ᵉThe craftsman-contractor operating independently is presumed to number 10 percent of the building trade force.

ᶠOnly 20 percent of mining and quarrying is assigned to the corporate sector even though 60 quarrying, coal, and other mining corporations were reported in 1844 because other evidence indicated that mining ventures were generally proprietorial and when incorporated, "investors were small local men . . . taking shares in mines they knew well" (Carus-Wilson 1954–1966, 1:354).

ᵍTransport was divided 60–40 because of the great number of seamen in the merchant marine, a large employment in omnibus, carter, cabman occupations, all mainly in "capitalist" production. Lesser numbers were employed in railroading, canal building, and telegraphy, the corporate sector.

ʰSee text pp. 132.

ⁱCiting budgetary estimates submitted to Parliament in February 1853 (Marx and Engels 1841–1870/1974–1986, 13:11; 14:416).

ʲSee text pp. 133.

ᵏA residual determined by subtracting item "free professions" from a total of professional and public service plus 50,000 for military serving abroad.

ᵐThe statistic is derived by supposing that 83 percent of all Irish persons in the 1841 Census reported as occupied in agricultural pursuits were in the landlord-tenant mode in various capacities: tenant-laborer, tenant-manager, craftsmen renting subsistence plot and doing occasional labor, etc. (Data from Mokyr 1983, Table 2.2.)

ⁿFor indoor "domestic service" Table 5.1 incorporates the enumerated totals for the United Kingdom of the 1851 Census as collated by Booth under the heading "domestic service indoor," which for the United Kingdom totalled 1,266,200 workers. I sought to exclude from this category those persons such as cooks, barmaids, domestics in hotels and institutions, which on the basis of the 1890 Census in Greater London amounted to some 17 percent of the category. I then sought to distribute that employment together with "extra" domestic employment as washerwomen, charwomen, office keeper under the "personal service" headings of the capitalist mode or the simple commodity producer mode. Extra and "outside" domestic employment in 1851 amounted to some 25 percent of total domestic service employment in 1851 involving altogether some 401,000 workers. Though the 1851 Census enumerated 1,667,400 for total domestic service (including "extra" and "outdoor"), I have cut this number down to 1,500,000 following Deane and Cole (1962, 147) where some employment in domestic service has evidently been transferred to other divisional headings.

Labor force employed, social product generated, final income received—all these leave out the dynamics of system metabolism that give some modes greater significance than others. A sense of these dynamics was eloquently put by David Landes (1969, 122) with which this section on "Modal Complex" closes:

> As described by occupation data, the British economy of 1851 may not seem very different from that of 1800. But these numbers merely describe the surface of the society—and even then in terms that define away change by using categories of unchanging nomenclature. Beneath this surface, the vital organs were transformed; and though they weighed but a fraction of the total—whether measured by people or wealth—it was they that determined the metabolism of the entire system. We have seen that, in so far as small-scale enterprise continued to flourish, it did so largely because of demand derived from the growth of concen-

trated manufacture: the demand of the large producers themselves; of their employees; and of the urban agglomerations that
grew up around them. But not only small industry was tied in this
way to the modern sector. Agriculture, trade, banking—all came
increasingly to depend on the needs, the products, the bills of
exchange, the investments of Lancashire, the Midlands, and the
other nodes of British factory industry. The people of the day were
not deceived by the pristine air of much of Britain's landscape.
They knew they had passed through a revolution.

Functional Priorities

Before probing further into the British capitalist economy, a pause
to consider the underlying functional priorities of British capitalist society is in order. These priorities lay out the emphasis and value as
reflected in literature, in political debate, in public opinion, which that
society had come to attach to the various goals and purposes fulfilled
by economic arrangements. For the British bourgeoisie the nineteenth
century was a time of fulfillment and maturity. In the seventeenth
century that bourgeoisie was still struggling with its monarch and
achieving firm control over all the British Isles with the establishment
of a national faith. It was deeply divided both between its English and
Scotch peoples and between its mercantile and landed elites. In the
eighteenth century that bourgeoisie was engaged in the relentless
struggle with the French—at the beginning with Louis XIV, with victory finally at Waterloo. Through that century they were still coping
with an independent artisanate and yeomanry, and latterly with Jacobinism and the terrors of the French Revolution. In the nineteenth century that bourgeoisie was triumphant abroad and at home. In thought
and feeling the long struggle with Jacobinism caused it to turn sharply
away from its own free-thinking traditions and to cling more closely
than ever to its orthodoxies and its established church as a bulwark of
the social order. A mode of production had become developed that
gradually cut down and undermined the artisan guilds. The village
community was torn to shreds by enclosure. Production of food,
minerals, and clothing had become more efficient, and the flow of
goods was more abundant. The balance of payments without effort
was secure. In this world thought took on a narrower focus, utilitarian
benefits became the benchmark of all behavior and self-betterment,
and enrichment became the universal norm. It was worked into the
fabric of a popular science called political economy whose doctrines
became almost household words generalized in the ideas of Freedom,
Equality, Property, and Bentham.

Freedom because both buyer and seller of a commodity are constrained only by their own free will. They contract as free agents, and the agreement they come to is but the form in which they give legal expression to their common will. Equality, because each enters into relation with the other, as with a simple owner of commodities, and they exchange equivalent for equivalent. Property because each disposes only of what is his own. And Bentham, because each looks only to himself . . . and no one troubles himself about the rest, and just because they do so, do they all . . . work together to their mutual advantage. (Marx 1863–1878/1967, 1:176)

In two visits to England in the 1830s and 1840s Ralph Waldo Emerson, the American philosopher and poet, found that the people had a "passion for utility." Steam he found "was almost an Englishman." When the Englishman wished for amusement, "he goes to work." The last term of insult was "beggar" (Emerson 1940, 573, 581, 590). And Malthus greatly weakened in that nation the power of Christian charity that had at times softened the hearts of rougher and stronger ruling classes. The only sure safeguard of a people to avoid ultimate misery and pestilence was to learn how to practice moral self-restraint in marriage or in the delay of marriage.[45] Even private charity should be guarded.[46] Thus the functional priorities of the capitalist epoch involved a minimum of taxation of upper-class income to widen the bounds of accumulation, avoidance of any action that might give false signals to the underlying population in field and workshop and weaken the tissue of moral self-restraint that needed to be cultivated, and zealous protection of property to maintain the incentive to progress itself.

Property, Money, and Regulation

The British capitalist economy of the mid–nineteenth century inherited from its predecessor mercantilist economy, briefly sketched in Chapter 4, institutions of property and money that suited its needs with some structural modification and minor adaptation. The holdovers of feudal forms of property – in landed estates, continuation of feudal revenues in manorial fines, rural public administration and church tithes, reserved status for game animals dedicated for landowner hunting parties – were attenuated and scaled down.[47] The open fields with shared commons so characteristic of feudal property in land had long been converted during the late Medieval and through the Mercantilist and Capitalist period into enclosed estates, usually to the loss of small tenants or copyholders who were being squeezed out or converted to farm laborers. By the mid–nineteenth century few open fields remained (Clapham 1926–1938, 2:499). The law encouraged proprietorial enterprise rather than the corporation with readily alienable share interests except for financial institutions and public utilities where a large aggregation of capital was required. But the public corporation had an established place, together with its ancillary institutions of the stock market and brokerage. In the middle of the nineteenth century, legal barriers hindering the development of the corporate form in business enterprise were removed so that the corporate mode of production was free to develop (see earlier n.n. 22–23). The bounds of private property were continually widened or narrowed as the law and public administration restricted or regulated the way property could be used, sold, leased, transferred, or inherited.

The institution of money as evolved in the later phase of the mercantilist economy took on matured form in the Capitalist period. The shift from a bimetallic to a monometallic standard of gold commenced in the eighteenth century when the free minting of silver coins was suspended and was further consolidated. The policy continued of restricting the issuance and circulation of paper bank notes to the higher denominations, at least in England and in Wales, thus building up a substantial metallic circulation in daily use by way of silver and gold coins that would tend to predominate in retail trade, in wage payments, and small payments generally. That policy was continued through the nineteenth century. The increased use of bank deposits transferable by check expanded the relative role of bank deposits rather than paper currency as a more economical form of money. Gradually through the Capitalist period the British began to centralize currency issuance in the Bank of England, and the bank in turn withdrew from a commercial banking business to take on more fully and deliberately the function of a central bank. In that capacity the bank was learning to coordinate its responsibilities with comparable institutions in other countries. It served as a depository for reserves acquired by commercial banks and financial institutions, which then cleared their accounts with each other through the central bank. In the discharge of this responsibility the Bank of England learned early on how to handle a banking panic through a policy of unqualified financial support by easy lending to panicky financial institutions pressed by their depositors.[48] And the bank learned that it had to keep relatively large cash reserves, much larger than other institutions, to meet shortage in the foreign accounts or demand for more coinage due to payrolls and retail trade. But the bank did not learn how to forecast economic developments with enough skill to slow down an expansionary movement before it had gone too far or how to ease the strains that cause a commercial crisis and thus a potential banking panic. The havoc of the business cycle had its full play in the Capitalist epoch. Ups and downs of business and commercial crises with their tendency to banking panics were experienced. Twice in the midcentury decades, in 1847 and 1857, the governors of the Bank of England had to ask the prime minister for an exculpatory letter waiving the statutory requirements of currency issue and gold reserves. The controlling statute was flawed, as banking school theorists and Marx pointed out, in linking gold reserves only to note circulation omitting deposit liabilities with which notes were for purposes of wholesale trade and finance substitutable. And the statute was uncomfortably rigid in supposing that every variation in gold reserves, arising even from transient causes, should be reflected in counterpart variations of like magnitude in central bank credit liabilities.[49] But then a central bank was a new phenomenon and the capitalist world was only groping its way in England, France, and the United States, and elsewhere for adequate principles to guide its policy and shape its institutional structure. The transformation of the Bank of England from a London commercial bank to a national central bank was paralleled by the opening up of banking to the corporate form, which at the high point of the capitalist economy became the predominant form of banking enterprise.

The regulatory complex of the capitalist economy emerged as a balance of two counteracting forces. One force unleashed early in the century was expressed in the repeal or withdrawal of the older mercantilist structure of commodity and resource control felt to be no longer needed and repugnant to the creed of free enterprise that Adam Smith and the new doctrines of political economy made so popular. This work was taken on in earnest after the Napoleonic Wars that left Britain triumphant in world politics and commerce with an ample gold coinage and a sound gold-backed currency. Decontrol was accelerated after the 1832 parliamentary reform. In the thirty-five years after Waterloo nearly all the protective tariffs were eliminated or scaled down or in effect repealed by reciprocity treaties negotiated with England's principal trading partners. Regulatory legislation for woolens, linens, and other products establishing how things should be made, measured, or bought and sold—legislation "still fashionable in the middle of the 18th century"—was allowed to lapse or was repealed. The attempt through Justices of Peace to regulate annually the wages of laborers and artisans and the price of bread and beer or ale was repealed early and as well prohibitory acts against combination by wage-laborers (Clapham 1926–1938, 1:133, 495, 337, 342). Repeal of interest-rate ceilings traditionally set by law and sanctified as late as 1776 by Adam Smith was resisted but allowed piecemeal for government borrowing, for the Bank of England, for building societies, and finally for everybody in the 1850s. The navigation acts having done their work were gradually repealed with Britain having on hand the world's largest merchant marine and shipbuilding industry; bounties on export of herring, linen, and grain and export prohibitions of wool and machines were withdrawn (Clapham 1926–1938, 1:330, 505, 327).

But almost as fast as the old regulatory complex was dismantled, new regulatory interests developed. The earliest harbinger of factory legislation was the bill in 1802 seeking to improve the treatment of apprenticed pauper children leased out to textile mills. The bill ordered that walls in all facilities be regularly whitewashed, that a sufficient number of windows be provided, that all apprentices be furnished with new sets of clothing once yearly, that hours of work not exceed twelve hours daily, and that religious instruction be provided for at least one hour on Sunday.[50] Other legislation followed, the interest widening from paupers to all juveniles and finally to females young and old, thus reaching the bulk of the labor force working in the textile factories.[51] Enforcement of the legislation in 1833 was devolved upon a specialized crew of factory inspectors who earned the hostility of manufacturers and the praise of Marx for their competence and freedom from "partisanship and respect of persons."[52]

Driven from now on not just by humanitarian interest but by an awakened working class with bold and devoted leaders and Tory pique at the withdrawal of corn tariffs in 1846, restrictive regulation moved on to establish in 1847–1850 the sixty-hour workweek or so-called ten-hour workday for British textile factories.[53] Coverage of the act was widened later to print works and then to bleach works, dye works, and lace works and finally in 1867 and later years to the whole of British industry where juveniles and women were employed.[54] The hours and conditions of work for adult men were unregulated except where exigent considerations of safety and sanitation were concerned as for seamen, underground mines, and the like.[55] Adult workmen were expected to speak and negotiate on their own behalf for acceptable working conditions and hours of work. Through their trade unions they did just that, following closely and even pushing the state regulatory model which established in 1876 a fifty-six and one-half-hour workweek as a norm (Clapham 1926–1938, 2:447). Apart from a first mild step by way of suggesting the principle of employers' liability for damage or loss caused by industrial accidents, legislation covering conditions, wages, and hours for industrial and shop workmen generally and adequate forms of security for old age, sickness, and unemployment had to await another social era and another century and the functioning of what is here regarded as another socioeconomic system (see Chap. 6).

An important focus of the regulatory work of the state was to reshape the state structure itself during the Capitalist epoch to reflect more adequately and to give more balanced representation to the sectors and strata of the capitalist or corporate mode of production. That state structure inherited by the Capitalist from the Mercantilist epoch was utterly inadequate. It excluded from representation in Parliament newer industrial areas which had grown up without corporate charter. It provided a pitifully small representation to greater London, the great metropolis which concentrated 15 percent of the United Kingdom population.

A substantial fraction of Commons representation came from old boroughs with a handful of voters controlled by the local landlord who sent one or two representatives to Parliament.[56] Members of Parliament were elected by show of hands at open meetings where large employers or landlords could exert undue influence over employees, partners or tenants.[57] In the chartered cities local government was predominantly in the hands of closed committees of local guilds or bourgeois notables who appointed their own successors. In the countryside county government consisted of controlled sessions of local notables commissioned by the crown to serve as justices of the peace and given arbitrary authority over persons, property, and local parish officers.

By a truly massive effort that almost reached the limits of revolutionary action, the representation to the Commons was in 1832 put on a more uniform property basis, though landed property was still allowed excessive representation.[58] By a municipal reform act of 1835 the archaic constitution of English boroughs was overhauled and a structure of representative government was provided to propertied citizens to permit responsible local government to function. By a succession of enactments the hated tithe was commuted, local urban authorities were empowered to levy rates on local property to raise funds to provide improved streets, sanitary facilities, and fresh water, to maintain a paid police service and in due course educational institutions and libraries. Not until the 1880s however was local government in rural areas taken away from commissioned justices of peace and put in the hands of elected representatives of local residents meeting suffrage qualifications. In the heyday of the British capitalist economy the suffrage was confined to persons of substantial property owned or rented and this was formalized but not altered much in the Reform Act of 1832.[59] The suffrage was brought down in 1867 to an intermediary level whereby the more well-to-do artisanate or salaried persons would vote. Only in 1884 was suffrage extended to reach most male wage earners to offset this plural voting by upper income individuals that was widely prevalent.[60]

Public Debt and Taxation

Redistributive patterns of British national income brought about by state action are in part structural—with continuous sustained resource flows—and in part episodic or conjunctural. The structural action may influence factor prices and thus may either be reversed or offset or reinforced if factor price changes are induced. The conjunctural impact is not likely to induce either counteracting or reinforcing factor price changes and hence the presentation of them may be briefer. There were three major structural factors of fiscal origin significantly affecting income distribution in capitalist Britain.

The first was a heritage of a century and a quarter of warfare which ended with Waterloo and a triumphant British empire. The government, Adam Smith believed (1776/1937, 862), was both "unwilling" to increase revenues promptly to pay for wars "for fear of offending the people" and "unable" to do so partly because of uncertainty over how much additional expenditure would be required. It was simply more convenient for both people and government to borrow the larger part of the expenses of war. That enabled the mercantile community to acquire new merchantable public debt available at high yields.[61] That also spares this community any need to severely cut back on their accustomed standard of living. Some of the cost of the war is thus silently financed by wartime inflation which, as we have seen, has potent redistributive effects for those classes who have the greatest control over their incomes (see p. 115).

The public debt commenced in 1688. By 1700 it was £14.2 million; by 1750, £78 million; by 1784, £243 million; by 1816 after Waterloo £778 million, and on the eve of the Crimean War it was brought down to £785.7 million.[62] The debt was paid off somewhat after Waterloo but additions to the debt for compensation for emancipation of West Indian slaves and relief of the Irish famine kept the total up (Clapham 1926–1938, 2:406). Most of the debt was funded in long-term or perpetual securities which relieved the treasury of the burden of continual reissue of securities. But debt service was heavy, especially heavy after Waterloo, as a percent of available national income, tax revenues, or fiscal potential.

The bulk of the pre-Waterloo debt was issued in exchange for depreciated paper pounds used for payment at an inflated price level. The debt had to be serviced at a lower price level in full-valued gold coin.[63] In 1827 the nominal value of the debt in face value was roughly double national income; annual debt service ran to over 6 percent of national income and accounted for one-half of the central government budget.[64] Thus the taxpayers paid one-sixth of their income in taxes and received one-twelfth back as interest.

If taxpayers and interest receivers were identical, the redistributive effect of the national debt and taxation to service it would have been slight though the disruptive and disincentive effects of raising and collecting the tax transfers could be substantial.[65] But taxpayers were different from interest receivers. The latter were predominantly upper-income groups and their favored institutions. Debt securities were especially favored for trustee investments to pay a secure income. Only about 13 percent of the tax revenues came in the 1820s from taxes concentrating on upper-income groups: chiefly the land tax impacting on landowners; duties on upper-class homes, carriages, and servants; and probate and legacy duties. This was raised to 17 percent in 1850–1853 by adoption in 1842 of a moderate 3 percent income tax, easily evaded and loosely administered.[66] Partly offsetting this upper-class taxation is the generous way the state budget treated royalty and its "civil list." Other tax revenues were indirect and took the form of business license fees, stamp duties on business transactions and documents, and a comprehensive network of excise and customs duties. This network taxed basic industrial materials—coal, leather, paper, building timber, glass, hemp, bricks—as well as consumer staples like sugar, tea, beer, spirits, imported grain, dried fruits, and printed cotton textiles. Indirect taxes entered into the general cost of production and affected price levels of most manufactured goods and housing. They probably reached consumers in rough proportion to their expenditure except that households abstaining from the heavily taxed alcoholic beverages, beer, or tobacco—accounting for some 38 percent of all customs and excise revenues—paid a much smaller share of indirect taxes. Clapham spoke of this concentration on indirect taxation as having "singularly little arrangement . . . according to the ability to pay"; Marx stigmatized it as the scheme of "modern fiscality" pivoting on taxes "on the most necessary means of subsistence."[67]

Agrarian Protection

The second structural factor affecting income redistribution—the highly protective grain tariff—operated through the early decades of the Capitalist epoch but after great struggles at the heyday of the system in 1846 was abolished. The British ruling class that throughout the post-1660 period but especially during the eighteenth century was dominated by its landed aristocracy, arranged a protective system assuring higher grain prices thus making for higher farm rentals. In the eighteenth century when British agriculture was sufficiently productive except in a bad crop year to export grain, this objective was achieved with a clever but wasteful system that combined a bounty on grain exports with a sliding scale protective duty on grain imports, the duty relaxing at higher prices.[68] But during the later years of the eighteenth century and very visibly during the years of the Napoleonic Wars, population growth had begun to outpace the limited capabilities of British agriculture, even with the addition of grain fields and pastures of Ireland. Hence at the end of the Napoleonic Wars when Britain had become dependent on grain imports, the policy of bounty was dropped and grain imports were permitted only when grain prices were maintained at the high (though not the highest) level reached in the Napoleonic War period, 80s. a quarter. That prevented, in Alfred Marshall's gentle words, "the peace from bringing its natural blessings to the English people" but it maintained high land prices and rents (Marshall 1919, 750). That 1815 price perch was eased a bit in 1828 when it was replaced by a sliding scale tariff, rather than a simple grain import prohibition. This started at 20s. duty when grain prices were 50s. and diminished to 1s. duty when grain prices reached 73s. per quarter, the scale being intermittently adjusted (Rostow 1948, 110). Under the conditions of wheat supply prevailing at the time, this made for very high and erratic grain prices and only a moderate fiscal yield for the treasury. The tariff was fully effective, the last year of grain exports being 1808. Wheat imports chiefly from the Baltic during 1830–1842 averaged 1.8 million quarters or the annual consumption of some 2 million persons (Mitchell 1962, 94). Though other raw material prices and price levels in general were falling, grain prices were held up to an exceptionally high level by this protective system. Grain prices in England for the decade of the 1830s were 27.5 percent higher than in France and 83.5 percent higher than in Prussia, which then supplied much of England's grain (Marshall 1919, 757 n.1).

The principal victims of this protective system were British wage earners and the lower middle-class for whom bread and cereal foodstuffs make up much of their total consumption outlay. Secondary victims were mercantile and industrial employers who reckoned that high food prices put pressure on sustainable wage levels and made their hired labor more expensive. The principal beneficiary was the landowner class whose property was made more valuable by the higher rentals it yielded. The capitalist farmers could be depended upon to make a great clamour to favor protection since their leases called for high rentals predicated upon the policy of protection and high food prices. They benefitted little from it in the long run. They would incur a transitory loss if protection should be cut down, by the decline of marginal cultivation, until leases would be readjusted.[69]

The victims became increasingly discontented especially after the Reform Bill of 1832 scaled down landlord influence in the elected Parliament. An organized agitation financed by manufacturers and merchants but supported by many Chartists grew up against the policy of taxing bread for the benefit of landowners. The agitation developed considerable popular support and electoral influence.[70] In 1846 the government and Parliament, feeling the pressure of need for increased food imports with the potato blight and Irish famine on their hands, repealed the corn tariff system. The repeal did not lead to a fall in corn prices, which held stable through the fifties and sixties at the level reached in 1831–1834. But the repeal prevented British corn prices from rising as elsewhere on the Continent and in world markets in the upward price swing of 1848–1873. In the decades following, with the assistance of American grain imports, British corn prices were 20 to 25 percent below French and German prices (Marshall 1919, 756). This made it easier for real wages to rise in the last half of the nineteenth century without injury to the British competitive position in world markets and it reduced the share of landlord food rents in British national income. There is no way to tell how real wage levels were affected in the long run by this redistributive change except on the doctrinaire premise that real wages always sink to or are unaffected by the cost of subsistence.[71] In any case wage earners were doubtless grateful for cheap bread, a blessing they could obtain without wage struggles with their employers or without much to do on their part.

The Poor House

The third structural force affecting income redistribution was relief out of public funds for destitute persons either unemployable, due to sickness or old age, or unemployment. In the Mercantilist period arrangements were made for such relief to be granted by local parish officers to bona fide local destitute residents. The relief could provide employment in a local parish workhouse where suitable work materials, chiefly yarns or textiles, could be provided or cash grants for the purchase of subsistence. Relief expenditures were to be financed as a public charge on occupiers of local property rated in accord with its market value. Where local parish officers were remiss in their relief duties, any justice of peace could order relief. The determination of residency entailing rights to relief was governed by law and generally called for prior public notice of residency and local employment for at least one year. As wage labor became the predominant source of income in England in the eighteenth century, reliance on relief in times of unemployment or food shortage with high bread prices became more common. By 1783 expenditure on poor relief in England and Wales ran to some £2 million or between 1 to 2 percent of national product.[72] The charge was high enough to be burdensome to rural capitalist farmers and tradesmen who as occupiers of property immediately paid for relief though the consumer picked up most of the cost in the long run.[73] Parish officers were instructed to monitor settlement of potential applicants for relief thus checking mobility of labor and restricting the freedom of occupation, as Adam Smith angrily charged (1776/1937, 137). The relief rolls swelled during the Napoleonic Wars due to high cost of foodstuffs (importation from the Baltic was hampered by the wars) and due also to the clearing of estates by enclosure that removed small holdings of cottagers who lost their rights to the commons and their small plots of land. To prevent building up of wage levels by agricultural laborers that might be difficult to scale down in the aftermath of war, English landlords and farmers thought it prudent to withhold increase of cash wages but to maintain subsistence by supplementary cash grants from the rates. This was the famous Speemhamland system initiated by a quarter session of justices at Berkshire and ratified by Parliament in 1791, awarding the average household 25 pounds of bread weekly, a standard later cut down.[74] This allotment system was maintained as a convenience to farmers and rate payers after the war and it persisted, though with increasing public criticism and academic attack, through the early 1830s when estimates indicate it provided for one-fifth of agricultural wages (Clapham 1926–1938, 1:364). At the wartime peak in 1813–1815 relief expenditure ran to some 2 percent of net national product and the amount was no less in current pounds in 1831 but was considerably greater in real resources due to the fall in prices and wages.[75]

Academic attack on the welfare system from the new science of "political economy" was partly on account of the check to mobility of labor associated with fixing residence, partly the absurdity of putting a substantial fraction of the agricultural wages on welfare allotments, and partly an increasing attack on the whole notion of public relief. The expectation that relief was available and could be obtained as a right induced—it was believed with little or no empirical investigation—imprudent expenditure on comfort goods or alcohol, earlier marriage and fertility in marriage, hence larger families and faster rates of population growth. Even the generous David Ricardo whom Marx so admired for his objectivity and his lack of class bias shared the widespread middle-class view spearheaded by T. R. Malthus that the abolition of poor law relief is to be sought by "the best friend of the poor and . . . the cause of humanity" (Ricardo 1817/1911, 128).

Under the practical circumstances of rapid industrialization in the United Kingdom with its industrial instability and its sudden displacement by mechanization of traditional handicrafts like weaving and spinning, which had given employment to hundreds of thousands of families, statesmen of England, even Whig statesmen elected after the 1832 Reform Act responding to middle-class interests and to Malthusian views, could not eliminate public relief. But they could make it more uncomfortable to its beneficiaries. This they did in the Poor Law of 1834 that shaped the British welfare system through the entire Capitalist epoch and well into the twentieth century.

That poor law took public welfare away from local parish officers or community notables and placed it in the hands of elected Boards of Guardians presiding over a poor law district that would usually include an entire urbanized area or a market town and parishes within a ten-mile radius. Some of the Districts had been established under earlier legislation but now they were spread over the entire country.[76] These boards in turn were made subject to a central government board at London with plenary authority over all public relief in England and Wales. Each district was supposed to construct a massive walled poorhouse with separate quarters for workshops or work yards, common dining rooms, and sleeping quarters separately for the sick and disabled and for women, men and children. By 1846 there were 707 poorhouses functioning with an average capacity of 270 inmates (Clapham 1926–1938, 1:466). Relief for the able-bodied, and for others on a space-available basis, was to be given indoors, that is, in the poorhouse. Inmates were avowedly to be under a virtual penal discipline. Adults were to be given task work, often breaking stones or picking oakum. Husband and wife were to be separately quartered and children were not allowed to stay with their parents. A uniform had to be worn. No communication was permitted during meals. Meat was allowed only three times weekly. No beer or tobacco was allowed even when provided from the outside.[77] It took an act of Parliament to permit aged couples over sixty to be quartered together. It violated the decorum of the institution to allow funeral bells to ring with a pauper burial (Hammond 1947, 111, 114).

The objective was to make acceptance of public relief as revolting and distasteful as possible. Achievement of that objective was thwarted by three factors. First, whereas earlier the prime need for poor law relief came from rural laborers, the process of industrialization created extensive need for welfare assistance in factory towns and industrial rural communities. Assistance was required for support of the many families whose main living had come from textile handicrafts, chiefly spinning and weaving, being superseded by factory production. Assistance was also required to cope with layoffs arising from periodically returning hard times. Irish immigration flooded industrial towns with destitute people looking for work and applying for welfare. It was not possible to build workhouses on a scale that could accommodate the throngs who applied for assistance. In 1839 there were 98,000 indoor paupers accommodated but 552,000 outdoor paupers (Webb and Webb 1903–1929, 8:59). By 1844 facilities were available for 231,000 indoor but some 1,247,000 outdoor paupers were assisted (Clapham 1926–1938, 1:582). Local guardians were unwilling especially in the industrial communities to invest resources on the scale needed to house and oversee some 10 percent of the English population. Hence most guardian boards and the London board itself, despite the philosophy of the Poor Act of 1834, continued with the more traditional policy of outdoor relief for persons temporarily unemployed or for the destitute aged or handloom weavers who could provide partly for themselves but needed supplementary assistance. A commonly used procedure for a needy family with an able-bodied male was to give a food allowance and a small cash wage to the male charged with daily task work in the work yards of the poorhouse. Sometimes work materials were taken home for the family to process. During the American Civil War when there was great distress in the cotton textile industry, outdoor relief was apparently generally provided to meet minimum nutrition needs. Welfare assistance fluctuated with economic conditions, rising and falling with the industrial business cycle.[78] In the low and high years alike, however, for the forties, fifties, and sixties, it appears that indoor paupers were about one in seven of the total number assisted. In Scotland by contrast a much more abstemious welfare policy was followed and only indoor relief was given, resulting for census years at least, in a lower fraction of population on relief than in England and Wales.[79] The workhouse test for handling welfare applicants was apparently employed frequently enough that there were instances of families choosing to die of starvation rather than accept the regime of the poorhouse.[80]

The welfare administration that emerged from the 1834 poor law reform certainly scaled down the relative role of welfare assistance in the British economy. The fraction of estimated national income used for poor relief expenditures is known with tolerable accuracy for censal years from 1811 onward (Deane and Cole 1962, 282). For the three censal years – 1811, 1821, 1831 – the fraction ranged between 2.00 and 2.39 percent. From 1841 onward after Poor Law reform the percent steadily declined as follows: 1841, 1.05; 1851, 0.95; 1861, 0.86; 1871, 0.86; 1881, 0.77.

This decline may partially reflect the rise in real wage levels that in the latter half of the century permitted increasing numbers of workmen to rise above the poverty level. But we know from the famous Booth survey of London poverty in the 1880s and 1890s that some one-third of the London wage-earning population was at or below the level of destitution and hence would need to apply for relief with any sustained adverse turn of fortune from ill health, industrial accident, or loss of a job. It seems then that welfare administration in England and Wales and Scotland kept the bulk of the poor alive but with sufficient deterrence to minimize redistribution from public funds to the poor.

Slavery and Sugar

Two conjunctural episodes of redistribution played a major role in the British capitalist economy; the one was a beneficent act that spoke to high moral purpose and touched the pocketbook as well, the other a deeply sordid act of near racial genocide. The beneficent act concerns the slave trade that was prohibited in 1808 and the liquidation of slavery in the British West Indies effective 1834–1838. The economic basis for a continued European slave trade had been undermined by the success of the trade itself, which by the end of the eighteenth century had filched from the continent of Africa an estimated population of 7.7 million blacks, nearly all transported to the New World. Here, they or their survivors and descendants manned the plantations producing tropical produce – sugar, cotton, tobacco, coffee – for Europe, which was the economic basis of the mercantilist economy that gave a profound stimulus to the development of the capitalist mode of production.[81] The older, well-manned colonies no longer needed infusion of slave immigrants if masters would only establish domestic arrangements that would permit reproduction.[82] The value of existing slave property could only be enhanced if cheap new slave supplies were restricted. Additionally, assimilation of the conquest of India opened up perspectives of development of empire in Southeast Asia with its vast population easily exploited, trained in social hierarchy, accustomed to a very low standard of subsistence, and with capabilities for production of the very tropical produce for which slavery was used in the New World.[83] Finally, the successful development especially by the French of their Caribbean sugar colonies had produced a relative glut of sugar in world markets so that even after the destruction by slave revolt of the productive plantations of St. Dominique (now Haiti), by 1799 the cultivation of sugar had been pushed to the point of a ruinous level of prices.[84]

Under these circumstances as soon as the British ruling class took a careful look at the realities of the slave trade, which exacted a fearful toll of its own merchant seamen and which was economically disorganizing along the whole coastal belt of Africa, they did not find it difficult to favor abolition of the slave trade, so eloquently preached among them and advocated in British public opinion by antislavery crusaders and moral reformers.[85] This trade had in any case diminished in importance as a branch of mercantile traffic and could be dropped without causing serious hardship to the British shipping industry (Williams 1964, 160). Hence the British ruling class followed the example of the slave-holding North American republic and enacted in 1808 a prohibition of the slave trade. The doctrine of prohibition was taken to with such zeal that the British government used its international political supremacy on the Continent and worldwide to induce other countries to subscribe to the doctrine. The British navy through the entire first half of the nineteenth century worked with energy and fidelity to suppress slave trading whether discovered on the coast of Africa or on the high seas.[86] A significant number of Africans captured in the nineteenth century by British ships of war, released from their slave carriers, and returned many of them to a part of Africa dedicated to freedom from slavery is witness to the tenacity of British antislave trade convictions.[87]

Slavery in the British Caribbean was spread over a host of islands, of which the largest was Jamaica with 320,000 slaves in 1833 and two mainland colonies, British Guyana and British Honduras, now Belize. The total slave population in 1830 may be estimated at 620,000 with a commercial value of £30 million. The white population was around 10 percent of the black. The bulk of the slaves lived and worked on large plantations and a good number of the owners, like Irish landlords, were absentee, especially in the older islands. As noted earlier, absentee British plantation owners had built up over the years a substantial representation in the House of Commons chiefly by purchase of pocket boroughs, which had been largely cut away by the Reform Act of 1832.[88] The regime slavery enforced was relatively harsh. Field labor tasks were heavy. The whip was generously used to enforce discipline. Manumission was discouraged by local law. Reproduction was poor, forcing reliance for maintenance of labor supply on the slave trade.

The British interest in supporting West Indian slavery had been undermined like the slave trade. Whereas in the seventeenth and eighteenth centuries without the supply of tropical produce from their Caribbean possessions British industry and shipping would have been badly hurt, by the second quarter of the nineteenth century other reliable sources of cheaper supply had opened up on more attractive terms. The independence following 1815 of mainland Latin American, Spanish and Portuguese colonies with which Britain established close commercial connections, the successful development of beet sugar on the Continent and of cotton in the American Southern states, and the flourishing of the India-China trade put the Caribbean West Indies trade in the shadows.[89] In the competition of sugar producers, the British West Indies became laggard in supply and exceedingly high cost. The preference duties on West Indies sugar cost the British consumer dearly.[90] As Williams put it in a phrase, the British Caribbean had not only become a sordid story of human oppression to which the British mind had become sensitive, but an economic anachronism and as such set for liquidation (Williams 1964, 138).

The antislavery movement first attempted amelioration of slavery by promotion of a reform slave code, imposed upon the crown colonies and urged upon the others, which abolished whipping for females, required time off for religious instruction, facilitated manumission, and established an outside protector. As this was resisted by the older colonies, the atmosphere was clouded by slave restlessness arising in part from missionary activities and from concern about their forthcoming emancipation.[91] In that setting the British ruling class egged on by missionaries and by a high tide of antislavery sentiment decided to go all the way and emancipate the West Indian slaves over a six-year transition period, beginning on 1 August 1834. During that period corporal punishment on plantations was prohibited, maximum hours were set with quarter time off provided for former slaves to work on their own provision grounds if compensation for provisions was not paid as wages.[92] Special magistrates were appointed to supervise the transition. At the end of the transition period full emancipation was stipulated. To compensate the planters for the loss of their property rights in slaves and to solicit their cooperation in working out the emancipation, the British ruling class appropriated £20 million to be paid to slaveholders when the requisite implementation ordinances were enacted. Since many West Indian assemblies believed that emancipation would be forced upon them if they resisted, the offer of compensation was accepted and the emancipation procedure was put into effect. It is hardly relevant to our present purposes to follow the process of emancipation and the way it was accelerated, becoming effective in four years, the struggles to prevent virtual slavery from being reintroduced via vagrancy or labor codes, the effort to establish rates of pay for labor and rental charges for slave quarters that would enable the former slaves to pay their way and not fall into arrears of debt that would lead to peonage as was happening on the Latin American continent with Indian cultivators. The economic emancipation of the slaves would have been promoted if on liberation the £20 million had been paid to them and not to their masters and if they were furnished with their own provision grounds that customarily throughout the Caribbean had been assigned to slaves on back lands that were not cultivated for sugar or commercial produce. The blacks with missionary help did seek to purchase small homesteads and garden plots. Planters were often unable to evict blacks from back lands.[93] But with their own resources the emancipated slaves could barely get a toehold for subsistence, although enough to weaken plantation output that over the transition period fell off by 10 percent partly due to cessation of field labor by women. With full emancipation in 1838, output in the following years fell off another 27 percent.[94] By that time Great Britain determined to terminate the preferential duties for West Indian sugar (effective in 1852) and became frankly dependent upon other supply sources (Mathieson 1932, 146, 160). Output in the West Indies was later partly recovered by importation of Chinese and East Indian coolie indentured labor and the installation of modernized production facilities on the plantations.[95]

Irish Famine

If British redistribution on account of slavery in the West Indies was generous if misdirected, redistribution to give relief to famine and pestilence in Ireland was altogether stingy and inadequate. Famine in Ireland had a threefold origin. The most dramatic source of hardship came from a new plant fungus that for some four years in a row attacked potato plants in Europe but especially in Ireland.[96] In the first year, 1845–1846, it destroyed in an unusually moist growing season about half of the crop; in successive plant years from two-thirds to three-quarters of the product of about 2 million statute acres perished (Mokyr 1983, 7). Acreage planted in grain and other food crops was near 3 million acres while hay and pasture land with 8.5 million acres supported grazing stock, work horses, sheep, and pigs.[97] Though only the potato acreage was damaged, that was critical because potatoes were the main carbohydrate food for the poorer Irish people. Probably most of the 1.2 million agricultural laborers listed in the 1841 Census and most of the nearly 1 million families depending chiefly on cottage industry drew their principal carbohydrate staple from a small potato patch up to an acre and a half in size. Potatoes also fed fowls and pigs. Irish diet however also drew upon oats, cabbages, green vegetables in season and some eggs. Milk, a staple of earlier centuries, had by 1846 grown very scarce.[98]

A small crop of barley and hops supplied thousands of illicit distilleries with Irish whiskey (poteen) that escaped the heavy excise duties, enriched the diet, and cheered up the social life of the Irish countryside.[99] If all Irish farmland had been owned and worked by Irish farmers, the potato blight would not have been so disastrous. Exports of grain, dairy produce, and livestock would have slowed down, the diet would have been pinched a bit, cash income would have declined, but the people would not have hungered. However, the agricultural laboring population did not own much of the livestock or of the grain crop or dairy products. What they raised of these was usually dedicated to paying their rent.

At the same time that the fungus attacked the Irish potato, mechanization was undermining the basis of livelihood of nearly a million families depending heavily on the earnings of cottage industry, either linen yarn spinning or linen and woolen hand weaving or needlework. Growing flax, decomposing and processing flax fibre, spinning linen yarn, and hand weaving of linen and woolen goods had been cottage crafts cultivated under British guidance, stimulated by a linen export bounty and worked up into major industries with distributive networks throughout Ireland but especially centered out of Belfast. A board of trustees for the encouragement of linen manufactures was established in 1710 and was operative in Ireland until 1828. An elaborate regulatory code was still in effect through the 1840s.[100] Irish linen output for 1770–1771 is estimated at about 38 million yards valued at £2,525,000. By 1806 Irish output would be raised some 60 percent and by 1840 the total would be still higher (Deane and Cole 1962, 202). Besides work in linen Irish hand weavers were active in woolen and flannel manufacture. Altogether the 1841 Census enumerated in the clothing and textile occupations a main source of breadwinning to nearly 900,000 workers of whom 573,000 were female, chiefly spinners, while some 122,800 were male, chiefly weavers. Another 200,000 cottage operatives were separately enumerated in the wearing apparel occupations, mostly woolen, flannel, and damask weavers (Booth 1886, App. A, B [3]).

Cottage textile industry was supplemented by other nonfarm sources of income like illicit distilling, migratory farm work in

England, and building and huckstering. All of them permitted rural households to become established without a main reliance upon agriculture and thus stimulated marriage and fertility, as has been convincingly shown by internal evidence from the Irish 1841 Census.[101]

Mechanization was delayed in its application to linen and wool spinning and weaving but by the 1840s it was working its way. Perhaps the work of the flax dresser and home spinner was the quickest to be undermined since mechanical spinning was speedier and more efficient. In his annotation to the analysis of census occupational drift over a fifty-year period, Charles Booth noted that the decline since 1841 in Irish textile employment was due chiefly to the "loss of this hand industry which passed to English machinery" (Booth 1886, 345). The production of effective flax spinning and fibre extraction machinery, which was commenced in the mid 1830s, doubled between 1835 and 1850.[102]

Weaving in worsted and linen was put under less pressure. A few branches of Irish cottage textile employment were sustained in the 1840s, there being apparently a rise in embroidering; in work with crepe, shawls, and fancy goods; and in woolen knitting. Some employment opened up in cotton textile mills. But over the decade the number of women returning their occupation as spinner shrank by 38 percent. The number of male textile workers, chiefly weavers, fell off by 20,000 and the number who could claim activity in clothing or wearing apparel fell by 13.5 percent. In the aggregate the whole activity in textile cottage industry was reduced by one-third, from 893,000 operatives to 595,000 operatives.[103] And many of those who still functioned could only drag out their existence with very low earnings in competition with the factory process that could handle and work fibers, spin yarns, weave cloth, and perform finishing operations much more efficiently than craft workers.

The potato famine tipped the balance in the British Parliament against the grain tariff, abolished in 1846. This action made it advantageous for Irish landowners to seek to modernize and reorganize the use of their agricultural lands that had drifted over the years into a mosaic of small holdings with very little large-scale capital investment in drainage, fencing, or soil improvement and with a husbandry that concentrated on cereal cultivation by tenant farmers employing large numbers of agricultural laborers set up as tenants. Frederick Engels in his 1845 book on the English workingclass noted the anomaly that though Irish farm acreage was 43 percent of British farm acreage, it produced only a fifth as much value product with as many tenant farmers and more agricultural laborers. This inefficient agriculture, which yielded substantial rental incomes by putting extreme pressure on living standards of Irish farm laborers, has been copiously investigated by Mokyr.[104]

The potato blight commencing in 1845 and the abolition of the corn laws in 1846 together gave a public signal to Irish landowners to commence the reorganization of their domains and husbandry; to clear the land of unprofitable small-scale subsistence agriculture; to establish modern large-scale farms properly capitalized and employing a much smaller labor force; and to shift away from cereal grains that could not be profitably grown in competition with cereal growers in the Baltic, in southern Russia, and in the New World. In lieu of anything better, it meant seeking to increase the emphasis on livestock care and dairy produce or, in Marx's words (1863–1878/1967, 1:712 n.), to turn "Irish arable into pasture land." That the share of pasture should be enlarged and that farms should be enclosed and modernized was a widely heralded development. In the decades to come, it actually occurred.[105] The indispensable preliminary was clearing the estates of agricultural laborers who had become established on the land with leasehold rights.[106]

British policy for the relief of the Irish Famine growing out of the potato blight was quite deliberately oriented to long-run reorganization of Irish agriculture by methods fully at home with the principles of the capitalist economy then becoming universally adopted as policy norms. These norms would not countenance indiscriminate giving of welfare assistance or outdoor relief anywhere but the poorhouses where "adequate" (penal) conditions could be established. These norms sought to interfere as little as possible with the methods of the free market. Hence there was great reluctance to allow government to undertake importing the lacking grain foodstuffs and distributing it by a nationwide relief program. One first step along that road was taken by the English prime minister when the full scope of the potato blight and approaching food shortage was brought home over the winter of 1845–1846. He ordered on his own the expenditure of £100,000 for the purchase of 800,000 bushels of maize in the United States for stocking and distribution in the spring and early summer months of 1846 when the full impact of the blight of the 1845 crop would be felt. It was not utilized directly for relief. Imported supplies over the next few years were dribbled out by sale in small allotments in those market towns where hunger had resulted in a sharp build-up of food prices, profiteering being a usual by-product of famine. In the relief plan of the Peel government that presided over the first two years of the Famine, government maize supplies were conceived of as a means of regulating market prices.[107] The British government not only sold its available relief supplies; it urged private charity groups who brought food into Ireland for relief purposes to do the same.[108] Government large-scale food imports would allegedly deter private dealers and grain merchants from their main business, handling and distributing foodstuffs, and private imports would disappear. For the same reason the government rejected requests of Irish leaders to prohibit continued distillation of grain to make alcoholic beverages or export of grain and foodstuffs including oats, butter, and wheat.[109]

To make up for deficiency of cash income among the Irish poor and to enable them to purchase relief or charity foodstuffs, the British government was willing to move ahead by a massive public works program launched in the spring 1846. Construction of railroads and land drainage badly needed in Ireland made sense only if planned and projected on a national or regional scale. They were not seriously considered.[110] Local public works that could be quickly improvised by local authorities would be financed by the British government – half by loan and half by grant – if the works projects after investigation would be found suitable, feasible, and sufficiently vested with public interest. Local Irish authorities were responsible for financing half the cost by a charge on local property taxes.[111] These public works projects which were slow to get started became the mainstay of Irish public relief efforts through 1846 and 1847 and employed at their peak some 700,000 persons (Woodham-Smith 1962, 166, 183). They hung over Irish landowners like an unpaid mortgage debt with interest accruing. They gave an immediate stimulus to landlords to carry through the clearing of their estates since only the Irish poor with legal residence in their parishes would be a chargeable liability.[112] After 1847 participants in public works were required as a condition of relief to renounce or give up their tenure rights in leaseholds, a condition written into the public works legislation for the purpose of helping to clear the estates.[113] Some of those evicted and cleared survived on the meager dole provided by public works; others died for lack of enough food even on that dole, while still others sought to flee the country and emigrate, some to England and Scotland that were near. Others, often with assistance from landlords or from remittances by relatives who had emigrated earlier, embarked for the New World. In 1847 the improvised public works were scrapped in favor of soup kitchens which, consistently with British relief principles, could be opened up as outdoor relief for the sick, the women, and the children. Able-bodied males were, by contrast, to be put in the crowded poor houses, with their capacity of little over 100,000. So the one class was taken out of the poorhouses and another class put in, a transfer often difficult to arrange. The average bowl of soup or pound of meal provided daily could only slow up but not impede the progress of starvation that had now become institutionalized (Woodham-Smith 1962, 307, 317, 374, 294). After approximately one year of soup kitchens, the relief program for famine in Ireland, now in the fourth year of potato blight, was terminated and the Famine was left to pursue its grim course countered only by relief provided by private charity or the Irish poorhouses with such finances as could be mustered by local authorities.

The consequences were ghastly. The total loss of population is estimated up to 1.5–2.0 million.[114] Hundreds of thousands died of starvation. At a certain stage of prolonged undernourishment, disease takes over, first typhus, relapsing fever, and finally cholera.[115] Since for purposes of relief or emigration the Irish poor were gathered in work gangs, around soup kitchens, in poorhouses, or in port facilities awaiting emigration, the speedy communication of contagious disease was facilitated. The poorhouses and "fever hospitals" became chambers of execution.[116] The dread typhus killed many doctors and nurses who sought to attend patients. Ships packed with emigrants to Glasgow or Liverpool or to the New World disembarked surviving passengers who had to be quarantined again and kept in isolation until release was safe.[117] Even after the Famine was past and food availability for the Irish poor was reestablished, the memory of the Famine haunted survivors. Steadily in the 1850s and 1860s emigrations continued out of Ireland—from 1851 through to 1865, 1.6 million persons, diminishing only slightly in succeeding decades (Marx 1863–1878/ 1967, 1:697).

Famine and pestilence were experienced not in Asiatic backwater provinces or deep in inland territories difficult to reach with provisions but right in the British Isles, next to the wealthiest country of Christendom, with the largest merchant marine and with ample financial resources, the absolute master of territories in Africa, the Indian Ocean, the Caribbean, North America, and the South Pacific. If the Irish were to be driven out of their homeland, could they not have been placed on fertile land abroad and given a helping hand? That act of redistribution was never carried out. Is it so strange that ill will lingers between the Irish and the English?

British Capitalist Economy and Multinational Capitalism

The British capitalist economy was not alone. Beyond its own outgrowths in its newly settled territories and its conquered colonial dependencies, it sooner or later faced rival capitalist economies. The first to emerge was the erstwhile child of British society, the United States. There machine technology and railroadization spread rapidly through the 1840s and 1850s creating a parallel capitalist economy in the New World.[118] On the Continent capitalist economies took shape more slowly but with notable acceleration in the 1850s and 1860s bringing into existence by the third quarter of the century capitalist economies in Holland, Belgium, France, Germany and by the 1890s or early 1900s probably also in Russia where the capitalist mode of production had a rapid development in agriculture, mining, and industry. And everywhere, even before the formal emergence of "capitalist economies" as defined in this work, there were capitalist sectors in mining, agriculture, and wholesale trade allowing mercantile interconnections and a growing volume of international trade and investment to develop with a common form of money in gold and silver. A single world market prevailed for primary product staples and by a unified metabolism great waves of prosperity or depression were propagated internationally. Though each of these societies had a distinctive economic system with varied modal complexes, distinctive forms of money and property, singular kinds of public economy and redistribution – as has been noted from time to time in this work – the capitalist modes of production operative in these systems were all linked together by trade and a shared development of science and technology, by migration of labor or investment of capital. They were alike subordinated to a world market by which they were disciplined and to which they were accommodated even when sheltered by tariff walls or high costs of transportation.

Nor was overt institutionalization lacking for this complex of interconnection, which we may tentatively call "multinational capitalism." The commercial treaties negotiated between the principal capitalist countries or imposed upon nominally independent tributary societies provided consular stations, access to ports of call, protection of alien nationals in the conduct of their business, juridical facilities for resolution of controversies. Many of these treaties made for a more rational world of international trade by providing for protection of rights in patents and copyright and for more uniform rates of tariff protection, giving to each signatory the tariff treatment provided the "most favoured nation."

The interconnections between central banks were beginning to build up the muscular tissue, which in another century would lead to the creation of the International Monetary Fund (Gottlieb 1984, 328–339). Though all efforts failed to develop a common bimetallic treatment of gold and silver as international monetary metals and as the worldwide basis for international commerce with uniform given parities, still a common gold standard linking together the stronger capitalist economies emerged and gold became its ruling money.

Certain major public works greatly facilitating the flow of international commerce made their way largely by international agreement—the Suez and Panama Canals linking the Indian and Mediterranean and the Atlantic and Pacific oceans. The Suez Canal was organized by a major international quasi-public corporation, a model of its kind, with international distribution of shareholdings. An international code evolved to govern the use of shared major rivers or strategic water passages—in the Baltic, the Dardanelles, the Danube, the Rhine and elsewhere.

This interwoven network of capitalist economies was colonialist like its predecessor mercantilist systems whose colonial empire it inherited. This empire was on one side curtailed in extent, on another side augmented, and in many significant respects was modified in its mode of operation. The scope of empire was curtailed because colonies predominantly settled by European peoples either asserted and fought early in the Capitalist period for their freedom and self-government as in North and South America. Later in the Capitalist period they were granted their freedom as British dominions in Australia, Canada, and elsewhere. These losses were counterbalanced by augmentation of empire in Africa, Asia, and elsewhere bringing vast populations and rich resources under Western capitalist control. This augmentation had a secure basis in the technology that the matured capitalist mode of production provided. The improvement in firepower, range, and accuracy of Western armaments resulted in deadly weapons like the machine gun and mortar or the great naval ships that could rapidly steam their way across oceans and up navigable rivers. The Western military became invulnerable in contests with older societies and less developed peoples. The Western colonialist achieved instant control of all port cities and navigable rivers. The steam railway permitted colonial penetration of vast inland territories facilitating travel and traffic. The electric telegraph made for instant flow of information over vast areas, facilitating public administration of unfriendly peoples.

The augmentation of empire was direct and crass in Africa, in Southeast Asia, and in northern Africa where Arabs were subjected to Western colonial power (Algeria). In these regions each colonial power sought steadily through the nineteenth century to enlarge its holdings, taking advantage of all opportunities. When empire already existed, as in India or Java, the scope of empire was rounded out by extension to outlying provinces, to distant Himalayan peoples, and to friendly local rulers. The British took the lead in the 1840s in battering down Chinese resistance in their vulnerable port cities. Later in the century the colonial powers teamed up together and jointly developed control of Chinese port cities and territories. They established territorial concessions in inland cities and control of Chinese customs administration, an essential organ of state power. In the Capitalist period colonial control extended over a much larger population of colored and non-European people than were subjected to mercantilist colonial control. The argument of V. I. Lenin that competitive nineteenth century capitalism was essentially noncolonialist is profoundly at variance with essential historical facts that tell a significantly different story (Lenin 1917–1922/1965, Chap. 6, 89–104). Our interpretation of these historical facts and Lenin's interpretation conflict so categorically that perhaps a more detailed exposition would be helpful.

Only very specious summary data enabled Lenin to conclude that *"it is precisely after this period"* [his italics] – the period of premonopolist Capitalism in which free competition was predominant and reached its limit in the 1860s and 1870s – "that the tremendous boom in colonial conquests began and their struggle for territorial division of the world becomes extraordinarily keen." That struggle was most intense in the seventeenth and eighteenth centuries. The struggle subsided in the first half of the nineteenth century to become especially keen as the nineteenth century closes and the decade following.

The struggle for colonies *did* intensify between 1890 and 1914 not because "premonopolist Capitalism" had died out but because new industrialized Capitalist economies had grown up with military capabilities (Germany, United States, Japan) anxious for a greater share in the world's colonial possessions and ready to fight to obtain them. The partition of inland Africa was consummated in the 1880s. This accounted for most of the great increase in gross square mileage in territorial possessions that Lenin marked off to the account of finance capital.

The preconditions for African imperial appropriation had all been achieved in the earlier capitalist or mercantilist period when much of the rimland of West and South Africa passed under imperial control. Then the slave trade had been scaled down and commercial development of palm produce, ground nuts, and cocoa showed great promise. Real economic development had to await transport to the elevated interior tablelands and speedy communication achieved by the railroad and electric telegraph, i.e. by investments that in Africa only became feasible in the second half of the nineteenth century (Hopkins 1973, Chap. 4, 124). In the period between 1840 and 1860 "the most flourishing period of free competition in Great Britain," was a period in which Lenin argues that "the leading British bourgeois politicians were opposed to colonial policy." Britain, riveted by famine and martial law its imperial control over Ireland, her first colony, brutally suppressed mutiny in India, extended the empire to Burma, tried to extend the empire to Afghanistan, gained a significant foothold in Egypt with a railway concession from Cairo to Suez, and jointly with the French and other European powers began the construction of the Suez Canal (the basis for Western colonial control of Egypt), fought a series of gunboat wars with China establishing Western administration of coastal enclaves, treaty ports, and customs administration, and thus began the transformation of China into a quasi-Western colony. It is odd that Lenin missed recognition of the extensive treatment that Marx gave to the forward movement of colonialism in the heyday of British capitalism or Marx's solemn declaration that "the veiled slavery of the wage-workers in Europe needed, for its pedestal, slavery pure and simple in the new world" (Marx 1863–1878/1967, 1:760); Marx and Engels 1850–1894/n.d., 24–77, 79–83, 130–208 [India]; 77 [Burma]; 91 [Persia]; 15–24, 108–30, 208–50 [China]. Lenin's analysis was thrown in the face of the 1913 (365, 368) masterwork of Rosa Luxemburg, *The Accumulation of Capital.* Her thesis was that "capitalism in its full maturity" depends "in all respects on non-capitalist strata and social organizations existing side by side with it," that capitalism arises "and develops historically amidst a non-capitalist society" laid out chiefly in the form of colonies and protectorates. Her two chapters, "The Struggle Against Natural Economy," "The Introduction of Commodity Economy" spell this out in vivid narration. Her work was flawed in its macroeconomic modeling and its analysis of depressions. But her work was insightful in its argument that capitalist production and colonialism went hand in hand.

The mode of operation of colonialism was also changed. The mercantilist philosophy was to channel all trade to the home country and thus enable its merchants, rulers, and producers to appropriate its main benefits. In the Capitalist period the exports and imports of colonies generally moved on nondiscriminatory terms. There was little or no exclusion of merchant shipping or trade by national flag of origin. Smaller capitalist countries without colonies could thus participate in some of the benefits of colonial development. The flag however governed the allocation of valuable lands for plantations or homestead settlement, reserved usually for nationals of the imperial power. Reserved also were opportunities for service in public administration or for access to public utility concessions such as building of railroads.

The altered mode of colonial exploitation that permitted some sharing of benefits with all Western powers – summarily expressed in the American formula of the "Open Door" – was associated with some form of consultation among imperial powers regarding disposition of imperial claims. A series of international conferences were held regarding Balkan, African, Asian, or Chinese affairs. Though British naval power was still supreme, she no longer believed it necessary that all desirable territorial acquisitions should be under the British flag. In the 1880s the entire continent of sub-Saharan Africa was allocated by agreement among the imperial powers.

But there were dissatisfied imperial powers whose aspirations were frustrated. Russian efforts to move south and achieve control of the Black Sea and its exit in the Mediterranean via the Dardanelles was consistently frustrated by Anglo-French interests in the same area and their fears of the Russian colossus. Later Russian expansion south of their Siberian wastelands into Korea and Manchuria was blocked by the aggressive thrust of Japanese power, newly industrialized and developed into a strong capitalist economy by the turn of the twentieth century.

The Germans, late in developing a strong national state, were frustrated at finding the world of colonial goodies nearly all divided up. The United States did not hesitate to make war upon the ailing and weak Spanish empire and appropriate some of her remaining choice territories in the Caribbean and in the Pacific. The Germans never found convenient occasion to do the same and thus their colonial hunger remained unsatisfied, a root cause of World War I. The same kind of colonial divisiveness was a source of rancor for the Japanese later in the twentieth century.

The contentiousness that marked colonial aspirations of leading capitalist powers indicates that the multinationalist capitalist order, though very real in critical respects, was also permeated with divisiveness. Great Britain had the lion's share of colonial wealth, not because she merited it, but simply because she had won it in earlier struggles and had a powerful navy difficult to challenge. Though certain major fluctuations were shared by most leading capitalist countries, the chronology of cyclical peaks and troughs of individual countries showed that each had its distinctive cyclical experiences. Most capital was still invested in the Capitalist period in the country of its origin. Though the labor movement of the time had profound internationalist sympathies, each country shaped a labor movement based upon its distinctive struggles, history, and the forms of resistance it encountered. So also were the economic systems, distinctive though joined together in a divisive order.

6

The
Mixed
Economy

Introduction

The label for this class of economy is admittedly awkward. It gives no clue as to what is mixed together or why. The label is however better than others suggested: "late capitalism," "managed" or "regulated," "market-oriented," "laboristic," "social-democratic."[1] The Marxist labels, "imperialism" or "state-monopoly-capital," are one-sided or misleading.[2] The principal connotation of our label is correct, namely that *many* characteristics are involved appearing in patterns varying considerably in individual countries. Chiefly for that reason I will not seek for the mixed economy to develop its characteristics by analysis of an individual country as I did for the capitalist economy. I will rather elucidate the characteristics that are strategic and shared by all and then indicate the different ways they are combined in the Western world. This broad treatment will involve omission of a detailed presentation of some system characteristics, such as property, which are distinctively national or which are not salient. It will be possible to treat fully the prevailing complex of modes of production, regulation, redistribution, the institution of money, and the guidance of economic growth and inflation.

The countries concerned are the leading countries of North America, Western Europe, the British Commonwealth, and Japan. In these countries the capitalist mode of production became well established during the nineteenth or early twentieth century. Industrial development became well rooted and agriculture accordingly subordinated in importance. Schooling of the population became universal.

166

The principles of the democratic state became dominant. These countries are commonly grouped together for statistical purposes as "advanced industrial countries." They have been conveniently associated together during the post World War II epoch as the Organization for Economic Cooperation and Development (OECD).[3] The economic systems of these countries will be considered in a well-bounded epoch, bordered at the lower end by the decade of the Great Depression followed by the catastrophe of World War II. At the upper end the epoch is bordered by the collapse of the Bretton Woods gold standard and by the explosion of oil prices and OPEC power in the seventies and the resulting ordeal of stagflation.[4]

Recovery in the 1940s from the disastrous experience of war and occupation was comparatively rapid. Political stability was achieved. The productive forces unfolded almost luxuriantly. The institutions of the mixed economy took deep root and flourished. Noteworthily, in this epoch the older layer of industrial corporations that emerged out of capitalist enterprise in the later nineteenth and early twentieth centuries outgrew their entrepreneurial character, became increasingly divorced from the dynastic family interests to which they were first subordinated, and achieved that diffusion of stockholdings and professionalization of management that is the true hallmark of the quasi-public corporation. Though entrepreneurial (capitalist) corporations still existed—they are continually in process of creation—their relative role was less and the role of the matured quasi-public corporation was larger in North America, Western Europe, and Japan.

American hegemony of the Western post-1946 mixed economy became somewhat weakened as the epoch wore on except for the superpower privilege readily conceded her in the investment of enormous economic resources in the improvement, positioning, and development of strategic atomic weapons whose use was ruled out, except as an act of national suicide, by counteracting atomic weapons held by the other superpower, the USSR. The remnants of military occupation in Western Europe and Japan relieved those societies of defense burdens, which instead weighed down the American economy. The erstwhile industrial competitors of the United States—Japan and Germany—rose from the dismal posture of total military subjugation with burned-out cities and a badly damaged industrial apparatus—to rebuild new and stronger economies. Their export industries had the advantage of low labor costs growing out of very favorable exchange rates, which made their labor very cheap. Western European economies developed a new and privileged form of tariff protection by adoption of a common market with nearly free movement of goods and services across European frontiers but a significant tariff for goods coming in from the outside. West European currencies by 1958 became freely convertible for all current and many noncurrent transactions, that is, became virtually hard currencies at set parities backed, except for the United Kingdom, by large and growing gold and dollar reserves. Industrial production for OECD apart from the United States reached prewar (1936–1939) levels by 1950 and by 1970 had considerably narrowed the gap in per capita GNP which, when computed at the more realistic exchange rates that prevailed after 1973, left the United States only a modest advantage.[5] Western Europe had discovered energy resources in the North Sea area that satisfied much of Western Europe's natural gas needs within this period and promised shortly after to reduce dependence upon outside petroleum resources. The new form of continental solidarity developed in Europe permitted all Common Market countries to share in building up a preferential system of trade with former African colonies; to utilize common resources for developing new peacetime uses for nuclear power; to stabilize the relative value of their currencies; and to facilitate personal travel, job search, and social security throughout the entire area. Though the Common Market was in some respects diluted by admission in the 1970s of the United Kingdom, it was strengthened overall since English ties with the Commonwealth were diminished and the strength and independence of the West European community was enhanced.

The continental solidarity developed in the Common Market has by no means rubbed out the distinctness of the individual economic systems that have developed in each of the Common Market countries and throughout the Western world. Each country has maintained a distinct regulatory complex, scheme of property, and public economy. The pattern of modes of production has varied considerably according to the degree of industrialization, the scheme of land tenure and forms of agricultural organization, the strength of the cooperative movement, and the penchant for nationalization. Prosperity and economic growth have pursued an uneven course among the advanced Western countries and that has left an imprint on the economic systems that have emerged. The influence of social democracy and related currents of progressive political action has been strong throughout the epoch. In several countries, notably Scandinavia and intermittently in France, West Germany, and Great Britain, social democracy has been politically triumphant and in a position to make progress in carrying out its political ideals including measures of nationalization, diluted schemes of economic planning, and wealth and income redistribution. Elsewhere and especially in the homeland of the mixed economy, the United States, social democracy has been a minor current of public policy.

While in recent years the direct imprint of American hegemony has been dissolved by economic growth outside the United States, in one significant respect that imprint is still maintained, namely use of the American dollar as an international money and for many purposes as the controlling form of domestic money within the Western world. The dominant position of the dollar has survived the fall of the gold standard and the demonetization of gold, 1971–1978 (Gottlieb 1984, 324). In a very significant way this has linked the economic metabolism of the Western world closely to the American economy, to its dominating urges and at times to its tantrums.

Decolonization

One significant feature of the mixed economy was that it became virtually stripped of colonial possessions that had been built up in the mercantilist and capitalist epochs. Decolonization had commenced in the eighteenth and nineteenth centuries. The American Revolution established the United States as an independent country in 1776–1783; the Latin American revolutions freed mainland American colonies from outside control. Great Britain later in the century established Canada, South Africa, Australia, and New Zealand as virtually independent states. But from then on progress in decolonization was slow and, as is well known, colonization became accelerated as choice areas in Asia and Africa were apportioned out. In his new version of Marx's Communist Manifesto, Lenin, the Russian revolutionary leader, was able in 1917 to portray colonialism and the struggle for colonies as a constituent feature of the "highest stage of capitalism" by which the advanced industrial nations were able to subjugate, manage, and exploit by the power of state control the population of the less developed areas of the world governed as colonies (see Chap. 5).

The dynamics of time itself tended to undermine colonial regimes since aspiration for self-government was stimulated by the development of colonial resources to make them available for Western use. Thus facilities for education so badly needed to fit young colonials for service as junior managers, clerks, administrators, and also as skilled producers brought into existence a stratum of intelligentsia touched by Western democratic and socialist ideas of self-government. Colonial landowners and businessmen appreciated the business opportunities created by colonialism but aspired to a national state that would promote their specific national interests. The railway network facilitating the movement of occupying troops and carrying bulk export produce out of the country helped to rub out provincial, racial, and caste feelings inherited from earlier centuries and laid the groundwork for the emergence of a new national consciousness. Hence sooner or later a nationalist movement sprang up in nearly all colonized areas continuing in some cases the resistance that initially greeted colonial takeovers. These movements usually sought by novel methods to agitate and educate people for the task of national liberation. These methods included organization of trade unions and peasant committees or cooperatives, the establishment of schools and study centers, the publication of newspapers, magazines and books and the formation of representative bodies or councils embodying a proposed national leadership.

These nationalist movements were many-sided, drawing disproportionately from the young, the more adventurous, and the less traditionally oriented of the old dispossessed ruling classes or intellectual elite strata who had access to education and the resources needed to carry on political activity. Where a tradition of peasant and popular resistance to despotic authority was deep rooted, as in China, the nationalist movement could veer off in the communist direction and seek both national liberation and domestic social revolution. More typically the movements would reflect the needs and aspirations of the rising middle classes of the colonies. While freely using the rhetoric of social revolt as in nineteenth century Ireland, these movements rarely transcended the class interests of the dominant possessing groups in the prevailing modes of production. That was especially true of the national liberation movements of South and Central America, which in the nineteenth century established classical property-owners' republics, often giving dictatorial power to a small class of landowners operating vast estates manned by peons. In the twentieth century the national liberation movements in the Arab world, in Africa, and in Southeast Asia followed the same pattern except where imperial power resisted change and forced the national liberation movement to resort to underground guerilla warfare as in the Caribbean region, Portuguese Africa, Algeria, and Vietnam.[6] The need to fight for national independence threw the leadership of the national movement into the hands of the most devoted, courageous, and militant nationalists who had generally to scrap their upper-class style of living and recruit followers from rebel workers and peasants who could adapt to a rough living style and survival tactics. These soldiers of revolt often became soldiers of revolution, the more readily since they would dominate the state power they were bringing into existence.

Under very favorable circumstances some colonial peoples, such as the Philippine people, were able to persuade their imperial rulers that they could establish a stable government on their own and their plea for national independence was acceded to. The colonizing country, the United States, had other favored sources of supply for the raw produce of the Philippines, chiefly sugar and pineapple, and the American national tradition did not favor outright imperial control (Spykman 1942, 139). But that was the exception and it required the explosion of World War II to loosen the reins of imperial control generally. The fate of war decided the outcome for Japanese and Italian colonial possessions. English imperial control had become untenable in India, whose dominant nationalist elites were in sympathy with the anti-fascist war but who sat out the war in prison camps because they could no longer stomach the dictatorial methods of colonial rule.[7] Since rule by martial law in peacetime was unpalatable to the British in their weakened condition, they bowed to the inevitable and in 1947 reluctantly undertook to withdraw from India though not before leaving relationships and institutions favorable to their cause. The French and Dutch resisted decolonization in Southeast Asia and in Algeria but by the midfifties conceded the inability to continue colonialism by the old means, especially since American principles favored some form of decolonization and Soviet funds and arms were readily available all over the world to nationalist movements willing to fight for liberation. The Portuguese held out until 1974–1975 when the African nationalist movement, led by its most militant sections, drove out the Portuguese whose will to power was broken in 1974 by revolution at home. The main colonial powers – the British and French – readily acceded to decolonization even of small island territories once they relinquished control of the major colonial possessions in India, Burma, Indo-China, and Algeria. A major theater of violent struggle is in the Caribbean and Central America where American hegemony is challenged by widespread popular insurgency which has established a secure base of power in Cuba (Pacca 1984; Chomsky 1985). A second theater is in southern Africa where a historic confrontation is being staged between an entrenched militant white settler society using violent means to unsettle and harass adjoining developing black peoples and a submerged African proletariat at home. Apart from South African settler society and the United States, the mixed economy as a form of economic system is distinguished from its forebears by a quite complete disestablishment of colonial empire. Decolonization proceeded vigorously throughout the entire quarter century under review – the epoch of the mixed economy – so that by the end of the epoch most of the 152 members of the United Nations (1980) are former colonial territories with self-governing status.

Decolonization is a complex process whose final forms are not yet clearly evident. Where a settler class made up chiefly of civil servants, plantation or estate owners, and professionals and business men had become well established as was typical in many African and Asiatic colonies, a departing metropolitan government would tend to settle authority on a local magistracy drawn from the settler community, older traditional ruling elites, native merchants who have allied themselves with foreign business interests (comprador class), and native landowners or landlords and others associated with colonial administration. These regimes would tend to be unstable where government was nondictatorial. Under conditions of an open society and mass suffrage political power would readily shift after a coup or civil war to parties and groups more responsive to mass interests and attitudes.[8] Even where an extended revolutionary struggle had prepared the way for a more complete eradication of imperial influence and had driven off most of the settler and comprador community, the interests of the emancipated colonial people would then depend upon the real activities, the developed industries, and the needs of the larger populations with new urban centers that frequently emerged from the colonial experience with hopes for modernization and higher living standards, both calling for importation of Western technology and capital resources. To scold these postcolonial regimes for still being concerned with "ground-nut harvests, with the cocoa crop and the olive yield" or with tea output or tourist revenues from animal parks and coral seashores is to reproach them for making use of the resources they have rather than imaginary resources they hope to get.[9] Some postcolonial regimes have developed native elites shaping a class solidarity with the white settlers.[10]

By 1980 I believe an authentic decolonization throughout the Western world has been in process even though the struggle for national liberation still continues and expectations of many nationalist revolutionaries are unfulfilled. More than "outward trappings of political independence" are involved (Vakhrushev 1973, 47). It is no longer possible to define advanced Western economic systems as resting in any fundamental sense on mobilization and exploitation of colonial peoples as was the case during the mercantilist and capitalist epochs.

Modal Complex

Six distinctive features characterize the modal complex of the mixed economy. In the first place the scope for certain modes of production that played so prominent a role in the nineteenth-century capitalist system—the village community with shared land tenure and open fields and pastures, the peonized plantation or estate and landlord tenant farming—is greatly scaled down. These modes have become archaic and either survive in attenuated form, rapidly diminishing, or they have completely disappeared by the 1960s, in the OECD countries. The parasitic scheme of landlord-tenant farming that was a centerpiece in the mid–nineteenth century of British capitalist agriculture in Ireland disappeared even before a national war of liberation, among the first fought with guerrilla methods in our century, drove the British out of most of Ireland and led in 1922 to the independent Irish Republic. The peonized scheme of landlord-tenant farming replacing the slave plantation in the American South finally gave way to a mechanized form of capitalist farming.[11] The black population, thinned out by massive migration to Northern cities, achieved by a remarkable struggle essential civil rights and terminated the most degrading forms of segregation.

A comparable kind of politicosocial emancipation occurred in Europe where remnants of feudal subjection were swept away and suffrage was extended with equality of representation.[12] Even the relative role of landlord-tenant farming is now very attenuated in the Western world since its substantial curtailment in the final decades of British rule in Ireland and its virtual liquidation by radical land reform carried out by American military government in Japan seeking to establish a broad base for social democracy in Japanese rural society.[13]

The second major feature of the mixed economy is the dominant position in industry and many urban services of the limited liability quasi-public corporation that as a form of business organization became readily available in the latter decades of the nineteenth century. An earlier presentation of the corporation as a mode of production has set forth a full account of rise to dominance of this mode in the United States, first in its entrepreneurial form dominated by wealthy capitalist magnates but latterly in its matured form as the quasi-public corporation (Gottlieb 1984, 105–28). While corporatization of British capitalist enterprise was slow to get started, it caught on very quickly on the continent where it served as a vehicle for conveying an interest to essential British or French investors. In one of his inspired journalistic flashes Marx (1859) called attention to the "rage of getting rich, . . . of opening new mines, of building new factories, of constructing new railways and above all of investing in and gambling with joint-stock company shares," a "passion of the day" that swept over Western Europe, infecting all classes "from the peasant even to the coronetted prince" (Marx and Engels 1841–1870/1974–1986, 16:161). The idea of the investment bank and of mobilizing savings for industrial investment by a public corporation was rooted in French thought and played a significant role in unleashing the industrial development of France and Germany, 1840–1870 (Cameron 1956, 281). In Europe banking was especially prone to corporatization. By 1913 commercial banking in Great Britain, France, Germany, and smaller European countries was controlled by a handful of nationwide banking chains with hundreds and in some cases thousands of branches.[14] Commercial banks in Germany combined investment and commercial banking functions and hence played a crucial role in shaping the great corporate combines that were landmark features of German industrial history.[15] The Japanese corporate combines had their earliest beginnings in the eighteenth and nineteenth centuries as *Zaibatsu,* family-controlled holding companies of which the largest four alone by 1970 controlled 25 percent of all industrial corporations, 50 percent of all financial, and 32.4 percent of all heavy industry.[16] In leading Western countries, the United States excepted, the formation of corporate combines or unions of enterprises drawn together in syndicates or cartels was until recently unrestrained by law.[17] In the United States antitrust restrictions, except in the field of commercial banking where chain banking was for a long time prohibited, had minimal effect, since relevant antitrust enactments were generally couched in vaporous language, enforced by a federal prosecutor starved of funds and staff, and were adjudicated in unfriendly courts (Hamilton 1940). American restrictions against negotiation of contracts and agreements in restraint of trade did discourage the formation within the American economy of those cartels and syndicates that flourished so widely in Europe and thus promoted in America the formation of the giant corporations. These achieved in the United States many of the purposes for which cartels were formed in Europe.

America's large corporations were hence generally much larger by the 1960s than their confreres of foreign vintage. A simple check of the largest ten nonfinancial corporations in eleven Western economies in 1968 showed that the average American top ten corporations were nearly three times the mean size of the British, six times that of West Germany and Japan, and eight times that of the French (Klein 1973, 80). America also had more than her share in terms of employed labor force or produced GNP of multinational corporations of which 60 percent in 1972 were of American vintage.[18]

A second ground for the lesser role and smaller size of the giant corporation outside the United States may be found in the larger role of public enterprise in the field of local, regional, and municipal utilities; in communication and transportation; power generation and railways; areas which in the USA helped to swell the corporate sector with the hybrid mode, regulated utilities (Gottlieb 1984, 158). Even before World War I the provision of rail and communication services in

Europe and Japan was commonly by public enterprise (Clapham 1928, 340, 363). This tendency to public ownership of utilities gained ground after World War II when in a widespread leftward surge Great Britain and France nationalized leading private utilities including electric power generation, the gas industry, communication services, port facilities. Nationalization went farther in both countries including coal mines, in the United Kingdom the steel industry, and in France the Renault car producing company, the aircraft industry, and the largest banking networks and insurance companies.[19] In Germany and Italy the fascist experience left a diversified heritage of nationalized enterprise, including in West Germany until 1960 the VW automotive company.[20]

Though the corporate sector outside the United States was of smaller size and had less international spread than in the United States, it was just as consequential. Existing measures of market shares held by leading corporations indicate that in comparable industries outside the United States they had larger—not smaller—market shares.[21] As in the United States the corporate sector grew both by a very high rate of profit retention, by generous capital consumption allowances, and by acquisition of capitalist enterprises compensated usually by stock issuance. [22] New stock issues sold in public markets played everywhere an unimportant role, providing less than one-twelfth of all external financing, an amount hardly equal to 1 percent of GNP (Goldsmith 1969, 121). Corporate mergers zoomed in the 1950s and 1960s, building both the multinational and conglomerate types of enterprises and cutting significantly into the capitalist sector.[23] Intermediary financial institutions such as pension funds and mutual investment trusts catering to the smaller investor played a significant but varied role, with the latter institutions chiefly active in the United States and in Great Britain (Goldsmith 1969, 248, 256).

A third major change in the modal complex of the mixed economy arises out of a general tendency for the reduced role of the simple commodity producer. The role of this mode has been undercut since its main occupational base, agriculture and rural society, has in all Western countries progressively shrunk in size, employing a falling fraction of the labor force. This relative decline of employment in agriculture is due to continuous technological progress with improved yields growing out of better seed selection; eradication of insect and fungus pests with new pesticides; and mechanization of plowing, seeding, cultivating, harvesting, and drying operations. In 1972 agriculture only accounted for 6.2 percent of domestic gross product in France, 5–8 percent for Scandinavia countries, 5.9 percent in Japan, 4.5 percent in the United States, and between 2.5 to 3 percent for United Kingdom and

West Germany.[24] The fraction of the labor force employed in agriculture, and the rural population it supports, has likewise declined though not to as low a level as contribution to social product. Since agriculture in the form of the family farm or peasant proprietor was the main home of the simple commodity producer generally, the decline of agriculture in the national economy carries with it the decline of that mode. The elimination of the plough animal and cart horse for which the tractor and motor truck are substitutes eliminates the large acreage devoted to growing fodder crops and permits this acreage to be used directly or intermediately for human consumption. Within the shrunken world of agriculture there is probably some increase indicated in the relative role of capitalist farming, always dominant in England though capitalist farming is still relatively minor in the United States.[25]

Almost as consequential as the decline of the simple commodity producer in farming is the decline of small-scale or petty capitalist enterprise in the field of agricultural processing and marketing. Involved here are potato and grain distilleries; vegetable oil extraction facilities; grain elevators and mills for grinding feed for cattle or rural household use; dairy enterprises; farm supply dealers handling fencing, bagging, fertilizers; cheese and butter factories. Commercial agriculture produced small craft and capitalist enterprise to conduct its processing, storage, and procurement operations.[26] Here was one of the major targets of the farmer's cooperative movement intended to enable farmers cooperatively through locally controlled organizations to do bulk-buying of needed farm supplies; to build the processing or assembly stations for specialized dairy products, fruits, vegetables where standardized grading and packing would be needed; to construct the dairy establishments for marketing fresh milk, butter, cream, and other dairy produce; and to construct the grain elevators to handle crop storage or convenient depots for shipment. Farmers' rural cooperation has gone a long way to undermine the small craft enterprise and rural dealer and has given this form of enterprise a much smaller role than it had in the nineteenth century (Gottlieb 1984, 139 ff).

A decline of the rural base of the simple commodity producer is complemented by a decline in his urban base by way of substitution of capitalist manufacture for craft services. The principal craft producers of a bygone capitalist era were the milliners, seamstresses, tailors, and shoemakers who produced our wearing apparel and shoes usually made to order to fit the needs of the individual customer. The blacksmiths and saddlers were indispensable in preparing and installing the horseshoes and leather harness for draft animals pulling wagons, carts, ploughs, or sleighs. Many of these simple commodity producers were drawn in the capitalist heyday to work for merchants. But most of these producers were still independent in the United States and United Kingdom between 1850 and 1870 and they survived more readily on the Continent and in Japan. By the era of the matured mixed economy they had largely disappeared and had been replaced by factories making ready-to-wear apparel and shoes of the range of sizes and shapes now selected by the consumer in a clothing or shoe store. The blacksmith has nearly disappeared along with the independent milliner, tailor, or seamstress making clothes now only for a small number of eccentric well-to-do customers who believe they cannot be well fitted by the factory-made product. The druggist now does not make the drug capsules or powders from the basic medicinal supplies procured in bulk. He has become merely a retailer and repackager of drugs manufactured in large factories or laboratories. While the small bakery survives for pastries and fine breads, the individual baker has largely been superseded by the large-scale capitalist bakery or corporate baking chain. In the same way only a small fraction of cattle and hogs and marketed poultry are now butchered by the local butcher or in a public abattoir that in the United States and elsewhere have been increasingly replaced by the capitalist or corporate meat factory (*Encyclopedia of Social Sciences* 1930–1934, 10:247). So also the small local dairy enterprise has often given way to the large sanitized capitalist or corporate dairy chain. Capitalist and corporate production create a supplementary need for local craft shops to handle and repair the domestic machinery now employed by the average household for transportation, house cleaning, water heating, home heating, refrigeration, cooking, air-conditioning, television, and the like. And with higher standards of living there is more call for small local enterprise to function as recreation establishments, pool halls, beauty shops, house repair and maintenance. But it is doubtful if the production functions lost to capitalist and corporate enterprise have been offset by the new activities gained in repair and consumer service.

An even more distinct loss for the simple commodity producer may be found in the shrinking role for the independent retail dealer who was, in the capitalist era, a main supply base of the urban simple commodity producer. The retail dealer found his place increasingly superseded by the capitalist department store (first established in France) or mail-order or chain stores and these in turn were soon in the twentieth century organized in regional and then nationwide chains. In the United States, the department store handles about 10 percent of all retail sales and multiunit chains some 44 percent. The scope for the small shopkeeper with less than four employees is shrunk to some 13.7 percent of all retail sales (U.S. Bureau of Census 1979, 833). And a good portion of these sales are found in gasoline service stations dependent upon integrated oil corporations for handling franchised supplies on such terms as the corporations find feasible.

Elsewhere in the Western world the mail-order or corporate-chain network is less powerful than in the United States though in recent decades the capitalist chain store has moved into high gear in Western Europe. And as formidable as the capitalist or corporate retailer is the cooperative store that plays a major role in Great Britain and in the Scandinavian countries. The cooperative trading movement has reached probably its outer limits of growth in Great Britain where it has achieved 10 percent of all retail sales (Gottlieb 1984, 136). Small retail shops in Japan have a somewhat larger role, accounting for over a third of all manpower employed in retail and wholesale trade, though capitalist and corporate enterprises in commerce clearly predominate.[27]

The growth of the corporate and decline of the simple commodity producer modes is complemented by the rise of the public mode. At the core of this is found a truly massive rise in the investment of resources in schooling. Schooling expenditures dominate government budgets in all Western countries except the United States where military expenditures have the ranking role. As a fraction of GNP in 1972–1976, public expenditure on education in OECD countries varies between 5 and 9 percent with peak expenditures in the Netherlands and Denmark and the lowest fraction in Italy (U.S. Bureau of Census 1979, 891, 161, 167). Education is provided almost entirely through the secondary level at public expense. Public support for higher education is an American specialty and has been carried a long way. The value of plant and grounds of institutions of higher learning so-called in United States in 1975 was $62 billion and in the aggregate 44 percent of all expenses were met with public funds. In nearly all major cities public institutions of higher education were available to qualified youth who seek it at minimal current expense. The contrast is striking with the capitalist economy where public education was grudgingly extended for a few years at the elementary level to a fraction of school youth taught at best to learn to read, write, and figure.

Rivaling education for governmental support is provisionment for transportation and its facilities in all its dimensions: urban and local roads to permit free and easy personal travel within and between urban communities; navigational facilities, traffic control arrangements, and airports for air travel now becoming the dominant mode of long-distance travel; improved waterway facilities on navigable or man-made waterways in most regions still optimal for bulk cargo. The increase in urban population in the Western world has called for a vast rise in public transportation facilities and transit fare subsidies financed on government budgets. Expenditures, both current and capital, are on a much smaller scale than for education, amounting in the United States in 1970 to 11.6 percent of all tax revenue or to 2.75 percent of GNP, that is, to little more than half the scale of education (U.S. Bureau of Census 1979, 284, 286, 307).

Competing strongly with transportation and education is the traditional field of defense that maintains a constant state of readiness for war with defense facilities, armed forces, an elaborate armament industry, information-detection systems, monitoring systems, and military capabilities on four levels: in water, in air, on ground, and in space. The need for an active national defense within the Western world has certainly fallen since World War II led to a kind of internal Western unification achieved under American hegemony based on the subjugation of the two most powerful dissenting Western nations, Germany and Japan. The Soviet Union survived the war, damaged, but with its armed forces spread over an immense territory in Asia, the Balkans, along the Danube, and eastern and central Europe. Along with the Soviet army came its political methods, its commissars, and the local communists who with their local allies organized the quisling governments in the war-torn territories to provide public services by which life was maintained, food rationed, and industrial production started up. Independent communist-led revolutions in Yugoslavia and mainland China and later on in Cuba, Vietnam, and elsewhere augmented the field of communist power and the threat this seemed to portend for the Western world: a vast expansion of the territory and population controlled by communist power and ideology reaching right into Germany, a core country of Western Europe.

This was the setting for the Cold War by which the Western world under American leadership undertook to mobilize its resources for a high state of military readiness to inhibit or resist further expansion of communist-controlled governments, to further develop the awesome power of atomic weapons, and to roll back Soviet power in eastern and central Europe or in Korea by all possible means short of outright war. The state of Cold War gradually emerged through a succession of crises from Iran in 1945–1946, Greece-Turkey 1947–1948, Berlin 1948–1949, and the first overt East-West armed conflict in Korea 1951–1953, which gave rise to the first major mobilization of American armed forces without a formal declaration of war. The development in the 1950s by the Soviets of a successful technology of atomic weapons production and as well of the means of their delivery by submarine, guided missiles, or long-distance bombers stepped up the pace of armament expenditure by both East and West. The competition puts the greatest strain on the two superpowers who bear the largest burden of military expenditure and production of strategic weapons and their costly delivery systems and technologies of strategic defense. Military expenditures per capita for 1975 and 1982, narrowly defined, were $659 and $798 for the United States, 5.8 percent and 6.4 of her GNP, and for selected Western countries much smaller amounts (see Table 6.1).

If the full cost of atomic weaponry and its means of production in uranium plants, so-called space exploration involving search for technologies of space warfare, military assistance to allied or friendly countries — if all these were counted as military expenditures, then the relative burden of armaments upon the American economy would be greater. The relative freedom of Japan from the burden of armaments and the lesser burden borne by American's leading West European allies — West Germany, France, and the United Kingdom — are part of the reason why the standard of living of Japanese and West European populations has risen in the postwar period at a much faster rate than the American standard of living and why the rate of accumulation or of capital formation is so high as compared with the United States.

Only brief comments are needed on the relative role of two modes of production whose economic positions were variously affected by hectic change. In the advanced Western world the cooperative thrived in agriculture where it cut into both capitalist and craft enterprise and helped to maintain the family farm as the primary production unit. In

TABLE 6.1. Military expenditures in selected Western countries per capita, 1975 and 1982, and as percent of GNP (1981 dollars)

| | Military expenditures per capita | | | | | |
| | In $[a] | | As % USA | | As % GNP PC | |
Country	1975	1982	1975	1982	1975	1982
United States	659	798	. . .	. . .	5.8	6.4
Belgium	266	334	40.3	41.8	3.0	3.4
Canada	193	235	29.2	29.4	1.9	2.2
France	352	444	53.4	55.6	3.8	4.2
West Germany	338	372	51.2	46.6	3.6	3.4
Italy	128	163	19.4	20.4	2.5	2.6
Japan	69	96	10.4	12.0	0.9	1.0
Netherlands	293	313	44.4	39.2	3.2	3.3
Scandinavia[b]	342	383	51.8	47.9	3.0	3.0
United Kingdom	411	461	62.3	57.7	4.9	5.1

Source: U.S. Bureau of Census, *Statistical Abstract of the United States*, 1985, 866.

Note: The comparative level of military expenditures will necessarily be affected by domestic military expenditures and by the exchange rate.

[a]Military expenditures are stated in dollars obtained for other countries than United States by computing the same in local currency and then converting to dollars at an internationally acceptable exchange rate for the year.

[b]The entry for Scandinavia is the arithmetic average for Denmark, Norway, and Sweden.

urban communities in the Western world the cooperative thrived mainly in the United Kingdom and in Western Europe. The capitalist mode gained by replacing craft or service producers or by taking over functions and activities formerly performed within the home, including food preparation, recreation, and care of the aged. On the other hand capitalist producers as soon as they matured as enterprises and gained size and stability were increasingly gathered into the corporate network either by purchase or exchange of stock.

The relative make up of the modal complex varies widely in the national members of the mixed economy. The capitalist and corporate sector together probably predominate in all, and within this sector the corporate clearly is uppermost. Looming far behind the capitalist and corporate sector is the simple commodity producer in agriculture, retail trade, and urban services, still potent especially where agriculture as in the United States, Japan, or in continental Europe is still important. Not far behind the latter mode is the public mode swollen by Cold War and by the vast educational responsibilities now undertaken by the state to prepare the entire population for the development of personal skills, endowments, and capabilities. The task of detailing the precise balance of modes in the individual Western mixed economies must be left to later monographic research.

Dichotomization

The major dichotomization in the mixed economy is probably created by the significant militarist corporate orientation of the American economy. The militarist bias arises because of the heavy concentration of public resources and foreign policy on military readiness and power, reinforced by the large role armament production in its "high technology" forms plays as an underlying support of American foreign trade. Military sales are, apart from agricultural surpluses, one of the categories of commodity exports in which American producers dominate Western markets. Military sales agreements publicly exposed in 1970–1978 ran to some $73 billion even though export sales are carefully screened to tie in with foreign policy. Military production is not generally directly in the public mode but is organized through a hybrid distinctively American mode—the "corporate-industrial-military complex" employing altogether some 4.6 million persons in the later 1970s (earlier, 18). Much of the initiative and driving force in this complex is played by armament producers who manage design, research, and sales promotion. In the United States, too, public utilities are privately operated thus swelling the corporate sector. Elsewhere the public mode is much more civilian and welfare-oriented in its make up, generally includes all the public utilities that are the core of the public sector, and has a minimal orientation to armaments especially limited by international agreement and constitutional prescription in the two major industrial Western powers of Japan and West Germany. Nationalization has carried the public sector into important fields of industry and banking—noteworthily in the United Kingdom and in France. Hence the mixed economy can be dichotomized between an American model with its primary penchant toward a militarized public sector based on a hybrid public utility and armament industry and a social-democratic model, pointing in the direction of another kind of society and economy.[28]

Both variants of the Western modal complex share three overriding characteristics. The first is the strong tendency to modify and revolutionize the mode of production by the systematic development of natural science in basic research and by cultivation in special laboratories of the arts of applying scientific knowledge to the improvement of methods of production and to the discovery or invention of new materials or new ways of using old materials. Modern science was utilized in the matured capitalist mode of production in the capitalist era based upon the discovery of the steam engine and of widespread use of iron in the construction of machines and mastery of the applied science of mechanics. But the key inventions of the capitalist mode of production were not spawned in laboratories. They were largely the improvisation of restless entrepreneurs tinkering and searching for improved ways of making or doing something, using in each case the materials that were at hand and the mechanical devices available and mostly combining these in different ways. The machine technology could be utilized and even improved by persons ignorant of the advanced principles of physics, chemistry or astronomy.[29] Hence most of the materials used in the capitalist era were traditional materials—cotton, iron, wool, coal, timber—in their natural forms. The great machines of the capitalist era—the spinning jenny, the power loom—are a more or less altered mechanical edition of the old handicraft tool. They have working parts that "are old acquaintances as spindles in a mule, needles in a stocking loom, saws in a sawing machine, knives in a chopping machine." Looking at the machines that made machines, Marx (1863–1878/1967, 373, 385) found "the manual implements re-appearing on a cyclopean scale," a boring machine being nothing but an immense drill operated by a steam engine, a steam-hammer an ordinary hammer head "but of such a weight that not Thor himself could wield it." The persistent struggle by ironmasters for improved methods of making steel with the use of coal derivatives proceeded by trial-and-error methods culminating in the Bessemer process found shortly after its discovery to be inapplicable to a whole range of ores (Rosenberg 1972, 121). The unfitness of the capitalist entrepreneur of the nineteenth century for using science to solve problems of industrial technology was interestingly disclosed by the complete frustration of the wealthy capitalist oligarchs of the oil refining industry in the young Standard Oil Trust when they moved from high-grade Pennsylvania oils to which their refining plants and procedures were adjusted to sulphurous Ohio Lima crude oils. None of these men who had grown rich by refining and marketing oil products could cope with the problem nor did they employ chemists with sufficient mastery of the young science to be of help. It was necessary to draw on a professional German chemist who after much laboratory experimentation developed a process of refining that separated sulphur from refinery products.[30]

German industry in the late nineteenth century was the first to draw extensively on academic training and laboratory research. These were especially applied to the newer industries of electrical and chemical engineering where, as Alfred Marshall (1919, 121, 133) put it, "mother wit counts for much but only on condition that it is equipped with thorough training and high-class laboratories." He observed that "Germany's zeal for solid education" laid "the foundation for her industrial progress." The British woke up to the backwardness of British industry during World War I when British industry was cut off from supplies of engineering and chemical products produced only in Germany. Hence legislation was shaped to establish a network of research institutes, cooperatively supported both by a government fund of £1 million and subscriptions from industry for the promotion of scientific and industrial research. Some twenty-six research associations were organized in the major industries. Though much progress was made, British backwardness in applying modern science to industrial research in the 1920s is indicated by the fact that total expenditures raised by industrial subscriptions were only at the rate in the early 1920s of barely £5000 per year. American expenditures for industrial research by trade associations and leading corporations amounted then to $75 million annually (Great Britain, Balfour Report 1927, 305–34).

The first American industrial laboratory dated only from 1880, and by 1900 only two major laboratories functioned.[31] They became common by World War I among the large industrial corporations dealing with electronic or chemical process. By 1920 some 526 industrial research laboratories were identified, operating either under auspices of trade associations, government bureaus, or large corporations; total research and development expenditures are estimated at $116 million.[32] By 1938 nearly 1800 concerns reported research departments employing altogether some 44,000 persons, mostly in relatively large corporations with large individual staffs (Perazich 1940, 9). The real takeoff of industrial development of laboratory science, now spawned and subsidized in universities on a large scale as well as in government and military laboratories, was during World War II, which witnessed all over the world a mobilization of science for war purposes.[33] Thereafter a vast infusion of scientific research into industry occurred, focused largely on war-related purposes but with significant spillovers for the civilian economy. The total number of R and D scientists and engineers employed in this effort was by 1954 some 237,000, and it more than doubled in the next quarter century with about two-thirds of the personnel employed in industry. Research and development expenditures by government in constant dollars in 1955 were 10.1 billion and tripled in the next quarter-century while industry with its own funds spent in 1970 $10 billion and by the end of the decade nearly twice that much (U.S. Census Bureau 1979, 623).

This infusion of science into the economy, though it concentrated on the development of war-related technology, was widely distributed in all fields of activity. It played a role in business administration where the scientific method was used in product research, quality control, production scheduling, marketing research, and management of workrooms and industrial operations. It played a massive role in facilitating and simplifying all record keeping and message communication permitting the rapid deployment of information and its analysis and tabulation in standardized form. It entered into banking where account keeping and fund transfer was greatly facilitated. It affected agriculture by developing new and more fertile seed strains (like hybrid corn), developing pesticides to destroy insects and organisms preying upon our cultivated plants and trees, designing equipment to carry on various agricultural operations, and designing livestock food mixes to provide high-grade nutrition at lower cost. In industry, it made available what Landes (1969, 514) quite aptly described as a "stunning array of new products and techniques." Plastics and synthetics have cut deeply into the market of vegetable and animal fibers, skins, or furs to provide our basic textiles and now provide many of our needs for building, packaging, and structural materials and containers. The computer has greatly extended the scope of research and has transformed communication. The science of medicine has been transformed by the new antibiotics spawned by the laboratory and by the miracle drugs that have helped the victims of a large number of degenerative diseases such as TB, Parkinsonism, and polio. The use of radioactive liquids which after injection permit internal photography of the organs and tissues of the human body has revolutionized medical diagnosis. A new technology has transformed life in the household by greatly reducing the time and effort needed to keep houses clean and comfortable, to do home laundry, or to store and prepare foodstuffs. This new technology has not only multiplied the number of basic discoveries and inventions but has greatly shortened the time for their industrial application and development into working technology. That time-span by one measure fell from thirty-seven years in 1885–1919 to twenty-four years in 1920–1939 to but fourteen years in the post–1946 period (Landes 1969, 519). Ways of working, ways of living, ways of communicating and computing, ways of playing, and even ways of having sex have been transformed by the scientific revolution, which through modern industry has entered into the life and soul of modern man. I thus agree with Simon Kuznets (1966, 9) in his wide generalization that the "epochal invention that distinguished the modern economic epoch is the extended application of science to problems of economic production."

It is unfortunate that little of the transformative effect of the massive application of science to production central to the modern mixed economy shows up in our defective statistical measures of aggregate industrial and service output. The design of these measures focuses attention on the changed quantities of the known and familiar but allows for only a small fraction of the transformative effects of innovation and invention. Hence our long-term production functions are biased in that they magnify the effect of the measured inputs like labor and capital and slight the unmeasurable effects of changed technology. Hence also in the recent decades of the mixed economy the biased statistical measure of productivity about which there has been some misplaced concern.[34]

The second distinguishing characteristic of the whole complex of the modes of production in the mixed economy is the shift in the character of the labor force at work in all medium or large-scale organizations whether in corporations, capitalist enterprises, schools, government offices or armies. The share of workers who are professional or technical or who function in administrative or clerical positions as "white collar" workers rises relative to the manual worker. In the early stages of this shift in the mixed economy for industry the fraction of administrative to production employees in industry for various Western countries around 1900 ranged from 6 to 11.8 percent. That fraction rose by 1925–1929 to 9.9–17 percent and by 1947–1948 to 20–21.6 percent (Bendix 1974, 214). In the United States by 1957 one-third of the total industrial payroll went to nonmanual workers; in West Germany by 1957 that ratio had risen to 30 percent and a similar rapid rise was indicated for Great Britain. Taking into account not only industry but employment in commerce, finance, agriculture, transportation and public utilities, "the number of non-manual workers in the industrial countries is approaching that of manual workers," a "fact of great political importance" (Varga 1961, 134). Of course such global aggregates based to a degree on dress or appearance are deceptive since we count as nonmanual workers an army of persons working in offices as bound to routine and mechanical repetition and limited discretion as many manual workers among whom are included operatives exercising considerable skill and artistry in their work (Braverman 1974, Chap. 15, 16). If we take merely the managerial strata of so-called "professional, technical and kindred workers" along with "managers and officials" and exclude from our consideration clerical, sales, and kindred workers, we then derive the following shift from 1900 to 1979 as fractions of the employed labor force in the United States (see Table 6.2).

TABLE 6.2. Selected white-collar classes, 1900–1979 as percentage of employed labor force, United States

Employed labor force	1900	1960	1970	1979
Professional, technical and kindred workers	5.7	11.4	14.2	15.9
Managers and officials	0.8	10.7	10.5	10.8

Source: Kuznets 1966, 192; U.S. Bureau of Census, *Statistical Abstract*, 1979, 415.
Note: Their work is supported by the army of clerical and kindred occupations, which as a fraction of employees of all kinds rose from 4.0 percent in 1900 to 18.3 percent in 1979.

That shift reflects the application of modern science to production; the rise of large-scale organization multiplying layers of management; and the professionalization of business management calling for detailed record keeping, statistical tabulation, and analysis to detect unfavorable trends to adapt policy guidance to continually changing conditions. Professionalization of management applies to administrative behavior in many places: government offices, schools, research laboratories, factories, mines, assembly plants, tax audit bureaus, hospitals and nursing homes. Hence the emergence of new sciences or quasi-sciences dealing with "administrative behavior" or devoted strictly to the work of "management" per se whether in the U.S. military organizations, in churches, in corporations, or in government bureaus. In many respects that shift in employment reduces to a rise in what German-schooled sociologists following Max Weber label "bureaucratization" (Bendix 1974, 211).

Democratization of Work

The third distinctive characteristic of all the modern modes of production calling for any form of associated labor is the widespread democratization of enterprise by the growth of labor organization developed by working people drawn into local trade unions. These are drawn together into regional and national and international organizations. Unions had their origin in the traditions of the self-acting guild association inherited from the medieval town culture of Western Europe. It was in this tradition that workmen in the same field of labor banded themselves together to deal with their capitalist employers as a group to resist the despotic power of capital against which a single worker was nearly helpless. The ability to quit a job and work for another employer who offered better terms would help to ameliorate the worst conditions of work. But few breadwinners with a family to support would take on the risk of quitting an existing job and looking for improved conditions of work and pay except in very good times with abundant job openings. Workers could have a say in determining the conditions and pay of their employment chiefly by banding together and speaking with one voice, realizing the social power of their numbers. Persecuted by law and bitterly opposed by middle-class society and by capitalist employers, the first unions had a hard time getting established and keeping their organization and unity intact.[35] Unions would spring up usually to counter some provocation of the employers. Because the savings and resources of the men are scanty, as Adam Smith noted (1776/1937, 67), they were forced to bring their conflicts to a "speedy decision." Hence they have "recourse to the loudest clamour and sometimes to the most shocking violence and outrage" for the purpose of course of preventing other men or women from taking their jobs. As Smith noted a bit sadly: "The workmen . . . very seldom derive any advantage from the violence of those tumultuous combinations which, partly from the interposition of the civil magistrate, partly from the superior steadiness of the masters, partly from the necessity which the greater part of the workmen are under of submitting for the sake of present subsistence, generally end in nothing but the punishment or ruin of ring-leaders."

If workmen widened the scope of their combination from the employees of a single employer to all the employees of a given trade, they would of course have a better chance at closing down any one plant or all the plants functioning in the area. But it was not easy to build an association of workmen by conspiratorial methods and secret meetings on such a large scale and to keep the loyalty of individual workmen while maintaining iron discipline and strong leadership with endless patience, infinite devotion, and steady purpose. Employers in the same field learned to counter these larger associations and to nip them in the bud by firing troublemakers and by banding together to give mutual support in their class battles, sometimes by arranging for the importation of strikebreakers from distant labor markets or even from other countries. Smith (1776/1937, 66) also noted the frequency and ease with which employers could combine, their numbers being fewer and their purposes more widely shared.

So difficult was the task of labor organization under these circumstances in the early nineteenth century that it was only rarely attempted in the newer factories employing large numbers of workers in close quarters largely because most of these workers were women or juveniles who would not undertake the difficult problems of association and organization and who could hardly undertake to stand up to their tough-minded employers. In Marx's day only the first toeholds of union organization were built, chiefly by skilled workmen with pride of craft. Few of them could pursue a national purpose and achieve combination on a scale that would embrace the entire industry and thus raise wages or improve working conditions in a way that would not injure any particular employer or group of employers and thus impair their ability effectively to compete in a national market. In fields of strictly local service such as the building or printing trades or local transportation, union power could be deployed effectively and as such it played a role in Marx's day, especially in England where the conspiracy laws against labor associations were partially lifted. But given its limitations, Marx and Engels held that unionism was powerless generally to do more than serve as "centers of resistance against the encroachments of capital," perhaps able to "retard the downward movements (of wages) but not change its directions," an excellent school for class organization but not by itself capable of changing conditions for most workmen. Even in England where Marx felt workers had by their class struggle and organization built up trade unions "of a certain degree of maturity and universality," these unions were an "aristocratic minority" to which "poor working people could not belong" and which could not organize the "great mass of workers" who are daily "driven from the villages into the cities." Hence it was that in his *Das Kapital* no role is allowed in the capitalist mode of production for the trade union to which Marx was personally sympathetic and with whose leaders he had some personal and political association, though an important place was allowed for factory regulation by the state.[36]

On many subjects Marx had a prophetic eye but not for the transformative power of labor organization and its ability to win over and organize the mass of wage earners. Yet that did occur, induced by the steady pressure of union organizers, the more favorable views of the general public, the lessened resistance of employers overwhelmed by the disaster of war, the decrees of governments seeking the support of organized labor, and finally the increased maturity and greater solidarity of the working class. Even so, only in Sweden is now virtually the entire body of wage and salary earners organized in trade unions (Klein 1973, 113). Among other Western countries the fraction of wage and salary earners in nonagricultural pursuits organized in trade unions ranges between 30 and 55 percent (Klein 1973, 110–15). But the authority and influence of labor organization radiates in these countries far beyond the scope of formal organization. Many employers and whole industries to deter unionization have made a practice of paying wages and establishing working conditions as favorable as or better than those won by unions. In industries where manual workers are organized and white collar or office workers are not organized, management commonly gave wage increases or nonwage benefits for their salaried employees on as liberal a scale as they have given for their organized employees.[37] Unionization is making definite inroads on the salaried worker class in white collar callings such as teaching, service institutions like hospitals and nursing homes, and branches of public service that have been traditionally nonunionist in their outlook. The principle adopted in the United States of allowing the determination of unionization to be made by secret ballot of the employees has facilitated the drive to unionization and reduced prolonged conflict over the issue of union recognition.

Over the years unions have matured. They gradually moved away from the rebellious creeds and the revolutionary attitudes that marked their origins and settled down to the prosaic business of slowly but steadily improving labor's share and stake in the economy (Perlman 1928). They have matured too in an organizational sense. They have evolved with employers a consensus on criteria that should guide collective bargaining. They have worked out techniques of grievance procedure to settle workshop hassles and controversies steadily arising. They have learned how to develop collective bargaining agreements covering many subjects beyond wages and hours: supplemental pay, vacations, union security, management security, and contract administration. They have developed within unions a form of democratic government by which adequate centralized authority can be built up on a national basis with sufficient control by members in their union locals with their elected officers. National referenda help to avoid excessive concentration of authority at the top. They have on the whole learned to accept and work with the institutions of a mixed economy and turn these to labor's advantage.

With maturity has come organizational strength. They have built up relatively enormous treasuries to finance membership growth, educational and propaganda activity, and such industrial conflict as may break out. They have evolved tribunals to adjudicate intraunion controversies where two or more unions are active in the same field of industry or trade. They have at their national levels built up technical staffs of great competence in the fields of economic research, industrial relationships, labor law. At the local and regional level they have learned to replace the volunteer officer with the paid full-time officer fairly compensated.[38]

The effect of unions on the mode of production and the way it operates has been profound. They have had revolutionary effects especially in the United States on the form of compensation, bringing about a larger share of compensation that is deferred partly in the form of retirement benefits, more frequent holidays or increased vacation time or sick leave provisions so that time off for sickness does not cause financial disaster. They have revolutionized industrial relations on the job, in the workroom, in the factory by providing new forms of job security, by opening up new channels by which worker protests or grievances may be ventilated and resolved, and they have carved out certain principles of tenure once a probationary period is completed (Gardner and Moore 1952, Chap. 8, 9, 15). In Europe especially unions have sought to provide new ways for worker participation in management through work councils or labor representation on directoral boards (Barkin 1969, 49). Finally, in naked economic terms unions have effected a revolution in the macroeconomic process. Wage levels do not decline invariably as in the days of capitalist enterprise during recessions though wage declines will occur under pressure of foreign competition and under circumstances of extended unemployment.[39] This change in macroeconomic process, which as we will see has its presuppositions in an altered and elastic institution of money and the development of price administration in the matured oligopolistic business world of the mixed economy, has invalidated the doctrine developed at great length by Marx fully in accord with all the principles of classical (Ricardian) economics that general changes in prevailing levels of wage rates only induce corresponding changes in prevailing profit levels but cannot alter price levels. If true, this would rule out one of the basic problems of the mixed economy and any tendency toward wage-price spiral.[40]

SOCIAL SECURITY

Redistribution in the mixed economy has a threefold makeup. Its largest sector relates to state programs enforcing a collection and pooling of a fraction of payroll income contributed usually jointly by employee and employer to meet special needs growing out of involuntary unemployment or inability to work. Involuntary unemployment is like a blind force that may strike at will from a wide range of causes: supersession of a craft or skill become outmoded, change of technology that destroys a line of business or the economic basis of a community, changing fashions, war or revolution at home or abroad, loss of patronage by key patrons, the downward turns of the business cycle. A worker may be laid off or terminated by a government agency, by a department of the army or branch of military service, by a local government agency, by a retail store, a clothing factory, a church, a legal firm. Ability to work and command income is also subject to interruption from numerous causes: accidents, illness, crippling effects of chronic disease, and finally the decline of energies of life coming at some stage with old age. Disability may be temporary and partial, it may be creeping like old age that sooner or later immobilizes nearly all.

In the capitalist economy these contingencies of unemployment and disability were met by voluntary saving assisted sometimes by insurance organized by some local friendly association of workmen. Many trade unions gained support from workmen by schemes of social insurance that the unions administered. But the funds made available in this way barely tided over the common short-term contingencies and left the people unprotected from those more severe or chronic in duration. Commercial insurance was available for only a few of these contingencies since mostly they involved uninsurable risks. But even where full insurance was available, as for ordinary death against which most families insured, for workmen the available funds sufficed for little more than the expenses of the funeral and the last illness; the larger the insurance nest egg the more generous the burial arrangements.[41] Borrowing from relatives and close neighbors and credit obtained from the local grocer and landlord might extend resources somewhat. In a few cases of industrial accidents where lawyers for the employees could prove no negligence on the employee side and employer fault, recovery of damage claims could be enforced against the employer. Beyond that there were only local charities or the official aid offered in the local poorhouse with its degrading conditions of life.

The provision of a fabric of social security was first undertaken by the German quasi-feudal ruling class in the late nineteenth century partly out of quest for social peace and partly to mitigate repressive antisocialist police measures not abandoned until 1890. Unlike the factory protection legislation pioneered by the British in the earlier nineteenth century decades (see Chap. 5) these measures were aimed not only at women and juveniles but also at adult male breadwinners treated in other capitalist countries as not needing state support or guidance. The Bismarck Reich first established accident and health insurance in 1883–1884 and in 1885 abolished the barbarous system of letting workers sue in courts to recover costs and damages for injuries suffered in work-related accidents. This was followed by schemes for old-age and disability pensions and finally insurance protection for family dependents and survivors.[42] Slowly other capitalist countries followed suit. The British late in the 1890s adopted workmen's compensation for work-related accidents and in 1911 they pioneered in establishing a comprehensive national scheme of unemployment insurance.[43] The United States was reluctant to follow these leads. A hostile judiciary left the field to state governments always anxious not to deter investment in a state by imposing social requirements in advance of those generally prevailing. Not until the Great Depression had revolutionized conditions in the United States and challenged traditional ways of thinking was a reform administration able to establish the kinds of social security pioneered by the Bismarck Reich a half-century before. Even then the forward step of health and sickness insurance was not attended to until the 1960s and was restricted to retired workers.

Social security is everywhere to some extent financed by a payroll tax on a base level of earnings, leaving higher salaried earnings outside the contributory and benefit system. The payroll tax is generally supplemented with public funds drawn from general revenues, on the lowest scale in the United States, but predominantly in the United Kingdom and Scandinavian countries.[44] The payroll tax is variously shared by employer and employee. The American preference for equal sharing is about as common as the French pattern for predominantly employer sharing or a weaker converse Scandinavian preference for heavier employee sharing.[45]

The economics of the shifting and incidence of the payroll tax has like all matters of taxation been extensively debated (Mieskowski 1969, 1103, 1106). Opinion is nearly unanimous, however, that the portion of the tax nominally shouldered by employees is borne by them. Under existing highly imperfect labor and product markets the ultimate incidence of the employer contributions is unknown. The most likely outcomes in order of probability are: (1) backward shifting to wages, (2) forward shifting to consumers in the form of higher prices and a larger body of nominal incomes, (3) a remote possibility that some fraction of the tax may persistently lower employer profit margins. Since hypothesis (2) of forward shifting reduces to burden sharing by labor, it is not unreasonable to suppose that the bulk of the employer contribution is predominantly shifted to labor. The tax thus generally is a levy on payrolls borne largely by payroll recipients. The form of an employer contribution makes the payroll levy psychologically acceptable and cushions its initial impact.[46]

Though the payroll tax is a regressive levy and was supplemented with little utilization of public funds to finance social security, it was in most countries an indispensable foundation for social security. Only if wage earners paid a good part of the cost would it be possible in most countries for them to receive benefits in later years without subjection to a traditional means test showing that their private resources and savings were inadequate.[47] Resistance to social security without wage-earner financing would have been especially intense from the self-employed simple commodity producers on farms or in shops and stores, with their strong faith in individual effort and self-reliance. Then too, clamor for improved benefits would meet little wage-earner resistance if wage earners did not shoulder an important share of the cost.

Moreover, even if the payroll tax meets the entire cost of social security so that transfer from nonwage incomes can be disregarded, there still would be significant benefits derived from the standard forms of social security because of the widespread inequality in wage and salary earnings. These inequalities are now and always have been much more circumscribed than inequalities in returns in the direct commodity producer mode or among capitalists or property-owning investors in that the range between which the bulk of the incomes are distributed is much narrower (Lydall 1968, 68). But within that range conventional measures of income inequality are quite high. One such measure widely used is the share of aggregate income received by the lowest one-fifth of wage-earning units and the highest one-fifth, ranking all receivers of wage or salary incomes in an array. For the years 1939, 1945, and 1951 in the United States the fractions of all wage and salary income (%) received by these respective quintiles were as follows (Budd 1967, 51):

	1939	1945	1951
Lowest quintile	3.4	2.9	3.0
Highest quintile	49.3	43.9	41.6

A very detailed analysis of a large sample of American households whose 1962 incomes were analyzed showed that the Gini coefficient of concentration (varying between 0 to 1.0, the closer to 1.0 the greater the inequality) was 0.43 for all income including pensions and transfer and 0.52 for all wage and salary income (Soltow 1969, 111).

Unequal distribution of wage and salary incomes arises from a number of factors. There is first the distribution of sociogenetic characteristics—health and body strength, mental ability, and qualities of self discipline—which has presumably a log-normal distribution with a concentration of wage-earner population at the medium bracket but long tails with wide range of variation at both ends. This distribution is of course subject to sociocultural warping due to the effects of inherited wealth, racial discrimination, and variations in the capacity of the family to nourish and nurture and adequately motivate the young worker. This range of human aptitudes and skills is matched with a similar wide range of pay differentials prevailing in different occupations because of varied training costs; greater instability of employment; varied degrees of trust and responsibility exercised; tradition; limited supply of genetic endowments capable of developing skills or talents called for as in expressive, healing, athletic, or teaching arts. Then there is a wide range of variation in the ability of families and individuals to benefit from, seek out, and master educational experiences that provide training and cultural enrichment required for higher-paying occupations. Equal investment in education and job training will always yield, even with uniform abilities, varied income levels due to essentially windfall variations in the prosperity of different industries, vocations, and particular locales impossible to project in advance but giving a wide range of income outcomes and income trajectories over time to different groups in the labor force, producing over a life cycle a wide range of income outcomes.

Unequal earnings arising from these sources will be compounded due to accidental factors like loss of a job in a factory closed by a fire, or a heavy load of illness or bad health or premature retirement due to technological displacement. Other families will enjoy windfall blessing and reap the advantage of both spouses working, yielding a double income, very difficult to achieve in communities with a limited supply of work opportunities for married women seeking to go back to the labor market.[48] Trade unions are believed to have increased earning differentials by creating greater job security for older workers and marked pay advantages for many classes of skilled workers (Mincer 1970, 4). As the share of wage and salary earnings in total household disposable income rises in importance—and it now runs in the mixed economy between two-thirds and three-quarters of total household disposable income—earning inequalities arising from windfalls, accidental factors, genetic imbalance, and socioeconomic capability of investing in education, evidence the need for some form of equalization within the universe of earnings.

This equalization is achieved by scaling social security benefits both to contributions and to social need. The role of need is uppermost in medical insurance where benefits are scaled wholly to need. Need and contribution join together in determining benefits for retirement, disability, survivorship, or unemployment insurance which have nearly everywhere been set with a low minimum benefit for eligible annuitants and rising slowly for higher earning levels up to a relatively low maximum benefit. Benefits are nearly always greater, regardless of contributions, where there is greater need to support dependents. This equalitarian bias is aptly illustrated by the original benefit scheme contemplated for the retirement annuity schedule for qualifying American worker-beneficiaries. The schedule awarded annuities made up of the following fractions of taxed earnings: 1/2 percent of the first $3000, 1/12 percent of the next $42,000, and 1/24 percent of the excess, with a minimum annuity of $10 per month and a maximum of $85 (Douglas 1936, 160). In all its protean modifications the American benefit schedule for our old age and survivorship insurance scheme never lost that pattern of limited graduation of benefit slowly rising from a set fraction of a base bracket of average monthly income with a much lower fraction of additional brackets of income.[49] Adoption in 1939 of survivorship benefits "gave a substantial advantage to the married worker" (Derthick 1979, 134). Since benefits are now usually computed only by taking taxable earnings for the most favorable twenty years of a recent twenty-five-year period, workers who have suffered much unemployment or have been out of the covered work force for an extended period, may qualify for a full set of benefits.[50]

Progressive Taxation

The second major focus of redistribution in the mixed economy grows out of the rise of income and wealth taxation at progressive rates, that is, rates which are higher with greater incomes or larger wealth holdings. Progressive income and wealth taxation was virtually unknown in the classical nineteenth century capitalist economy. The then prevailing mode of taxation in peacetime for national purposes was indirect, favoring excise or customs on goods crossing the frontier or domestically produced and suitable for taxation (see Chap. 5). Local revenues were usually drawn from license fees or occupation taxes on local businesses and various forms of the local property tax applicable chiefly to homes, farms, shops, and business properties, with emphasis on tangible lands, buildings, and inventories. The American constitution actually prohibited any direct tax levy for national purposes other than a uniform head or poll tax.[51] Properties passing at death were often subject to a legacy duty but these again were partial in coverage and usually with very low and flat charges. When strained by wartime need, income levies were raised but they were promptly dropped after the war.[52] In its heyday the British ruling class levied a peacetime income tax upon itself in 1842 and this was made more or less permanent in 1874, but the levy was a flat levy at a uniform rate on all income over a set exempt amount. Similar income taxes at a flat rate on upper-class income were adopted elsewhere in the nineteenth century. Individual American states sought to tax corporate incomes and succeeded in doing so here and there partly to make up for the way corporate securities and financial assets escaped the local property tax and partly because it was widely felt that the lucrative privilege of incorporation should contribute to public funds. But the tax rates involved were low and at a flat proportional levy (Seligman 1892, 270). The capitalist mode of production in the nineteenth century was only slightly checked and in the United States was virtually uninhibited by taxation in its tendency to accumulate and concentrate property in large holdings, freely transmitted to heirs of one's choice.

However, as the capitalist epoch matured, the resistance to progressive income and wealth taxation weakened. There was widespread dissatisfaction with the inequalities of wealth and income. There was also awareness of resources being foregone. The British in 1909 made their 1842 income tax formally progressive by adding a second layer of rates. An American corporate profits tax assessed and administered nationally was established in 1909. By an extraordinary political effort the American Constitution was amended in 1913 in the heyday of the Progressive revolt to permit national direct income taxation and following shortly after the amendment a personal income tax was enacted. A few years later the first national inheritance tax was enacted, applicable to estates of $50,000 or more. In France and Italy, where there was great reluctance to move ahead on income taxation, taxation of inheritances at progressive rates was established early in the 1900s. By the time of World War I the more advanced countries of the Western world (including Japan) had established a going tax administration that had opened up the fiscal potentialities of inheritances, corporate profits, and personal incomes, and had acculturated people to the idea of the graduated scale, once so bitterly attacked as outrageous or as a form of graduated robbery but which had over time become more familiar if not entirely acceptable. That great war with its massive conscription of soldiers was naturally accompanied by conscription of wealth and income achieved by imposition of drastic income and wealth taxes at progressive rates. Even if this was not called for to appease social discontent, it was required to collect taxes on the largest possible scale; and persons and corporations with large incomes were obviously in a position to pay large taxes. In this respect, as in so many others, that war and the war which followed two decades later were locomotives of history.

Nor was it easy to relinquish these wartime taxes after the hostilities had ceased. In countries where combat operations were carried on, the requirements of peace were almost as great as the needs of war. A vast public debt had built up, a considerable population of war wounded or injured or refugees needed supportive care, areas ravaged by combat needed assistance in rebuilding. The expanded military could not readily be shrunk to prewar dimensions, and new social programs or public needs in education, welfare, transportation, and resource development inevitably made their way and could not be denied even by conservative governments.

Of these three new fields of taxation, the inheritance tax most easily succeeded. The hold of property is least felt at the time of property succession when even legacies that are greatly reduced appear attractive to heirs. States had an ancient tradition going all the way back to the Roman Empire and the principles of feudal property of taxing succession. The proprieties of determining the adequacy of a will or testament and the plan of disposition of an estate had always been worked out under the auspices of the state and had imposed considerable costs and long delays before new entitlements to an estate were granted. The unworthiness of many heirs to great fortunes had deeply impressed itself upon the popular mind and had caused many wealthy persons to sidestep their immediate family in planning estate disposition. Hence there grew up in the capitalist world a pervasive state of mind that since the fiscal needs of the state were pressing it would be well to retain high levels of estate taxation on the wealthy. Quite unmerited is the jibe that only about 3 percent of the estates and less than one-quarter of their value in any one year are now in the United States subject to estate taxes that average a bare 10 percent though nominal rate levels run as high as 70 percent for taxable estates over the $10 million bracket (O'Connor 1973, 207). So few estates are subject to taxation because the estate tax was intended for the wealthy, not the working or middle class. Hence the spouse exemption of $100,000 and exemption of $175,000 (formerly $60,000) of gross estate value before an estate becomes taxable. The average rate of taxation is low on net taxable estates partly because charitable bequests, running from 10 to 14 percent of gross estate value, are excluded from taxable estate (U.S. Bureau of Census 1960, 717). But bequests proper to intended heirs especially from the larger estates are drastically cut down by inheritance taxation on a scale that probably facilitates corporate concentration by promoting sale of capitalist property to gain the necessary liquidity to pay inheritance taxes.

Taxation of corporate profits is a similar case. Here the essential target was raised not by the corporate form as such or the vast number of little corporations in which guise capitalist enterprise clothed itself.

The essential target was the world of Big Business evolved into the quasi-public corporation which by the third decade of the twentieth century was passing from an entrepreneurial phase into a matured phase where there was an effective divorce between ownership and control and where professional management or control by oligarchies or financial groups was becoming prevalent. It was very clear to knowledgeable persons that the great corporation typically acquired more earning power than could be dislodged or eroded by the ordinary working of the market. A real element of monopoly had evolved, wide in some instances, narrow in others, not readily controlled by courts or abolishable by edicts of law. Why not tax the privilege of association, bearing an express charter of the state, which had borne such fruit? That would in effect socialize a portion of corporate profits without clothing the state in the guise of stockholder. It would be easier to do this by leaving a wartime tax at high levels since in the interim much corporate stock had been bought and sold and passed to new owners with appropriate discount taken of the likely course of corporate earning power and dividend passout. If the tax was a burden on stockholders, it was a burden felt by the holder of corporate securities at the time corporate profits taxation was established but not by a later security holder who bought the security making allowance for the new hazard of corporate profits taxation (Goode 1951, 26, 68). Corporate leaders appreciated that the corporate profits tax was basically a flat tax, however high its level might be. For the same reason smaller private corporations became reconciled to the corporate income tax since in part it could be evaded by setting high scales of entrepreneurial withdrawals in the form of executive salaries, in part because a lower rate of corporate tax was eventually established for the first bracket of earnings of small corporations, and finally because the privilege of accumulation, by reinvestment of retained earnings without income taxation at progressive rates, was valuable for growing capitalist enterprise.[53] Finally, corporate earnings like inheritances touched very few voters directly and were extraordinarily easy to assess and collect (Colm 1955, 96). The business affairs of the quasi-public corporation had become a matter of public record bearing the constant scrutiny of the entire financial community and normally subject to outside audit. Taxes could be avoided by seeking a favorable set of capital consumption allowances and write-off charges for bad debts and the like but they could not ordinarily be evaded by simply not booking incomes or by making up false ledgers.

Heavy corporate profits taxes in recent decades in most Western countries have exceeded dividends paid out to stockholders, an undeniable fact that cannot be shuffled aside.[54] Nor can the fiscal significance be denied of such taxes running on an arithmetic average to some 3.5 percent of gross national product in advanced Western countries and to a full third of total indirect taxation (1954–1960) (Kuznets 1966, Table 4.1). For the United States alone corporate profit taxes have been running yearly in the late 1970s to some $80 billion. It can however be claimed that the tax is not effective in the sense that it is shifted forward like a sales tax to purchasers of corporate products and services by widening the gross profit margin taken over costs.[55] The existence of ability to shift corporate profit taxes and the extent to which that ability, if existing, was utilized has been a much debated theme during the past half century. The many investigations of that ability or of its use are all inconclusive, especially econometric models and before-and-after studies of the major wartime periods when corporate profits tax rates were boosted up due to changes in business conditions, in the stages of the business cycle concerned, shifts in price levels, and in world market conditions.[56] For certain classes of corporations shifting seems very likely, as with American public utility corporations subject to regulated standards of earnings generally calculated on an after-tax basis (Goode 1951, 51). Too, corporations competing in a closed market against each other all subject to drainage from the corporate profits tax tend to be able to raise before-tax profit markups to yield target levels of earnings. But shifting of the corporate tax would be handicapped in fields where corporate profit making was uneven so that many market suppliers earned relatively low corporate profits that would not enter into their price calculations.[57] Similarly, corporate enterprise would have less ability to shift corporate profit taxes in markets where it has been competing aggressively with capitalist enterprise as in retail trade, oil wildcatting, banking, insurance, urban services, dairy products, bakeries, and the like. Then again in limited monopoly fields where corporate enterprise rigorously maximized its profit potential, a corporate profits tax would in conformity with the principles of monopolistic pricing leave profit markups unaffected. Finally, as one of our wisest fiscal analysts has suggested, the ability to shift corporate income taxes has been stronger when overall economic policy was expansive and the price level could float upwards without meeting either domestic (internal) or external (foreign balance) resistance (Colm 1955, 91). In the light of these pros and cons it seems unlikely that all of the corporate profits taxes were shifted or that none of them were shifted. Perhaps we can accept the judgment of Richard Musgrave, the outstanding public finance theorist and practitioner of this generation, that one-third of the corporate profits tax was shifted forward to consumers.[58] We cannot accept his further assumption that stockholders bore two-thirds of the tax since corporate retentions and reinvestment probably bore much of that burden. As a result of the corporate income tax stockholders probably have enjoyed via their dividends a smaller share of national income than they otherwise might have had and probably the corporate sector vis-à-vis the capitalist sector of the economy has grown at a somewhat slower rate.

The development of personal income taxation rests on a different basis than either inheritance or corporate profits taxation. The personal income tax has a very mixed assortment of taxpayers drawn from different modes of production. Income receivers drawn from the simple commodity or self-employed mode or the allied world of small capitalist enterprise are important or dominant in agriculture, retail trade, housing rentals, urban services, and the free professions. These taxpayers usually make up their own records and tax statements, often keep their own books, and handle enough cash transactions to make strict accounting for income and outgo difficult to audit except by very expensive detective procedures. Over the years many self-employed proprietors – traders, landlords, farmers, professionals – have submitted ridiculously low income statements understating revenues and overstating expenses.[59] Tax audits in this field are generally rewarding and even when conducted with superficial methods bring in substantial corrections.[60] Little or no effort is made to crack down on violations by imposing punitive fines or criminal punishment for malefactors or to actively solicit information from employees, suppliers, customers, or neighbors or to conduct public campaigns designed to step up compliance with the tax laws.

With regard to other categories of incomes such as wage and salary incomes the personal income tax system works very well. Employers are generally scrupulous in reporting payroll incomes and deducting from the source since these incomes are geared to social security and employment records which it is in the interest of employee as well as employer to maintain. Employers can provide benefits in kind to employees or salaried officers by way of housing, health benefits, or transportation to reduce the flow of reported taxable income. Generous travel and entertainment allowances add their little show of corruption to the white-collar world. But the great bulk of the income paid out is fully reported. Hence wages and salaries reported for taxation now make up 83 to 84 percent of reported gross incomes.[61]

With rentier revenues, such as dividends, royalties, and interest, there is more scope for evasion of income taxes, especially among smaller investors, when payers are not required to report payments to the tax authorities. The bulk of the dividends are received by upper income households and even before reporting at the source has been required some three-quarters of dividends paid out were entered in income tax returns (Holland 1962). The income and its record was too public to risk the chance of evasion. The mere notification by corporations to the tax authorities of the names of parties who receive stated amounts of dividends has further boosted the compliance record. But interest payments – much of it accruing on investment or deposit accounts and originating with households or small businesses – has been traditionally underreported, almost on the same scale as landlord incomes from farm and residential or business rentals. Before reporting at the source for institutional payers of interest over a certain amount, only a third of taxable interest, exclusive of tax-exempt interest or interest accruing on federal savings bonds, was entered in tax returns. Avoidance was indicated more widely where smaller amounts of interest were involved rather than the larger investors. Accrued rather than paid interest and interest payments from noninstitutional sources was neglected (Selzer 1955, 1275, 1286). The record of compliance has been improved since notification to tax authorities was required by institutional payers but even then nonreporting is on a considerable scale running to half or more of interest earned. Rentier investors do not have the facilities available to many large or small business proprietors for converting earned income into capital gains, which in most tax systems is only partially taxed.

The general role of progressive taxation in the mixed economy is set forth in Table 6.3 providing a distribution of tax receipts for leading Western countries in the period 1962–1964.

Entries in the first column exhibit the relative magnitude of state drainage in taxes from national income not counting social security

TABLE 6.3. Tax receipts of general government, selected mixed economies, 1962–1964

Country	Tax receipts (%) of GNP	Share in total tax receipts (%)			Indirect taxes
		Total	Direct taxes		
			Household	Other	
Denmark	26.0	48.0	43.4	4.6	52.0
France	23.3	25.7	16.9	8.7	74.3
West Germany	25.4	43.3	32.0	11.2	56.7
Italy	19.8	30.8			69.2
Netherlands	22.5	55.5	43.6	11.9	44.5
Norway	28.0	47.2	41.4	5.8	52.7
Sweden	30.5	58.6	51.4	7.6	41.8
United Kingdom	24.8	45.6	33.9	11.7	54.4
United States	23.4	59.7	41.3	18.2	40.3
Japan[a]	13.4	45.2	21.5	23.7	54.8
Austria	27.1	43.4	34.3	9.1	56.6

Source: Klein 1974, 179; Japan 1972, 99, 101.

Note: Japan's local government tax revenues were estimated at 37 percent of their expenditures and were all booked as indirect taxes.

[a]Years averaged were 1960, 1965.

contributions or gross receipts or surpluses of proprietorial enterprises. For European countries and the United States the fraction varies between 20 and 30 percent with the Scandinavian countries with their penchant for social democracy leading the way. The unusually low position of Japan on this scale partly owes to her miniscule expenditures for national defense growing out of the disarmament enforced upon her after World War II and the virtual write-off at that time of public debt resulting in low present charges for national debt service. The extent to which the countries involved have moved away from the capitalist pattern of taxation with its concentration on indirect levies is shown by the relative height of the direct levy contribution to national taxes. By that measure the United States, Sweden, and Netherlands lead the way with France and Italy a long way behind, reflecting in part the traditional unwillingness of the French bourgeoisie to submit themselves to income taxation. Noteworthily Japan leads the way in relative emphasis on corporate taxation, though at the time American corporate profits tax rates were among the highest, 52 percent.

It is by no means to be concluded that indirect taxation need always have a regressive effect on income distribution. The use of annually reported incomes for purposes of tax analysis tends to overstate the regressive nature of much indirect taxation.[62] Similarly, differential taxation common in excise and customs may be slanted toward luxury products commonly purchased by the well-to-do while subsistence staples are sometimes exempted from taxation. And as we have seen, the American income tax bears with extraordinary severity upon wages and salaries and rentier incomes but not very heavily upon many self-employed proprietors. A fraction of the corporate income tax is shifted to consumers like most indirect taxes especially in fields where large corporations compete against each other at markups they determine and where corporate losers play a limited market role in shaping product price levels. But making all these allowances, it is still true that the enormous revenues collected from upper salaried, rentier, corporate, and upper capitalist incomes plays an important role in the mixed economy and tends to reduce the after-tax income inequality of income distribution.

THE WELFARE STATE

Graduated taxation of income and wealth may reduce the inequalities of income distribution but it does not directly improve the standard of living of the lower income groups or equalize the flow of benefits to people growing out of resources utilized by the state. The capitalist economy was distinguished for a minimal use of state resources to improve the common life or to channel benefits that would have an equalitarian bias. Medical aid and assistance, apart from exigent measures of public health to avoid the spread of contagious diseases, were minimal as was the use of state monies for educational purposes. Welfare assistance to the poor and needy was channelled into the institution of the poorhouse, the great welfare reform of the nineteenth century in the English-speaking world (see Chap. 5).

Partly in reaction to this neglect of social and ameliorative services, as the mixed economy emerged it was associated with a rich menu of social programs. Grounds for the emergence of welfare expenditure were twofold. There was first a growth and pervasive spread of social sentiments looking with disfavor on any form of hardship or suffering almost regardless of circumstances barring only association with a hated enemy, such as communism, or with enemy peoples during a period of active combat in a proclaimed war. These sentiments are evoked by any form of life with which humans can identify and extend even to landscapes and wilderness settings arousing almost passionate forms of attachment. The development of this extreme sentimentality has gone hand in hand with tolerance for development of technologies of destruction that can lay waste human habitation over wide areas and make the earth lethal for life at large. These sentiments perhaps developed as defense reactions in conformity to the laws of psychoanalysis to aid the psyche in accommodating itself to a condition of latent horror the psyche cannot directly face. It is in conformity to these sentiments that in the United States electric power plants are forbidden to release into lakes or rivers warmed waters used for cooling purposes to avoid disturbing the living conditions of marine life inhabiting those particular waters and causing discomfort or inconvenience, thus compelling migration.[63] So also obscure species of life hardly ever noticed are invested with absolute rights of survival even when public works on which hundreds of millions of dollars have been spent are at stake.[64] Though the United States was in the latter years of the 1960s and increasingly thereafter moving into a state of rising dependence upon insecure supplies of Persian Gulf oil, for five years after the celebrated discoveries of North Slope Alaskan oil in 1968, development was blocked chiefly by ecological concerns of devotees of wild life and ecology who were able to tie the project in knots by recourse to the courts.[65] Later on, environmental issues were critical in blocking the most economical and shortest (Arctic) route for the gas pipeline to bring both Prudhoe Bay and Mackenzie Delta gas to the lower United States, along the coastal plain of the Arctic Sea and up the Mackenzie River valley. The pipeline was to be buried except for four compressor stations but it would need to traverse an Arctic

Wildlife Range. The pipes and pumping stations would trespass upon (but hardly harm) caribou herds, a snow geese staging area, and a light settlement of native Indian tribes with unsettled land claims in the area. The pipeline would invade pristine wilderness and that was the paramount consideration. Hence the decision was made for the less productive, more roundabout and expensive Alcan route that is still (1987) unfunded.[66] Hence also a great sensitivity has developed to improve conditions for the handicapped or for all minority peoples regardless of where they came from or whether they deserve special privilege. This admirable sentiment has at times taken such extreme form that facilities for urban transport—which can be barely afforded by the able-bodied population who need to use buses—have been denied until they are modified for use by the crippled or handicapped. It is these sentiments that have led to a continuous decline since the 1930s in the number of executions under civil authority of the United States from 1667 in the decade of the thirties to 77 percent of that number in the forties, 43 percent in the fifties, 11.4 percent in the sixties, at which time civil executions for premeditated murder or rape practically disappeared (U.S. Census, Statistical Abstract 1979, 199). Combined with these social sentiments and associated states of consciousness was the political rise of labor organization with an insistent demand that a larger share of national income be dedicated to purposes of social amelioration. Whether mediated by social democratic parties as in Sweden, Norway, and Great Britain, or by democratic party leadership under such figures as De Gaulle, Truman, Eisenhower, and Kennedy, or by Christian Democratic parties in West Germany and France, the outcome was much the same: adoption on a wide variety of fronts of programs using public funds to ameliorate social conditions.

Leading the way in this amelioration were programs for improving, widening, and deepening educational effort, extending now to higher education, universal secondary education, and vocational education in all lines of work. Health care is another focus of social amelioration. The United States did not extend its social security system to include health care for all and not only for the aged as did other Western democracies. Yet national responsibility for health care promotion and financing was undertaken in a wide variety of programs. These have embraced funding for construction of new medical schools; partial financing of physician eduction; vocational rehabilitation of disabled persons including treatment of blindness, orthopedic impairments, deafness, mental illness, mental retardation, and other disabilities, annually affecting several hundred thousand persons in the decade of the seventies. Medical vendor payments for most of the welfare population in the United States getting case-load assistance are now handled under programs financed and regulated in large measure by national standards and funded at a cost that in the decade of the seventies ran between 15 to 20 billion dollars annually. Facilities and programs for treatment of mental illness have mushroomed largely at governmental expense so that since 1955 patient care in professionally manned treatment facilities has risen on a per capita basis threefold.

In Europe larger families have been a center of social concern and outright grants. Employer organizations in France in the 1920s pioneered a program of supplemental wages by an extra allowance for a dependent child. These allowances were universalized under law in the 1930s and extended and enlarged after World War II (French Embassy 1980, 80, 662). The United States has a form of family allowance for low-income families in the ADC program (Aid to Dependent Children) instituted in the 1930s when the national government first became committed to using federal tax funds for direct welfare purposes. In the conservative Nixon Administration a major effort was made to get a national scheme of graduated family allowances paying a "negative income tax" to low income families, turning at a certain point in the income scale into a positive income tax (Moynihan 1973). Both the aged and the young have become central objects of national concern in the United States. Federal and local funding is obtained for school lunches while retired persons are attracted to federally subsidized lunches in the effort to provide stimulation and a nutritious meal in a governmentally constructed network of retirement centers built up over the nation to provide social and transportation services to retired persons, without any show of a means test.

In this context the old poorhouse or workhouse system for relieving need, temporary or chronic, is definitely out. In the United States there is a constant tendency to regress to primitive and inefficient forms of "workfare" rather than "welfare." The attempt to organize efficient forms of productive work rather than costly forms of "make-work" is necessarily self-defeating in view of the capital costs of efficient work and the total lack of any scheme of adequate incentives at either management or worker level.[67]

Finally, all through the Western world an immense public responsibility has been assumed to promote and help fund better housing for urban populations. This has partly been achieved chiefly by credit underwriting in the United States to guarantee the loans of borrowers and thus to channel credit to small borrowers for longer terms, small down payments, and for low interest.[68] Programs of slum removal and development of public housing have been slow to develop in the United States and after some forty years have only provided up to 1.7 and 1.8 percent of the housing stock.[69] In the European democracies publicly assisted housing has played a much larger role especially since tenant and collective housing in larger apartments is more prevalent than in the United States and since housing shortages and rent control have been experienced in some instances continuously since 1914–1918.[70]

Regulation

Regulatory functions of the state have been vastly extended in the mixed economy which has returned to the pattern of state overlordship and guidance characteristic of the mercantilist economy. The forces underlying this extension of state power are varied. The competence of the state to develop and successfully administer regulatory controls over economic life has greatly increased. A large supply of professional and technically schooled personnel is now available for public service. Difficulties of regulation are partly eased by careful drafting of regulations usually screened by prior hearing and often pretested with an advisory council of the public directly concerned. In the United States enactment of regulatory authority is generally preceded by exhaustive legislative and executive investigations and public hearings at which comprehensive knowledge of the subject matter is built up. The need for regulation has increased since sensitivity to long-term effects, generally ignored by the market, of production and resource use on the welfare of future generations has grown. The possibilities of fraud and deception are now much greater due to the greater complexity of goods and services and the disparity of knowledge between users, investors, and producers. Instances have multiplied where price and cost do not match in market exchange because some costs are borne by parties who are not beneficiaries and other parties are benefitted without making appropriate contributions.

Methods of regulation are varied. They will generally include some form of licensing or registration to establish effective contact with the subject activity. In some fields as in certain professions it may be sufficient to define with some care conditions of eligibility for those seeking to practice a given profession or trade where protection to the public, readily duped especially in a condition of distress, is or may seem to be required. In most fields of regulation licensing and registration are insufficient. Usually one or more types of activity will be prohibited or limited to specified uses and circumstances, sometimes merely requiring adequate disclosure of accurate information. Disclosure is the keynote of large American regulatory programs dealing with loan charges, ingredients contained in food, many consumer products, drugs and pharmaceuticals, and protection of investors from corporate management. Disclosure weakens the tendency for corporate insiders to benefit from privileged information. Disclosure provides a good deal of protection for corporate investors contemplating purchase of newly issued securities that must be accompanied by public disclosure of relevant facts and background. Beyond disclosure there may be further requirements calling for professional prescription of drugs by a licensed medical practitioner. And certain practices, products or byproducts may be directly curtailed or prohibited as with programs of environmental protection. These prohibitions and curtailments took on a new twist in the American campaign to improve the ambient air quality over most metropolitan and industrial regions by phasing in over an advance ten-year period a program of declining emissions of pollutants annually to be projected from the successive fleets of automobiles produced in coming periods. Producers were given time to adjust the makeup of their automotive lines offered to consumers and of their production technology that over time would be reworked with continuous capital investment and research. Some schemes of regulation call for detailed policing. Other schemes tend to be self-policing where one or more of the parties immediately involved has an interest in enforcing rights provided by regulation. Much regulation is achieved by way of tax-exemption or tax-levy, which mobilizes incentives calibrated to promote abstention from or indulgence in programs, activities, objects, from philanthropy to pollution, liquor, education, gambling, and whatnot.

Targets of regulation are all over the economic system. One major focus of regulation had its origin in the capitalist economy in comprehensive factory regulation pioneered by the British initially for the protection of juveniles and women workers but ultimately extending over the entire labor force. From an initial concern with preventing excessive hours of labor, the corrective concern of the state shifted to imposition of requirements for healthy working conditions; safety requirements and adequate ventilation; prevention of accidents; and minimum wages especially for unskilled workers, juvenile workers, migratory farm workers, and others in the labor force whose conditions of life make it unlikely that they can adequately protect their own interests in their employment relationships. Where industrial safety is concerned, intervention of the state is often critical in setting proper safety standards since lack of adequate knowledge would make it expensive and difficult for the parties immediately concerned to protect their interests. Newer targets of regulation are found in the fields of agriculture, environmental pollution, consumer protection, and finally investor protection. Some of these regulatory programs have been touched upon in other contexts. The hints and suggestions made there may suffice for present purposes if we examine in detail the scope for and nature of regulatory programs in agriculture as evolved in the mixed economy.

Agriculture Control

The need for regulation in agriculture grew out of continuous instability that characterized pricing of agricultural staples disposed of in agricultural world markets. The rate of consumption and production of agricultural staple products is relatively insensitive in the short run to even substantial changes in prices especially downward. These tend only slightly to induce compensatory shifts in either farmers' responses to expected lower prices or consumers' responses to actual price reductions.[71] Consumer response to farmers' price change is limited partly because the processing and marketing margin between what farmers get and what retail buyers pay has risen over time and in the short run is relatively constant. A large percentage change in farm prices results in a much smaller percentage in retail food prices.[72] Both demand and supply elasticities of response are, moreover, growing smaller over time so that it becomes ever more difficult for the price mechanism to work in the field of agriculture.[73] The resulting price instability has in turn been magnified by the need to hold large inventories of agricultural stocks to even out consumption within and between crop years or seasons. In the capitalist market economy these inventories were held by speculative investors based upon their forecasts of likely movements of worldwide demand and supply; the cost in terms of storage, wastage, and interest payments of holding inventories; and the likelihood of sufficient capital gains to make the speculative investment worthwhile. J. M. Keynes who created the science of macroeconomics also discovered the equation that explains why, to use his language, "redundant stocks exercise a disproportionate effect on prices and therefore on new production."[74] Experience has taught these speculators that when the market starts to move downward "it is safer and more profitable to await a further decline," the primary producer being usually "unable or unwilling to hold so that if the speculative purchaser holds back he will get the commodity still cheaper."[75] Even within a single year these speculative markets traverse a very wide range. Keynes (1930, 1:450) once calculated for a number of basic staple products over a ten-year period spanning the twenties and thirties the high-low range of market price, expressed as a percent of the mean price for the year. He found that for cotton, rubber, and wheat the mean percent was 42, 96, and 70, and that for wheat and rubber in only one year of ten was the percent less than 47 and 70 respectively. The year-to-year fluctuation of mean prices is also very considerable.[76]

This background explains why even small shifts in market supply—unfavorable or favorable—along with ripples in speculative sentiment produce an exaggerated movement of price. Though the characteristic movements of the business cycle involving recession and expansion only touch lightly on expenditure for foodstuffs, yet even these small fluctuations induce substantial fluctuations in wholesale and retail food prices.[77] As Keynes (1930, 2:141) pointed out, "where production is inelastic or where a particular product is so large a proportion of the national business that alternative occupations cannot be found a miscalculation leading to heavy redundant stocks may prove ruinous, if matters are allowed to take their course on principles of *laissez-faire.*"

The year-to-year variations in farm prices have an exaggerated effect on farmers' net earnings. For the prices of farm supplies, fertilizers, taxes, insecticides, transport, and other services including hired labor will change very little from year to year. Even a small fluctuation in gross farm receipts will thus translate itself into a sizable fluctuation of net income. Some of this fluctuation may be neutralized or offset by diversification of husbandry and relying on a broad mix of field crops, dairy produce, and livestock returns with basic subsistence grown and consumed on the farm. But that kind of diversified general farming is incompatible with use of specialized machinery that saves labor and permits the cultivation of large acreages and achievement of high levels of productivity. The diversified general farmer is being phased out of agriculture in the mixed economy making for more specialized forms of production, lesser diversification in husbandry, and greater risks if market prices are free to fluctuate.

These risks would be vexatious even if prices fluctuated in random fashion around a constant level. But the yearly variations are subject to upward or downward drift depending upon the cumulative balance in world markets between long-run forces of demand and supply. This balance is slowly changing with shifts in food habits, growth in nonfarm urban populations and their standard of living, the opening up of new arable acreage, the development of synthetic fibers that have displaced agricultural fibers or of fossil fuels which have displaced the draught horse, and the improvement of agricultural yields by better seeds, insecticides, and fertilizers (see Chap. 4). When this drift is in the farmer's favor so that the yearly fluctuations of market price are on an upward trend, the work of the market is found acceptable and the rhetoric of market freedom has a persuasive ring. But when these fluctuations are on a downward path, the farmer's discontent about his "income treadmill" becomes bitter.[78] Adjustment to a downward price trend is possible if the need for adjustment is confined to one or a few product lines and if some farmers are able to divert cultivation or husbandry to more favored lines. When the need for adjustment is more general, weaker farm families may be forced from the land or will voluntarily leave. The land will rarely go out of production since a neighboring farm can by increasing acreage make more efficient use of farm machinery. Nonuse of improved land is itself costly since the results of past tillage will be dissipated as fields become infested with weeds, fencing decays, and the capital invested in housing for the farm family and livestock wastes. The discontent of the farmer is aggravated since the urban population whom he supplies with food and fiber have in the mixed economy organized their life to obtain greater security of livelihood and income. Farmer discontent with the capitalist methods of economic organization came to a head in the long period of agrarian price decline commencing early in the 1920s and became intensified during the world depression of 1929–1933 when farmer net earnings from their work reached absurdly low levels.

Farmers learned then that they could not individually or through their cooperatives achieve a comparable security of livelihood. Farmers needed to establish some method of regulating the supply of farm produce by periodic organized regulation nationwide of production to prevent surpluses from accumulating. And those surpluses needed to be withdrawn from the speculative whirlpool of world markets and put under managed control. For some products international control of production has been attempted. Supply and inventory management could only be achieved by farmers wielding the resources of government and deliberately separating national markets for farm produce from world markets. Programs of inventory storage, price stabilization, supply management, and export pricing multiplied in the Western world during the latter 1920s and through the 1930s.[79] Perhaps these programs were most fully developed in countries like the United States with a large export agriculture and an aggressive and capable farmer's movement with political clout. Under Franklin D. Roosevelt farmers found a national leader willing to improvise new solutions and deliberately take up methods of economic organization that challenged the hallowed precepts of capitalist economics suited for the pristine capitalist economy of the nineteenth century. A decisive change in agricultural political economy was feasible in the United States because agricultural economics in the United States was a well-developed discipline with an intricate network of supply and marketing information and with knowledge of supply and demand adjustments needed to develop effective farm management and pricing programs.

The new agricultural political economy is based upon certain principles. Responsibility is shared between national and state governments. State governments take responsibility for controlling supply usually by license, by acreage allotment, or poundage limits for the growing and marketing of produce of milksheds or of special kinds of fruits and vegetables produced chiefly within a few states.[80] The national government undertakes responsibility for regulating supply and price in most milksheds and for managing storage of surplus dried or canned milk and butterfat. For crop staples only certain pivotal storable products are selected for stabilization operations of which wheat, feed grains, upland cotton, tobacco, wool, peanuts, sugar and rice are the most consequential. For certain of these products such as for peanuts and tobacco, control of supply is achieved by issuance of what are virtually poundage or acreage allotments.[81] For the leading crop staples such as wheat, upland cotton, and feed grains, control of supply has been achieved by selective cropping cutbacks to reduce forthcoming supply and onerous storage burdens. For the some twenty years after 1956 some 6 percent of available crop land (chiefly whole farms) were entirely taken out of current production or reduced to pasturage thus cutting back somewhat on farm output potential and easing farm supply across the board.[82] For price-supported products the government established support price levels and provided storage for that part of current supply that did not sell commercially. For the earlier decades storage was undertaken chiefly by government agencies, though in the first instance the farmer could hold title to the product and retrieve it from storage if market price should turn more favorably. Most of the inventory ended up under government control. In later years storage is primarily under the immediate control of the producer who since 1977 may be induced to release to market by varying the rate of government subsidization of storage costs chiefly for interest, handling charges, and shrinkage. Rates of subsidization in case of low farm prices are outlined in advance with a corridor of floor-ceiling prices offering a degree of security to farmers that the free market entirely lacked.[83] By 1973 farmers had to take out of cultivation up to 60 million acres in set-asides and crop limitations, including the soil bank, to obtain the price stabilization programs developed by the Federal government.

During most of the years of price support and stabilization, foreign trade in farm staples—both exports and imports—have moved under comprehensive controls to protect the domestic farm program from the world market. Most farm exports moved abroad with substantial but partial subsidy on so-called commercial sales but total and outright subsidy when surplus products were given to needy countries who fitted into a pattern of American foreign policy.[84] Some of the more benevolent and kindly sides of American foreign policy have arisen from the peculiar need to contrive ways and means of disposing of farm surpluses through channels that would not appreciably undercut commercial disposition.[85] Likewise, programs of nutritional support to school children and to the aged and poor have obtained much of their legislative support from the need to cut back on surpluses. When domestic prices are above world market prices—the case for years with sugar, cotton and wheat—variable tariffs or import quotas were imposed to limit foreign supply and maintain the necessary price differential.

The devaluation of the dollar in 1972–1973 had the immediate effect of raising domestic farm prices on the same scale and thus making it possible to eliminate all cropland or general supply restrictions. The gap between support prices and market prices narrowed so that farm price stabilization programs became relatively less expensive. Since farm productivity was continually increasing at a faster rate than demand for farm output, pressure on farm prices ultimately returned near the turn of the decade and the tendency to surplus and the need for supply management along with it. Though the rhetoric of the conservative political turn that put Ronald Reagan in the White House— and made his British counterpart, Mrs. Thatcher, the First Lord of the Treasury and Prime Minister of her Majesty's Government—would seem to call for total and outright abolition of this new political economy of agriculture, that was simply not feasible. Farming has become too specialized, investment in production has become too great, and too many collateral interests of bankers and industrial producers servicing farmers would be endangered to return to the instability of the old agricultural political economy. Credit margins of farmers and farm produce would shrivel up, and the market for farm equipment and supplies now running into billions of dollars annually and intricately interlaced with industrial farm supply operations would collapse. Conservative rhetoric can, however, cut the appropriations and lower the corridor of price support that is working havoc on farm net incomes and causing farm mortgage foreclosures not seen since the Great Depression.[86]

A corresponding structure of agricultural political economy was shaped up in postwar Europe and Japan. Wartime food shortage drove home the overriding national need to maintain a local reliable supply of foodstuffs and to improve incentives for rising levels of farm investment and productivity. Both objectives called for farm price support or subsidy payments to farmers competing against world market supply.

In the creation of the European Common Market these uneven structures of price support, subsidies, and tariffs created the greatest obstacle to the unification of economic institutions which was essential to carrying through the creation of an economically integrated Western Europe. The 1957 Rome Treaty to launch the Common Market called for continuing negotiations to create a Common Agricultural Policy (CAP) and set forth the agreed premises and certain procedural undertakings to guide the negotiations (such as the universal use of tariffs rather than import quotas). The agreed premises were that agricultural markets will be jointly regulated by a system of common rules to control competition implemented by "price controls, subsidies on marketing and production, stock-piling and carry-over systems, common mechanisms for import and export stabilization, and a common fund or funds for agricultural guidance and market support."[87] The negotiations for CAP when it was first achieved in the early Sixties and later modified when the British and other new members were taken into the Common Market were troubling and extended.

The CAP has evolved into a comprehensive integrated agricultural political economy for the Western European states, originally the six partner states who came together with the Rome Treaty, now the nine partners with subsequent members coming later. Its agricultural support operations are facilitated by the basic fact that the Common Market as a whole is a food-deficit area that must import agricultural produce on a large scale and is plagued consequently with only minor problems of surplus adjustment and disposal. Its basic principles are fourfold:

1. Free movement of agricultural products in the CAP area unobstructed by quotas or tariffs
2. Agreed uniform basic prices established annually for leading agricultural staples in the Common Market area with differentials permitted in special situations due to exchange rate variations
3. A variable import duty or "levy" on leading agricultural products imported into the Common Market area to adjust the world market price to the fixed price
4. Deposit of levy proceeds, together with a portion of the value-added tax applicable through the entire area, into a common segregated fund providing for financial management of the markets, handling of surplus product inventories and the structural reform of agriculture in member states.[88]

The operation of the Common Market calls for the annual fixing of prices for the leading crop staples produced and marketed in the

Common Market area and a variable import tariff levy to allow for necessary imports to sustain that price. Direct public expenditures as a percent of the value of agriculture output for Common Market countries has ranged for a representative recent year, 1968, between 10 and 18 percent. A similar pattern prevails for non-Common Market counties such as Japan or Sweden that support agriculture by price stabilizing and market-control operations (Klein 1973, 142). Since costs of production on small European farms are much higher than in modern mechanized New World farms, the import duty levy is considerable.[89]

The newer political economy of agriculture developed by the mixed economy is nearly everywhere an imperfect instrument for achieving its purposes. Controls are often expensive to administer fairly and when they are developed by democratic processes in an open society various pressure groups tend to obtain unfair advantages.[90] Government administration of carryover inventories tends to make foreign trade in agricultural products a dumper's paradise.[91] The annual setting of target or support prices tends to become involved with campaigns for election support. In the United States, where all these faults reinforce each other, the system has with all its infirmities helped to lift up farmer incomes to the neighborhood of nonfarm incomes. Farm price instability has been reduced. Farm income instability is much greater than nonfarm income instability but it has become lessened and farmers have been able to become more specialized, mechanized, and efficient in their agricultural practices.[92] Whether the new political economy of agriculture can withstand the efforts of laissez-faire dogmatists to dismantle it remains to be seen.

Stability and Full Employment

The capitalist economy was plagued with instability and chronic unemployment irregularly rising and falling with the tides of the business cycle and longer wave movements. A very persistent short-term fluctuation between 30 to 44 months in duration was recorded in the United Kingdom as far back as the 1790s. It was well marked in American business history and appeared more or less distinctly wherever capitalist enterprise was well developed (Gottlieb 1984, 101). That fluctuation was driven mainly by desire to hold, obtain, or reduce business inventories. A more irregular decennial-type movement centering largely in building, industrial, and railway investment ran its course in and out of the shortwave movement, now coalescing with it, now running apart. Often these longer more pervasive fluctuations would have a more international sweep and a climactic phase of commercial crisis sometimes culminating in financial panic or breakdown of banking credit.[93] Sometimes coalescing with these movements of industrial investment was another cyclical wave centering in residential construction and urban growth with a time period from crest to crest of ten up to thirty years and carrying with it a stream of speculation in urban real-estate values and urban development.[94] Many of our major depressions such as 1929–1933 were characterized by interweaving of contraction phases of two or more distinctive waves, reinforcing each other as they combined. Running through this instability were surges of growth of the underlying monetary base of the capitalist economy – gold and silver enlarged by the use of bank credit. Tendencies to instability were heightened whenever new sources of alluvial gold or new technologies of working gold-bearing ores were discovered. The unstable flow of precious metals into the system generated an upward trend of rising money value in 1847–1873 and again for the twenty years after 1897, followed by periods of falling trends of money value.

All this instability was long regarded in the capitalist world as natural phenomena that human society must adjust to but could not alter. The fundamental statistics of economic growth were only beginning to become available chiefly as byproducts of decennial censuses or government collection of taxes or monitoring of foreign trade at the frontiers. The study of economic behavior focused on patterns of distribution of income among classes or analysis of fundamental concepts and their relationships. Inferior minds attracted to the study of economics were more concerned to pronounce upon the eternal rightness of current arrangements than to investigate ways to improve these arrangements. During most of the nineteenth and some of the twentieth century, probably the majority of economic theorists actually believed business cycles were impossible, that they could not occur, that markets would always be provided for producers who were producing the right things or combinations of things, and that the deep-lying instability around them was a mirage or was the product of disturbing events such as wars, manias, drouths, or the foolish antics of government "tinkering" with the currency.[95] These widely held views predisposed government leaders to abjure responsibility for guiding economic affairs. When major credit breakdowns and crises aroused government attention, they tended to be investigated and studied as isolated events unique to a particular era or combination of circumstances to be accounted for, as Marx notes, "by incidents, movements and agencies altogether peculiar or presumed to be peculiar to the one period just elapsed" (Marx and Engels 1841–1870/1974–1986, 16:34). That made diagnosis and treatment difficult even if the will were there to play an active role. Given that will, the ability of government in the capitalist economy to influence the course of economic events was limited. With a declining tide of business, tax revenues would tend to fall off and the first requirement of government under such circumstances by all their principles was either to add new revenues – very difficult to do precipitately – or curtail expenditures, failing which distress borrowing would be needed. While for most of the capitalist countries access to a central bank would provide credit accommodation even in a time of cyclical tension, the whole scale on which governments were organized made cyclical shifting in their scale of borrowing a matter of negligible impact upon the course of economic events. The potential power of government armed with knowledge and given the necessary institutional support was considerable. The actual power of government in the pristine capitalist economy was near miniscule.

As the capitalist economy matured, the groundwork was laid for a more active role by government to moderate the instability of the capitalist economy and to give it a steadier course of movement. Firstly, the statistics began to be collected, processed, and published on a more current basis permitting diagnosis of the current business situation to be undertaken and at least the beginnings of therapy provided. The clearinghouses established by commercial banks in the larger financial centers disclosed their returns thereby providing a continuous record of the gross turnover of business payments. Security exchanges required public corporations with listed securities traded in public markets to regularly disclose earnings and dividends. Security market agencies computed crude indexes of security prices and bond yields so that the daily disclosure of security prices could be more meaningfully digested by interested investors. Building contractors were in time serviced by trade journals publishing current records of newly negotiated building contract awards yielding information about building activity. Trade associations began to collect and publish information about various industries – its production, marketing, prices, and other activity – to facilitate intelligent market action by industry members. Progressive states like Massachusetts, New York, and Ohio embarked on statistical research and current economic statistics to which public officers had access.[96] All this was in addition to economic information increasingly collected and published by the federal government concerning emigration, foreign trade (both imports and exports by class of commodity), taxes, debt serviced or issued, patents issued, money and banking statistics, agricultural crop and marketing statistics. An abstract of these data was annually compiled and published from 1878 onward as a *Statistical Abstract of the United States.* The formation in the United States of the major governmental departments of cabinet rank for agriculture, commerce, and labor and the establishment of the Federal Reserve System in 1914 gave prominence to the supporting role of government in these fields and at least the need regularly to collect and publish current economic information. Soon these departments embarked on comprehensive schemes of data collection. The labor statistics collected by the Bureau of Labor Statistics were published in the *Monthly Labor Review.* The memorable *Survey of Current Business,* which began publication in 1921, and the *Federal Reserve Bulletin,* whose publication dates from 1914, all aroused curiosity and nurtured the growing interest in current economic developments.

Collection of statistics was accompanied by refinement in their presentation. The simple device of the arithmetic mean and its coefficient of variation obtained popular exposition in statistical presentations late in the nineteenth century. It was in the second half of the nineteenth century that time series of prices expressed in the form of index numbers became common. Refined treatment of index numbers became possible on the basis of comparatively recent twentieth century debate. The use of correlation analysis as a method of measuring correlated behavior of different objects or processes was developed as a scientific instrument of statistical theory only late in the nineteenth century. It was put to use in economic analysis in the twentieth century. The use of harmonic analysis to discover hidden periodicities in different time series was applied to economic data in the twentieth century (Mitchell 1927, 189). The regular graphing of time series and smoothing for seasonal variations became well-established in the twentieth century.

As more information about economic instability became available and as wider circles of public opinion showed greater concern, professional students of economics and business finally began to study the subject with the seriousness it deserved. The first histories appearing in 1858–1860 of the phenomena concentrated only on the dramatic crisis phase of credit breakdown but at least this was shown as a recurring dislocation.[97] German and Russian students by the last decade of the 1890s and the first decade of the twentieth century were deeply influenced by Marx's work and shifted attention from the crisis itself to underlying industrial cycles.[98] By World War I a number of major monographs on the subject were published of which the most outstanding was the 1913 treatise, *Business Cycles,* by the American economist, Wesley Clair Mitchell, who later founded the National Bureau of Economic Research devoted largely in its earlier decades to research on this very subject.[99] By the 1920s a large number of investigators were engaged in analysis, debate, and publication. A number of scientific institutes were established principally for the purpose of engaging in current research and publishing monographs and periodicals on the subject. Theoretical debate illuminated the subject and at the same time confused it for there was thereby created a "new puzzle . . . the relations among a lot of theories" (Mitchell 1927, 45).

This research into business cycles culminated in and in a sense was completed by three major theoretical developments. The first was a practical research which laid out a scheme and a set of current measurements of national income accounts showing the comprehensive relationships between interrelated quantities of production, spending, and income payments. Estimates of national income were not new but this was the first time statistical enquiry sought to measure the continually shifting magnitudes at first annually and then quarterly of income flow and how the different items in the national income accounts changed and shifted about over time.[100]

Coming about at the same time was the theory of national income accounts – how they form and reshape – developed by that seminal mind of our era, John Maynard Keynes, and published at first in an immature form in 1930 as the two volume *Treatise on Money* (1930) and then in matured form as a theoretical treatise, remarkably compact and concise, remote and yet exact, the *General Theory of Employment, Interest and Money* (1936).

It was no coincidence that the first reliable time series of the flow of national income and expenditure for a major country appeared while the *General Theory* was in the making (Keynes 1936, 102). Keynes taught economists to look behind the recorded national income accounts into a well-known volitional force, "demand" which entered into the making of expenditures. Having in mind industrial production, which is closely tailored to anticipated demand and its current expression by way of "orders," he showed that the determinants of demand were laid out differently for consumer goods and services and for investment goods. Similarly he showed that the stock of money had to be broken down according to the purposes for which money balances are held. Keynes's own results were stillborn. He did not undertake to put together the various parts of his model to see how they would fit and function together. His model moreover was absurdly limited. It was without a field of agriculture, foreign trade, or government. As originally formulated his model yielded only a statical solution holding for given values of the determinants of its variables. Many of the equations setting forth the determinants of his variables presupposed unlikely or highly simplified conditions such as the strict dependence of changes in price on changes in marginal cost or the assumption of diminishing returns as the scale of output expanded or the assumption that all investment expenditure was financed by borrowing. Milton

Friedman had a field day showing that one of Keynes's basic behavioral laws—that the volume of consumption expenditure does not change proportionately with the level of disposable income—did not hold over a cumulative period so that at best the law was a transitory phenomenon (Friedman 1957, Chap. 1).

However, despite its weaknesses and flaws—the struggle against Keynes, the effort to refute him, the desire to supplement his results and enrich his model or to work out its equilibrium properties—created the field of ferment that brought into existence the new discipline of macroeconomics. In the final outcome the Keynesian model became purified, enriched with new empirical and theoretical studies. The Keynesian "multiplier" in the *General Theory* was the process of amplification of an increment of investment expenditure as it elicited a succession of rounds of incremental consumption expenditure. In the more general theory any increment of new expenditure resulting in additional production was found to elicit successive rounds of expenditure of all kinds by households, governments, enterprises at home and abroad with corresponding tendencies to elicit additional processes of production. Likewise, the rigid line that Keynes drew between consumer and investment outlay—the one chiefly governed by household income, the other by bond yields—was modified since some classes of household expenditure are substantially affected by consumer credit, its availability, and its terms. Much business investment in working capital especially is influenced by terms of and availability of short-term bank lending and by available retained earnings.

This rich development of macroeconomic theory was soon accompanied by empirical investigations laid out in the new discipline of econometrics, which in effect joined the newly flowing information on national income accounts with Keynesian macroeconomic theory.[101] In the form these reached in the forties, econometric models were intellectual curiosities, too simple to use for practical diagnosis or projection purposes. But these models were soon enlarged and came in the 1960s to yield excellent service to the mixed economy by increasing the ability to diagnose business-cycle situations and trends and especially to project the cumulative effects of discrete policy changes in taxes, expenditures, interest rates and the like. Use of these econometric models has been widely distributed throughout the business and corporate world. Most of the larger firms now regularly consult high-grade econometric models for forecasting and diagnostic purposes. Model builders are paraded before congressional committees exhibiting and defending their talent and their wares.[102]

Keynes's *General Theory* and the rich development of econometric model building came too late to influence government policy and liberal thinking during the Great Depression itself. Its central message, its theoretical scheme, was too novel and took too long to assimilate to have much practical effect then. Perhaps Keynesian doctrine concerning the gold standard, which Keynes proclaimed a "barbarous relic" and against which Keynes had fought in the 1920s, was taken to heart. Great Britain went off the gold standard in 1931 and adjusted the gold value of the pound to what she could afford and keep her economy going. The Roosevelt New Deal commenced its program of economic reform and recovery with a massive 65 percent devaluation of the dollar on a scale sufficient to allow national income to have a full and vigorous recovery without meeting gold restraints.[103] This devaluation was accompanied by nationalization of the gold supply so that the profits of devaluation were collected by the nation and not by the wealthy persons or bankers who hoarded gold. The devaluation was also accompanied by a boost in hourly wage rates by some 25 percent associated with the reduction in the legal work week. Easy terms of credit encouraged investment expenditure. But the private inducement to invest had been crippled by the harrowing experiences of the depression itself. At the shrunken level of real income prevailing, much higher money wage rates and the disorganized condition of the world economy even cheap terms of credit did not elicit much investment expenditure. The Roosevelt New Deal was willing to incur some deficit financing of public investment expenditure but on a pitifully small scale in relation to the higher level of wages and farm prices that had been established. Thus that part of the Keynesian message in the decade of the thirties did not bear fruit and create a strong recovery reaching full employment except perhaps in Nazi Germany where the unleashing of the war economy with its massive public expenditure and price control did the trick.

After the war stability and growth prospects for both the American and for Western world economy were on a different footing. By war's end the generation that lived through the Great Depression and the war accepted the responsibility of government to manage or guide the economy to maintain prosperity and stable economic growth and accepted the combined and balanced use of monetary and fiscal policy to achieve that end with such direct controls as were needed to suppress inflation if it should become troublesome.[104] By international agreement a multinational institution, the International Monetary Fund (IMF), was established to assure the orderly behavior of exchange rates changed from time to time when needed by individual countries to balance their accounts and to preside over a system of international monetary assets made up of gold or dollar claims pinned to each other at a set parity and convertible into each other by member governments at will. That seemed to resolve the gold problem for the Western world. If gold supplies themselves were becoming short, raising the currency price of gold would make the existing supply of monetary gold more valuable in terms of available currencies and price and income levels. If an individual member state was in foreign exchange trouble, it would not have to go through depression or isolate itself in autarchy. It could devalue its currency in terms of gold or dollars. The United States whose national money was thus made into an international monetary asset entering directly into the exchange reserves of other countries was supposed to manage its affairs and avoid persistent or excessive deficits. Apparently this was easy enough for an economy traditionally running a balance of payments surplus, enjoying overwhelming technological superiority in most mass production industries, undamaged by the Great War that laid waste its main competitors, and with exportable surpluses of most major commodities: petroleum, coal, steel, vehicles, armaments, food grains – you name it.

The damage and destructiveness of the war in Europe, Japan, Asia, and North Africa assured a relatively intense inducement to invest. In the United States investment needs were created by the large increase in the volume of employment and the resulting boom of marriages and child births delayed by the Depression and the war. Besides, during the war wasting structures and equipment in homes, stores, and factories could not be renewed or replaced unless needed for the war effort. So the inducement to invest was strong everywhere. The relatively high progressive personal income and corporate profits taxation and the widespread use of payroll social security taxation made public revenues very sensitive to a changed flow of gross national product. A converse relationship existed for major fields of government expenditure for welfare support, retirement programs, unemployment insurance, and agricultural price support tending to vary inversely with a downward or upward movement in GNP. All this made the fiscal balance sensitive to even slight changes in the rate of growth of GNP, corporate profits, and payrolls. An acceleration of GNP growth would tend to produce sizable budget surpluses, which themselves brake the expansion or stabilize its course. An unanticipated or unbudgeted recession produced large deficits. These surpluses and deficits on fiscal account tend to shield personal income and expenditure and thus they tend to prevent any oscillation from becoming diffused and multiplied as it works its way. Such an automatic stabilizer does not prevent cyclical oscillation or tendencies to depression.[105] But these are slowed down and filtered out, thus allowing more time for discretionary action to take effect. Automatic stabilizers on government account have been supplemented by similar stabilizers developed chiefly (but not exclusively) in the corporate mode of production, which has stabilized the flow of payroll and dividend income. A higher fraction of the labor force is employed in staff or overhead capacities. Corporations have often stabilized the flow of dividends into personal incomes despite fluctuations of corporate earnings. This has contributed to stabilization of planning for corporate investments now budgeted over long time periods based on long-term forecasts of economic growth rather than immediate market need (Burns 1969, 101).

The arsenal for discretionary stabilizing policy has grown wider over the years and has varied considerably according to the political climate and the style of national life in the Western world. In Europe where central banks had a much more organic hold on commercial banking by active participation in loan markets and continuous provisionment of reserves by rediscounting or loan operations and where integration of central bank policy into overall economic management was more acceptable, changed central bank action by way of credit restraint or loosening could be targeted more directly on sagging or surging areas of the economy. In the United States the role of central banking was weakened by reliance entirely upon creation or withdrawal of liquid reserves by purchase of government bills. Rediscounting had become an ineffectual instrument because its use was discouraged. A special form of fiscal policy was developed and applied in West Germany: tax concessions and export allowances or tax relief on incomes invested in housing and shipbuilding (Shonfield 1965, 282). Countries whose economic growth and productivity lagged were able to avert the need to throw themselves into depression to relieve balance of payment pressure both by imposition of direct export or import controls and even more by deliberate variation of exchange rates widely undertaken by European countries in the epoch prior to 1973. The first major round of exchange rate adjustment came in 1949 and a second round in 1967. In both cases the initiative was taken by Great Britain but involved many other countries. Exchange rate changes are not magic. They result in a one-sided shift of pricing relationships between countries for all categories of goods, services, and financial transfers, cheapening them or making them more expensive depending upon whether exchange rates are revalued or devalued. To be effective the price changes must be accepted and not resisted by the principal economic classes concerned. A widespread effort to shift adjustment burdens, noteworthily the case in the unprogrammed exchange rate changes that occurred after 1972–1973, became institutionalized when a policy of floating was embarked upon with greatly diminished management and integration of exchange rate policy into overall economic guidance.

Beyond these measures of policy a whole range of policies sprang into life with different forms of wage and price control to weaken or suspend a tendency toward the development of a wage-price spiral, the one feeding on the other. Again this varied widely by countries depending upon the style of national leadership and its doctrinal attachment to the verities of the nineteenth century, the closeness of ties of the trade union movement to the political leadership, and the mechanics of collective bargaining. In countries such as Sweden where a master collective wage bargain was negotiated by national spokesmen for organized labor and business very evidently the wage-price spiral is nearly cut off at its source. In a system such as United States where even industry-wide bargaining is rare and where individual firm or single area negotiations are the rule, it is easier to ignore the effects of a wage bargain on concurrent bargains or on prices, and the inducements to wage-price spiralling are magnified.[106]

In the entire postwar epoch extending over a third of a century the achievement of the mixed economy in greatly reducing cyclical instability and achieving stable growth and relatively high rates of development of economic life is written large in the historical statistics of our time. There has been a nearly continuous play of a minor cycle tendency in most Western countries running its course in thirty-five to forty-four months with relatively short recessions. Many of these were so mild that they only show up in actual statistics as a slowdown of growth and not an absolute decline in industrial production or employment.[107] The mean duration of the seven recessions in the American economy since 1946 has been eleven months and only one of the recessions—that of 1973–1975—can be regarded as severe in intensity or duration. There was very little international synchronization of cycle movements—that chiefly in the 1957–1958 and 1973–1975 recessions—in itself exerting a smoothing effect.[108] Nothing remotely approaching the extended, continuous wave of decline registered in the great depressions of the capitalist epoch has occurred. Virtually any tendency toward a long-wave of urban development or building cycles has been obliterated by the greater role of public construction and credit aids to building, by the greater maturity of the real estate and building industry, and by the greater planfulness of economic life in the mixed economy.[109] For many of the countries of the mixed economy it seemed as if the very tendency toward cyclical oscillation had become smoothed out, predominantly in the 1960s for the United States, for Japan, and for many European countries[110] The very phenomena of waves of bank failures that once so plagued capitalist economic life and regularly rose to the front in periods of financial tension was eliminated either by development of gigantic monopoly networks privately owned or nationalized as in Europe or by the development of bank deposit insurance, which as in the United States cuts short the need for runs against deposits in institutions believed liable to failure.[111]

Mixed Economy and Friedmanism

The record of stable growth until 1973–1974 with only minor relatively short recessional phases applies to the aggregate of the mixed economy but not to all its individual countries. The Western world has been uneven in its growth tendencies for reasons not too well understood. The unprecedented surge of growth in Japan and Western Europe has come near lifting in many areas per capita real household disposable income to near the highest level in the Western world. That surge has enabled Western Europe to draw in on a vast scale immigrant labor from southeastern Europe and the Balkans, playing in the mid-twentieth century the role of migrant employer that the United States played in the late nineteenth and early twentieth century.

Those growth surges have been complemented by tendencies to slowdown in the erstwhile leading countries, United States and United Kingdom. There the recessions became sharper and more aggravated, unemployment greater, the growth of productivity lagging, and the tendency toward balance of payment deficit sharper. In these two countries sound economic policies have been undermined by the rapid development in the last two decades of conservative and monetarist doctrine that has slowly been erasing all the gains in understanding of macroeconomic process inherited from the work of Keynes. Friedmanism with its cult of market freedom has led to a profound retrogression in the ability to guide and plan macroeconomic development in the Western world. Friedmanism called for release of restraints on capital exports from the United States in 1969–1970 and rationalizing the flood of private dollar capital transfers to Europe and Japan that by 1971 had nearly doubled the quantity of international currency reserves equated to gold as backing and cover for domestic monetary expansion.[112] Friedmanism glorified the role of floating currencies and denied any responsibility of government or of its central bank for setting or adjusting the foreign exchange value of its currency. Friedmanism condemned any effort by government to diagnose business conditions or to seek to offset any unfavorable economic trend by either fiscal or monetary action. Friedmanism has sought to narrow the role of a central bank, deny it any responsibility for previsioning economic development or seeking to influence the level or the term structure of interest rates by use of its immense credit resources in bond and loan markets. The only fiscal initiative approved by Friedman is the reduction of tax rates advocated on all occasions to reduce spending resources available to democratic legislatures. Reduction of tax rates may seem to have worked well in the United States in recent years. The resulting immense budget deficits and armament spending have produced a growth in employment and real income exceeding that of Western Europe. But our growth has been fueled by massive and unbalancing borrowing from abroad, raising interest rates all over the world, and laying the foundation for financial crisis in United States and abroad.

It is not possible to write the epitaph of the mixed economy and to declare that it will expire in a wave of endless stagflation, high unemployment, wage-price spiral, and financial crisis. Monetarism with its crude relationships between gross aggregates and its submerging of the metabolic processes interweaving the varied activities of the Western world economy is hardly the last word in macroeconomic theory and practice. Healthier forms of mixed economy will stand out as an example to the others. The effort to return to simpler, almost primitive, forms of economic policy now dominant in the United States and in Great Britain cannot long persist without producing an awakening of mind and conscience. Healthy common sense will be aghast at the lost opportunities and hardships imposed upon millions of younger and weaker people in the Western world by virtually suspending economic growth. But we cannot now foresee when this will occur, or in what forms or after how much dislocation and disturbance.

7

The Socialist Economy

Commanding Heights

We seek to describe, by the term "socialist economy," the structured economic arrangements and institutions governing economic life in the Soviet Union since it emerged victorious from the Civil War of 1917–1921 and the many countries taking the socialist path since and during World War II. Out of the disorder and struggles marking the course of that war, socialist resistance movements mobilized their people, fought their way into power, and established governments in the Balkans (Yugoslavia and Albania) and in the Far East (mainland China and in Indochina). Over large areas of the Balkans, eastern and central Europe, and in Korea Soviet armies pushed back or conquered German and Japanese armed forces that had overrun the whole of Europe and penetrated deep into the Russian and Chinese heartland. In the process these Soviet armies established supporting civilian governments. Understandably these civilian governments were drawn from domestic political movements opposing Fascist or Japanese power in the great confrontations of World War II. They would unflinchingly carry out Soviet directives and they drew largely upon local or domestic Communists ideologically attracted to the Soviet banner and willing to function under, temporarily at least, Soviet control. The line between Socialist regimes initially established by domestic revolution as distinct from those established by victorious Soviet armies is fluid. Everywhere in the war-torn territories there were resistance movements predominantly led by Communists destined to play a significant political role once invading foreign armies were removed and the potential for revolutionary change opened up. In some areas these movements came to independent power. In other areas they were assisted to power by Soviet armies.[1]

Our analysis leaves out of account the Third World countries in Asia, Africa, and Latin America in which revolutionary governments are seeking to turn their economies in a socialist direction and are aligned to varying degrees with the socialist camp. The principal countries concerned are Cuba, Nicaragua, Angola, Mozambique, South Yemen, Ethiopia. The socioeconomic level of these regimes is much lower than the earlier countries that have taken the socialist direction. Soviet influence and control is of a different character. And political leadership is not in each case in the hands of an authentic Communist party with its distinctive ideology and its tendency to follow Soviet institutional patterns.

The characterization of socialist economy is not intended to include the first stages of the new regimes dominated by considerations of military security, the first sweeping steps of nationalization, the seizure of properties and facilities, the reopening of railway transport and of electrical service, and organization of food supplies. For the Soviet Union this initial transition extends through the period of so-called "military or war communism" dominated by all-out mobilization for civil war and terminating in the establishment of the New Economic Policy (NEP). This is here considered the first phase of the Soviet socialist economy. For the other countries the socialist economy proper commences with the dissolution of the early transition forms of coalition government and the commencement of government regimes wholly dominated by the Communist party, certainly well in hand by 1948–1949 for most of eastern and central Europe.[2] For mainland China the period instituting the new regime was extended by gradual enlargement of Communist-controlled "base areas" established in the early 1930s. Thus considerable segments of the new China had been on hand for some time when the People's Republic was launched by ceremonies in Peiping in September 1949. The revolutionary work of land reform continued through 1950 and the Chinese mobilization of "volunteers" to fight the Korean war in many ways extended the Chinese civil war to a new adjoining theater.

The takeover of state power by a government pledged to socialist objectives is the political presupposition of a socialist economy. To carry out those objectives there must be a takeover of the commanding heights of the economy: banks and mints, large-scale industry and mining, major wholesale trade establishments, transportation and communication networks including power stations, and finally channelling of all foreign trade and handling of foreign exchange to state agencies specialized for those functions. In large part this takeover occurs automatically as capitalists, corporate owners, and bankers abandon their properties and flee upon the advent of a socialist government or the approach of socialist armed forces. Sometimes takeover results from suppression of capitalist sabotage or from encouraging programs of worker control. As Soviet armies crossed frontiers in pursuit of Axis-led forces in eastern and central Europe, the Soviets automatically sequestered all industrial properties owned and operated by German nationals or by large German or Japanese corporations or by the Axis state powers. If not dismantled at the war's end, these properties were later turned over to the socialist regimes set up in the wake of Soviet armies.

In China the process of takeover of commanding heights of the economy was more gradual. There was immediate nationalization of all Japanese-owned or administered properties that were extensive especially in the port cities conquered by Japan early in the war or in Manchuria, the most industrially advanced region of China. Likewise there was nationalization of Chinese state properties or properties closely associated with the ousted Kuomintang regime. Industrial or commercial enterprises joining in the support of the anti-Japanese resistance and not closely attached to the Kuomintang regime were left in private ownership. Owners who had fled were sometimes invited back to resume control of their enterprises.[3] In the first year (1949) of the China People's Republic (CPR) 48.7 percent of nonagricultural commodity production was reported from 123,000 private enterprises, closely watched by workers' councils and trade unions and subject to control by state organs. State organs provided work materials and often purchased the finished product. In 1952 the share of industrial output from privately owned plants was 39 percent and of wholesale trade 36 percent.[4] State controls tightened after a campaign in 1951–1952 to enforce compliance with state regulations and to wipe out black marketing and tax evasion (Mao 1961–1977, 5:64). Already the juridical status of private enterprises had shifted in many cases into joint private-public enterprises with the state paying an interest return for a set period of years (at first limited to seven years but later extended with interest claiming 20.5 percent of earned profits).[5] The strength of the state sector was great enough in 1956 to apply the partnership principle to virtually all private industrial or wholesale trade enterprises. Embracing a labor force of some 3.8 million employees, the Communist state leadership was able to retain the good will of the bulk of the capitalist cadres remaining in the country and utilized their managerial skills and knowledge at the cost of a fraction of industrial output. Mao argued that "the capitalists plus the democrats and intellectuals associated with them have a higher level of cultural and technical knowledge." With "remoulding" and under close control, he found this class useful, explaining that by "buying over this class . . . and giving them jobs" we have deprived them of their "political capital and kept their mouths shut" for a small price in fixed interest and annual salaries.[6] Though the position of the private capitalists and their interest income was somewhat damaged during the Cultural Revolution, it is indicated that their positions were often quietly held. They are still active though with little national importance in the program of "modernizing" China.[7]

Communist Party Dictatorship

The decisive characteristics of a socialist economy run far beyond merely the uncontested functioning in a given territory of a communist-controlled governmental regime and takeover of the "commanding heights" of the economy. Uppermost of these characteristics is the dominating role of a Communist party, that association of conscious and willing adherents of the communist creed who pledge their good faith, their abilities, and their personal resources to cooperate with their party comrades in whatever theater of action they are engaged—be it a village community, an army unit, a local government, an electrical utility, a price-control office, a steel mill, or a hospital—to carry out the communist program. Concerting their activities in local associations holding regular private meetings; using where necessary the power of the state or police to win control of local public organizations where election or nomination may be required from some assembly or meeting; continually upholding the authority of government and propagandizing continually on its behalf; capable of deciding on policies by open group discussion but mobilizing all resolutely to carry out agreed decisions; in constant communication with higher levels of the party that are nominally established in hierarchic fashion by periodic congresses or conventions of elected party representatives meeting locally, districtwide, provincially, and finally nationally to elect the guiding committees and officers (including formidable secretaries and chairmen); pledged to instant obedience to all directives issued by higher party authorities; constantly purging itself of members deemed unworthy or unreliable; constantly soliciting new members from those drawn to the activity and programs of the party; subscribing to a dogmatic creed with its pantheon of martyrs and heroes and its assembly of devils and heretics; inspired by its messianic hopes for an ideal society, this brotherhood is less a political party than what the

Webbs four decades ago properly called it, "the vocation of leadership" with a commitment equal in intensity to that of religious conviction.[8] The main outlines and principles of the Communist party as an instrument of political action were shaped and theoretically formulated by V. I. Lenin, the founder and teacher of the Russian Communist party and the first leader of the Communist international.[9] Joseph Stalin made of this party a powerful instrument wholly dedicated to his will, as Mao did in China. Membership in the Communist party is categorically proscribed for capitalists, landowners, property owners. Its original Russian members were mostly professional revolutionaries and worker-militants. Except in the Far East where peasant guerrilla fighters predominated two to one or better in Communist party membership both during the period of civil war and after victory, the Communist movement has little representation in peasant communities but it draws well from workers engaged in modern industry, from public administration, and the professions. Khrushchev (1961a, 133) could well boast that the strength of the socialist economies was an outgrowth of the "most powerful force of our times," namely, the united will of Communist parties with a membership of about 40 million adults in eighty-seven countries. He added: "What vast numbers of people follow the Communists, share their views and convictions and approve and support their policies." For the Soviet Union itself Khrushchev could express pride in the nearly 10 million members active in the Communist party in October 1961, 40.7 percent being factory workers, 22.7 percent collective farmers, and 35.6 percent office and professional workers (Khrushchev 1961b, 156). The Chinese Communist party built up its membership after coming to national power in 1949 from 4.5 to 17 million members in 1961 to a reputed 28 million members in 1973 and 39 million members in 1981.[10] The faith of party members and the ties that bind them in fellowship are sufficiently strong to endure such great shocks and disruptions as the Russian Purges whipped up by Stalin and his henchmen who destroyed most of the state and party leadership in the country between 1935–1938, the Cultural Revolution in China that broke up many party organizations and dispersed much of the leadership evolved during the prior quarter of a century, and finally the startling revelations that came later and exposed the personal tyranny, abuse of power, and damage that the great idols of the Party, Stalin and Mao Tse Tung had wrought.[11] One of the indications in 1981 of the disintegration of the Communist political regime in Poland—and thus of its socialist economy—is the apparent loss of faith by working Communists in their party and its apparent inability to rally party members, much less the general population or most blue-collar workers, to its side.

The leading role of the Communist party is expressly written into the state constitution of the USSR, which in its 1936 version set forth the right of "the most active and politically conscious citizens" to unite in the Communist party as "the vanguard of the working people in their struggle to strengthen and develop the socialist system," thus forming the "leading nucleus of all organizations of the working people, both social and state."[12] That merely gave juridical expression to the fact that the Communist party destroyed all of its political rivals and even its coalition partners with whom it made the 1917 revolution and expressly prohibited any tendency toward association of citizens for the purpose of dislodging or replacing the Communist party. After destroying its rivals the Communist leadership prohibited its own members from coalescing into organized factions for the purpose of opposing the leadership or seeking to win over delegates to a communist congress or central committee. Efforts to coalesce could be nipped in the bud. The Communist leadership in China was more flexible. It asserts the "leadership principle" more indirectly. And it permits persons who had opposed the Chiang Kai-Shek regime and joined the establishment of the new republic to function in some form of political organization, to hold public office in a kind of united front movement under the leadership of the Communist party.[13]

The tendency to a paramount Communist position in the socialist economies is reinforced by certain deeply ingrained tenets and habits of thought of the Communist creed and the background of Marxism-Leninism from which it stems and to which it is adapted. The resolute conviction fortifying and strengthening Communist activists tends to give them a constant sense of categorical assurance that makes them intolerant of opposition and contemptuous of criticism. The Marxist doctrine of unconscious class action permits public action of almost any genre to be construed as drawing from a hostile class position. This makes it easy to condemn any opposition or criticism as inspired by enemies of the working class, the repository of all virtue in the Communist creed. Nor did this creed warn against undue centralization of power or abuse of power by those who wield the authority of the state. The Marxist formula of "Proletarian Dictatorship" serves rather to encourage the unrestricted use of power to achieve the purposes of the revolution and to build positions of strength for creation of a new society. In Marxist theory the state was regarded as an agent of a ruling class. Marxian theory did not deal with problems of abuse of state power or the complex means by which cliques or charismatic persons might seek to rule through political instrumentalities. The entire historical effort of bourgeois society extending over centuries to checkmate the absolutist power of the state, to limit its power of taxation, to subject it to standing rules, to work up a specialization of functions that would fragment and not centralize political authority, to weaken not to strengthen the power of the state, and to seek to provide safeguards against the abuse of that power—all this passed Marxism by as irrelevant to the strategy of building a new socialist economy and state. Marxian theory forecast the disintegration or "withering away" of state power as such once the foundation stones of the new society were laid though the nature of that society called for a greater role for state authority.

Three simple remedies were hailed in Marxism as "infallible" for the purpose of preventing "the transformation of the state" and its organs "from servants of society into masters": (1) universal suffrage, (2) the right of recall of elected officials at any time, and (3) imposition for all officials high or low of only workingmen's wages as an "effective barrier against place-hunting and careerism." Workingmen's wages must become differentiated to provide adequate incentives for persons undertaking the more difficult, strenuous, or costly forms of work. Any scheme of universal suffrage with or without recall is worthless as an antidote against a repressive state unless a code of civil rights is enforced, unless the power of the state is sufficiently dispersed that it may become accessible to minorities, and unless some access to media and rights of political association are assured. It was not accidental that Lenin's *State and Revolution,* the study that gathered together the gems of Marxism on the state and its role in history and its eventual "withering away" was itself composed in the summer of 1917, the heyday of revolutionary excitement, with its promises and illusions laid out in warmest hues for the buildup of the power of dictatorship without a glimmer of insight into the potential for abuse that this would make possible (Lenin 1917/1932, 64, 86).

Finally, the ingrained tendency for Communist rule to become unrestrained and centralized under the elastic formula of "dictatorship of the proletariat" was steadily reinforced by the exigent need to enforce a regimen of austerity. This was needed to repair the damage and disruption occasioned by the devastation of war—the staging for the advent of communist regimes—and to speed up industrialization that was in an advanced state only in parts of Eastern Germany and Czechoslovakia and provide for the common defense. The Soviet peoples had twice—after 1920 and again after 1945—to bear the burden of austerity in which they had lived for some fifteen years while adjusting to Stalin's war on the Russian peasantry and the first ordeals of accelerated industrialization. Nowhere in the communist world could personal comforts of good living be widely enjoyed except by the Communist elite nor could the vast new urban populations that were to be crowded into old cities or their newly built suburbs be housed adequately or even respectably. Only a small fraction of the upper classes could enjoy the comfort of a personal vehicle or of a small personal apartment or a summer cottage in vacation country.[14] The Soviets could hardly tolerate a rise in the standard of living for the satellite population much above that possible for their own people, though by the 1960s precisely that began to emerge in the more fortunate or better managed communist satellites. The flow of foodstuffs to the cities was not likely to be bountiful even with good harvests for peasant populations do not take readily to standard Communist management. Significant improvement in the standard of living for the people of China was pretty much undermined at the outset by the high rate of population growth, unrestrained in the early period of the Communist regime, which more than doubled China's population in thirty-one years between 1949 and 1980.[15]

The burden of austerity upon these Communist regimes was intensified by the hostility of the outside world to newly established socialist governments. The historical record will show that during World War I, the new Soviet regime was recognized and dealt with only for the purpose of negotiating treaties by which its territory could be annexed. Once the Western powers had settled their fratricidal conflict, the Soviets were encircled with trade and diplomatic boycott. The domestic enemies of the new regime were aided and abetted by foreign intervention on every front possible: in Asia, along the Black or Caspian Sea, in the Arctic, and via Poland and the Baltic states. Only the jealousy of the intervening powers of each other, a general sense of war exhaustion, the strong support of the European labor movement for the young Soviet republic, and the truly heroic mobilization of revolutionary armies on the Soviet side pushed out the invading armies and put an end to civil war. The Soviets never had any real assurance that intervention might not be resumed at any time. Only gradually did individual European countries establish normal diplomatic relations with the Soviet regime, defeated Germany leading the way, United States waiting until 1933 for this simple act. The victory of fascism in Europe, first in Italy in the early 1920s and later in Germany in 1933, the rise of authoritarian anti-Soviet regimes in central and eastern Europe all kept alive the fear of intervention this time foreshadowed by the building up of a German war machine. The American diplomatic recognition of the USSR in 1933 and admission to the League of Nations did little to ease the sense of outside hostility. To counter this and to prepare for seemingly inevitable onslaught the Communist leadership had constantly to whip up its population to a fever pitch of fear of foreign spies, to guard against all association with possible enemy forces, and to build strong defense forces. And when the feared intervention finally occurred and after long struggles and much sacrifice was finally repulsed by the coordinated efforts of the Soviet Union and her West European and American allies, the long-sought consolidation of peace was frustrated by confrontation with the United States. Armed with the formidable power of strategic nuclear weapons that brought Japan to her knees, United States led the Western allies into the Cold War with its inevitable accompaniments: intelligence infiltration for purposes of military espionage, internal subversion and sabotage, economic harassment by trade boycott and nonintercourse. Thus any potential for liberalization of the Communist regime in Russia and for the cultivation of a code of legality and belief in civil rights for expression of dissenting ideas and political criticism was dried up at the source or curbed because of fears that any Cold War crisis could become explosive in one theater or another or in all concurrently. Twice, popular revolt against austerity and repression in the Communist satellite world led to Soviet military intervention: in Hungary in 1956 and in Czechoslovakia in 1968. While the internal schism between Russia and China has lately relieved the Chinese Communist leadership of fear of American-led intervention, this was a latent menace while fighting in Korea in the early 1950s and in Vietnam until 1973. The latent American threat was replaced by menace on the Soviet frontier due to conflicts over borders, over doctrines, and rivalry for leadership in the Communist world. The self-assurance of the communist leadership in the Soviet Union has grown stronger with their successful mastery of nuclear weaponry and their remarkable breakthroughs in missile power, demonstrated in 1957 by their orbiting Sputnik. They could begin to relax under Khrushchev the repressive controls built up under Stalin.[16] The censorship over their creative writers was lifted sufficiently to bring out a new generation of dissenting intellectuals headed by such prophetic figures as Solzhenitsyn and Sakharov. The power of the secret police with its informer network was curbed. Ordinary judicial process with greater respect than previously for standing law was again restored. The concentration camps were if not emptied at least greatly thinned out. Former inmates were held guiltless of wrongdoing. A more normal form of collective leadership was restored. Much of this progress was reversed when Khrushchev was ousted in 1964. Short of a major breakthrough which would ease the burden of armament and the Cold War, the Soviet regime is not likely to move beyond Khrushchev's first steps of liberalization. That leaves the socialist world with all the earmarks of an authoritarian political regime, with media expression and the power of government wholly in the hands of the Communist party.

A Socialist Regime?

Are we entitled to denominate the economic system of an authoritarian political regime as "socialist" in the proper sense of that term? That denomination deeply offends two groups. One group comprises those whose faith in socialism is linked with a conjunct faith in democracy as a principle of political and industrial organization. A great many socialist parties in the generation that followed Marx deliberately chose to emphasize the conjunct character of their aims and faith by labeling themselves "social democrats." That was noteworthily true of Lenin's own party, which bore the label "Social Democracy" through the Communist takeover of power in Russia in 1918.

The second group who are offended by the socialist label applied to the Soviet and associated economies are inclined to withhold the label "socialist" until fairly high standards of industrial and political development are fulfilled. The leader of Soviet Communism, V. I. Lenin, was very cautious about applying the socialist label to the Soviet states that he had championed or to the far-reaching nationalization of industrial and commercial property that had been carried through. Quite clearly he believed the socialist economy was a thing to be "built up" during a prolonged transition period.[17] His only formal characterization in 1922 of the kind of economic system which was being built up under the rubric of the New Economic Policy (NEP) was a "special kind" of "state capitalism."[18] Even after one and a half decades of further development and construction, a dedicated Marxist-Leninist such as L. D. Trotsky believed the socialist standard was not yet achieved. The Soviet dictator, however, proudly proclaimed in 1936 that socialism had been achieved in at least its initial stages. A generation later Soviet leaders proclaimed that a further development of a socialist economy into a "Communist" economy was in process.

It is not our concern in this work to pass upon issues of logical construction in Communist doctrine or Marxist debate. Neither do we wish to offend in our terminology the views of persons with refined political sensitivities. Yet clearly we have a need for a simple and suitable label for the kind of economic system that has been built up in the Soviet Union and its allied states. That system is characterized by three basic underpinnings: (1) a political dictatorship with rule by a Communist party, (2) almost complete nationalization of industry and natural resources, (3) development of a regime of central growth planning to guide economic activity and especially the process of accumulation. These underpinnings are also embraced in the Marxian version of socialism as essential to the construction of socialism. It seems reasonable then to label "socialist" the economic system of economies built upon these three underpinnings without in any way presupposing that "socialism" itself has been achieved. What we are designating as a "socialist economy" may include nonsocialist modes of production especially in the fields of agriculture, urban and artisan services, and trade and commerce. Outstanding here is the world of direct commodity producers that dominated the producing population in agriculture and retail trade of both the Soviet Union and the People's Republic of China especially during their earlier years. The cooperative mode of production, which plays a decisive role in the agriculture of the Communist world, is a distinct mode of production even when it is state-directed and guided provided that cooperative members have the means to exert significant influence on the organization of production, the selection of management, the distribution of benefits, and the use of cooperative income. Nor should the role in a socialist economy of overt capitalist enterprise be excluded, especially in wholesale and retail trade and light industry such as Lenin sought to promote under the NEP, which Mao successfully for over a decade utilized in Chinese economic development, and which the Yugoslavs have successfully assimilated into their economic system. The mixture of modes or their hybridization will differ in the various socialist economies – just as they do in other economic systems.

Moreover, just as there are phases or stages in the development of other economic systems, so the socialist economies may have one or more phasing sequences. Some form of phasing occurs almost automatically since all the socialist regimes commenced under conditions of poverty and hardship, emerging generally out of the chaos of war and often in backward countries with a relatively low level of culture and of productive forces. This called for an initial set of policies, priorities, and institutions that could function under conditions of extreme austerity and central control. This contrasts paradoxically with the classical assumption of Marxian socialism as a "classless society based upon solidarity and the harmonious satisfaction of all needs."[19] Austerity and economic strain would also influence the role of state power and the margins or resources available to meet social concerns and the relative emphasis given to material incentives that are more pressing in their urgency at lower living standards. We may also expect the pressure for conformity to be greater when the risk of outside intervention is greater and before the new institutions have taken deep root. The habits of conformity and repression are psychologically difficult to throw off even when the need for them has been largely outgrown until some striking event or some liberating force clears the way to new horizons. Yet the history of the socialist states has pointed to an underlying thirst for freedom of expression and opportunities for self-government, sometimes even at the price of heavy personal sacrifices. The intellectual culture of the socialist world and some of their sacred texts provide constant incitement to rebellious attitudes, favor widespread participation in public decision making and reject passive acquiescence in rulings of authority. Hence I would close here with an earlier generalization I once ventured on this theme (Gottlieb 1972, 88).

> Whether the socialist economy will develop in a democratic or authoritarian direction and with egalitarian distributive patterns depends upon factors which are extremely varied: the traditions of the society embarking on the socialist path, the political institutions devised for allocating power and competing for office, access to the mass media, openness of courts and independence of the judiciary, differential access to education and other factors as well. . . . A socialist economy may thus be more or less class-bound or egalitarian, democratic or authoritarian. Certainly the dimensions of egalitarian-democratic response need not be unvarying but may have a dynamic of its own. The capitalist economy functioned in a wide variety of social settings and political arrangements. The political development under capitalism was not static or uniform. Though launched with a class-bound political state in which the underlying population was denied all participation in the political process, capitalism developed in England, in North America and in most of Western Europe a surprisingly large potential for democratization. Later this was followed by tendencies to fascism or authoritarian rule. A similar variety of social and political patterns may be expected for the socialist economy.

Growth Planning

A socialist economy rests upon two fundamental institutions: (1) a new form of accumulation achieved by comprehensive growth planning, (2) universal price control. If socialization of industrial or commercial property is not merely nominal, it must channel to the central treasury—that is, to the financial custodian of the socializing state—surpluses or profits earned by the enterprises. These profits must not be appropriated by local management or the local labor force or community with whose immediate aid production was carried on. These surpluses or profits include allowances for consumption of capital since it is quite open to question where and when replacement of capital should be carried out, in what form, and in which industry. Of course some discretion would be allowed local management to carry out the more routine kinds of maintenance to replace particular items of equipment or structure necessary for continued operations, and to carry out small-scale projects utilizing local materials not in scarce supply.[20]

The pecuniary resources of central investment planning will be extended considerably by mobilizing other available sources: general budget revenues ordinarily channeled for public works, newly created bank credit extensible without generating inflation, and thrift and pension funds channeled for new investment. This mobilization of savings to finance accumulation was energetically pursued by the NEP under Lenin and by the successor Stalinist regime in the Soviet Union. Central control of socialist finance was allowed to disintegrate in China during the period of Cultural Revolution. Special state measures were needed to centralize investment decisions in the modernization course of the post-Mao regime.[21]

Mobilization of funding is only the precondition for comprehensive central investment planning. The funds can only be used if a real economic basis exists by way of facilities that can produce capital goods. These facilities are organized in three broad branches of industry: construction materials, equipment, and the construction industry itself. The principal products of the construction-materials industry are building timber, cement, bricks, glass, roofing, fabrication steel, copper wire, steel pipe and copper tubing, insulation, specialized building hardware, electric fixtures, meters, fittings, wallboard. Each of these products is made by specialized producers drawing upon many kinds of raw materials. The principal products of the equipment industries are: vehicles, ships, locomotives, engines, pumps, printing presses, weaving looms, knitting machines, electric motors, diesel engines, drilling rigs, machinery and instruments of all kinds. The construction industry proper carries out building and construction projects. These projects mobilize a skilled labor force, equipped with the necessary tools and instruments for building. To carry out construction the necessary equipment for digging, mining, and excavating must be used. To assemble and install equipment as designed, light engineering skills are required, the work going hand in hand with heavy construction.

Some form of building industry will almost always be on hand in most countries though often lacking the capacity to carry out industrial or engineering construction. In many socialist economies even where an adequate construction industry is available with modern construction skills and capabilities there is very scanty availability of specialized industrial equipment production facilities. In these cases some capital accumulation can only go forward through the operations of foreign trade. An export trading surplus must be generated to provide funds for purchase of requisite industrial equipment from foreign producers. The scale of this export surplus or the extent to which other importation can be suppressed will then govern the scale and dictate the form of accumulation. The Soviet economy in its early years had domestic capabilities for heavy construction work and advanced engineering and it soon provided itself with a broad variety of specialized equipment producing facilities. Yet Soviet economic planners found it desirable to import many specialized kinds of industrial equipment (including outfitting of entire factories) that could only have been produced domestically at very high cost and with long delays. The equipment and engineering capabilities of the socialist world have been considerably augmented since 1946 by specialized engineering industries developed in the more advanced socialist economies (such as East Germany) so that mutual trade among them can now provide most of their advanced engineering needs.

A construction and equipment industry properly diversified will only function in the work of accumulation if it is adequately supported with transport and energy. Construction will always call for additional energy utilization since building materials, especially cement or bricks, can only be produced by high temperatures and construction materials and equipment are by their nature bulky for their value and must often be transported long distances. Hence the real work of capital accumulation in the modern economy can only go forward on a widened scale if facilities for transportation and for generating and distributing power are extended concurrently.

The broad character and scope for capital accumulation in the socialist economy will thus be determined, apart from the flexibility given it through foreign trade and the export surpluses not already required for procurement of essential imports or for service of outstanding foreign indebtedness, by the volume and built-in capabilities of the building materials industry, the construction industry, the transport and power network, and the machinery-building and equipment industries. The plan of capital investment is very important for it will provide the leeway for further expansion of transport and energy and widen the bounds for further accumulation. It will pinpoint the site of new investment and the pattern of geographical specialization that will be emerging, the scale of investment in particular enterprises and the diversity of industrial specialization permitted. The plan will offer a choice between improving particular types of equipment capabilities (say between making tractors, trucks, or mining equipment). To a limited extent the current investment plan can channel resources into further production of primary metals—steel, aluminum, copper that are the main components of all equipment—or into further production of additional kinds of equipment specialized to make consumer or producer goods or that will service agricultural production and the level of subsistence this makes available.

Whatever its strategical pattern, the investment plan must look forward to more than a single year because most investment activity is carried on for relatively long periods before bearing fruit. This gestation period between the initiation of an investment project and its materialization will be longest for major railway lines, hydroelectric structures damming a great river, or a canal. Even for a single plant encompassing a variety of integrated production processes, the gestation period will be appreciable. Informed estimates of Soviet experience indicated that average "total elapsed time between project initiation and full scale production" ranged between five to eight years.[22] Some Western students of those industrial business cycles with a duration between eight to ten years have even hypothesized that the duration of the cycle expansion or "boom" was governed by the predominant gestation period concerned. The hypothesis seems dubious indeed because of the variability of gestation periods for different kinds of industrial investment.[23] In recent Chinese experience only some 10.6 percent of the total number of big or medium-sized investment projects in process were completed within a given year (*Beijing Review,* 27 May 1982, 13). Fewer than half of the 890 large or medium-sized investment projects projected in the sixth Chinese Five-Year Plan (1981–1985) are scheduled for completion during that period and this despite efforts to accelerate construction activity and to commence fewer projects. Hence each planning period commences with carrying forward undigested investment projects still in process and scheduled to come to fruition at different points of time, some immediately, some within a few months, some within the year, and others in more remote periods. A more rapid process of completion may be expected for projects of betterments and extensions of existing enterprises, a category of investment boosted in recent Chinese planning from the prior pattern of one-fifth to a little over one-third of gross capital outlay.

The diversity of gestation periods and the continued role of small-scale projects and of extensions of existing enterprises going hand in hand with whole new parcels of investment means that a plan for new investment must concurrently be interwoven with a plan for the entire industrial economy. That plan must be prepared not only as a sequence of investment projects but as a flow chart of industrial output in each forthcoming time period pinpointing the new production facilities scheduled to become serviceable and go into operation. Allowance must hence be made for supporting transport and energy, for supplies and materials, and for the labor force needed to activate new facilities. Place must also be found for their outputs that will become, except for finished consumer goods, inputs for other industrial use. Hence the forward planning of industrial output up and down the line for a succession of projected time periods is fully essential for the forward planning and proper placement of investment projects. What is more, there must not only be balance between inputs available and output projected at the termination of the planning period but continuously throughout its course.

Where the pace of new investment is very limited compared to the extant stock of production facilities, new investment for the forward period may safely be geared to the needs and requirements experienced and perceived at the outset of the planning period. The socialist economies of our time have mobilized such a large fraction of their national income for accumulation and have built up an industrial economy with so ample a capacity for accumulative output, as to preclude adaptation of the pattern or norms of investment to the preexisting conditions that are the immediate environment of plan takeoff.[24] The modeling must allow for continuous change in the technical norms conditioned by prevailing technology and engineering practice, by the relative scarcities of goods and supplies, by skills accumulated in the labor force, and by structured incentives for innovative performance. These norms are expressed in many ways: as productivity norms governing piece-rate pay schedules, input requirements for given amounts of output, durability or life serviceability of equipment and products. These norms will themselves change significantly during a plan period.

Then, too, planning must allow for the projected needs and requirements of the transformed industrial environment that will materialize at the end of the plan period and for the side effects that will cumulate. This may call for significant research and laboratory capabilities and for higher levels of technical schooling for manpower engaged in industry. The accumulation of wealth and the improvement in technology will usually call for and be associated with a redistribution of population between town and country and the creation of new or enlargement of old urban centers. The most essential of the investment needs of this ramifying course of economic development must be anticipated by an optimal investment plan.

An optimal investment plan cannot merely be concocted by an agency of central planners though its final form must be determined by these planners. It is in that respect like a government budget, which though drawn up by a central budget bureau will embody budget programming carried on by innumerable agencies and bureaus of government. Central staff planners could never develop close knowledge of prevailing needs and resource gaps of various industries and regions, of the potential capabilities of new technology, of the triggering role that small investments can play, of trends in technology that may safely be projected. This knowledge is often concrete, local, and scattered all over the industrial economy: in management levels of many industrial enterprises, in design bureaus, in research institutions, in government ministries or bureaus with immediate responsibility for branches of industry or commerce, in provincial governments. Even in the worst days of the Stalinist tyranny central economic planning in the Soviet Union was conducted as a kind of nationwide symphony, with all bureaus, institutions, firms, ministries responding critically or creatively to government guidelines with a draft five-year plan for their industry, their enterprise, their region.[25] This surge of information and planning—which expresses itself in vast numbers of investment projects growing out of a widespread investment drive or "hunger"—is the major raw material out of which a plan is eventually made.[26]

The task of central planners is then to orchestrate this raw material, to review its various projects and programs critically, to carefully screen cost and yield estimates, to develop criteria for selection and rejection of projects in terms of yield or priority, and finally to carry through the necessary iterations that will finally achieve economic and material balance at higher levels of social product and productivity.

This planning task would be extremely difficult if technology were held constant so that methods and designs of products and services were unchanged. The task is rendered immeasurably more difficult by the need to utilize new investment to lift levels of productivity and improve the performance, durability, and quality of products; to utilize new production resources and materials; and to develop higher levels of technology. Investment yields where new technology is concerned must be estimated or projected beyond the realm of familiar experience. The established tables of input–output coefficients cannot be utilized without modification to schedule the quantities of inputs for each additional unit of output. Nor can investment funds be neatly dichotomized into two categories of projects: (1) to enlarge productive capacity at a constant technology, (2) to improve technology itself. Some form of technical innovation will probably be embodied in most investment projects carried out in each planning period. The role of innovation will tend to be large in the socialist economy partly because the socialist programs ascribed immense importance to the task of lifting productivity to higher levels by the application of scientific research. Socialism was virtually identified with high levels of production achieved by accumulating capital embodying a higher technology based upon scientific research. This theme stood out very strongly in the writings of Lenin during the early years of the Soviet regime. The industrial trusts and ministries were generally equipped and staffed with first-rate laboratories and research institutes. Soviet higher institutions of learning readily collaborated in many instances with enthusiasm and devotion if only to overtake and surpass American productivity or more simply to overcome traditional Russian backwardness.[27]

Critics of the Soviet economy generally concede that its cultural and political norms favor technical progress. This is especially true of Kornai (1980, 2:54) treating East European socialist economies and particularly Hungary prior to the 1968 Reform. But he contends enterprise managers facing "soft" budgets foster investment projects of all kinds, tend to overstate prospective investment yields or payoffs, and in negotiations with higher levels of authority seek approval of wasteful projects.[28] That there is some merit to these contentions is conceded by many Soviet observers and leaders who charge many enterprise managers with carelessly hoarding equipment and manpower, obtaining unduly low output target objectives, and generally acting irresponsibly.[29] Soviet planners and design institutes continue year after year to schedule an excessive number of new construction projects. State property is widely misused.[30] We have known for a long time that central economic growth planning has been virtually since its inception far from optimal or ideal in the socialist economies of our time. For decades the allocation of investment resources in variant designs had no way to scale adequately for investment yield of design variants because of denial of the concept of incremental capital productivity and the unsatisfactory measure of product value devoid of capital charges or differential resource rents. Overtaut planning was encouraged by scheduling levels of productivity or of norms for capacity utilization to keep enterprise managers and trust managements up to the mark.

However, the evidence on the quality of socialist central growth planning and investment decision making is not all negative. Claims that all or most enterprise directors and trust or combine or ministry management are self-seeking or act irresponsibly in their proposals for capital investment are hardly consistent with the record of sustained economic growth even in the most terrible years of the Stalin dictatorship. The remarkably speedy rebuilding and industrial recovery within two decades after the ending of World War II, which devastated immense areas of European Russia and took over 20 million lives, testifies to the contrary. Even in industrial activities such as petroleum and gas exploration, which are not readily subject to bureaucratic management of large corporations in the Western world and which in the United States have been largely reserved for private entrepreneurial ventures, the Soviet state has done remarkably well in developing in a very difficult environment the world's largest oil and gas industry operating in one country. Output of crude oil has risen through the late seventies and early eighties to over 12 million barrels daily.[31] Beside developing a large petrochemical industry for fibres and synthetics and providing fuel for transportation and electric power thermal stations both for itself and its European socialist states, petroleum and natural gas now make up a leading export providing hard currency for Soviet trade needs. This remarkable achievement in investment and output growth does not appear to have resulted from a special planning regime unique to that industry. So also Soviet achievement in space travel and nuclear weaponry was not the product of sleezy or irresponsible behavior up and down the line in investment planning. Noteworthily, many of the gross deficiencies characterizing Soviet economic planning under Stalin have been corrected in recent decades. The newer socialist economies have not recapitulated the entire sequence of errors and crudities that marked the Soviet pioneering effort to master socialist growth planning. Finally, all the socialist economies are now making full use of the resources of computerized science, of optimal programming, and of econometric modeling that are now playing a significant role in socialist planning (Gottlieb 1984, 215 n.80).

Socialist central investment planning is not the only form of planning embodied in economic systems. Western economies had earlier and concurrently developed three partial ingredients of socialist growth planning: short-term planning for production and inventory schedules by business firms, long-term capital planning by larger corporations extending in special cases over five years, and institutionalized forward yearly or biennial planning of revenues and expenditures by central and local governments. Both the short- and long-term planning by businesses and governments are based upon forecasts of national income or industrial output. Capital budgeting by large corporations is a crucial management device by which topside management is able to retain control over ramifying networks of individual enterprises scattered over an immense territory and engaging often in unrelated fields. These plans are not, however, cleared, much less integrated with each other. The plans of different corporations are not geared to maintaining full employment of national resources; they are based on varying levels of forecast activity. Commitments are rarely made beyond a coming period ahead. Planning generally is influenced disproportionately by recent trends or by immediately felt or experienced shortages or surpluses. Hence planning in the mixed economy and in the socialist economy are profoundly different.[32]

PRICE CONTROL

The second major institution of the socialist economy is universal price control. The role for central price control as a normal method of economic management was spelled out in my recent work, *Theory of an Economic System* (1984, 234) and this is quoted in extenso:

> In the socialist economies price control as a central state function is called for as a normal method of economic management by a double set of reinforcing pressures. One of these pressures grows out of state socialization of industry which usually takes the form of comprehensive industrial trusts or combines managing all enterprises making the same line of products or perhaps using the same manufacturing technology. Even when more than one trust operates in a given commodity field, they cannot be expected to compete with each other for markets, patronage, or supplies. And certainly other enterprises cannot be expected to be attracted to a given field which appears profitable and be able in a well-organized socialist economy to set themselves up in business. Nor can competition be expected from foreign producers who are not allowed free entrance into the economic system and the right to establish enterprises, make profits and withdraw them as they please. Industrial undertakings will thus possess an uncommon degree of monopoly power in their commodity area. If they would have the right to set prices with a free hand, that monopoly power could take a frightful toll at critical points in the commodity field. If industrial profits are all commandeered by higher state authority, then the motive to exercise this monopoly power would be weakened and it would probably not be so harmful.
>
> Such commandeering brings into play the second set of pressures which in the socialist economy calls for price control. The leaders of the Soviet economy realized as their industrialization proceeded that they needed to provide incentives up and down the line in socialized enterprises to manage resources efficiently, to strive for cost reductions or for improvements in quality. These incentives it was found could best take the form of "profit-sharing" arrangements with which the Soviet economy is littered. Profit-sharing involves bonuses for meeting state targets and one of the best available and most generalized targets is precisely the earning of extra profits or the achievement of cost-cutting goals while maintaining output and quality targets. Bonuses for meeting these targets are paid out and provide incentives not only to management personnel but to the entire regular work staff of the enterprise. If management is not constrained as to the prices that may be charged, there is no assurance that additional profits earned are not the result of use of monopoly power in pricing rather than of efficient management or high work morale.

The two pressures converge to the same outcome. If competition cannot become the organizing force to control price levels and if profit is to serve as a motivating force for innovation and improved productivity, then pricing must be taken out of the hands of enterprise management and converted into a central state function operating by uniform principles through the entire economy.

A socialist economy may need centrally administered price control but this control need not be applicable to all exchange transactions and to all commodity markets. If the socialist economy includes direct commodity producers in urban crafts and services, on farms and in petty retail trade, then pricing by those producers may in principle remain free except at a time of national emergency or for a very limited period under special conditions. Any control that is needed must be achieved by indirect methods that include taxation, licensing, and state entrance into the commodity field offering products and services moving prices in the desired direction. If capitalist or foreign-operated businesses are licensed to conduct operations in a socialist economy, as they were in the Soviet Union in the NEP or in the present Chinese economy, then those operations would be hampered considerably if prices were subject to control by the socialist central authorities. So also sale of personal possessions by households or sale of houses, lots, or personal services rendered to individuals should in principle be free of state control though it may be desirable for certain classes of these transactions to be a matter of public record.

The field of price control as a principle of socialist economic organization relates to prices of socialized enterprises selling or disposing of goods or services primarily to other socialist enterprises or to what we can generally label state interfirm transactions. Certainly, terms of sale to "foreign" or external buyers would be controlled in a different way; and terms of sale to final consumers at the retail household level can be regulated by imposition of retail margin or markup requirements over retail delivered cost. Some preticketing of final retail price may be a feasible distribution strategy where rationing has been imposed or for certain goods and services in short supply. Since such preticketing does not readily allow for transportation costs that are an essential element of retail price, preticketing of price should only be considered in special cases.[33]

Central price control obviously does not mean that every commodity entering into interfirm transactions would in some catalogue issued by the central pricing office be ticketed or listed with a selling price. Where products are produced in set moulds or models with little variation for individual buyers, then such products and their prices would be specified in some appropriate form. But where materials, size, and other features of the product are variable, then the central authorities would fix not the price itself but the pricing formula or the rule by which a price would be determined. Such pricing by formula was well known and frequently used in the now distant days (1942–1946) when price-control functioned in the American scene. Formula pricing may merely embody a procedure for determining prime costs for labor and material; a mark up for indirect charges; and an allowance for selling, administrative expense, and profit. The formulae must be known to buyers as well as sellers and there must be sufficient reporting of formula use and sample audit to assure compliance.[34]

Objection has been raised to this principle of central price control for the socialist economy, whether for good or bad, that it is "largely simply a myth." Prices for "standard mass produced" industrial goods, such as coal, cement, granulated sugar, or milk may be specified unambiguously. But it is contended by an economist who has worked professionally in the Hungarian economy that for the vast mass of "differentiated products," such as a "portable radio," a "relatively simple device" yet one that can be produced in a "thousand variations," price control is not feasible. There is too much variability of its component parts, its finishing materials, and even its packaging. "Hidden price increases" are possible since "quality is not prescribed in every detail" nor can it be expected that the price control authorities will "test the product in every detail."[35]

While industrial products can be altered in innumerable ways, once processes of production, equipment, and a stockpile of component parts and materials have been assembled and organized for the production of a given set of models, styles, or line items, stability is then imposed upon product makeup. Customers or would-be customers, higher authorities, and distributors are all informed of the product makeup usually embodied in a catalogue, bulletin, or other descriptive literature with the necessary specifications, warranties, quantity limits and the like. It is this product makeup, with appropriate samples, photographs, detailed description, and necessary cost information, that will be passed upon by price-control authorities and given the necessary approval. Maintenance of this price and of product specifications will be assisted by the stability of plant technology and by resistance of customers or product users to unscheduled and unannounced deterioration of quality by the use of substitute materials or appearance of seconds or rejects in product deliveries. If price-control authorities monitor product markets and keep in touch with buyers, weak spots in price control can be readily detected.

If managers of socialist enterprises act with the mentality and drives of petty traders or with utter disrespect for the laws and directives of the socialist state, then the administration of that economy would be a very costly affair. A certain degree of congruence must be presupposed in any economic system between its human functionaries and its guiding principles. While there are limits to the extent that self-seeking propensities can be denied expression, it would appear that provision of bonuses, profit-sharing plans, and the hope for promotion would resolve any tension caused by price control.

The Socialist Ruling Class

The socialist economic system has a ruling class, of course. This class is made up of the persons who preside over and direct public enterprises and institutions who comprise the higher level of the military and civil service and the apparatus of the Communist party, who approve publications and work out the line taken by the public media, who at the higher level decide periodically on the allocation of national income for different purposes and arrangements for financing public services, who enact generally applicable legislation covering such topics as state organization and distribution of functions to central and local organs, arrangement of the judiciary, education, family and divorce, and whatnot. The persons discharging these offices cannot be chosen by lot or indiscriminately from the public as was assumed in the early days of the Russian Revolution.[36] Only a limited number of persons have the aptitudes, the abilities, the drives, the professional schooling to qualify for these positions. And once qualified persons have had operative experience, they will have an enormous advantage over others without experience. That the socialist economy calls for large-scale economic and cultural organization and involves a high degree of specialization and expertise – whether the work is in marketing, industrial production, transportation, schooling or publications or planning – means that a broad diversity of directive personnel throughout the executive and managerial stratum of the society must be employed.

Apart from periods of revolutionary change such as occurred in the Soviet Union between 1927 and 1931 (when the Communist opposition groups and specialists were "purged"), or during the Great Purge of 1935–1939 (when the entire Soviet elite was purged), or in China between 1966–1976 during what is now called the "catastrophe" of the Cultural Revolution, the composition of the ruling class will be relatively stable. Annually a small fraction of positions will be emptied because of promotion, illness, retirement, or premature death. A large number of new entrants to the ruling class—which may be assumed to grow steadily in magnitude—will become placed in their entering positions. Ceaselessly positions are reshuffled between incumbents who advance up the hierarchy or shift about in it to find more satisfactory niches. But the entire class assimilating its new members and dropping its old ones has a truly monolithic form and character.

The ruling class is not homogeneous and its different members have varied responsibilities and scope for decision making according to their sphere of activities. At the highest level is the Secretariat of the Communist party in continuous session, executing party decisions, assigning party personnel to their respective posts, making up the agenda of high-level agencies. Nearly at the level of the Secretariat and integrated with it is the politbureau or Presidium, the summit of Communist decision makers, meeting weekly and engaged more or less continuously on important national issues. From there the scope of authority and the range of decision making falls off drastically. The central committee of the Communist party is a large representative body that has at times played a central role since it elects the Secretariat and Politbureaus and other higher executive organs of the party. If it were in continuous session it could play a quasi-parliamentary role as the holder of sovereign authority. But its members are geographically dispersed, it is elected indirectly, and its sessions are convened only twice yearly in recent years, and more for the purpose of ventilating issues and collecting views than working out compromise enactments subject to actual voting.[37] At the same national level a series of other bodies are engaged in decision making but only within a restricted sphere: finance, taxation or price control, economic planning, the conduct of foreign trade, editing of newspapers, direction of scientific research, or administration of business and industrial enterprises grouped into broad divisions under ministries and trusts. At the regional level encompassed by the various Soviet Republics and so on down to the level of municipalities and rural areas the same duality of all-purpose leadership organizations and specialized organizations is found.

The social and income statistics of the Soviet Union and other Communist-controlled countries do not disclose patterns of income distribution or numbers of the ruling class. We can gauge the magnitudes involved from rough estimates of the social physiognomy of the ruling stratum, prepared by a former Communist leader, L. D. Trotsky, who played an important role in the first decade of the Soviet state. In 1935 midway in its growth he estimated the "commanding upper circles of dignitaries and leaders" of the Soviet Union and its individual republics numbered "near half a million." Going on to the "heavy administrative pyramid" at the local and district level of the state, army and public services he believed would swell the ruling stratum to some 2 million. The administrative and technical personnel including foremen of economic enterprises and collective farms with their party and trade union leaderships—who do not engage directly in productive labor but "administer, order, command, pardon, and punish"—is estimated at 5 or 6 million, for a sum total of 7–8 million persons of which the Communist party activists amounted to only 1.5–2 million persons. With their families he believed that as many as 25 million persons were involved or some 12–15 percent of the Soviet population.[38] A more contemporary estimate of social stratification in the USSR emerges with a directive stratum of some 12 million employed persons or nearly double that of 1935–1936 with a larger proportion in the Communist party that in 1973 included among its members 6.6 million white-collar workers including clerical and lower-rung office personnel and professional service workers.[39]

The income distributive share drawn by the socialist ruling class, as disclosed by official wage and salary statistics, widened considerably in the Stalin period. Though detailed income data were not published after 1934, astute Western investigators have been able to piece out the statistical patterns of income distribution for nonfarm incomes (Wiles 1974, 20). It is believed that the top 0.6 percent of nonfarm income receivers, numbering in 1966 some 430,000 persons, had monthly incomes over 260 rubles, compared with a mean earning level of about 100 rubles and a minimum wage bracket of about 40 rubles monthly. The characteristics of income distribution among that topmost stratum is not known though in 1934, as patterns of inequality were settling in, the top bracket salaries were some 28.3 times minimum wage brackets (Bergson 1944, 129). That multiple must have grown considerably as the Stalin regime matured. Inequality of income distribution for the bulk of Soviet income receivers is measured in decile ratios, which span the range of inequality for the middle 80 percent of income receivers with the bottom and top 10 percent of the array sliced off. The ninetieth percentile income position in the array of income receivers as a multiple of the tenth percentile position rose from 3.82 in 1928 to 4.15 in 1934 and reached the unusual height of 7.24 in 1946.[40] Under Khrushchev it appears considerable inroads were made on income inequality with substantial boosts of low wage rates and retirement and disability pensions. On good authority we are told that no "other country can show a more rapid and sweeping progress toward equality" (Wiles 1974, 25). Beside boosting low wage brackets, pensioner, and kolhoznik incomes, an effort was made to curb special consumption privileges of the upper stratum by special stores, summer homes, and personal use of state cars. Measured inequality for the decile range fell to 4.4 in 1956 and 3.7 in 1964 and to levels of 3.2 under Brezhnev in 1970.[41]

There are three significant offsets to the measured range of income inequality which still allow a considerable fraction of Soviet disposable household money income to go to the upper class. In the first place total real income including social services is distributed more equally than disposable household money income. Pricing policies as well as the quirks of sales taxation establish relatively low prices on basic household necessities such as basic housing space, bread grains, and rough clothing and when these necessities are in short supply they are rationed. At times bread was priced so cheaply it was purchased for livestock feed.[42] Correspondingly, luxury goods in exceptionally short supply were sold at high markups and some were burdened with heavy turnover taxes. Certain vital services such as social security, education, schooling, and health care have been largely if not entirely financed by state budgets and not from payments out of household income. Stratification in distribution of these social services has been relatively limited.[43] Then, too, upper-stratum incomes are subject to personal income taxes (10–11 percent) (Nove 1968, 116).

There were many offsets to the higher standard of living that the Soviet ruling class took for itself under Stalin and still retain, though on a lesser scale under successor regimes. Managerial or directive service in the Communist state was itself a trying experience. It called for an extraordinary amount of work, a continual preoccupation with party affairs apart from one's regular work, readiness to be jerked out of friendly surroundings and dispatched on party assignments with little advance notice, making oneself a target for a host of auditors and informers searching for weak spots or "deviations." In the earlier years of the Stalin regime high office often turned into misfortune not blessing except for persons with a cruel streak or a craving for high adventure. Some antidote by way of personal comforts must have been indispensable in maintaining psychic equilibrium, though for most members of the ruling class on a hedonic scale the benefits of high office were hardly worth the strains and pressures entailed.

Mass Education and Class Structure

Finally, in the period when incumbency within the ruling class is not so stressful, then the relative position of the ruling class must be weakened by the vast relative increase in levels of education and technical skills that have become increasingly a prerequisite for high position in the Communist world. Facilities for secondary and higher education have been given lavish support in the Soviet Union and elsewhere in the socialist world so that a growing fraction of the Soviet adult population is now schooled for entrance into lower levels of the ruling class. The first Five-Year Plan put a major emphasis on the acceleration of schooling and vocational education to upgrade the skills of the labor force and acknowledged that "failure to give due attention" to skill development was the "principal defect in the long-term planning thus far done" (Gosplan 1929, 114). From 1940 onward a near constant 12 percent of Soviet government budgets was allocated for education giving rise to a monumental increase in the amount and diffusion of schooling especially in the younger generation. Complete primary school education was nearly universal in the Soviet Union by 1940 and by 1970 some 60 percent of primary school graduates went on to formal secondary schooling or vocational education. In 1980 Brezhnev could proudly announce the latter figure was 100 percent (Communist Party Soviet Union 1981, 78).

By 1960 the Soviets were graduating from higher educational establishments nearly as many persons with advanced degrees as in the United States.[44] In addition to full-time residential schooling there is enormous participation especially by younger workers in correspondence and extension courses.[45] Admission to higher institutions of learning from secondary schools is on the basis of merit screening and entrance examination with some quota admission of students proposed by their factory or farm.[46] The pressure of financial need to pay tuition is now obviated by the remission of tuition requirements imposed during the Stalin period.[47] Understandably students coming from homes with a more advanced cultural background and more comfortable personal circumstances are more inclined, and possibly more able, to qualify for higher educational institutions. Hence in the Soviet Union as in the United States higher education is socially selective and tends to build up a stratified society of manual workers and peasants on the one side, professional and technically schooled or directive personnel on the other, both usually marrying within their cultural class and watching their children follow in their footsteps (Lane 1976, 185). But unlike the United States the gates to higher education are financially unimpeded for ambitious and able younger men and women coming from working class or peasant homes. A very high percentage of college students in the USSR come from families of manual workers or peasants.[48] The multiplication of training for white collar pursuits and professional careers in the socialist world as elsewhere will tend to lessen the economic value such careers will bring, and will help to strengthen the move for income equalization. It should also tend to unsettle a political regime that does not allow significant scope for political self-expression.[49]

Wider access to higher education, which is becoming the critical requirement of the ruling class of the Communist world, is joined to another fact of strategic importance, namely that manual workers and peasant producers still are welcomed and drawn to the Communist party and permitted entrance in it – the concentrated cadre of the ruling class of the socialist economy. In the Stalin period the role in the party of manual workers had according to one report considerably declined (Crankshaw 1959, 65). During the Khrushchev years manual workers and collective farmers made up between 50 to 63 percent of Communist party membership.[50] The giant Communist party of China was reported in 1956–1957 with a membership in 1957 of 12.7 million members of whom 67 percent were of peasant origin and 13.4 percent of worker origin.[51] To the extent that channels of upward mobility are fully operating within a Communist party with this social composition, a closed stratum of a ruling class cannot crystalize. But it may be expected that as Chinese Communist society matures a much greater proportion of the membership of its ruling party will be drawn from persons who are born and raised in households, as in the Soviet Union and the East European satellite states, where the higher occupations and white-collar pursuits predominate.

The Chinese Cultural Revolution

The consolidation of a ruling class in the Communist world has met outright challenge only in Communist China. There for a decade a profound effort was made to uproot the tendencies to social crystalization of an elite ruling stratum. This effort partly stemmed from the unique agrarian background of the Chinese revolution, the predominance in its party cadres of peasant militants, and its tradition of the Civil War with its celebrated episodes of stamina, combat heroism, and guerilla warfare. It stemmed more largely however from the special philosophy of its great revolutionary leader, Mao Zedong, whose thought could not outgrow the nurturing conditions of three decades of revolutionary struggle and Civil War. He remained committed to the goal not merely of building a socialist China but of engaging in nearly continual revolution. He declared many times that his primary mission was to "make revolution," the revolution in "permanence" since he felt the revolution was continuously tending to backslide.[52] As he grew older he became more attached to the irrepressible enthusiasm and zealotry of youth who alone in history and usually "without learning" created new schools of thought, who "recognize new things at a glance and opened fire on the old fogies." (Schram 1974, 83, 119, 123, 210, 215). He began to be suspicious of formal learning and of universities where the professional and technical stratum were being schooled and prepared for their work. They read too much and became "bookworms." The ruling class who dominated the government offices were "eating well, dressing well and not ever doing any walking." He came to despise all appeals to material incentives dominating Soviet economic methods of income payment and which to him made "capitalism unbeatable." There were two ways of building socialism—one "coldly and deliberately," the other "boldly and joyfully" (Mao 1977, 79, 84, 89). It was obvious the way he favored.

This revolutionary-romantic side of Mao was submerged in the early work of consolidating the new regime. When this was well along in 1957–1958, Mao went on his first Left binge. He pulled the party with him on communal forms of collectivization that suppressed private plots. He whipped up the Great Leap Forward, which prescribed wild targets of iron and steel output and building of small iron and steel mills in the countryside. Incentive pay systems were drastically cut back. In 1961 output levels had fallen from 1958 levels 26.3 percent in agriculture and 38.2 in industry.[53]

Mao resigned the chairmanship of the government but retained his high party post, bided his time, built up a following in the People's Liberation Army. In 1966 the opportunity arose to appeal to the masses of student and army and working youth to take to the streets, establish revolutionary committees, "bombard headquarters," displace the party and government authorities who were "taking the capitalist road" and be guided by the "great red banner" of Mao's thought as set forth especially in a little red book.

A central target of institutional reform carried out in the Cultural Revolution was a revolutionary transformation of schooling. "While their main task is to study, students should also learn industrial work, farming and military affairs and take part in the struggles of the Cultural Revolution."[54] An extended period of manual farm work and rural living became a central phase of all programs of higher education and a form of retraining or "reeducation" imposed upon "old fogeys" who were not sufficiently enthusiastic about the Cultural Revolution. A virtual ban was put on material incentives. A full effort was made to undo the work of class stratification that had been built up over the past decade and a half.[55] Yet with Mao's death, after a short time of adjustment, the whole structure collapsed. The previous social pattern and cultural values were reinstated.

The Chinese experience of the Cultural Revolution shows nega-
tively what the experience of other socialist countries has shown posi-
tively that the socialist economy will be governed by a ruling class with
changing characteristics but linked with manual workers in fields, factories, and offices by institutionalized channels of upward mobility.
The economy as we have also seen will have its phases of greater or
lesser adaptation to austerity and repression. Beyond these features of
variation the socialist economy is subject to variation in a number of
other respects. Its composition of modes may vary considerably according as private property in farmland has been abolished (as in the
Soviet Union) or curtailed by pooling of farm properties in local
cooperative farms variously hybridized with state agencies and thus
having a dual character—on the one side a true producer cooperative,
on the other a state agency for enforcing and managing farm labor and
collecting surplus agricultural product. In urban industry and services
a varying role for private enterprise may be recognized or a uniform
and heavy-handed socialization may be enforced. Finally, the balance
in allocating resources between market methods and rationing may
vary. The Soviet economy in the NEP period, present-day Yugoslavia,
and it appears Hungary have worked out schemes for accommodating
central control of investment of national saving with decentralization
of decision making in procuring and marketing output with a greater
emphasis on prices and market transactions as organizing forces. In all
these respects we have almost as many distinctive socialist economies
as we have socialist countries and stages of development. That is fully
consistent with the central hypothesis of this work that economic systems even of the same broad class are varied in significant respects
and are continually changing.

Yugoslav Breakaway

So powerful is this tendency to system evolution and differentiation within the socialist world that it is just possible that it has carried
at least one socialist country outside the bounds of the socialist community. This has occurred in the judgment of well-qualified observers
in the case of Yugoslavia.[56] Differential evolution here partly took off
from the heavy-handed attempt of Stalin to impose his will by abrupt
trade boycott on the Yugoslav Communist leadership that had come to
power by its own strength in leading a national resistance to the Nazis
in World War II. The Yugoslav Communists defied Stalin and sought to
break with the centralist pattern of Soviet socialism by giving support
to the principle of worker self-management in their economic and

cultural enterprises.[57] The Yugoslavs went beyond Soviet and Western practice in allowing workers through some form of elected works council to advise with management or to negotiate with management on terms of employment and working conditions.[58] The Yugoslav leadership took seriously Marx's claim that by socialization of enterprise workers "freely associated" would control the process of production. They subordinated plant directors to elected worker's councils and they required that plant directors be appointed or dismissed by these councils that would have plenary authority over current plant operations, subject to restrictions in standing law about the working day, injury to environment, and current controls on selling prices and wage rates. It is not easy to tell from a distance how effectively these elected councils attended to their duties, to what extent they affected business policies or altered the course of management decisions. Since most plant directors and technicians and professional staff, together with a substantial number of worker council members, were members of the Communist party (or "League of Communists" as it is called in Yugoslavia), state interests endorsed by the party might well get tender consideration (Brzezinski 1967, 191). As everywhere, it is easier for popular lay councils to merely ratify ready-made programs put before them by informed staff than venture out on new courses. There is no evidence that business management was warped by the immediate interests of worker councils and there is evidence that on the whole council input was constructive and helped build morale and worker support for the enterprise.

In 1965 the Yugoslav leadership decided to base their economic regime even more fully on the policy of workers' self-government. This policy was then targeted on the entire process of accumulation, until then primarily managed by the central authorities on the basis of a far-reaching fiscal mobilization of national savings and central investment planning. This strategic shift in direction was announced by Tito during the Eighth Party Congress meeting in December 1964. Looking backward over the fifteen-year period that had elapsed since worker self-administration was introduced, he proclaimed it "as the most efficacious system in the development of our socialist community" that had "proved to be the real foundation upon which alone our socialist society can be further developed." On this basis he declared we should give the work collectives "the necessary material resources" to tackle the problem of accumulation and the whole work of augmenting production. "It is the work collectives" he declared, "which are best able to assess whether or not the construction of new enterprises, often requiring large-scale investment at the expense of the standard of living of both producers and the community as a whole are going to be economically sound." He went on to indict the whole system of centralized growth planning, of saving mobilization and "the system of centralized accumulation." "There is no denying that we have for years been bleeding industry white with levies, even on the depreciation fund, thus preventing renovation in industry, while the funds accumulated by us in this way were sometimes allocated to unprofitable investments," causing "major dislocations in our economic development," "dissatisfaction among our working people," and "friction between the republics." Thus he contended that they needed to "radically expand the self-management rights of the direct producers in the field of enlarged reproduction," making it possible "for work collectives to create and earn incomes in an increasingly independent and free manner as well as to distribute such incomes in accordance with their own and the general interests of the community, in an increasingly direct fashion" (League of Communists 1965, 30).

In the following address given by Tito's second in command, A. Kardelj, some of the practical implications of this approach were spelled out. There is no need "to secure resources for expanded reproduction by taxation of income." "Production relationships themselves and the system of income distribution" deriving from them, "are the most powerful incentive to work collectives to invest rationally." The collectives should be given freedom to utilize depreciation funds with minimum rates properly set by law. "It is most essential that the resources of expanded reproduction which accumulate in the work organizations will be inalienable from them," Additional funds for social reproduction will be available through the credit system "for all who guarantee to use them efficaciously . . . in accord with the economic policy to be determined by the economic plan." Credit institutions should be independent, "autonomous," "able to bear the full responsibility for their financial affairs and for their obligations and able . . . to say 'no' even to the organs of the socio-political communities" (League of Communists 1965, 81).

This drastic forward move to extend the work of collective self-government was carried out. Credit institutions were reshaped and consolidated, greatly reduced in number, and converted into powerful organs to administer the funds of savings and credits put in their possession for both short-term and long-term investment purposes.[59] Enterprises were given more freedom in setting prices and production decisions and were even permitted to merge or to establish branch enterprises or trade abroad. Corporate income tax was scaled down if not eliminated except on foreign concessions or joint enterprises. Use of depreciation reserves and of retained earnings was left up to the firms guided by decisions of their governing boards and workers' councils. Though total investment expenditure, as a fraction of gross domestic output, declined in the period following reorganization of the economy to effectuate the planned reforms, the decline proved only temporary and the share of investment in GDP remained surprisingly high, between 35 and 40 percent in 1974–1975.[60] From 1964 to 1970 the fraction of business earnings allocated to the wage fund rose to 80 percent, but there was a corresponding upward surge in the financing of capital outlay by expansion of bank credit, that is, by inflationary means (Furubotn and Pejovich 1973, 281).

The share of financing for capital outlay coming from central government budgets greatly declined to only 17 percent, 1970–1975.[61] The total share of private and collective consumption in gross social product since the reform has stabilized at around the prereform level, about 60 percent, ensuring adequate funding for business expansion that in turn has activated a steady growth in social product at a rate that official Yugoslav reports measure out at 8.4 percent per year, 1967–1975, but that Western critics have recalculated at 7.0 percent.[62]

The transformation of the economic system around the theme of worker's self-administration has affected all aspects of economic and political life. To function properly, controls on prices and wages have been relaxed so that enterprises are free to engage in business dealings on terms which they help to determine. A series of changes introduced in 1965 helped to rationalize the price system in conformity with the premise announced by Kardelj that "since we live in a market economy, . . . the primary distribution of national income should be effected through the market and prices" (League of Communists 1965, 86). A single sales tax was established to replace multiple sales tax rates, subsidies were abolished to industrial enterprises for sales to domestic markets, multiple exchange rates in foreign exchange markets were abolished in favor of a single exchange rate applicable to all classes of transactions for goods and services, and individual enterprises were encouraged to initiate and carry on foreign trade activities and were able to retain a fraction of the foreign exchange generated for firm purposes.[63] A world of small enterprise with less than five employees is tolerated in the urban service or handicraft sector along with a rural world of private farming enterprises (Bornstein 1974, 209). A greater role was allowed for competition among enterprises especially suited to an economy highly dependent on foreign trade. A central economic plan was compiled and enacted into law but it no longer exerts obligatory force though plan forecasts have conformed closely to actual outcomes, in the large if not in detail (Gruchy 1977, 564).

This more decentralized, loosely coordinated economy with social ownership of means of production is very obviously a socialist economy of a special kind. It has suffered from inflation, ups and downs in business, and a growing and substantial amount of unemployment despite the rather high rate of growth of social product and investment in fixed capital.[64] Perhaps worker self-management has induced a more capital-intensive plan of investment making for greater productivity and improved working conditions but failing to augment employment at the desired rate.[65] Surplus Yugoslavs have had to migrate to Western Europe and take up industrial opportunities there.[66] This opening of their frontier to free movement of their people testifies to the obviously deep-rooted loyalty of the people to the regime but it also indicates that worker's self-management may favor the employed or tenured, not the disadvantaged worker. Yugoslavia still retains the "leadership" principle for its Communist party but this has splintered into rival national provincial parties with a form of single party reign similar to that of Mexico rather than the USSR.[67]

The evolution in Yugoslavia is detailed only as a special case of structural change that has characterized the entire socialist world. In the six decades of the socialist history of the Soviet Union three more or less distinct forms of socialist economy have taken shape: the NEP economy that developed and flourished between 1922–1929, the mobilized overplanned Stalinist economy of 1930–1952, and the more democratized and advanced Khrushchev-Brezhnev regimes. The Chinese socialist economy has experienced its own kind of NEP (1949–1958), its highly mobilized and disrupted phase of Cultural Revolution, and finally its present regime of "modernization." East European satellite regimes have had similar ups and downs. A review of these special forms of socialist economy in this work will not be made. It will suffice here to trace out two of the most important lines of structural differentiation: (1) the mode of production evolved within agriculture and (2) the relative scope for decentralized decision making in industrial and commercial enterprise.

Agricultural Modes of Production

The historical basis for the development of agricultural modes of production in the socialist economy was created by the agrarian revolution accompanying the establishment of a socialist regime. The objective of this revolution was to liberate peasant producers from earlier modes of production in agriculture—whether feudal, landlord-tenant, or capitalist estate farming—that were deemed burdensome or oppressive. Farm properties of landlords, estate owners or capitalist farmers were generally confiscated and divided up into small farms allocated to former tenants or farm laborers or some ex-city dwellers returning to the countryside because of the decline of the urban economy. Agrarian land reform was a primary target for Chinese Communist-led armies engaged for two decades in civil war. As territory was liberated by the Red armies land reform was concurrently carried out. In the Russian Revolution the delayed process of revolution—which laid low Czarist power in February 1917 but did not see a Soviet regime established until October, eight months later—allowed wave after wave of elemental peasant revolt to seize estate properties and distribute the same to land-hungry peasants (Trotsky 1932, 1:392, 403). Much of the land reform was carried out before it was validated by an early decree of the young Soviet state that nationalized all land and provided for the confiscation and division of estate properties by local peasant committees.[68] In the Soviet Union hardly more than 1 or 2 percent of arable farmland was withheld from peasant distribution and was retained for state-farm purposes. In China the amount withheld was even smaller. In many East European satellite states, where advanced forms of capitalist farming were more developed, significant acreage was withheld from peasant land distribution and served as a basis for what later became a "state-farm" sector.[69]

Russian land reform went farther than merely seizure and distribution among peasant households of landlord and capitalist estate properties. The peasant communities undertaking land reform also seized and reallocated landholdings previously set aside from the open fields of the village community under earlier Czarist legislation. This legislation withdrew the support previously given by the Czarist regime to the village community as a viable form of land tenure. It enabled peasants who wished to operate individual farms as full private property to withdraw their landholdings from the authority of the village community and to acquire a consolidated tract capable of being enclosed and separately operated. By 1916 it is estimated that some 2.5 million peasant households, generally more prosperous and of larger size who had previously been acquiring land by lease or purchase from the estates, availed themselves of their legal rights under Stolypin legislation and put 46 million acres of farmland outside the jurisdiction of the village community, often against its will.[70]

The revolutionary discontent of the Russian peasantry in 1917–1919 evened up scores not only with landed estates and the gentry but also with their individualized comrades. The drive against individualized landholdings was encouraged by the Soviet regime, which in 1918 established "poor peasant" committees as the basis for Soviet power in the countryside to check on land reform and to better collect grain taxes.[71] In consequence it appears that a far-reaching degree of equalization of landholding occurred over the period 1917–1921, most thoroughly in Russia proper, more weakly in outlying provinces like Siberia and the Ukraine.[72] Everywhere the authority of the village community was extended over all farmland except cooperative farm colonies and state farms operated under direct state control. These village communities were made up of household heads of farming families, operating under traditional law but with authority recognized by Soviet law to regulate land allocation and other matters of village concern such as schemes of crop rotation, handling of common pasture and woodland wastes, and land reallocation to provide for new households or to utilize vacated holdings.[73]

The Chinese agrarian revolution like the Russian extended its equalizing scope to the more well-to-do peasants who either employed regular wage labor or leased lands to tenant farmers. In some of its phases the agrarian revolution merely reduced rent and interest and spared the category of "rich peasants."[74] They were generally reached sooner or later so that altogether some 43 percent of China's cultivated area was caught up in land reform that affected, it is believed, "a significant part of rich-peasant land" (Nolan 1976, 203). The extent of differentiation persisting after land reform between peasant strata appears very limited in the light of larger family size and increased number of workers in the so-called rich peasant class. In terms of arable area, income, and draft animals, so-called rich peasant households on a per capita basis were only a bit better off than so-called middle peasants involving for every ten rich peasant households 2.4 more acres of arable land, 3.1 more draft animals, and 543 more yuan income over a corresponding group of ten middle peasants. All the farms were minuscule in size ranging from a mean rich peasant holding of 4.22 acres per household against 3.22 for middle peasants and 2.26 acres for poor peasants and hired hands. Even rich peasants did not have a full plough or waterwheel per household.[75]

In East European countries and in Russia peasant landholdings emerging from land reform were generally of much larger size than in China. But relative to the scale of farm size evolved in the New World, the resulting farms were mere subsistence plots generally not exceeding 12–20 acres (Woytinsky 1953, 497). Beyond their small size suited to the wooden plow, hand scythe, and other traditional implements, these petty farming establishments were generally handicapped by the customary allocation of farmland in separate strips or plots scattered in different sections of the open fields evolved from the village community. Partible schemes of inheritance and piecemeal acquisition by lease or purchase of tracts of land becoming available at different times reinforced the tendency to partition farm holdings in numerous strips or plots. Though this partitioning tendency was perhaps strongest in Russia proper, it was also found in Chinese agriculture where farm holdings of less than 1 acre would be divided into 6 or 7 plots. In Czechoslovakia 1.4 million farms had 33 million plots averaging in size 5/8 of an acre each (Woytinsky 1953, 492; Eckstein 1968, 78). These inefficiently laid out, manually operated farms suffered from all the disabilities of traditional agriculture: low crop yields, poor seed selection, pitifully low milk output per dairy cow, traditional crop rotation schemes that involved relatively large fallow land, overuse of the limited amount of natural pasturage, use of only traditional fertilizer from animal husbandry.

Economic relations of socialist industry with peasant agriculture under conditions of impoverishment and austerity necessarily raised major issues of incentives and credibility. Peasant villages after agrarian reform would tend to support a socialist regime that liberated the village from landlords, debt usury, and oppressive local government (which in both Russia and China traditionally relied heavily on corporal punishment, in China the bamboo, in Russia the knout to collect taxes). Russian and Chinese peasants manned Red armies and the symbol of the Soviet state was the union of workers and peasants, the hammer and sickle.

But villagers were accustomed to sell or trade their small surplus production for bona-fide money that could be used to acquire necessary supplies for the farm and the household and to pay taxes and dues. They would need to believe the conditions of trade and the money used as a medium of exchange were such as to assure them a fair market so their work would bring them reasonable compensation and access to goods and services produced by urban communities. Once the conditions of civil war in Russia and international conflict had terminated, Lenin became convinced that peasant incentives to work, save, and market could only be assured if a market economy were restored with freedom to trade in open markets both by peasant proprietors, their cooperatives, and by licensed private traders or merchants and industrial producers, mostly state owned but including privately operated smaller firms. The peasant villages had enormous capacity for craft production, which needed to become galvanized into action. Capitalist producers if available and willing would be licensed for operation if they had some special skill or resource helpful in reactivating production. To carry his party with him and to turn the party around in its way of thinking "inside out," Lenin found it helpful to depict a socialist economy tolerating private traders, cooperative institutions, licensed capitalist producers, and state enterprises competing on an open market as "state capitalism"—capitalism guided by a proletarian state building up socialist industry.

Though Lenin planned to retain banking and foreign trade as a field of state enterprise, it was important that bank credits and foreign exchange resources be used commercially and prudently. Credit could only be granted to gainful enterprises that would repay their loans and contribute to economic expansion. That was Lenin's strategy of a New Economic Policy (NEP) in which trade was the link between the "new economy that we have begun to create," the "peasant economy by which millions and millions of peasants obtain their livelihood," and large numbers of bourgeois producers and traders whose enterprise and skills must be utilized in economic development.[76]

The "new economy" was to be based upon state enterprises operating in competitive markets subject to the test of market profitability. But the "new economy" was nonetheless to be guided by central state planning. Its investable resources were to be pooled, augmented by whatever could be squeezed out of the budget, and new accumulation was to be guided by a systemwide forecast, based upon comprehensive information and scientific judgments worked up by an independent staff whose judgments would have quasi-legislative force. Lenin's enthusiastic support for the plan of electrification developed in the midst of the Russian civil war foreshadows the extent to which planned investment under NEP was to be combined with the task of transformation of technology to higher levels.[77]

The Lenin strategy launched in the fourth year of the Russian Revolution was the strategy developed by Mao at the outset of the Chinese Revolution when prospects opened up for achieving a democratic coalition to mobilize resistance to the Japanese invasion. Thus the Chinese carefully targeted their nationalization to abandoned bourgeois, former Nationalist, or foreign-owned properties but exempted the ordinary run of small business, urban real estate and industrial enterprises that would cooperate with the new regime. The currency issued by the revolutionary forces was always carefully calibrated to what could be absorbed by the requirements of commodity circulation so that cumulative inflation was avoided partly by fiscal austerity and partly by high effective rates of taxation. The Chinese Communist leadership shied away from the policy and philosophy of "military Communism," which enticed the Soviet leadership. In the interest of promoting broad and deep incentives for restoration of productive effort the regime in 1949–1950 proclaimed a Chinese NEP of "four freedoms"—to buy and sell land, to rent land, to make loans at interest, and to hire labor.[78] To a considerable degree the Lenin NEP strategy was also widely adopted in the earlier stages of the East European socialist economies during their formative period when the methods and ideas of coalition government still prevailed. And especially in China where the political basis and acceptability of the new regime was stronger, economic recovery was most rapid from the disturbed conditions of nearly two decades of civil war and national resistance to Japanese intervention.[79]

Drive for Collectivization

The recovery of aggregate village output by the extraordinary efforts of millions of peasant producers was understandably very uneven. The wartime conditions from which agrarian reform evolved necessarily handicapped many of the newly established farms because of shortage of suitable equipment including in some cases plows, draught animals strong enough to work the fields, seed suitable for planting. A startling fraction of the Russian peasant households were horseless even by the late 1920s.[80] While village mutual self-help schemes, neighborly assistance, and governmental aids provided some amelioration of extreme shortages, the general level of productive activity was low and the restoration of earlier productive levels was uneven. Considerable advantages were thus created for the particular regions and farms that were less handicapped in starting operations under the new regime and were favored with good weather. Under conditions of impoverishment and shortage, even modest surpluses, especially if they cumulate, take on extraordinary importance and market value. It is hence not surprising that as economic recovery in agriculture worked its course in communist-controlled economies that the issues of capitalist development and kulak enrichment should become paramount objects of public concern. Russian Marxism and especially Lenin had in theoretical works and applied economic investigation before the Revolution laid considerable emphasis on the tendency of peasant villages to differentiate and to secrete a layer of well-off peasant bourgeoisie.[81] The theoretical category of rich peasants was also well developed by Chinese Marxists and had passed into the common currency of Marxist discourse in the world Communist movement.[82] The fact that hiring of labor and leasing of land was severely limited in the Soviet Union and that banking credits and tax policy favored the poorer peasant and laid burdens on more prosperous rural households did not hinder the fear of class differentiation. This was envisaged as pushing its way covertly if not overtly so as to belie official investigations and statistics.[83] The rich peasant combined with the private trader, both operating in free markets, conjured up the vision of capitalism being born and reborn in their very midst.[84]

A second problem worried the Communist leadership. They perceived that recovery of agricultural output to prewar levels by a universe of smallholding peasant farmers using traditional farming technology inevitably limited the fraction of farm output that could be extracted or drawn as market surpluses to give provisionment to urban population and urban industry. Without feudal lords or usurers the villagers especially in Russia were living better under the Communist regime. They were consuming at home or investing in growing livestock herds, and were marketing a smaller overall fraction of their output. The Communist leadership believed that this marketing fraction could not be pushed upward by administrative tax measures or by raising prices of industrial goods and services bought by peasant villages.[85] They believed that the marketing fraction could be increased appreciably only by getting direct hold of the productive forces operating in the village so that a larger share of the harvest could be siphoned off just as payroll taxes are taken from Western workmen's wages by schemes of withholding. That hold on village productive forces would require a new organization of village labor and land tenure so that the state through its local agents or loyal village cadres could organize farm labor and control the allocation and use of farm output.

Such a reorganization of village productive forces could achieve two other objectives. It would sweep away the innumerable boundaries of petty farm holdings and allow scientific agriculture and mechanical power to substitute for human and animal labor. Reorganization would also make it easier to utilize surplus working time that abounds in traditional peasant agriculture in nonpeak periods of labor utilization for communal public work projects involving road building, tree planting on high slopes, water-conservancy projects, or preparation of new farm fields on hillsides or wetlands by drainage or embankment. In the Soviet Union and in Eastern Europe emphasis was given to the first of these two objectives. In China and in the Orient, with its age-old tradition of corvée labor on public works and its relative overpopulation and small arable acreage per capita, emphasis was given the second of the two objectives. A third byproduct of a reorganization of village production that obliterated private property holdings in the countryside is that emigration out of villages would be facilitated since emigrants would not be held back by property rights in small farms.

Marxist leaders had always stated that a victorious proletarian revolution would never expropriate its self-employed peasant proprietors and force them into state-controlled collective farms. To alienate the village population in this way was envisaged as an act of madness to be abjured under all circumstances. The Communist leadership was fully aware of this doctrinal tradition.[86] Nevertheless their fear of class differentiation and of kulak enrichment was equally potent and traditionally enshrined. They were lured on by the obvious advantage of achieving a greater control over the allocation of village output to assure provisionment of the growing cities and expanding industry. They were inspired by the ultimate vision of achieving a higher level of the productive forces in agriculture thus enriching the nation and in the long run all of its citizens.

By this conjuncture of doctrine and circumstance, a bold and somewhat panicky Soviet leadership in 1928–1929 turned away from the Leninist strategy of NEP. They closed out private traders from food or grain markets, seized control of peasant landholdings and major farm means of production including draught animals, drove out of the countryside those better-off peasant households labeled as kulaks, imposed discriminatory taxes on refractory peasant households, and over a series of years organized village agriculture into collective farms. This agrarian revolution was led by local Soviet officials and police units, a small number of loyal Soviet villagers who were either indoctrinated Communists or poor peasants attracted to the new regime by their poverty, and by an army of urban worker-militants dispatched to the villages to reorganize village productive forces. Only gradually over the next decade were the tractors, harvesters, and combines made available for the mechanization of collective farm field work for preparing, cultivating, and harvesting the major field crops, especially bread grains, animal feeds, and cotton. Blowing hot and cold, the Soviet leaders finally worked out the compromises assuring peasant households a small private plot on which could be maintained a dairy cow, small livestock and poultry, and the right to free markets for the disposal of their private output or share of collective farm produce available for sale.[87]

Collectivization in China

The Chinese NEP did not last as long as the Russian. The Chinese leadership quickly became dissatisfied with its outcome. By the end of the third year of the new regime some 40 percent of peasant households participated, and it appears for the most part voluntarily, in mutual-aid teams typically made up of from half dozen to a dozen households undertaking to combine certain farming operations and their separate pools of equipment or stock while retaining separate identity and landownership. The proceeds of joint operations were generally allocated by separate agreement of the parties making allowance for the quality and quantity of effort and the value of the land and equipment furnished. Two years later the participation fraction rose to 58 percent. This spread of a new form of social organization of production was too rapid to be wholly the result of voluntary dealings by peasant households, but it is indicated that no unusual degree of force or pressure was called for.[88]

The Communist leadership was not content with these inchoate locally improvised peasant associations in which separate farm identity and ownership rights were preserved. Hence while pushing ahead with "team" organization they simultaneously launched a succession of drives calling for conversion of teams into larger formal cooperatives, generally running from thirty to fifty households or more, and involving permanent dedication of property to the new organization that would embrace all farming operations outside of small garden plots not to exceed 5 percent of farm acreage and livestock holdings allowed the members. Cooperative distribution still allowed for remuneration of land or capital provided as well as work services.

From late 1954 through 1955 a series of campaigns by the redoubtable chairman, Mao Zedong (1961–1977, 5:187, 239, 200), led to the transformation of individual farming into cooperative farming. In October 1954 the number of cooperatives was to be boosted from 100,000 to 600,000 and in the spring of 1955, to a million. By year's end 1955, 63 percent of China's peasant households or over 50 million were "cooperatized." Mao in midsummer 1955 boasted that forming cooperatives did not appear to reduce the output of the year before. He claimed before good data was available that in some 80 percent of cooperatives output "actually increased from 10 to 30 percent." Hence while scheduling the extension of cooperatization to the as yet unorganized households, found chiefly by then in the more newly liberated provinces and among distant minority peoples with predominantly pastoral agriculture, the Communist leadership pushed ahead for the elimination in existing cooperatives of the principle of distribution of income to reward differential contributions of property. That was achieved during 1956 thus resulting in "fully socialist agricultural producer cooperatives" which by December 1956 embraced 87.3 percent of China's peasant households. This expropriation of the small capital accumulated by better-off peasant households must have been resented but the movement was so rapid and the authority of Communist village cadres with their backing of former guerrilla fighters and demobilized soldiers was so great that local opposition was overcome.

The year 1957 was used to consolidate gains and stabilize the cooperative institutions that had been created. In 1958 the forward movement of agricultural reorganization was resumed. Cadre control was reinforced by federation of cooperatives into a smaller number of cooperative-control agencies called "communes" embracing from 1400 to 9800 households and a considerable territory usually coinciding with what in Anglo-American usage would correspond to a township or county (*hsiang* or *ch'u*). In the commune phase private plots with their pig breeding and gardening were eliminated, conscription for public works was greatly stepped up, control over rural income distribution was centralized, and for a time there was extensive experimentation with public feeding or canteens when wives were drawn into field work.[89] This period of agrarian policy in China has been labeled by a friendly observer as "peasant militarization" (Schurmann 1968, 479). A mass campaign was launched under cadre direction to squeeze in another round of crop sowing by double cropping or by interrow planting (Eckstein 1968, 329–96). Additional output was not proportionate to the added effort partly due to deterioration of soil fertility, by thinner spreading of manure and restricted cultivation and crowded work schedules. The supply of pigs especially fell off; grain output in 1960–1961 fell off by one quarter. Food availability nationwide deteriorated, and peasant dissatisfaction became acute.[90] The private plots and local food markets were restored. The leadership at party headquarters appeared to shift from Mao to party moderates. Authority over most farming operations was shifted back to the former teams and cooperatives. The commune headquarters was left to function chiefly to mobilize labor for emergency public works; to maintain a pool of farm equipment and high-grade repair facilities; to plan for water-conservancy schemes going beyond the natural village; to operate small industrial establishments processing locally grown agricultural products or local raw materials; and to carry out standard functions of rural local government including public health, roads, militia control, and communications.[91] Apart from a relatively small state farm sector virtually all of Chinese agriculture was reorganized into socialist-type cooperatives, closely linked through commune management to state guidance and direction but in internal operations run by annual meetings and elected officers with private agriculture confined to the small garden plots, fruit orchards, and pig and poultry raising around the homestead. In the Cultural Revolution period it is indicated that private plots were abolished again but after 1979–1980 they were reestablished with up to 15 percent of available acreage so utilized (*Beijing Review,* 29 June 1981). The private plots in 1980 averaged nationwide some 7.1 percent of farm acreage (Perkins and Yusuf 1984, 83). They are now overshadowed by the so-called "responsibility system" which in the post-Mao regime of Deng Ziaoping has revolutionized rural

China. Commencing in 1978 farm procurement prices were boosted substantially and some collective farmland was leased by cooperative management to peasant families on the basis of a stipulated plan of land use for a set quantum of farm produce with relatively free disposal of the surplus. Peasant response to the opportunity to work the land individually was so phenomenal that the system was extended nationwide and made more attractive. Lease terms now run up to fifteen years, fixing of a plan of land use has been dropped except for specification of the product used in lease payment, and that payment has at least in some areas been set at a tenth of total crop yield. The open markets for sale of farm products are open to all buyers and peasant producers and their cooperatives but the dominant party in such markets are the government buying agencies that control the great warehouses and granaries for storing or refrigerating farm produce or for transporting it to the cities and to main consuming regions.[92]

Collectivization in Eastern Europe

East European governments terminated the NEP as the Cold War intensified in 1948–1949 with Marshall Plan consolidation of Western Europe. Since recovery of agricultural production to prewar levels was substantially achieved, the stage was set for the Communist attack on private property in the countryside. Resistance was considerable and forced reversal of the policy of collectivization in two Communist-controlled countries after the first threshold of peasant resistance was broken. The Communist leadership in Yugoslavia and in Poland pulled back, pressure to collectivize was dropped, and the bulk of the collective farms fell apart. In Yugoslavia the pullback was part of a general retreat toward more democratic forms of social organization. In Poland the retreat was partly due to moral conviction of the Communist leader Gomulka who was willing to go to prison when he opposed the forced collectivization policy (Brzezinski 1967, 254, 340). The proprietorial instincts of the Polish peasant, for whom the village community was a long dissolved social form, had been reinforced by the Code Napoleon and later by special Russian liberation programs intended to weaken the Polish nobility.[93] It is significant that Khrushchev (1974, 208) who as a Ukrainian understood something of the Polish character recognized the validity of the Gomulka position and was willing to allow the Polish Communists to handle collectivization as an internal matter.[94]

In the other eastern countries, each following a somewhat different course and mingling differently the carrot and the stick, collectivization was pushed through only with liberal allowances for the private plot, the Communist safety valve for collective farming. While only amounting to 1.5 percent of Soviet arable acreage, these plots amount to 10.3 percent in Bulgaria, 15.3 percent in Hungary, 10.4 percent in East Germany, 8.3 percent in Czechoslovakia, and 15.8 percent in Romania (Shmelv 1979, 79). The fraction of farm output originating on private plots and of peasant income generated is correspondingly greater since the private plot tends to draw fodder and have well-fertilized fields for vegetable growing, orchards, vineyards, and the like. Though levels of productivity per worker and per crop acre or producing animal in the five Eastern European countries with socialized agriculture were at a somewhat higher level than in the two countries with private agriculture, the latter experienced a somewhat faster rate of growth of agricultural output. By 1973 the two countries with private agriculture achieved agricultural output levels for field crops of 183.8 percent of 1934–1938 levels against a socialized output index of 149.7 and the relative output rates of livestock output were 234.2 to 171.4.[95]

In all Communist countries except Yugoslavia and Poland the institutionalized collective farm with its common ownership of the means of production, sometimes shared with the state in farm machinery stations, with its sideline of private garden plots, is the dominant mode of production in agriculture. It clearly functions to a considerable degree as a state enterprise managed by state-appointed personnel with control of farmland and basic means of production and authority to direct the labor of villagers to produce farm output and to turn over a substantial share of that output to the state. Effective state control of directoral personnel in collective farms has been well attested to both in the Soviet Union and in mainland China. In the Soviet Union the operative managers of collective farms are formally elected by a twofold procedure: election by a membership meeting and confirmation or approval by a higher state organ. In China the procedural order is reversed. The initial appointment is proffered by the state organ and an executive board of the cooperative or commune confirms (Eckstein 1977, 77). In both cases it is apparently working practice for the will of the state organ to prevail though in many cases where membership preference seems strong and where no major state advantage by reversing local preference seems indicated it will be tolerated. In the first year of collectivization in the Soviet Union a small army of 25,000 urban worker-militants were sent to the countryside to take over directoral positions in newly formed collective farms. This practice of dispatching trusted urban party members to the countryside continued during the entire first decade of the formative period of Soviet collectivization.[96]

Most membership meetings automatically approved higher-level nominations.[97] The search for suitable personnel for collective-farm chairmen became a major preoccupation of lower cadres of Soviet Party officialdom.[98] Since good appointments were scarce, provincial party leaders would sometimes overlook marked "irregularities" in behavior (Fainsod 1963, 273). Yet Soviet leaders could also perceive that the "best directors" were not those who were sent unwillingly and accepted the post for "reasons of party discipline."[99] So the preference apparently was for local villagers suitably indoctrinated, loyal to the state, and with the indicated personal capacities. As the collective-farm system matured, these were found on an increasing scale. By 1939 it is indicated that 76 percent of directors originated from local villages, many of them having been given special schooling or training in the Soviet army (Bienstock 1944, 182).

Commandeering of a large fraction of collective-farm output by way of compulsory crop, meat, and milk deliveries at relatively low state-set procurement prices, which for most of the Stalin years were of nominal value in terms of effective purchasing power, was the major outward mark of state control. Collective-farm directors had the responsibility for fulfillment of these delivery quotas. Yet if the farms did well, it was common experience for their delivery quotas to be increased partly because district and regional food procurement agencies were under continual pressure to meet higher delivery schedules. Though it was continually promised that delivery quotas were "permanent" so as to create incentives to expand farm output with beneficial effects for the food growers involved, the continual change of "quotas" belied the promise.[100]

State control is also indicated by the facility with which boundaries of collective farms could be changed and sometimes revolutionized in a short time period. Thus in 1949–1950 Soviet authorities decided to consolidate their 236,900 collective farms with a mean size of 81 households. In one region within a few months in early 1950 some 2956 kolkhozi were reduced to 849. In the same period in the Moscow region 6069 Kolkhozi were reduced to 1668 (Vucinich 1952, 76). In the entire country in one year the number of collective farm units shrunk by nearly a third and the average number of households embraced reached 165 by the end of 1950. Merger activity continued and though the total number of peasant households countrywide declined, the average number in a collective farm rose to 275 in 1958, and to 383 in 1960, reaching in 1965, 421, and in 1979, 496 members and over 3,000 hectares.[101] Similarly the Chinese collective farms suddenly in one year, 1958, consolidated themselves into very widespread organizations that embraced an extended territory that precluded face-to-face dealings of commune members with very many of their fellow members living in different villages of the commune. In no way could these sudden displacements be rationalized as a process by which "collective farms began to merge, to pool their material and labor resources to accelerate the expansion of production on stronger economic and technical foundations" (Makhov and Frish 1969, 123).

While in these respects the collective farm functioned as a state-managed enterprise, in other respects it functioned as a producer's cooperative. Once the delivery quotas were met, the cooperative at its regularly held membership meetings and through its elected officers and governing board had authority, subject to broad state rules, to approve all production plans, output quotas, budgets, the disposal of output, and allocation of income. The board has authority to engage in direct marketing in nearby towns and cities of its surplus farm produce and to arrange for procurement of suitable or desired supplies and materials. There was considerable local autonomy about assignment of personnel to different responsibilities of brigade and team leaders; to set up or modify private plots and gardens; to control local affairs; and arrange local utilities for streets or roads, stores, and shops, repair facilities, and craft undertakings.

While in the Soviet Union initial resistance to collectivization was intense as in China during the heyday of the "commune" great leap forward, 1958–1960, the institutionalization of private plots and private marketing for that output in free markets helped to relieve acute discontent by preserving a remnant of the private farm. And as collectivization exhibited its great advantages by permitting use of mechanical power either to draw water or plow or cultivate huge fields previously worked by hand labor, opposition to it diminished especially in the younger generation attracted to the new technology. In the Soviet Union the collective farm was a special form of joint husbandry whose value was traditionally upheld by the village community. In China where there was no live tradition of a village community, the minuscule size of farms which often made it difficult to support a plough animal prodded interest in finding a way out of rural poverty while the large number of indoctrinated peasant Communists provided strong local leadership for collective-farm work. Finally, the collective-farm system with its nationwide schemes of farm procurement made it easier for collective farms in favored regions with fertile fields or with especially good leadership and high morale to achieve strong results and thus attain high earning levels serving as a beaconlight for weaker collective farms.[102] Though the Soviet state attempts to siphon off differential rents arising out of natural advantage in climate or soil fertility, only in recent years is a careful land cadastre in process of being developed. The absence of a land market with its ready capitalization of earning capabilities makes it possible for favored collective farms with natural advantages to achieve higher income levels and more satisfactory living conditions.[103] The collective farm is more attractive to peasant households if as in Hungary the autonomy of the local organization is given wide credence by supervising officials of government and if the state allows cooperatives wide scope for arranging plans of production and marketing.[104] At its best, however, the socialist collective farm harbors significant elements of coercion stemming from the mode of its creation and the use made by the state of the producing cooperative to appropriate a substantial share of agricultural output with only a semblance of market trading. Perhaps that accounts for the striking fact that in Soviet economic development, agriculture has been the weakest sector of the economy with the slowest rate of growth.

Rationing and Markets

If rationing were the sole or predominant method of resource allocation in the socialist economy, that economy would fully deserve the somewhat pejorative label "command economy" now widely applied to it.[105] For rationing essentially reduces to an authoritative distribution of resources by order or command, barring or greatly restricting freedom of choice except for the allocator. Throughout most of its history the socialist economy eschewed the use of rationing in distribution of most goods to individual consumers. Formal rationing of essential consumer goods, especially basic foodstuffs, was instituted during Russia's collectivization ordeal, the war period, and its immediate aftermath. It has been reapplied during relatively short crisis periods in the Soviet Union and eastern Europe.[106]

The tight food balance of China has given rationing a more persistent place there. Informal rationing by recurring shortages, in effect favoring consumers on a first-come, first-served basis, has prevailed more widely. But with further economic recovery in recent decades, the predominant method of consumer goods and services distribution is by optional purchase in quantities designated by the consumer using chiefly payment of money to finance the transfer.

In the Soviet Union the previous endemic seller's market for consumer goods began in the 1960s to shift for many classes of consumer goods into something like a buyer's market. As consumer stockpiles of clothing, consumer durables, and house furnishings became more widespread, selective buying increasingly appeared. Varieties of products that were slow selling because poorly designed or lacking in the proper finish or assortment of sizes or colors began to accumulate unsold on store shelves and in dealer stocks. The phenomenon of mark-down sales to dispose of old slow-selling inventories made its appearance for the first time.[107]

The principal field of consumer living dependent upon allocation by ration and not by free purchase is nonfarm housing. In the Soviet Union, village and farm housing has remained under the control of farm households either directly or through the kolkhoz. But in the cities a different pattern prevails. Urban real estate including housing and shops but especially apartment and tenement houses characteristically was socialized in the 1917–1921 takeover and was managed by local soviets or socialized enterprises. In the NEP period (1922–1928), new residential construction was predominantly built by workers or employees or their cooperatives at their own expense or with the aid of state credits.[108] In the Stalinist period with its great boom in urban development, private house construction was greatly curtailed and amounted in square footage to a quarter of officially constructed housing. Except for a well-to-do elite class or higher level working-class families, the typical Soviet worker and employee was dependent upon a rented flat or a bedroom with access to a kitchen and bathroom. This was allocated or dispensed chiefly in conjunction with employment and was sometimes used to reward favored employees or as an incentive for loyal performance. Since in a particular community allocated housing will be locally controlled by a few or even just one state agency – factory managers or local commune officials – allocated housing is bound up with a kind of personal dependency. Upper level or elite employees are allocated higher grade housing as an elite prerogative but it is received not without a sense of obligation.[109] In the postwar (1948–) heyday, restrictions on building private housing were eased and private housing under Khrushchev ran to a bit better than half of state-controlled housing. In the Brezhnev period strictly private housing was again curtailed though privately controlled cooperatives offset some of that curtailment.[110] Over the entire Soviet period of from 1917 to 1979, privately constructed and occupied nonfarm housing has run to about 30 percent of allocated state housing (USSR, Central Statistical Board 1979, 184).

Private housing had to compete against highly subsidized public allocated housing in which the rent charge covers barely a third of housing upkeep and maintenance. Owner-occupied housing cannot be sold or openly leased to others though it can be bequeathed upon death.[111] Private housing cannot be built in duplex form to help cover the cost and huge down payments must be accumulated in advance since state mortgage credit aids are very limited. Nevertheless, so strong is the hunger for home ownership – treasured for its privacy, its opportunity for self-help, its security of life, the opportunity for garden and for expression of personal taste – that a significant fraction of newly constructed Soviet housing has been private. The same pressures that have opened up Soviet housing markets have been experienced in China and throughout the East European satellite world.[112]

The impulse to ration has also been felt in Soviet labor, as in the housing market, but there it has been more resisted. One of the great political struggles in the early years of the Soviet Union prior to NEP concerned this issue of state labor mobilization sponsored by Leon Trotsky. It was strongly fought by Lenin and the Communist Party turned the proposal down.[113] The decision was that employees would be assembled and put in place by voluntary dealings of employer and employee, the one usually designating and controlling the proffered "job," the other usually agreeing to try to fill it on terms applicable to other jobs of the same class. Once employed, workers had powerful assistance in the NEP period from their local trade union in resisting management encroachments and keeping working conditions and pay rates substantially in line with earning possibilities in comparable fields as sanctioned by prevailing wage norms. Even after unions were curbed under Stalin, the worker through his union local had an opportunity to participate in protection of job tenure. Through his union the worker also had some say in the allocation of available bonus revenues and in the administration of various fringe benefits in money and in kind that are part of the wage package. The worker through his union no longer enjoyed full-fledged collective bargaining rights. Any use of the strike weapon was a criminal offense. Acceptance of the officially laid down plan for the enterprise and its wage norms was obligatory. But the worker had the right to quit the job and look for other employment. That right was abridged by cumulative encroachments built up in the Stalin period to a regime where workers were required to have at all times not only a valid passport for personal identification but a workbook normally held by the employer giving their employment history, job records and reasons, if any, for shifting from one enterprise to another. The outbreak of World War II in 1939 stimulated the further move toward labor mobilization. In 1940 workers generally were denied the privilege of leaving their jobs without permission of the employer and were made available for transfer to other jobs at the direction of labor offices. Young workers were made subject to outright labor mobilization (Schwartz 1954, 523).

These Stalinist restrictions on the freedom of labor became increasingly resented after the war, and after Stalin's death in 1953 these restrictions were permitted to lapse without enforcement and were then withdrawn (Nove 1968, 135). Even the limited 2–3 year period for labor mobilization for graduates of higher educational institutions or technical schools, as a compensation presumably for state-financed schooling, was poorly enforced. Some 90 percent of all hiring in the late 1960s of new accessions in the Soviet labor market was by means of free recruitment and not by allocation or mobilization. Since job openings are relatively abundant there is a good deal of labor turnover. Unplanned labor turnover annually in industry runs to 20 percent and in construction to 33 percent.[114] Management efforts to recruit needed labor to meet production targets and labor pressure for improved wage benefits or working conditions has in the past resulted in a continuous process of wage inflation, from time to time stimulated and generalized by nationwide wage boosts and corresponding price changes, which during the entire Stalin period of industrialization lifted wage levels over tenfold (Schwartz 1954, 170). Though the process was slowed down appreciably in the Khrushchev-Brezhnev period, in the two decades between 1960 and 1979 average monthly earnings have about doubled, rising faster than real wage levels or the improved quality mix in the labor force (USSR, Central Statistical Board 1979, 171). Inability to recruit or hold an adequate labor supply has hindered economic development in the northern and western portions of the country. Industrial investment has to a significant degree been pinpointed to areas of labor availability to ease the strain in labor recruitment, which has had to be achieved not by measures of coercion or rationing but largely by market methods or inducements.

The "Documentary" Economy

The field of economic life where rationing became most deeply entrenched under the Stalin regime and has most strongly resisted reform is marketing of industrial products and services between enterprises and through channels of wholesale distribution. The process of central economic planning requires that output of goods and services of all enterprises be projected over forward time periods so that additional producing capacity can be fitted into the producing complex at the right time and with the proper makeup of raw materials, power and transportation, intermediate products, equipment and construction. All intermediate outputs need to be scheduled for use as an appropriate input to contribute to an output of final goods and services of the planned type earmarked for a certain class of final user. But that scheduling of intermediate goods and of final products and services is only for the purpose of carrying out the investment plan at the right time and place. That scheduling need not be realized in actual distribution if a money economy is in place, if disposable incomes received by final users are sufficient in amount to purchase the final goods and services becoming available, if the right goods have been produced, if firms and export agencies have been prohibited from carrying out capital investment projects other than those approved by the plan, and if banks are alert not to expand credits for unauthorized investment purposes.

The scheduling of final products and services destined for household consumers was not carried through at the final distribution stage to particular consumers once finished output was available. But intermediary products and capital equipment and construction materials and services were ticketed for disposition by planning or supply agencies who would dispense warrants or specific authorization to designated enterprises for purchase and use. That a particular enterprise was equipped and established to utilize the particular intermediary products and equipment and that the plan authorized capital expansion or the production process in question was not a sufficient entitlement for purchase. A specific authorization or warrant from a proper planning or supply agency would also be needed. In this respect the Stalinist model of a socialist economy has been properly denominated a "war economy" (Lange 1962) or a "documentary" economy (Berliner 1976, 18). Intermediary products could only move through the industrial system with elaborate documentation all the way. A variety of agencies were in charge of issuing this documentation and their organization and mutual responsibility was frequently shuffled as political leaders sought for an improved organizational setup. In the version shaped in 1965–1967 the all-Union Gosplan prepared input-output allocation tables and allocated supplies under some 2,000 commodity designations (Nove 1968, 92; Berri 1977, 1:72). These commodities have nationwide use and were considered industrially strategic. A special administrative organization (Gossnab) with the sole function of product supply and allocation and with a large number of local and provincial subagencies and warehouse depots handled input-output balance and commodity allocations for some 13,000 to 18,000 commodity designations (Berri 1977, 1:74). Besides there are autonomous distributive networks in the fields of construction materials, agricultural supply, and certain ministries.

Since the annual production and investment plan is prepared by a different staff and at different times than the annual supply and allocations plan, they are frequently found to disagree, causing interruption of supply and production slowdowns.[115] Buildings will be completed before the equipment to be installed in them is available or equipment will be delivered and stockpiled long before the construction is completed. Delivery schedules are rarely synchronized properly. Hence the endemic tendency of Soviet producing organizations to seek to provide for many of their own needs for repair equipment, replacement parts, and the like to avoid dependency upon the supply network but at the cost of holding excessive inventories. The sheer number of producing enterprises to be accommodated, now running at 130,000 (as of 1976), and the huge monetary turnover involved (over 140 billion rubles) are part of the problem since the difficulties of organizing supply tend to increase geometrically as the firms and products involved in the supply network multiply (Berri 1977, 1:79).

The main lines of reform needed to resolve these difficulties of supply planning have been developed by a school of Soviet economists. Reform must involve shifting responsibility for supply alignment, marketing, and procurement back to the producing enterprise or the corporate combine to which the enterprise belongs for management purposes. It is widely understood that this would only be possible if pricing and investment policy would be reformed. Relative commodity prices facing buyers and administered by sellers would need to be more closely aligned than they have been with social and resource costs directly experienced or foregone. The main lines of pricing policy were reformed early in the 1960s by a series of measures including in price a charge on working and fixed capital utilized based on an up-to-date inventory, by an equalization of fuel prices to be aligned with BTU values, by allowances for regional or product royalties or rents, and other measures designed to make price a more significant indicator of economic value. Investment policy was recast to make sure that investment analysis included feasible variants, that it allowed for the time lost in construction or in resources tied up for future use, and that variants selected were optimal in terms of their effectiveness. Here, too, investment analysis was recast expressly to allow for marginal efficiency and the revival of the concept of interest discounting to reduce future benefits and costs to a uniform measure of present value.[116]

On the basis of reform of pricing and investment policy Soviet reformers hoped that the bureaucratic supply system could be swept away, returning initiative in product disposal and supply procurement back to the firms, combines, and wholesale establishments already operating. A move in that direction was made in the 1965–1970 period and certain fields of industry were experimentally opened up to the new methods.[117] In Hungary and to a lesser degree in East Germany a far-reaching reform of supply administration was carried out. In some fields the application of linear programming models has optimized supply flows and transportation arrangements.[118] But in the Soviet Union and in most of the East European satellite economies reform was stymied because old habits and institutions resisted change. The top leadership was apparently afraid that decentralization would become disruptive and perhaps that enterprises were not ready or able to carry out the function of marketing and supply and still not neglect basic state priorities.

The next stage of economic reform in the socialist economies will surely call for drastic reduction of rationing as the normal method of supply and procurement administration in interindustrial relationships. The burgeoning science of socialist political economy now centered on the theory of optimal economic planning with intensive use of market methods and price incentives premised on commodity circulation is fully aware of the need for such a reform and focuses continual attention on reform.[119] Practical business administration is hampered by retention of outworn dogmas of Stalinist planning theory. Oscar Lange who helped to guide the attempt at reform in Poland in 1957–1960 quite properly stigmatized the use of physical planning in supply procurement and end-product distribution as a feature not of the socialist economy but of the "war economy" inherited from the capitalist epoch.[120] The old rationing system lays a heavy burden on public administration even with the aid of computerized schemes of calculation. It now appears as if under a new dynamic leader, Michael Gorbachev, a comprehensive restructuring of the Soviet economy is in process promising the liquidation of the "war economy." But how far this reform will go it is not now possible to tell.

Notes

Chapter 1

1. Hence committed Marxists may be very uncomfortable about my use of the term (Resnick 1986, 305).

2. As this manuscript was going to press, I learned through Elizabeth Kohlenberg of the doctoral dissertation in geography submitted in 1987 at the University of Washington by James E. Randall giving a comprehensive account of the household mode of production, its major theoretical problems, and its empirical basis (Randall, 1987). Randall's work has exceptionally wide scope, both methodologically and substantively, drawing freely on formal economic theory, on historical accounts, on sociological literature, and on many relevant writings in economic geography and anthropology. He has conducted an illuminating survey of three Washington communities of "self-service" activities in or around the home, the car, and personal or household possessions (Randall 1987, Chap. 7). Randall's work makes it clear that the "mixed economy" which has matured and taken shape in the fifth and sixth decades of this century is distinguished by a significant movement in urban communities for the widespread growth of the household mode of production arising from the greatly reduced workweek, the development of cheap electrical energy and electrically powered tools around the house, the spread of home ownership and widespread ownership of automobiles and home appliances which call for frequent repair and servicing. Important also was an adaptive response by the business world which has developed models and techniques that have facilitated self-servicing or has made available on a rental basis needed equipment or machines.

3. When this labeling was suggested in my earlier work (Gottlieb 1984, 89, 96), several reviewers implied I unduly diluted or multiplied unwisely or unnecessarily the modes of production classically enumerated by Marx (see Eggertsson 1986, 96; Zimbalist 1986, 188). Confusion was worse confounded when a reviewer indicated that "agrarian capitalism" and "mercantile capitalism" were among my ten modes of production around which "the whole book is organized" (Eggertsson 1986).

Chapter 2

1. See Jolowicz and Nichols 1972, Chap. 19, 95; Anderson 1974a, 67.

2. The relative decline of the slave plantation and of the slave's role in the Roman labor force by the fourth century A.D. is now well-established in Western historiography and is coming to be conceded by Marxist historians. See Anderson 1974a, 77, 82 n. 42, 99; Petit 1976, 247; Engels 1884/1978, 181; Finley 1973, 77; Jolowicz and Nichols 1972, 82; Jones 1966, 2:794.

3. Jones 1966, 1:18, 64; Jolowicz 1972, 345.

4. On this class ordering, see Jones 1966, 525, 527, 738; Jolowicz 1972, 434; Finley 1973, 46.

5. See the magisterial work (still in process) by the great Sinologist and historian-scientist, Joseph Needham, *Science and Civilization in China,* 5 vols. 1954–1978, especially 1:79–90. See also Goodrich 1969, 7–17. For an appreciation of the work of Needham see Elvin 1980, 17–53.

6. Needham 1954/1978, 1:90–99; Book 3, 4:258. The warring-states period is well illuminated in standard historical works. See Eberhard 1977, Chap. 3.

7. Needham 1954–1978, 1:90–99; Eberhard 1977, Chap. 4.

8. Needham 1954–1978, 1:112–14; Fitzgerald 1943, Chap. 11; Goodrich 1969, 58–113.

9. See Gibbon 1776–1778/1932, 2:494; Needham 1954–1978, 1:181; Curtin 1981, 91.

10. See Finley 1973, 30; Dudley 1960, 179; Bury 1925/1958, 1:62; Kolb 1971, 112; Bozan et al. 1981, 26; Twitchett 1953/1970, 27, 251.

11. See Needham 1954–1978, 1:240; Needham 1964, 46.

12. We have no statistics of enumeration of urban population or the number of urban places. But the population size of the great metropolitan centers was massive though probably greater in China. According to Jones (1966, 2:1040) the population of Rome and Constantinople in the Late Empire was between 500,000 and 750,000 persons. The T'ang capitol, Chhang-an, was around 2 million persons (Fitzgerald 1942, 320). Hangkow, in the middle of the thirteenth century, an improvised capitol after the Mongols had captured their northern capitol, is estimated at 500,000 "at the very least" (Balazs 1964, 72). For the eastern half of the Roman Empire a document survives based on an official register drawn up in the middle of the fifth century indicating that there were about 900 units of local government involving cities (Jones 1966, 2:713).

13. The Christian message was infectious. The younger Pliny learned from his experience as proconsul in Asia Minor in 111–113 A.D. that the "wretched cult," as Pliny called it, had spread widely over the towns and rural areas (Pliny, Book 10:96). The Chinese reception was more tolerant. Many Chinese, especially after Buddhist faith had spread to Tibetan and related peoples of Inner Mongolia and present Sinkiang, were attracted to the new philosophy. Even amidst the Buddhist persecution that broke out in the mid-ninth century, the diary of a Japanese Buddhist monk's travels in China shows how pervasive Buddhist practices and ideas had become (Reischauer 1955).

14. For the Roman Empire see n. 2. Though certainly there was no general regime of slavery in early China, slavery is indicated by the elaborate law codes covering the slave relationship (T'ung Tsu Ch'u 1961, 186–200). A careful survey of the sources in the Han period indicates that slaves made up only

1–5 percent of the labor force (Wilbur 1943, 57). The Tunhuang documents of the eighth century also point to a small slave population held mainly by the upper income groups (Wright and Twitchett 1973, 137). The northern Wei regime in the Yellow River valley (the immediate predecessor of the Sui-T'ang dynasty) issued in 485 A.D. a basic land reform statute, which assumed a typical household beside parents and children of four male slaves employed as field hands and four female slaves employed as weavers. In a land law of 564 A.D. allowance was also made for slaves in amounts of land allotted to common people (Balazs 1964, 107–11). Apparently slavery prevailed in the far northwest regions among minority nationalities where according to an 1183 A.D. statistical document among the 6.7 million Ju-chen people the average family had 2.2 slaves and 170 aristocratic families had 163 slaves each (Balazs, 123).

15. Balazs 1964, 118, 120, 122; Twitchett 1953/1970, 19; Jones 1966, 2:792.

16. The endowment of veterans with landholdings prevailed all through the Republic, was prominent in the Principate, and lasted through to the Late Empire (Jones 1966: 1:64, 149, 635; 2:778, 813.) As Finley notes "veterans constantly demanded land grants upon demobilization"; a quarter of a million veteran families were given land in the last century of the Republic (Finley 1973, 80). There were also spasmodic efforts both East and West to check foreclosure on peasant holdings due to usury and to limit abuses connected with client-patron relations. The Chinese did not lay the same emphasis on veteran's grants but all through the early Chin-Han period and up through the middle T'ang period authority over land allocation was used to promote independent peasant proprietorships where vacant land was available for distribution by local authorities (Balazs 1964, 101; Elvin 1973, 56).

17. Restrictions in China on land sale were undermined by evasion and were finally dropped in the middle of the T'ang period and pressures to rural class differentiation worked their way, resulting in larger landholdings worked by tenants, by wage-labor, or tenants bound in peonage. While some go so far as to speak of systems of "villa" estate farming taking over (Balazs) and of a wholesale "manorialism without feudalism" (Elvin), yet substantial evidence indicates that a widespread class of peasant proprietors held their own for they clearly show up again in the late Sung period (Balazs 1964, 119; Twitchett 1953/1970, 18; Elvin 1973, Chap. 6; Golas 1980, 300).

18. See Wittfogel 1931, 145–58, 158, 174, 337–51, 390.

19. The social grouping in local clans that typically combined families tied by kinship in different economic circumstances—including scholars, poor peasants, landowners, officials, or merchants, or dealers—played a powerful role in rural society with joint property and temples, festivals, and various forms of mutual support that probably sheltered peasant proprietorship. All descriptive accounts of Chinese rural society emphasize the role of the clan. Weber and Moore attribute the stability of Chinese peasant proprietorship to the close ties of the clan association (Weber 1916/1964, 88; Moore 1967, 207; Hsiao Kung-Chuan 1960, Chap. 8).

20. As officially tabulated in 1952, but not well publicized, we learned that some 112 million acres or 43 percent of China's cultivated acreage were confiscated from landlords and richer peasants (Cheng Shih 1974, 8); and this agrees with Soviet and Western reports (Larsen 1967, 214; Nolan 1976, 203; USSR, Academy of Sciences 1957, 790). The reform redistributed lands of richer peasants officially defined as having 25 percent or more of their income

from exploitive sources. The final land reform law of 1950 directed the confiscation of only those lands of richer peasants that were leased out (Mao Tse-Tung, 4:183, 175 n. 6). That the land reform was drastic is indicated by the relatively meager holdings of so-called rich peasants who survived the reform with an average farm of 4.22 acres of arable land, 2.68 head of draft animals, 1.3 ploughs, and an annual income of 1300 yuan (Nolan 1976, 203). Mao (1:87, 4:164) specifically and the Communist analysis generally contended that between 60 and 80 percent of arable land was held by landlords and rich peasants.

21. Balazs 1964, Chaps. 7, 8; Jones 1966, 2:781; Fei Hsiao-Tung 1953. On the guild-organized craftsmen and their profusion and free character, see Jones (1966, 2:855; 1974, 45–57). On free Babylonian craft guilds, see Driver and Miles (1952, 394). The Chinese guild was "undertaken by and for the common people" and belonged to the "plebian order" (Needham 1954–1978, Part 4, 2:21, 42, 17; Balazs 1964, 14, 17). Weber (1909/1976, 47) certainly erred in contending that "a guild or something similar in Antiquity [is] nearly always essentially a state organization for the forced imposition of public tasks."

22. The highway networks East and West in the second century A.D. were estimated by Needham, using reliable authorities, at more than an doubled mileage in the West (48,500 miles compared to 22,000 miles in the East) or to mileage per square mile 27.5 miles for the West over 14.3 miles in the East. Eastern roads were wider and involved more rough terrain (Needham 1954–1978, Part 3, 4:35; Jones 1966, 830).

23. Jones copiously backs up with an extended survey of the Western public economy his broad generalization that "the imperial government . . . made virtually no use of the private merchant, supplying the major needs of its hundreds of thousands of employees by levies in kind upon the producers, by manufacturing some parts of its requirements in state factories and by conveying the goods thus levied or manufactured to their recipients by means of state transport services" (Jones 1966, 1:671; 2:827, 834–55).

24. Corvée labor and its role in Chinese classical public works is well known. It played a major role in bringing down the first Chin dynasty. A guild of shippers with tax privileges, under the control of special praetorian prefects, handled freight shipments of grain from Egypt to the imperial cities at greatly reduced rates as compared to commercial shipping, in convoys under military guard (Gilmore 1953, 18; Jones 1966, 2:827). The Chinese grain fleet was under the control of a state "Directorate of Grain Transport" (Needham 1954–1978, Part 3, 4:312 n. 2).

25. Astronomical observatories besides their scientific functions had practical responsibilities connected with making of calendars and weather forecasting (Needham 1954–1978, 3:127, 186, 192, 194; Part 4, 2:10). The Western empire also had state academies such as the State University of Constantinople, inaugurated in about 425, with ten chairs of Latin grammar alone (Jones, 1966, 2:990). The church had its own training institutes after it became a state religion with tax immunity, state and private endowments, great wealth and the beginning of monasteries.

26. Needham 1954–1978, Part 3, 4:30, 211–378.

27. Balazs (1964, 77); Needham (1954–1978, Part 3, 4:71); Fei Hsaio-Tung (1953, 95).

28. State control of salt and iron was initiated in the early Han period,

was opposed by Confucian scholars, and was debated in a fascinating conference reported in a contemporary volume, "Discourses on the State Control of Salt and Iron." Nationalization was favored by the "legalist" school (Hsaio 1975, 116–41; Balazs 1964, 45; Needham 1954–1978, Part 2, 4:17b). In the Chinese Empire foreign trade was actually carried on by state agencies; in the Roman Empire it was merely controlled, though closely, by state bureaus (Jones 1966, 2:826).

29. There was established in Rome in the late fourth century A.D. public salaried doctors, one for each region of the city. They were later established by Justinian for Carthage, and they are reported for other cities (Jones 1966, 2:1012). China did not experience public feeding. This began in the late Republic, was systematized under Augustus with formal tickets, became hereditary and saleable in the early third century, was extended from grain to baked bread and oil, and was supplemented at times by provision of pork for five months of the year. Feeding in Rome supplied from 120,000 up to 320,000 recipients and it is indicated nearly as many in Constantinople and other major cities (Jones 1966, 1:695–705, 2:1045). Amazingly, public feeding was continued under early Gothic rule when grain supply from Africa was available (Gibbon 1776–1788/1932, 2:461). For a deeper analysis of the role of public feeding of the Roman lumpenproletariat, see Anderson (1974a, 68).

30. Of 915 scholars in the nineteenth century who passed high-ranking examinations for imperial degrees, roughly one-half had fathers who also held degrees, more in the rural areas than in towns (Fei 1953, 132). In the T'ang period only 10 percent of official posts are estimated to have filled through competitive examinations (Twitchett and Fairbanks 1979, 3:328).

31. By the nineteenth century, corruption in office had become institutionalized. The side earning of the some 25,000 officeholders was some ten times the official salaries (Chang 1962, 42). See references and discussion in Gottlieb (1984, 78 n. 116, 151 n. 17).

32. Beside monthly pay and support given in cash or goods, there was a "donative" of five gold solidi and a pound of silver paid on the accession to the throne and quinquennially thereafter (Jones 1966, 1:624).

33. Jolowicz 1972, 276; Gibbon 1776–1788/1932, 2:151; Plutarch 1864, 651.

34. Twitchett 1953/1970, Chaps. 1, 4, and Wright and Twitchett 1973, 121–50.

35. On the revolution in land tenure see the full account in Twitchett (1953/1970, 17). The great reformer of the late Sung period, Wang An-Shih, later sought to reverse the process but his efforts were stillborn (Fitzgerald 1942, Chap. 29; Needham 1954–1978, 1:138).

36. Balazs (1964, 71, 77, 88); Weber (1916/1964, 13); Yoshinabu (1970, 132); Elvin (1973, 175).

37. See Radin 1917, Chaps. 22–25. Distribution of a major estate in the Roman world was a public event of first importance and was often the subject of public comment. If "legacy hunters" were disappointed, disapproval would be vehement and efforts would be made to break the will. See e.g., the comments of the younger Pliny on a major case of a large estate, which "is all we talk about" (Pliny 1963, Book 8, no. 18). Pliny's letters describe four legacies he had received: Book 2, no. 17; Book 3, no. 6; Book 4, no. 1; Book 5, no. 7. Cicero was famous for receipt of many legacies.

38. The legal standing of plural Chinese marriage is set forth in T'ung-

Tsu Ch'u (1961, 35, 36, 66, 91, 119, 123–27). Among feudal nobility a strict rule of primogeniture was followed giving a special place to the "main" wife, the *tsung-fa* system. "With the collapse of feudalism, the *tsung-fa* system collapsed also. . . ." Among notables formal plural marriage was recognized "since this was common custom [and] the law did not insist upon annulment of the second marriage." Among common people plural marriage was proscribed but a woman could be purchased as concubine (ch'ieh) and cut off from her family but fully incorporated into the master's family with the title "father-concubine" and after children were born, "concubine-mother." Jealousy by a "main" wife or attitudes hostile to a concubine were strongly reprobated and grounds for divorce. A tendency to plural marriage was probably stimulated by the many incursions into China of Mongol, Tartar, and Turkic peoples (ultimately assimilated into the Han people) who commonly in Central Asia had plural marriage with varying distinctions between main wives, concubines, and "little wives." Second and later wives have been dubbed in English translations of Chinese texts "concubines" but the expression "little wives" might be better since all wives had a low status in classical Chinese society and were under the domination of fathers and husbands. On this difference in translation, see Briffault (1927, 2:323, especially 328 n. 6). Briffault (328–29) found children born of concubines legitimate and capable of inheriting, especially among the Mongol and Manchu peoples. In China the children of little wives and concubines were protected by statute from partiality. The perceptive John Dewey who observed and lived in China for a while in the 1920s found "the attempt to support a number of wives extravagantly . . . one of the chief sources of political corruption." Even ordinary laborers were found "from ancient times to have two wives or more." The number of progeny frequently would be augmented by the practice of adoption illustrated by the family of a well-to-do official who adopted no less than twenty-six "brothers" and nine "daughters," fully assimilated into the family (Yu-Tang 1963, 449).

39. The role of equal sharing among sons has frequently been pointed to as a source of partition of landholdings. "In the absence of primogeniture, a wealthy family might find itself reduced to penury in a few generations through equal division at inheritance" (Moore 1967, 170). "In the long run, the hereditary partitioning of land greatly democratized landownership" (Weber 1916/1964, 830); "China's traditional system of land inheritance—whereby land was subdivided among the various heirs . . . —prevented large accumulation of land in the hands of a few" (Larsen 1967, 213; Kolb 1971, 113, 145; Fei, Hsiao-Tung 1939, 196, 66; Myers 1970, 125).

40. Bolin 1958, 47; Jones 1974, 195.

41. Jones 1966, 107, 435, 445; Jones 1974, 68.

42. Local copper and silver coins were minted or issued for local use and were valid for payments of only a small amount (Jones 1966, 1:438; Bolin 1958, 238).

43. Ku Pan 1950, 220, 228, 270, 327, 352; Twitchett 1953/1970, 70; Yang 1952, 2, 27.

44. The Japanese court supplied their envoys visiting in T'ang China with bags of gold dust. Being readily concealed and accepted in China, this stood the monk Ennin, who spent many years traveling in China, in good stead (Reischauer 1955, 33, 41, 318).

45. Twitchett 1953/1970, App. 4. Older sources credit T'ang China with a larger number of mints but the Twitchett account is more trustworthy.

46. The high cost of minting was widely noted in Chinese sources and is

reported for two periods in T'ang China to run at 75 and 100 percent of the face value of the coins (Twitchett 1953/1970; Eberhard 1977, 213).

47. This remarkable experience of the Han period was described fully in Pan Ku 1950, 232–37.

48. The celebrated chapters of Gibbons (1776–1788/1932, 1: Chaps. 10, 20, 21, 28) treating the main effects of Christianization trace out in almost morbid detail how it stifled worldly interests in science or technology, led to refined theological debates on the relationship of supernatural entities to each other, and promoted an arid Scholasticism that nearly buried the promising beginnings of scientific thought.

49. The profoundly disruptive role of the sport enthusiasts of Constantinople caused Justinian to put the city under martial law and close the hippodrome (where the great chariot-racing contests were held) (Gibbon 1776–1788/ 1932, 2:486). On another occasion the disappointment of the hippodrome mob in the arrest of a favorite charioteer led to street disorders that took the life of the local military commander (Gibbon 1776–1788/1932, 2:33). Romans inherited the games complex from the Greeks for whom it was a participant sport. The Romans developed it in the Late Republic and Principate into a massive spectator sport, thus providing the people with the famous "bread and circuses." The games, says Jones (1966, 2:1016), "despite the thunders of the church, retained a central place in the life of the empire." He illustrates this curiously. After the disastrous barbaric invasions of Gaul at the beginning of the fifth century, the first request of the city of Treviri to the imperial government was for resumption of chariot races. Strikingly, the Americans in their latter-day imperial visitation developed a like passion for spectator sports, shifting from the earlier style of participant sports.

50. This concern for abundance and for improved arts and crafts continually shows up in the many volumes of Needham as touching many emperors themselves, their highest officers of government, and many ordinary officials.

51. "'What about death?' was the next question, and Confucius said 'We don't know yet about life, how can we know about death?'" (Yu-Tang 1963, 292 [from the Analects]).

52. "Let mulberry-trees be planted about the homesteads with their five acres, and persons of fifty years will be able to wear silk. In keeping fowls, pigs, dogs and swine, let not their times of breeding be neglected, and persons of seventy years will be able to eat flesh" (Yu T'ang 1963, 265 [Mencius]).

53. Marx (1863–1878/1967, 3:791; Marx and Engels (1841–1870/1974– 1986, 12:127). These statements are key underpinnings in an elaborate construction by Marx and Engels of the so-called Asiatic Mode of Production. For a full presentation of the texts in the various writings of Marx and Engels, see Krader (1975). For a critical evaluation of these writings and of predecessor writings of earlier theorists and commentators such as Hegel and Montesquieu, see Anderson (1974b, 462–549); Bailey and Llobera (1981, 109); Gottlieb (1984, 36 n. 1).

54. For the elaborate, exacting, and punishing scheme of Roman taxation in Egypt, applied precisely to the Roman province where private ownership of land and rental relations were fully developed, see Wallace (1938); Max Weber (1909/1976, 249). In an earlier stage of Egyptian history full state property in farmland is indicated though smallholdings and alienable estates were found in the late Rameses times (Hawkes 1973, 390).

55. It suffices to mention Babylonia where irrigated agriculture with state control of public works subsisted with heavy taxation, with private property in

land (alongside crown property) alienable, mortgageable, and hereditable with a considerable development of landlord-tenant share crop farming (Driver and Miles 1952, 111, 136, 145, 173; Hawkes 1973, 91, 158).

56. Marx noted that the "necessity to calculate the periodic movements of the Nile created Egyptian astronomy and with it the rule of the priest caste as leader of agriculture" (Marx 1863–1878/1967, 1:514 n. 1). Needham found similar connections in the work on calendars, meterological analysis and astronomy and the practical needs of hydrological control. (Needham 1954–1978, 3:186, 514).

57. The Yellow River carried a prodigious amount of silt estimated at a billion tons per year, causing the river channel in the wider reaches of the river to steadily rise with silt deposit and thus readily overflow channels (Needham 1954–1978, Part 4, 3:211–47). In the Yangtze valley water control was needed to permit wetland cultivation of rice. The early presentation of Wittfogel (1931, 410) on the state as "superintending organ of agricultural production in China" is still valuable.

58. Some fifty national minority peoples have survived, making up 6 percent of the total population (Foreign Language Press 1974, 6). That includes outlying Mongol, Korean, Manchu, Tibetan peoples. Kolb (1971, 99) believes that the count of minority peoples should be larger.

59. In late Ching times the miner had developed techniques of underground illumination, poisonous gas could be drawn off to the surface, seams could be supported by timber construction, and shafts and tunnels could penetrate up to some 200 feet deep (Sung Yang-Hsing 1966, 236; Collins 1922, 7).

60. Needham (1954–1978, 1:109, Book 2, 5:510; Sung Yang-Hsing 1966, 237; Chien 93 B.C./1979, 30, 63, 153, 235, 257, 263) citing only use of gold or silver as present or as reward.

61. See Twitchett 1968, 66; T'ung-Tsu Ch'u 1961, 128; Weber 1916/1964, Chaps. 5, 6; T'ung-Tsu Ch'u 1962, Chap. 10.

62. Balazs 1964, 70; T'ung-Tsu Ch'u 1961, 135–54, 166.

63. Thus the emperor is asked whether the public bath at Prusa, which is "old and Dilapidated" can be rebuilt; whether a local community which has experienced loss from a severe fire would be permitted to form a fireman company and obtain fire engines or other equipment; whether a local town can build an aqueduct for which it has ample funds (Pliny 1963, 271, 268, 291).

64. Twitchett 1953/1970, Chap. 11; Weber 1916/1964, 55–62.

65. See Chap. 2, n. 34.

66. Jones 1966, 1:460, 468; see also Ste. 1981, 488.

67. Jones 1966, 1:429, 2:871.

68. On the record of remission of arrears, largely to clear public accounts by "writing off bad debts," see Jones (1966, 1:467). Tax collectors were empowered to use coercive means to bring in the revenue. Among Egyptians "a man is ashamed if he cannot display many weals on his body earned by refusing to pay taxes." Ibid., 2:811.

69. "The Roman state had become a huge, complicated machine, exclusively for bleeding its subjects. Taxes, compulsory service for the state and tributes of every kind pressed the mass of people always deeper into poverty; the pressure was intensified until the exactions of governors, tax-collectors and soldiers made it unbearable. . . . The more the empire declined, the higher rose the taxes and levies and the more shamelessly the officials robbed and extorted" (Engels 1884/1978, 178).

70. Fitzgerald (1942, 353, 377); Eberhard 1977, 191); Twitchett 1953/1970, 106).

71. A statistical study of the number of hydraulic projects of all provinces as shown by topographical histories in the various dynastic regimes, expressed as the number of projects carried through per year, shows a noticeable acceleration of projects to levels seven to eight times higher than in the Chin-Han period, only surpassed by the later Sung and Yuan (Mongol) regimes. Perhaps the giving up of walled defensive fortifications on the northern frontier led to a diversion of corvée effort from defense to productive purposes (Needham 1954–1978, Book 3, 4:282, 306).

72. The celebrated royal family of a great Manchu emperor in the seventeenth century included 56 offspring and the 28 survivors were equipped with proper domiciles (Spence 1975, 120, 173). He kept only 300 women around the palace and had over 100 sons and grandsons. Under the earlier Emperor Outy the number of wives and concubines in the royal palace is said to have exceeded 10,000 (Briffault 1927, 2:327 n. 5).

73. Imperial residences at the time of Constantine were found in Trier, Milan, Sardica, or Nicomedia "which all had their palaces." To these should be added the former palaces at Rome, the new Western palaces at Ravenna, fixed in the fifth century as the main capitol of the Western Empire. Other eastern palatial residences are found in Antioch, Oesia, Marcianopolis (Jones 1966, 1:83, 366).

74. The Christian emperors and especially Constantine himself were generous in endowing institutions of the church. By the middle of the third century the local churches were wealthy enough to permit their higher clergy to be salaried (Jones 1966, 2:907). By the fifth century it was "well worth while to be a priest or deacon on the establishment of a great see." The sixty clergy of Ravenna received an annual stipend of 50 solidi each "without taking their share of offerings into account." Jones (1966, 2:908) believes an index of "the growing wealth of the church" was the emergence of simony and related abuses of taking fees for consecrations, ordinations, and the like. Gibbons reports that bishops received an annual income of nearly 10 pounds of gold yearly. The rent roll of the Roman church included properties with an annual rental income of 305 pounds of gold (Gibbon 1776–1788, 1932, 1:633).

75. A concrete measure of this encapsulated wealth is provided by the T'ang campaign 845 A.D. against "foreign" religions. 4600 monasteries were destroyed, 265,000 bonzes and 150,000 temple slaves were laicized (registered as taxpayers) and millions of acres of farmland were seized (Balazs 1964, 122; Eberhard 1977, 192).

76. The coronarial offering (*aurum oblaticum*), supposedly voluntary, struck hard. One collection nipped the entire senatorial order some 1600 pounds of gold. The curial offering (*aurum cornarium*) was also contributed by curial members or decurions and in the third century was almost the sole source from which the government obtained gold (Jones 1966, 1:430).

77. A later Roman Senate allegedly bought off the Visigoth leader Alaric with 5,000 pounds of gold, 30,000 pounds of silver, 3,000 pounds of pepper, and other gifts. This payoff, famous in history, must have nearly wiped out treasure hoards of senators and of town merchants (Jones 1966, 1:186, 193, 204, 206; Gibbon 1776–1788/1932, 1:152).

78. Finley 1973, 150; Jones 1966, 1:537, 705.

Chapter 3

1. Anderson 1974a, 147–55. A generalized "feudal synthesis" based on a "feudal mode of production" resulted in a threefold "typology": (1) northern Europe with its slower transition to "feudalism" and its predominantly Germanic heritage, (2) southern Europe "where the dissolution and recombination of barbarian and ancient modes of production occurred under the dominant legacy of Antiquity," and (3) an intermediary zone in the homeland of the Carolingian empire centered on the Rhineland and northern France.

2. Our text speaks of the Roman Catholic church and not a diffuse "European Christianity" because the church was organized and centered precisely in the city of Rome.

3. See Gibbon 1776–1788/1932, 2:757; Mitchell and Leys 1963, 36; Lopez and Raymond 1967, 60–73.

4. The rationalist Gibbons (1776–1788, 1932, 3:367) searched the record for clerical delinquencies to memorialize and pays eloquent tribute to the fostering role of the church in keeping alive the intellectual heritage of classical antiquity.

5. A fourth century rule, laxly administered, forbade marriage in the orders. We know that bishops were required to be celibate at the beginning of the seventh century. By 1000 A.D. celibacy was uncommon and the laws enforcing it almost obsolete. Yet respect for the principle persisted and in the eleventh century regeneration of the church the rule of clerical celibacy began to be strictly enforced (Gibbon 1776–1788/1932, 2:754; Bury et al. 1929–1936, 5:12).

6. The predominant form embodied in the Deuteronomic code, prescribed a tenth of the grain harvest and a more restricted share of livestock "firstlings," fruits, and wine. This tithe was to be delivered to the Levites who would retain a share for their use with the rest going to the Sanctuary where tithe offerings would be used for the preparation of a festive meal. Every third year the tithe was to be stored locally for use by the Levites and the needy. In the later days of the high priesthood, tithes passed under the control of the high priests. (Gehrman 1970, 952). Neither Jesus nor Paul urged a tithe, and Jesus' one reference to tithing was scathing (Matt. 23: 25–27).

7. In early Anglo-Saxon England these fees and dues included church scot – a certain measure of grain or produce delivered annually – plow alms, light scot, and Peter's pence – a silver coin of low denomination for transfer to Rome – (Roundell 1888, 180, 218). Doubtless burial fees, marriage and baptism fees were levied and in later times they were of considerable magnitude (Hill 1956, Chap. 7).

8. In England in the early nineteenth century about one-half of all parish ministers were nominated and presented with their "living" by the local landlord or estate-owner acting as "avowson" (Halévy 1912/1937, 16). The right of avowson was so ancient and deeprooted a practice that the English thirteen-century church leaders threatened to separate themselves from the Roman connection rather than abolish lay patronage. (Roundell 1888, 293). The Gregorian Reform in Italy and throughout the Catholic world generally required that patronage appointment of a priest be confirmed by the bishop (Boyd 1952, 154). On avowson generally, see Coulton (1923–1950, 3:156, 387) and Hill (1956, 53).

9. The barons of England made the crown certify to their rights of

avowson to monasteries in the Magna Carta of which clause forty-six reads: "All barons who have founded abbeys for which they have charters of the Kings of England, or ancient right of tenure, shall have as much as they ought to have, their custody when vacant" (Downs 1959, 128). For the domination of monastic lands or "lay abbacies," see Boussard (1969, 76).

10. See for the detailed story of the feudalization of church tithes and properties in the tenth century (Boyd 1952, Chap. 5). Italian ecclesiastical property holdings as recorded in property transaction records declined by 50 percent from the ninth to the twelfth centuries (Herlihy 1978, 586, 93).

11. The office of the archbishop in the diocese of Auch in Gascon France was found in a survey of tithe revenues and distribution in the Eighteenth Century to draw a tithal share from two-thirds of the reporting parishes, yielding 308,000 livres, about 43 percent of the tithes concerned (Rives 1976, 61–104). The Cathedral Chapter of the Archbishopric collected a quarter of that amount from a much smaller number of parishes, resulting from earlier awards by archbishops of their tithal revenues (Rives 1976, 22). In the area of Toulouse the archbishopric drew a share from 38 percent of his parishes (Frêche 1974, 521). For the contrary pattern of wholesale divestment of tithal revenues by the episcopate of Italy during the tenth century A.D., see earlier n. 10.

12. Including collegial chapters of central cathedrals, French monastic institutions are credited with receiving in 1789 some two-thirds of some 120 million livres. The corresponding fraction in England on the eve of the Reformation in the 1530s was one-third (Evans 1976, 17; Coulton 1923–1950, 3:145; Lefebvre 1939/1967, 137).

13. Duby 1974, 62; Bautier 1971, 18; Clapham and Powers 1941–1978, 3:376.

14. Clapham and Powers 1941–1978, 2:576; Bautier 1971, 21, 59; Duby 1974, 49.

15. Lombard customs in the Kingdom of Italy in the early eleventh century at Pavia were payable in money at the tenth of the value (Lopez and Raymond 1967, 56).

16. The English church under Alfred paid 300 marks (about 20,000 shillings) to the papal legate for transmission to Rome, an arrangement continued under William (Bury 1929–1936, 6:554). The popes entrusted by the twelfth century the great Tuscan banking houses with the transmission to Italy of ecclesiastical revenues collected throughout Europe (Bury 1929–1936, 6:317; Miskimin 1975, 144; Herlihy 1969, 43). One financial settlement reached in 1215 specified one living in every metropolitan and episcopal district be reserved for the curia plus 10 percent of income from all the benefices and ecclesiastical property plus certain direct revenues previously collected from outlying domains.

17. After the Conquest "the kings received from their estates not weights of gold or silver but only payments in kind" (Herlihy 1970, 40).

18. A two-sided motivation accounts for the shift to money rent; peasants complaining of the cartage requirement, the king anxious for his estate revenue to be more fungible for waging foreign wars (Herlihy 1970, 41).

19. Lopez and Raymond 1967, 13, 146; Clapham 1941–1978, 3:583.

20. In a fascinating study of the beginnings of banking and loan finance in Medieval Bruges, De Roover (1948) has shown by a meticulous examination of local records that Bruges banking was an import from sophisticated Italian

banking, that in the fourteenth century banking and organized finance seem well rooted, and that banking houses operated typically on a small scale had organized "clearing" of local payments.

21. Anderson 1974a, 147, 184. Anderson holds that a "feudal mode of production appearing as 'feudalism'" emerged in Western Europe in the tenth century, expanded during the eleventh, "and reached its zenith in the later twelfth and thirteenth centuries."

22. Bautier 1971, 82; Duby 1968, 53, 87; Cipolla 1972–1976, 1:212; Clapham 1941–1978, 1:18, 330.

23. Bautier 1971, 47; Postan 1975, 176, 330; Duby 1968, 55.

24. Duby 1974, 142; Clapham 1941–1978, 1:346; Bloch 1939–1940/1961, 186; Anderson 1974a, 168.

25. Bloch 1939–1940/1961, 265; Postan 1975, 180; Clapham 1941–1978, 1:173, 485, 491; Bautier 1971, 47; Anderson 1974a, 173.

26. On Anglo-Saxon Franklins or Sokemen, see Homans 1941/1975, 248, Chap. 11; Thierry 1825/1907, 1:86, 91, 357; Postan 1975, 162, 164, 165.

27. Duby 1968, Doc. 91; Postan 1975, 91.

28. For possibly an exaggerated account of such purchases by magnates from small holders, see Postan 1975, 155.

29. Waxing eloquent on this theme, Duby writes that "on the continent free peasant properties were being reassembled in a hundred different ways" (Duby 1968, 170).

30. Postan 1975, 12, 92; Bautier 1971, 22, 56; Duby 1974, 31, 39, 85.

31. Mundy and Riesenberg 1958, 15.

32. See Bautier 1971, 49–57; Bloch 1939–1940/1961, 3–56. In the hundred years after 850 or so nearly every West European or Mediterranean urban settlement reachable from navigable waters opening to the North Sea or Mediterranean was raided and pillaged many times. Lightning Hungarian cavalry raids penetrated deep into Western Europe from the Carpathians.

33. Weber 1923/1950, 220; Clapham 1941–1978, 3:126; Lopez and Raymond 1967, 79. The fairs in Champagne stretching on for nearly the entire year cleared merchandise and debt settlements for all of Europe.

34. The capitalist character of entrepreneurial leadership emerged as a later stage in the development of a cloth-making industry using wool, silk, and linen. Such an industry required the assembly from distant areas of the raw materials needed and the coordination of the "putting out" arrangements with craft specialists like fullers, dyers, weavers, shearers. The merchant took on the adventure of marketing. See the masterful account by E. Carus-Wilson (1941–1978, 2:355–429) of the wool industry in these terms, and a fascinating case study of one such merchant-entrepreneur by Origo (1957).

35. The available fragmentary information on crop yields of the Carolingian period as compared with yields of the later twelfth or thirteenth centuries suggests that net disposable output, after laying aside seed for next year's sowing, more than doubled and possibly tripled (Duby 1968, 25, 99, especially 103; Duby 1974, 28, 194, 198; Cipolla 1972, 1:196; White 1962, 39–79).

36. I draw here from that remarkable monograph of White (1962, 41–56). White's emphasis on technology is by no means "fetishistic" (Anderson 1974a, 135, 183).

37. White (1962, 57–63). On the superiority of the Chinese harness, see the more detailed fascinating account in Needham 1954–1978, Part 2, 4:304–28.

38. White 1962, 69–76; Duby 1974, 189; Homans 1941/1975, Chap. 5.

39. Duby 1974, 189; Homans 1941/1975, 40, 91; Gimpel 1977, 44.

40. See the illuminating essay by M. Bloch, "The Advent and Triumph of the Watermill" (1967, 136–68). The spread of the water mill over the countryside is indicated by the reliable English statistic enumerating 5624 mills in Anglo-Saxon England at the time of the Conquest. White 1962, 81, especially 84. For the general history of water mills East and West, see Needham (1954–1978 Part 2, 4:366–80). The Roman mill utilized a vertical waterwheel with vanes pushed by a stream of water working millstones with right-angled gearing. The Chinese developed a horizontal waterwheel requiring no gearing but involving channelling the force of falling waters in to a jet stream hitting vanes with turbine force. Both originated East and West at about the same time.

41. Bloch 1967, 148; Needham 1954–1978, Part 2, 4:555–68.

42. Bloch 1967, 153; Needham 1954–1978, Part 2, 4:400; Homans 1941/1975, 225, 285.

43. This precis draws on the informed surveys by Gimpel (1977, 59–74), Clapham (1941–1978, 2:433, 435), and Max Weber (1923/1950, 181).

44. White 1962, 132; Needham 1954–1978, Part 3, 4:563; Lane 1966, 331; Clapham 1941–1978, 2:149.

45. This runs through the entire fabulous history of the Venetian state fortunately in its economic and related bearings brought to us by the detailed researches of F. C. Lane.

46. The widespread use of "commenda" or "colleganzia" contracts is indicated by existing notarial records (Lopez and Raymond 1967, 168–84; Clapham 1941–78, 2:173, 306; Weber 1923/1950, 206, 225). Max Weber devoted a monograph to the legal aspects of the commenda contract as a phase of the development of partnership and corporate law. See his *Zur Geschichte des Handelegesellschaften im Mittelalter* (1924, 312–43). It was commenda ventures that Antonio in Shakespeare's *Merchant of Venice* counted on to make good his promissory note to Shylock.

47. The record of chartering and debate about town formation in Anglo-Saxon England is interestingly presented in essays and documents collected in Benton (1968, 19–42; for debate and for a sampling of documents see 42–105).

48. See especially Rörig (1967, 30, 72, 98; Clapham 1941–1978, 3:389).

49. "The town could force rural lords to free their serfs as happened on a large scale in fifteenth century Italy . . ." (Cipolla 1972–1976, 1:79). See also Anderson (1974b, 152). The menace to republics in tolerating in their domain "lords possessing castles" or country gentlemen "who live idly upon the proceeds of their extensive possessions" was a cardinal theme of Machiavelli who distinguished the region of Tuscany where there are "no lords possessing castles and exceedingly few or no gentlemen" from the kingdom of Naples, the Romagna, or Lombardy, where these "enemies of all civil government" abound (Machiavelli 1513–1521/1950, 255). But Machiavelli shied away from agrarian reform à la Grachii (see his Discourse 47). Max Weber (1921/1968, 2:1320) notes that shattering by burger towns of "traditional seigneurial" authority went hand in hand with the development of landlord-tenant farming (*mezzadria*).

50. Waley 1969, 56, 110, 221; Pirenne 1936, 16, 40, 169; Bury 1929–1936, 5:208–24.

51. That later development, of which there were premonitions, was su-

perbly portrayed in Burckhardt 1860/1958, Part I, Chaps 3–5. See also Anderson 1974a, 143–72.

52. Herlihy 1970, 219. The allocation of manorial domains after the Norman conquest left 24 percent of the available revenues in the royal family (Bury 1929–1936, 5:508). The two largest receipts in the first available set of English treasury records are manor farm revenues and fees from justice administration and estates (Harriss 1975, 4; Benton 1968, 98; Herlihy 1970, 243).

53. Herlihy 1970, 185; Postan 1975, 188; Bloch 1939–1940/1961, 221.

54. The representative Normandy code of law of 1258 bound vassals to take arms to support the duke "to repel an attack of the enemy" but at the expense of the duke after forty days of service (Herlihy 1970, 179).

55. Formally the share of the Carolingian count was a third (ibid). The Norman sheriffs in England collected the king's revenues from domain and other sources at a set "farm" and recouped themselves by scaling their collections accordingly. The disciplining of sheriffs' collections was an involved process spread over many centuries with a key role played by administrative inquests and reforms of Henry II (Bury 1929–1936, 5:509, 582; Harriss 1975, 132; Bloch 1939–1940/1961, 430).

56. Bloch 1939–1940/1961, 61; Boussard 1969, 61.

57. The evidence for this development was assembled and brilliantly set forth by White (1962, 1–28).

58. White 1962, 30. William the Conqueror in return for the manorial domains given to his barons and ecclesiastical authorities obtained the commitment for 5,000 armed knights to be on call annually for forty-days service (Bury 1929–1936, 5:51).

59. The pros and cons of artillery, which could readily batter down "even the strongest walls," were illuminatingly treated at the close of the Medieval epoch by Machiavelli (1513–1521/1950, Discourse XVII).

60. Cipolla 1972–1976, 1:88, Pirenne 1936, 62, 89; Mumford 1961, 309; Rörig 1967, 72.

61. Italian *contado* or rural hinterland, brought under town control in Germany and Switzerland sometimes by outright purchase, was summarily reviewed by Rörig 1967, 168. Lübeck had by 1350 acquired rights to 240 villages; Erfurt some 83 villages in over 610 square kilometers. The Swiss towns of Zurich, Berne, Lucerne, and Basle acquired extensive rural domains. See for a contrary view, Anderson 1974b, 150 n. 12.

62. Waley 1969, 95, 107; Rörig 1967, 172.

63. Waley 1969, 93; Lane 1973, 59; Rörig 1967, 114; Braudel 1975, 1:329.

64. In 1252 Genoa commenced coinage of the gold genovion; a year later the Florentine florin followed; in 1284 Venice came out with her famous ducat (Clapham 1941–1978, 3:590).

65. Lane 1973, 14; Gottlieb 1984, 157.

66. I draw here on chapters and essays by Lane on Venetian shipping and maritime administration (1966, 3, 143, 193, 253; 1973, 58, 126).

67. Lane 1973, 58. Like English wool, Venice treated salt as an excised export (Rörig 1967, 163; Waley 1969, 78).

68. Waley 1969, 79; Rörig 1967, 162. For Siena's experience between 1287 and 1355 with direct income taxation, see Herlihy (1969, 205).

69. Brucker 1962, 31, 92, 195, 201, 315, and Chap. 8. See also Machiavelli (1525/1909, 109–35). The outline in the text of the feudal institution of property as an ensemble of rights and tenures is drawn chiefly from the

law summary of Normandy authored by an unknown lawyer about 1258 (Herlihy 1970, 177–87).

70. For an illuminating description of the process of the "triumph of hereditability" of "social forces over an obsolescent right" see Bloch 1939–1940, 1961, 190. Max Weber noted the "appropriation" of benefices reached a point where even the heirs received a compensation for the loss of revenues derived from the benefice (Weber 1923/1950, 2:1074).

71. Homans 1941/1975, 73.

72. Precisely that is the theme of "Raoul of Cambrai," a heroic Medieval epic from the early Medieval period (Herlihy 1970, 131–76).

73. On copyhold tenures in open field manors that were unenclosed and persisted through to modern times, see Taylor 1919, 305. Rules of descent, services prescribed, and quitrents if any were regulated by custom. Under the provisions of the Copyhold Act of 1894 and earlier acts, copyhold tenures were largely abolished.

74. Relief payments could sometimes be "exceptionally extortionate" and wardship could be administered "rapaciously" (Postan 1975). "One of the complaints in 1234 had been of the disposal of wardships and marriages to Poitevins." The king was once openly rebuked for his collection of "untold wealth from the vacancies of abbeys, earldoms, and baronies, wardships and escheats." (Harriss 1957, 138). Often it seems wardships and escheats were farmed out for the highest price.

75. For a brief treatment of that puzzling "conveyance to use" – the technical name given to the legal means for evading wardship and relief by arranging for the transmission of property to heirs through the device of a prior nominal grant to third parties masquerading as a sale – see Tigar and Levy 1977, 209. See also Bean 1968, Chaps. 3, 4, 8. The presently valid Statute of Uses and of Wills and the Statute of Enrollments resulting from the controversy left one-third of knightly and baronial estates subject to relief and wardship. For texts of statutes which still have some legal validity even in the United States, see any standard text on real property law, e.g., Vance 1971, 232–67. These feudal drainages were however finally abolished by the sweeping grant of the Restoration Parliament of "allodial" status to feudal holders of property in England, "an act of usurpation," wrote Marx, which vindicated for the landed proprietors of England the "rights of modern private property in estates to which they had only a feudal title" (Marx 1863–1878/1967, 1:723).

76. Homans 1941/1975, 109; Duby 1974, 227; Downs 1959, 57; Coulton 1923–1950, 3:292. Feudal death duties lingered in Western Europe long after formal serfdom had disappeared (Blum 1978, 60).

77. Miskinin 1975, 60; Homans 1941/1975, 35, 240, 259, 282; Duby 1974, 203, 222; Postan 1975, 167. The problematics of commutation and the degree it was implicated by the rise of a money economy and markets is exhaustively discussed in Dobb (1963, 38).

78. The old tradition of holding borough court was "the most prized among Municipal jurisdictions" that "more than any other . . . determined the evolution and working constitution of the Municipal constitution." Some forty municipal corporations had sole jurisdiction in 1689 of petty sessions or minor charges and suits. Some fifteen corporations could try all misdemeanors, however grave, but no felonies. Some eighty-seven corporations could try felonies except the most heinous; and forty-seven corporations could try all felonies. High municipal officials were generally given ex-officio authority as JP; and for

ample London JP arrangements (Webb and Webb 1903–1929, 2:278, 328; 3:577, 662 n. 2, 667).

79. Max Weber (1921/1968, 2:1325) generalized: "autonomous law creation by the city and within it again by the [old] guilds and the [later] crafts was a right fully exercised by the politically independent Italian cities and at times by the Spanish, English, and a considerable part of the French and German cities."

80. Internal divisiveness multiplied toll stations along the great rivers and thus hindered economic unification in northern Italy. The constant fighting to enlarge territorial domains – especially the long fratricidal wars between Pisa and Genoa, Genoa and Venice, and between various Lombard and Tuscan states – checked economic development, kept industry on a small scale, and hindered the development of a strong regional economy.

81. See Max Weber 1921/1968, 2:1322. "The circular path of the Italian cities from a stage in which they were component parts of patrimonial or feudal structures, through a period of independence obtained by revolution with a government of local notables and then of the craft guilds, followed by the *signoria* and finally again by a position as component parts of relatively rational patrimonial associations – this cycle has no exact counterpart in the Occident."

82. For the decline of Medieval and domain revenues and the gradual rise of national taxation, especially headed up by the powerful wool levy uniting the crown with a merchant-monopoly, see Harriss (1975, 509). Wool revenues had been fiscally exploited at the turn of the twelfth century when the ransom for King Richard was raised with a wool levy of 50,000 sacks. The rising value of English raw wool in export markets of Italy and Flanders made it possible to exploit a monopoly position benefiting both crown and merchantry, taking up to 40 percent of the export value of the crop (Postan 1975, 214, 238, 245; Harriss 1975, 235, Chap. 18). The crown obtained not only a tax on wool exports but a share in the profits of monopoly sale granted to a company of merchants together with a loan in anticipation of its sale. This is not to gainsay the importance of the development of national "aids" or "subsidies," which were in effect a levy at flat rates on property and income on all free subjects and communities throughout the realm, subject to assent of Parliament (Harriss 1975, 435; 3). On the quite exceptional position of Medieval England see the still useful investigation of Heckscher (1955, 1:46–55).

83. Anderson 1974a. I differ from Anderson chiefly in his effort to construe these varied social formations as manifestations of a unitary feudalism.

Chapter 4

1. Periodizations are approximate or, as Wallerstein (1974, 67) put it, "historical centuries are not necessarily chronological ones." I follow Eric Williams (1964, 120) in interpreting the American Revolution of 1776–1783 as a smashing blow to the English mercantilist system just at the time its theoretical premises were undermined by the critical work of Adam Smith (Schumpeter 1954, 374 n. 20).

2. Schumpeter (1954, 335) in his introductory remarks commented on a certain "pontifical attitude" toward "The Mercantilist' Literature." J. M.

Keynes (1936, 334) commented he was "brought up to believe" that mercantilist theory was "little better than nonsense."

3. Marx 1858/1971, 54, 157, 168; 1857–1858/1974, 174, 283; 1863–1878/1967, 3:337, 785.

4. That is the express message of the famous Part 8 of *Capital* (1:713–74), "The So-called Primitive Accumulation."

5. Cipolla 1980, 104, 176, 275; Wallerstein 1974/1980, 2:43; Braudel 1982–1984, 3:191.

6. De Vries 1976, 93, 192.

7. Islamic culture and traditions give abundant testimony to an old and well-established export of slaves across the Sahara as well as to an indigenous development of slavery in Muslim Africa (Hopkins 1973, 23, 82; Ibn Kahldun 1377/1968, 117). The adaptation of African society in the Western Sudan to the arrival of Portuguese marines, soldiers, and traders was not without its indigenous African protest, but on the whole the Marxist Walter Rodney (1970, 88, 102, 253) agrees with Hopkins (1973, 87–116) that the Atlantic African slave trade primarily rested on merchandising between Western traders and West African rulers and dominant states especially Dahomey and the Ashanti. A wide selection of goods was used for African slave trading involving heavy emphasis on copper produced in Germany and Hungary, European textiles including British woolens, Indian cotton goods, copper, colored glass and beads, iron bars, alcoholic beverages (emphasized in recent research); and guns and staple hardware items (Williams 1964, 65, 81; Miskimin 1977, 125–28; Thomas and Bean 1974, 901).

8. The Atlantic slave trade was thus a commercial venture with elaborate markets on the basis of price up and down the line.

9. Thomas and Bean (1974, 902) pointed out that on one 100-mile stretch of beach there were twenty-two permanent forts or lodges manned by Europeans and up and down the coast no point was more than 10 miles from a fort of both Dutch and English nationalities, the competition between them "being intense." For a similar evaluation, see Anderson and Richardson and a "Reply" by Inikori (1983).

10. Williams 1964, 73; Cole 1939, 2:50.

11. As is well known, the French evinced a special aptitude for this skill.

12. Estimates of the great Brazilian gold strikes between 1695 and the 1720s vary widely because of uncertainty as to the percent of legal marketing (Boxer 1962, 3–60, App. 2). Allowing for 30 pounds to the arroba, the legally recorded output subject to royal tax amounted between 1700 and 1750 to 797 tons of gold, the bulk of this being recorded in the period 1714–1724.

13. These estimates do not allow for the large amount of New World silver that escaped the taxing net of the Spanish crown and was smuggled to Europe by sailors, soldiers, and traders, or was acquired by West European merchants trading in Spanish dependencies where goods were scarce but silver abundant. The great work of E. J. Hamilton (1934, Table 3) in appraising the impact of Spanish silver inflow on Spanish economic life and price levels holds up well and has been enriched, not at all rebutted, by criticism. That measured inflow amounted to 18,575 tons between 1503 and 1660. The estimate of 50 percent by Braudel and Spooner as the increase of domestic European money supply from inflow is well regarded by other analysts (Clapham 1941–1978, 4:442; Miskimin 1977, 32; Wallerstein 1974, 70, 170).

14. I agree with the famous judgment of G. Schmoller (1884/1967, 57)

that the mercantilist system is basically nation building.

15. Estimates of population drawn from contemporary records of the mercantilist period are known to be very unreliable even for advanced cities such as Venice that actually took a population census in 1509 (Cipolla 1972–1976, 2:21). The estimated increase of Western European population between 1500 and 1700 by 32 percent is a "guesstimate" with an unspecifiable margin of error. It is known, however, that two abnormal factors reduced the share of net growth between 1600 and 1700: (1) heavy loss from extended wars, (2) massive European migration to the New World. One abnormal factor reduced the share of net growth between 1500 and 1600 – relatively frequent outbreaks of bubonic plague.

16. The number of wars by count or years of formal warfare were probably not greater than in previous centuries but certainly the size and effectiveness of armies and fleets were greater. For Europe as a whole Pitirim Sorokin (1937, Chaps. 9–11) recorded a quantum jump in the number of war casualties per million of population: 9.5, 15, and 45 in the fifteenth, sixteenth, and seventeenth centuries. With political authority on the Continent notably more centralized, standing professional armies of trained soldiery were much larger. Improvement in weaponry, art of fortification, artillery continued apace since the beginning of the seventeenth century (Marx and Engels 1841–1870/1974–1986, 18:317–40, 340–56, 429–59).

17. De Vries 1976, 35; Cipolla 1972–1976, 2:399. In England the share of farmland operated as manorial estates by church and crown sharply fell off, which probably made for a more productive agriculture. With enclosures gradually accumulating, by 1700 half of the English open fields were enclosed (Coleman 1977, 43, 124). This partly resulted in more high-grade pasture and more capitalist farming. In the course of the eighteenth century English yearly wheat output rose from 19 to 50 million bushels because of the rise in yields to 20 to 22 bushels per acre, from 3 to 4 times the late medieval level (Deane and Cole 1962, 62).

18. On the potato plant the enthusiastic comments of Adam Smith (1776–1937, 160) are well known: "The strongest men and the most beautiful women perhaps in the British dominions are . . . generally fed with this root." The traditional administration of tithes, which did not assess tithes on new plants until they encroached too much on the standard plants, favored the more rapid spread of new plants. Maize cultivation made rapid headway in southern France and in the highland region of the Spanish-French border. We are told this permitted the eradication of subsistence crises in the region by 1653. See Goy and Ladurie 1972, 228; Goy and Ladurie 1982, 138; Frêche 1974, 213; Appleby 1979, 875; Cipolla 1972–1976, 2:125, 252, 311, 316, 318, 327; Clapham 1941–1978, 4:276, 285, 299; Braudel 1982–1984, 1:158.

19. The waters of the North Atlantic in the shallow banks of the North Sea off Iceland and Newfoundland are unusually rich in seafood and support a teeming marine population, which accounts for a very high fraction of the world's fisheries. For comparison with the more sterile waters of the Mediterranean, see Braudel 1973, 1:138; Braudel 1982–1984, 1:214; Clapham 1941–1978, 5:133–84; Smith 1776/1937, 487.

20. Annual per capita fish consumption in Italy is estimated at 27–28 grams per day for both rich and poor. Fish consumption must have been higher for European peoples with Atlantic Ocean ports or with active fishing fleets such as England, Scotland, the Scandinavian countries, Holland, France,

Spain, and Portugal. Adam Smith (1776/1937, 487) noted that in many parts of Scotland "herring makes no inconsiderable part of the food of the common people."

21. See especially Unger 1980, 25; Wallerstein 1980, 39; Clapham 1941–1978, 4:171, 268.

22. De Vries 1976, 108, 109. This expansion in iron output "signifies a notable increase in the usage of iron in such goods as wagons, farm equipment, and of course military hardware." Nef estimated European iron production in 1525 in the neighborhood of 100,000 tons, which rose by 1700 by some 60 percent, with faster progress in the eighteenth century. Braudel 1982–1984, 1:377. Iron production between 1350 and 1550 rose seven- to eightfold (Cipolla 1980, 129).

23. Genuine blast furnaces with their continuous output of molten iron were developed in the fifteenth century and come extensively into use in the sixteenth and seventeenth centuries, with notable results especially in cannon manufacture. See Clapham 1941–1978, 2:464; Cipolla 1965, 39, 56; Cipolla 1972–1976, 2:262, 391.

24. Cipolla 1972–1976, 2:398.

25. It suffices to cite the record of the amazing surge of English coal output from 200,000 tons at the mid-sixteenth century to 3 million tons in the 1690s (Cipolla 1972–1976, 2:394). On the Dutch peat industry, drawing upon the near surface supplies of burnable decayed plant life found in marshes and bogs, see De Vries 1976, 164. Coal mining in southern and central France, in Westphalia, and especially around Liege developed notably in the mercantilist period (Clapham 1941–1978, 2:472).

26. Cipolla 1972–1976, 2:383, 401; De Vries 1976, 90, 105; Coleman 1977, 151.

27. Clapham 1941–1978, 4:112, 117.

28. Not only did printers, printshops, and printed books multiply in the sixteenth and seventeenth centuries and on a mammoth scale – an estimated 35,000 editions appearing in 15 million copies produced in 236 localities – but an *industry* emerged with specialized producers of movable type. Printing shops grew in size and became capitalist enterprises (Cipolla 1972–1976, 2:379).

29. In an interesting chapter Max Weber (1923/1950, 286) cited the tulip craze of Holland in the 1630s as often included among the earliest speculative crises.

30. For a general presentation, see Ashton (1955a). Lewis (1965, 10–39) makes a convincing case for British building cycles taking off in the early 1700s. In my later study I found three long building and real estate development swings running their course in England in the eighteenth century (Gottlieb 1976, 215).

31. Ashton's first two themes in his analysis of economic fluctuations in England in the eighteenth century were "the elements" and "the harvests" for these predominated in bringing good fortune or bad times to the country (Ashton 1955a, Chaps. 1, 2). A careful study of thirty "crises" or "depressions" in English business between 1558 and 1720 traced nearly all to famines, outbreaks of the plague, wars, civil disorders, irregularities of public finance, or high-handed acts of government" (Mitchell 1927, 75; see also Cipolla 1978, 360–66).

32. In the 1920s the standard authorities on "agricultural depression"

were Conrad (1909) and Sering (1925). Two Russians have since joined them: Lyuboshits (1949) and Spectator (1929). I owe the Lyuboshits reference to Y. Varga who praised the reference. The *Spectator* reference was discussed in an unpublished draft manuscript on agricultural depression which E. Altschul, a German economist with a special interest in business cycles, prepared under the auspices of the National Bureau of Economic Research. This draft manuscript in incomplete form was passed on to me, a former student and at the time (1957) a colleague at the University of Kansas City. Dr. Altschul's only published work on the subject to my knowledge appeared in 1937 and in 1938. The latter item was a review of a work by S. Ciriacy-Wantrup. Though Altschul felt that Ciriacy-Wantrup linked agricultural depressions too closely with industrial slowdowns, he believed the work was "remarkable," deserving an "outstanding place" in the "growing literature on agricultural depressions." Of this literature the only work that has survived with interest to our day is by W. Abel, *Agrarkrisen und Agrarstruktur im Mittel Europa von 13th bis zum 19th Jahrhundert* (1935). This has gone through a third edition (1980) and is now translated into English.

33. This version of price determination in capitalist enterprise is set forth more fully and with appropriate qualifications and references in Gottlieb 1984, 194.

34. Laying out average wage rates paid on the manorial estates of the bishop of Winchester, Postan (1973, 200; 1975, 145) questions whether these wage data are very relevant to "movements from villages to towns."

35. This is a manifestation of the paradoxical and well-known "back-bending supply curve" by which over a limited stretch of values a lesser return elicits not a reduced but a greater supply effort (Marshall 1890/1920, 335; Perlman 1979, 4).

36. See especially Varga 1968, 247; Schumpeter 1939, 1:266; Gates 1960, 104.

37. For references to inability in earlier centuries for cities to reproduce their population without net rural inflows, see Gottlieb 1984, 61 n. 68. For delayed marriage patterns among European villagers back through the mercantilist and late Medieval period, see Hajnal 1965, 101–43. Since Le Roy Ladurie's (1974, 213, 311; 1979b, 239–53) own data for Languedoc show until 1740 mortality rates at about the same level as birth rates, that Languedoc fertility began to decline with the Revolutionary years, and that any tendency to population growth in Languedoc (where fertility was somewhat higher than in the rest of France) was offset in whole or in part elsewhere in the country, he has little justification to speak of the province as "swarming" with children.

38. Peasant Medieval obligations, insists that master of French rural history Marc Bloch (1931/1966, 120), were always for "so many pounds, shillings and pence" (Carolingian units) and not for "a certain weight in gold or silver." The English pound and penny contain at present, reported Adam Smith (1776/1937, 27) in 1776, "about a third only" of its original precious metal endowment, the French pound and penny about a sixty-sixth part; and the Scots pound and penny about a thirty-sixth part.

39. Simiand 1932. For an appreciation of his work, see Lane 1953, 464.

40. Kondratieff 1935, 105–15. For a summary of debate on the Kondratieff theory, see Garvey 1935, 101–25. While these long cycles were found to pervade the capitalist economy, Kondratieff emphasized that their core was the agrarian depression. "During the recession of the long waves, agriculture,

as a rule, suffers an especially pronounced and long depression. This is what happened after the Napoleonic wars, it happened again from the beginnings of the 1870s onward and the same can be observed in the years after the World War."

41. This is well-recognized in specialized works on the Great Depression. See especially Timoshenko 1935; Kindelberger 1973, Chap. 4; Schumpeter 1939, 2:732. The contribution of agrarian depression was three fold: (1) it created "depression poles" that generated contraction (e.g., agricultural machinery industry, rural nonfarm businesses); (2) it disrupted foreign exchange relationships, leading in 1930 to currency defaults and exchange devaluation by agricultural export countries whose ability to pay for industrial imports had greatly declined; (3) it led to bank failures in rural U.S. banks contributing to loss of depositor confidence that ultimately in the United States exploded in banking collapse.

42. See especially Varga 1968, 244; Schumpeter 1939, 1:216; Gates 1960, 104.

43. For sharp criticism that Kondratieff received from his Soviet confreres, see Garvey 1935. For Western economists, see the appraisals of Burns 1969, 9; Hansen 1951, 53; and Johr 1952, 50. Fellner (1956, 37–43) declared: "Most investigators now feel that the Kondratieff findings depended too much on particular trend-elimination procedures and on arbitrary decisions of dating."

44. The established records of improvement in crop yields in England and in the Low Countries through the late seventeenth and early eighteenth century was phenomenal. For older accounts see Rogers 1883, 468; Lord Ernle 1912/1961. For more recent accounts, see Ashton 1955a, 30; Coleman 1977, 111; Slichter van Bath 1967, 43, Graph 6, 55; Thirsk 1984–1985, 2:9, 82.

45. Smith 1776/1937, 437–82. As critics have pointed out, price supports and a floor ceiling would tend to encourage extension of cultivation and diversion of capital into agricultural improvement subsidized by the export bounties that burdened British taxpayers. Smith himself argued rather mechanically that the bounty-tariff system raised the cost of living and thus tended to raise wage levels. This was inconsistent with his own empirical findings on wage-rate determinants (see Gould 1962, 330). Since even with this support system, grain prices in England and Wales had fallen from 1680 levels and since, as we shall notice later (n. 46) there were two decades of price distress for many English farmers, it may be doubted that much additional agricultural investment in poorer lands was encouraged. The main effect of the bounty system was to reward efficient producers and minimize the distress otherwise unavoidable.

46. See especially Mingay 1956, 323–38; Chambers 1957, 41, 43. But even in these two decades there were some intermissions in the low price years and Chambers assures us that the "larger tenants," who accumulated most of the rent arrears, "usually were able to weather the storm." See also qualifications to Mingay's research in Thirsk 1984–1985, 2:81.

47. For an example of the "nominal" in contrast to the deflated price returns for tithes in France through the 1685–1717 period see Goy and Le Roy Ladurie 1972, 222 (for Toulouse region).

48. This hostility to royal taxation exploded in the sixteenth century in an insurrectionary movement in Dauphiné on which Le Roy Ladurie (1979b, Chaps. 2, 3, 13, 14) has written. On seventeenth century peasant revolts, see

Mousnier 1970; Le Roy Ladurie 1974, 265–86; Goubert 1986, Chap. 16. In between revolts, peasant proprietors "crushed by the higher taxes sold out to privileged investors" (Hoffman 1986, 45).

49. Scoville 1960, Chap. 5, 156–210.

50. On population decline between 1685 and 1715, see Le Roy Ladurie 1974, 239; Scoville 1960, 411.

51. There is little basis for attributing much of the output decline to bad weather which over the entire period, 1550–1730, was of a normal range (Hoffman 1986, 41). The trend to colder winters and more extended glaciers, a trend detected by many writers from 1540 on, persisted to 1850 not the early 1700s as Goubert contends (1986, 123). Colder winters hurt agriculture in Alpine terrain or in far northern Europe, but it did not appreciably injure French agriculture (Le Roy Ladurie 1971, Chap. 7). The recurrence of the plague in 1720–1722 was a disaster for the Marseilles region; but the plague was visiting more extensively through the first half of the seventeenth century (see Le Roy Ladurie 1981, 68; Braudel 1982–1984, 1:83). There has been no refined statistical analysis of crop shortages, as measured or indicated by extreme variations of market price, and it does appear that French agriculture in the three decades before 1715 was more afflicted than usual. An extreme winter in 1709 destroyed nearly all Mediterranean French olive groves for nearly a generation (Le Roy Ladurie 1974, 230). Hence the text specifies a 2 percent allowance for reduced farm output over the three decades for ecological and weather effects.

52. In his *Peasants Languedoc,* (1974, 227, 234) Le Roy Ladurie etched a portrait of the decline of agricultural output by product groups (wine, grains, olive oil) and repeatedly suggested that the "plunge" as he called it of farm output was "brutal." He wrote that from 1680 onward an "irremissible decline of the gross product," reached by 1710–1715 one-half of its previous level. In his latest work, based upon extensive studies by students and associates, the proportion of decline is considerably cut down. In at least three provinces – Brittany, port of St. Malo, Alsace, and Burgundy, no decline seems to have occurred. Decline was "relatively slight in the countryside around Paris where the . . . rents fell by only about 15 percent. Elsewhere in the north and south of France the tithe and rents fell by between 25 percent and . . . 35 percent" (Goy and Le Roy Ladurie 1982, 18).

53. M. Morineau, M. T. Lorcin, M. Nicolas, G. Frêche, J. Rives. For samples of this writing, see the two collections: Goy and Le Roy Ladurie 1972 and 1982; Rives 1976, 144. For a measured reply to criticism, see Goy and Le Roy Ladurie 1982, 26–34.

54. Coulton 1926, 291; Hill 1956, 77–88; Cobbett 1835, 77; Evans 1976, 17, 144; Boyd 1952, 181, 197; Frêche 1974, 522.

55. Coulton 1923–1950, 3:224. See also Goy and Le Roy Ladurie 1972, 105. Church manuals instructed priests to throw out a sweeping curse many times yearly on tithe evaders (Coulton 1923–1950, 3:211, 251, 294, 335). Church mortuary taxes on peasant households – taking the second-best beast or some equivalent value – was supposedly compensation to the church for evasion of tithes in the deceased's lifetime (Homans 1941/1975, 385).

56. Wastelands were in 1761 given limited exemption from tithes for up to twenty years for marshland and this exemption was widely used and stirred up much controversy. Rives 1976, 124; McManners 1985, 158–59.

57. Le Roy Ladurie 1979c; Coulton 1923–1950, 2:113, 137; Latourette 1953, 453–56.

58. Assignment of tithe collection to contractors in exchange for a set fee has been traced to the early and late medieval years. The role of contractors became larger in the mercantilist years, their contract terms became lengthened, their operating methods became more sophisticated. The net return of contractors is not of course known but informed estimates range between 20 and 40 percent. I am inclined to find the higher figure more credible. Coulton 1923–1950, 3:255, 297, 644; Neveaux 1980, 43; Rives 1976, 59, 147; Bois 1984, 119; Goy and Le Roy Ladurie 1972, 216.

59. This neglect of traditional objectives of tithing was especially resented. Coulton 1923–1950, 3:220–28.; Goy and Le Roy Ladurie 1982, 230; McManners 1985, 153–55.

60. Altar dues (*dieu-d'autel*) in Cambrésis were over twice the tithe rate of 8 percent as a drain on village income. Altar and parish fees in England in the mercantilist period included rents for gravesites, bells at funerals, Easter offerings, pew rents, mortuary fees so heavy they were regulated by statute under Henry VIII and christening fees of 11.5d subject to reduction if the child died. (Hill 1956, Chap. 7).

61. Even in the Vendeé where peasants joined priest and noble to fight the French Revolution, the "few places" where monastic institutions were found became "patriot centers" (Tilly 1964, 189).

62. Le Roy Ladurie 1977, 172.

63. Goy and Le Roy Ladurie 1972, 15; Le Roy Ladurie 1977, 184.

64. Goy and Le Roy Ladurie 1972, 255-73.

65. Le Roy Ladurie 1979a, 379 n. 80; Goy and Le Roy Ladurie 1972, 27, 232; 1982, 603.

66. Warren Scoville's interest had been aroused by his graduate studies in the economic effects on French economic development of her religious civil wars of the sixteenth and seventeenth centuries climaxed by the Revocation of the Edict of Nantes in 1685. He turned away from this topic on the advice of the distinguished economic historian John Nef who advised him that the study was too extended for a doctoral dissertation. Scoville was glad that he passed up that thesis opportunity because in the preface to his book he testified that it required "ten years of continuous work" (Scoville 1960, viii). His work surveyed the Huguenot position in industry, finance, and agriculture, and the role of other factors contributing to the stagnation of 1684–1717 (see Chap. 11, 465–533).

67. We thus rule out the entire hypothesis of Wallerstein (1980, 2–35, 19, 13) that the seventeenth century phase of capitalist-mercantile development was in a chronic state of "crisis" or that it was subject through most of the period 1600–1750 to "the B-Phase," i.e., the long-swing decline or contraction phase of a "long wave."

68. Aston (1965) republishing articles published in *Past and Present* in response to two leading papers by E. J. Hobsbawm and H. R. Trevor-Roper.

69. Postan 1975, 171; Duby 1968, 332. See Engels's (1850/1926, App., 157) vivid though outdated account of the German peasant rebellion of the sixteenth century, a belated manifestation of the same kind of discontent that exploded earlier in England and France. The revolt was a mass outbreak reliably estimated to have resulted in the death of 100,000 persons (Clapham 1941–1978, 4:72). The various suggestions at causation reviewed by Wallerstein (1974, 23) are not very persuasive. An immense literature has arisen on Luther's involvement with the Peasants War and its implications for Protestant theology (see Arnal 1980–1981, 443).

70. On this policy of *Bauernschutz* so-called, variously exhibited by royal power in England by Tudors and Stuarts, and in Germany and France . . . see De Vries 1976, 61, 66; Tawney 1926/1947, 118; Marx 1863–1878/1967, 1:748; Blum 1978, 206; Brenner 1976, 70. "Let States that aime at Greatnesse, take heed how their Nobility and Gentlemen, doe multiply too fast. For that maketh the Common Subject, grow to be but a peasant and Base Swaine, driven out of heart and in effect but the Gentlemen's Labourer. . . . And you will bring it to that, that not the hundred poll will be fit for an Helmut especially as to the Infantery which is the Nerve of an Army" (Bacon 1625/1903, 137).

71. Boon works and revenues from *heriot* still were collected in the late sixteenth and early seventeenth century (Deane and Cole 1962, 301; Carus-Wilson 1954–1966, 2:210; Gottlieb 1984, 65).

72. The evolution of the English capitalist farmer was traced out by Marx (1863–1878/1967, 1:Chap. 29) in one of his pithy master genetic sketches. Their numbers were estimated at 150,000 by Gregory King in 1688 (Coleman 1977, 6). See briefly De Vries 1976, 75; Cipolla 1972–1976, 2:300.

73. Sometimes these were detached properties, sometimes a formal estate operated by dependent share-cropping households settled on small plots, the *mezzadria* of the Italian or Iberian countryside or the *metairie* of France (Braudel 1973, 1:75; Cipolla 1972–1976, 2:297).

74. Gregory King's estimate of 140,000 freeholders is widely accepted. Marx explained the survival in the English countryside of peasant smallholders who cultivate the soil as an accessory. Their chief occupation was some form of cottage industry (Marx 1863–1878/1967, 1:748). Many smallholders were descendants of the "franklins" of an earlier epoch.

75. In the Mediterranean world of the sixteenth century, Braudel (1973, 1:40) finds a kind of "freedom of the hills" that has "survived into our own time" with its relative freedom from estate farming and a drift to equalitarian holdings, while conversely "large estates have remained the rule in the plains." Max Weber (1923/1950, 76) reported the Rhenish or southwest German peasant "became in fact his own master, able to sell his holdings or transmit to his heirs." A substantial stratum of large German farmers, the *Grossbauern,* emerged in central and southern Germany (De Vries 1976, 61).

76. The fulling mill had become widespread in England and Wales during the thirteenth century and by 1327 over 100 mills chiefly in the hilly northern and western parts of England have been identified where a new clothing industry had sprung up along capitalist "putting out" lines. See the remarkable investigations of Carus-Wilson (1967, 183, 211).

77. Cipolla (1972–1976, 2:399; 1980, 104).

78. De Vries 1976, 92; Cipolla 1972–1976, 2:216; Marx 1863–1878/1967, 1:428.

79. This theme is developed in a number of early papers of J. U. Nef. See especially his "The Progress of Technology and the Growth of Large Scale Industry in Great Britain, 1500–1600," (Carus-Wilson 1954–1966, 1:88–107); Nef, "The Industrial Revolution Reconsidered" (1943); Nef, *Industry and Government in France and England 1540–1640* (1940/1957, 1).

80. Dobb 1963, 139.

81. Coleman 1977, 152; Clapham 1941–1978, 4:362; Cipolla 1972–1976, 2:181.

82. Coleman 1977, 87. Waterpowered French paper mills are believed to have functioned in the early 1700s mostly with a single vat and employing

from three to ten persons making from two to ten reams of paper daily (Scoville 1967, 283).

83. Cipolla 1972–1976, 2:221; Nef 1957, 76, 101.

84. Nef 1957, 59, 88; Cipolla 1965, 39.

85. Coleman 1977, 180; Heckscher 1955, 1:227, 233. Smith (1776/1937, 119, 128) described the apprenticeship and guild system as an active though declining force in English economic life.

86. Heckscher 1955, 1:137; Nef 1940/1957, 14; Cole 1939, 1:65, 2:441.

87. See especially the extended investigations of W. Sombart (1902, 1:423) in the first edition of his *Der Moderne Kapitalismus,* and especially in textiles (424), clothing and footwear (449), food preparation (447), building trades (462). Apprentices still resided in the household of the master (476).

88. Heckscher 1955, 1:393; Cipolla 1972–1976, 2:408.

89. This was the case in England and France where the merchants, aristocracy, and crown played a leading role in corporate development (Clapham 1941–1978, 4:240, 250; Heckscher 1955, 1:349, 394, 398). To bring together the landowning aristocracy of France under the lead of the monarchy into a close alliance with the aggressive mercantile and industrial bourgeoisie was indeed the heart of the Colbertian strategy for promoting economic development in seventeenth century France (Cole 1939, Chaps. 8, 9). The warm welcome by Louis XIV given the initial petitioners for the forming of the East India Company "impressed the courtiers" (1:477). Three-quarters of the directors had to be merchants "actually engaged in commerce and who do not hold government offices" (482). In selling stock an aggressive effort was made to "arouse the interest of the landed proprietors" (485). The royal family and the higher nobility "especially . . . connected with the court" invested handsomely (496). The later companies formed followed the same pattern. This aspect of mercantilist development in the emergence of royal power in England and in France is quite neglected in the account of Perry Anderson who stressed the "integrating" of the "nascent French bourgeoisie" into the "circuit of the feudal state" by the purchase of offices and tax farms (Anderson 1974b, 97). Yet the fantastic financial adventuring of John Law in France (1715–1720) is only understandable in the light of this bourgeoisification of the French court and nobility under the tutelage of Sully, Richelieu, and Colbert. This bourgeoisification was noted by E. Preobrazhensky (1925/1965, 243) "through the process of circulation, through the banks, through the form of joint-stock companies and so on, the two classes, the industrial capitalists and the landlords have to a considerable extent become transformed into a single class, the receivers of dividends." This overstated the case though the class fusion was especially strong in England. In the two preceding centuries landed estates had been purchased on an appreciable scale by successful town business men who also shared in the distribution of crown estates and of landed property seized both from the monasteries in the sixteenth century and from the Irish during the sixteenth and seventeenth century. Moreover, the whole industrial development in Great Britain was founded on the remarkable growth of coal production and marketing. This rested on close relationships, as Nef (1932, Part 4, 1:347, 133) has made very clear, between landowners (on whose estates the mineral deposits were located) and mining undertakers with the skill and ability to work the mines and organize coal marketing.

90. Thus in effect chartered corporations for Africa, for the Levant, for the East Indies trade were carved out of the "regulated trades" and made into

independent joint-stock corporations. The Dutch East India Company, which grew out of a network of provincial trading companies, was formed with a much larger capital than the corresponding English company. Though Marx and Engels (1841–1870/1974–1986, 12:148–57) dated the "true commencement of the East India Company" to a no more remote epoch than the year 1702 when the different East-India trading societies were united under a single corporation, for most of the seventeenth century the older East India Company whose stock was regularly exchanged in London and whose mercantile operations were on a large scale was the dominant English party in the India trade.

91. Stockholders of the East India companies could sell their shares but no longer expect to redeem them at the company by 1612 for the Dutch, 1623 for the English (Cipolla 1972–1976, 2:556). To be effective the new security purchaser had to be "accepted" into the "fellowship" of the company, which in England until the middle of the seventeenth century was not a mere formality (Heckscher 1955, 1:413; De Vries 1976, 224).

92. Cipolla 1972–1976, 2:557; De Vries 1976, 121. A true Paris bourse did not develop until the early years of the 1700s.

93. See Cole 1939, 2: Chap. 9, 130, 634. Besides the companies for the East and West Indies there were companies for Canada, Equinox, St. Pierre, Madagascar, etc.

94. That was especially true in England where Whig finance under the new dynasty of William and Mary pivoted on grant of corporate charters for easy terms on purchase of public debt, – e.g., the Bank of England, the South Sea Company, and the United East India Company. "This epoch in the history of England bears . . . an extreme likeness to the epoch of Louis Philippe in France, the old landed aristocracy having been defeated, and the bourgeoisie not being able to take its place except under the banner of the moneyocracy or the 'haute finance' " (Marx and Engels 1841–1870/1974–1986, 12, 148).

95. De Vries 1976, 224; Cipolla 1972–1976, 2:582; Hamilton 1967.

96. The so-called "Bubble Act" enacted in 1720.

97. Thus the ranking East India companies, both Dutch and English, became losers in the eighteenth century though their colonial servants and staffs gained immensely (Clapham 1941–1978, 4:271).

98. That was in fact the express judgment of Adam Smith (1776/1937, 699).

99. De Vries 1796, 229. John R. Commons (1924, 251, 253) declared that "modern capitalism begins with the assignment and negotiability of contract." He traced the first legal recognition of the right to negotiate the bill of exchange in England to 1603 but the achievement of a fully assignable promissory note, good to bearer, only to 1704.

100. As Hamilton (1934, 73) put it, Castile "passed through her golden age in the sixteenth century" and her "bronze age" in the seventeenth. See also his sequel study (1947, 9–35).

101. Illicit overdraft facilities led to the failure of the Dutch Wisselbank and to earlier failures of the Bank of Valencia and Barcelona. See De Vries 1976, 262; Hamilton 1934, 134; Usher 1943.

102. See the illuminating "Introduction" by Tawney to Wilson 1925, 155; Tawney 1926/1947, 137, 192, 243, 244.

103. Private bankers by the middle of the seventeenth century were accepting deposits, making loans, or discounting bills and accepting checks (Carus-Wilson 1954–1966, 2:341). John Locke (1690/1691, 562) found incredi-

ble that "it be very true, yet it is almost beyond belief, that one private gold-smith of London have of credit, upon his single security (being usually nothing but a note under one of his servant's hands) for above 1 million pounds." Private banking was "notoriously unstable." The disappearance or bankruptcy of firms was "quite common" and about one-third of the London bankers disappeared in the 1720 Bubble Crash (Carus-Wilson 1954–1966, 2:374).

104. The judgment of Thomas Hobbes (1651/1914, 184) was typical. "For what reason is there that he which laboureth much, and sparing the fruits of his labour, consumeth little, should be more charged, than he that living idly, getteth little, and spendeth all he gets; seeing the one hath no more protection from the Common-wealth, then the other? But when the Impositions are layd upon those things which men consume, every man payeth Equally for what he useth. . . ." The "pivot" of "modern fiscality," wrote Marx (1863–1878/1967, 1:756), "is the most necessary means of subsistence. . . ." Montesquieu generalized (1748/1899, 1, Book 13, 215) "The natural tax of moderate governments is the duty laid on merchandise."

105. Smith 1776/1937, 871; De Vries 1976, 202; Braudel 1953, 2:855.

106. Hamilton 1947, 9; Carus-Wilson 1954–1966, 1:223.

107. Perhaps as Braudel indicates the term "bankruptcy" is misleading since what is involved is a unilateral readjustment of indebtedness, sometimes stretching out payments or scaling down interest and hence not decisively breaking with creditors who continued to hang around and deal with the crown (Braudel 1953, 1:505; 2:897, 960; Hamilton 1947, 128).

108. Commencing in the mid-seventeenth century and ending up in 1838 with some 22,000 miles of turnpike road, 1,116 trusts employed some 20,000 collectors at 7,796 tollgates. The terminal mortgage indebtedness was some £7 million. The turnpike system produced for England a serviceable highway network with very little aid from the central state, though many abuses developed out of local jobbery, contract manipulation, toll overcharges (Webb 1903–1929, 4:154–221). Daniel Defoe (1724–1726/1928, 2:117), whose travels over England brought him in close touch with this road network, praised it highly.

109. Cole 1939, 1:379; Clapham 1941–1978, 4:190; Smith 1776/1937, 683; Summerson 1962, 52, Chap. 6; Reddaway 1940.

110. Altogether some 80 million livres were invested in royal edifices (Cole 1939, 1:292, 340, 374; 2:458; 1:117–35). By contrast the allowance for highway building was raised from 40,000 to 600,000 livres annually; and though navigation conditions on some twenty-two rivers were allegedly "improved," very little of the ambitious program to develop mineral resources was ever carried through. The grandiose du Noyer program approved under Henry IV was neglected in execution.

111. Heckscher (1955, 1:20) simply defines mercantilism as "economic policy of the time between the Middle Ages and the age of laissez-faire." Dobb (1963, 209) defines it in a twofold way: as a "system of state-regulated exploitation through trade" and as the "economic policy of the age of primitive accumulation."

112. Marx 1863–1878/1967, 3:785; see also Weber 1923/1950, 347–49.

113. As John Locke (1690–1691, 612) put it plainly: "all the imaginable ways of increasing money in any country are these two: either to dig it in the mines of our own or get it from our neighbors . . . by force, borrowing or trade."

114. Sketching out the creative analysis which later went by the name

"cash balance approach" to the velocity of circulation of money, the brilliant Petty (in a writing Marx deemed a masterpiece of analysis) followed by John Locke showed that at a given price and wage level the expansion of a country's income or production called for a determinate increase in the stock of money (Schumpeter 1954, 212, 316; Marx, "From the Critical History" included in Engels 1877–1878, 265; Locke 1690–1691, 573).

115. If we wish to know why "in every kingdom in which money begins to flow in greater abundance than formerly, everything takes a new face: labor and industry gain life; the merchant becomes more enterprising, the manufacturer more diligent and skillful," we must, says Hume (1752/1955, 37), have regard to the "interval" between the "acquisition of money and rise of prices" when the "diligence" of producers is "quickened." See also Locke (1690–1691, 607).

116. Keynes 1936, 335. Heckscher added to the revised (1955, 204) edition an addendum chapter, "Keynes and Mercantilism," which illustrates how valid criticisms sometimes yield invalid conclusions.

117. As Keynes (1936, 337) put it sharply, "the economic history of Spain in the latter part of the fifteenth and in the sixteenth centuries provides an example of a country whose foreign trade was destroyed by the effect on the wage unit [Keynesian language to describe the level of wages] of an excessive abundance of the precious metals." This outcome was adequately demonstrated by the remarkable researches of Hamilton (1934, Part II).

118. Recognition was in "time" because for most of the sixteenth century Spanish public opinion and contemporary debate put the blame, as Hamilton (1934, 393) makes clear, on quite secondary factors or symptoms of inflation and looked for measures of punishment and regulation to stop price advances. The famous French writer, Jean Bodin, was the first in 1568 to give an extended statement of the hypothesis that increased American silver was the main cause of the price revolution that had swept Spain (Schumpeter 1954, 312).

119. Debasement of currencies in the mercantilist period is graphically presented in Clapham 1941–1978, 4:458; Cipolla 1980, 200.

120. Hence declining real wages in the mercantilist period up to 1650 are indicated by our best available measures of monetary wage rates but are always difficult to couple to an acceptable cost-of-living price series. See here the recent work of Braudel and Spooner in Clapham 1941–1978, 4:425. J. M. Keynes (1930, 2:163) with his eye for key statistical facts was quick to notice that this first great price inflation increased profits and lowered real wages, though he believed that the extent of real wage decline thrown up by the statistical research of Hamilton seemed exaggerated. The more careful later studies of Nef (1940/1957) and Felix (1956) indicate the reduced proportions of this decline without eliminating it altogether. The extent of real wage decline will of course depend upon the margin of real wages over bare subsistence, changes in productivity, turnover practices in employment, and varying practices of giving wage supplements in kind by way of rations, housing, and the like. Marx (1862–1863/1963–1971, 1:154) correctly argued that money wages did not rise in proportion to the prices of commodities . . . "and because of this relative surplus-labor increased and the rate of profit rose." It was this, "though they were only dimly aware of it," that led the mercantilists to favor monetary expansion policies.

121. As Adam Smith (1776/1937, 400) noted, the policy of prohibition of

gold and silver export was anciently the policy of all European nations and was not specifically mercantilist. Nor was the policy enforceable. Locke (1690–1691, 607) noted laconically that "it is the death in Spain to export money; and yet they who furnish all the world with gold and silver have the least of it amongst themselves."

122. This differentiation between an earlier and cruder "monetary system" and its later outgrowth into "mercantilism" proper is variously expressed in Marx's writings (Marx 1859/1971, 54, 157; 1857–1858/1973, 225, 327; 1863–1878/1967, 3:785).

123. Cole 1939, 2:472–502; Webb 1903–1929, 7:29, 399.

124. It was these discriminatory trade arrangements favoring Portuguese over French wines that practically destroyed Anglo-French wine trade (Smith 1776/1937, 441, 460).

125. Clapham (1941–1978, 4:470) shows wheat prices and ten-year averages between 1440 and 1760 for various commercial centers in Europe.

126. "Why should the rise of capitalist industry require a whole period of prior accumulation?" (Dobb 1963, 177). "The wealth of the nabob returning home from India to England was more likely to go into land and office than into trade, the experience of colonial exaction was a poor training for risk-taking ventures in a competitive market" (Landes 1969, 36). See also Max Weber 1923/1950, 300. In his analysis of "primitive accumulation" Werner Sombart (1902, 1:277, 251, 299) pointed to other sources of wealth accumulation arising out of the normal working of the late medieval economy including high mark-ups on Asian spices, fees from handling international papal revenues, tax farming, and enrichment through rise in the value of town real estate.

127. The need for such a transition system has been expressed in different languages by others. "How are we to speak of the economic system in the intervening period . . . which . . . seems to have been neither feudal nor yet capitalist?" "What is the correct definition of the historical period which extends approximately from the fifteenth to the sixteenth centuries during which feudalism was dead or dying but when no real elements or signs of the capitalist mode of production were yet present?" (Dobb 1963, 19; Procacci, "A Survey of the Debate," in Hilton 1976, 129; Amin 1976, 51, 64). The most compact formulation of this transition hypothesis was worked out by Preobrazhensky: "Capitalism was able to pass through its period of primitive accumulation in the age of absolutism in politics and of simple commodity production and feudal-serfdom-relations in the economic sphere" (Preobrazhensky 1925/1965, 19. See also Gerschenkron 1952, 31–51, 90, 118).

Chapter 5

1. The penal laws dated from 1695. The laws were provoked by Irish armed support of the Stuart aspirant for the British throne after the Protestant William of Orange was seated in 1688 on the British throne. They were not repealed in entirety until Catholic Emancipation in 1829. The penal laws aimed at the virtual destruction of a distinctive Irish Catholic society. (See Costigan 1969, 91; Young 1776–1779/1892, 2: 60. On the relaxation of the penal laws, see Halévy 1912/1937, Book 3, 96).

2. A votary of the new cliometric economic history, Joel Mokyr, believes that the penal laws had only a transitory effect and have little to do with the question of Irish poverty. He in the first place confuses the question "why Ireland starved" in the Great Famine with the question of structural Irish poverty in the prefamine period (Mokyr 1983, 15, 278). He finds it only "conceivable" that the era of "land confiscation and penal mercantilism" – in the seventeenth and eighteenth centuries when Ireland's economic interests were flagrantly violated and when "Irish Catholics were ruthlessly dispossessed and persecuted" – caused such "irreparable damage to the delicate basis of Irish economy that nothing could make Ireland prosperous again after 1780." He finds a "kernel of truth in this line of reasoning" but gives this kernel narrow scope: the deterioration of entrepreneurship "lay at the heart of the economic shortcomings of the rural upper class in eighteenth and nineteenth century Ireland." This deterioration sprung from the emergence of "a new class of parvenu proprietors" who became owners and masters of Irish farmland (212, 287). Firstly, is not 1780 a bit early to date the removal of the penal acts? Wolf Tone (1973, 102) wrote his eloquent plea – "Argument on Behalf of the Catholics of Ireland," which led to the formation of the United Irishmen movement and the attempted revolt of 1798 – to remove the disabilities still in place on Irish Catholics. The Irish Catholic Relief Act of 1793, sponsored by the British government to draw support from Irish Catholics but never enacted into law, has been characterized as "the largest single installment of emancipation ever gained for the Catholics of Ireland" (Jackson 1970, 125). Removal of legal disabilities when it came in 1829 did not extinguish their cumulative effect, just as the Emancipation Proclamation and the Fifteenth Amendment to the U.S. Constitution did not by themselves undo the effects of slavery in handicapping black advance. The Irish economy was not "delicate." But for over a century Irish schooling was proscribed and a public primary school system was only commenced in 1831 chiefly for the purpose of undermining Gaelic (Jackson 1970, 183). This did not bar literacy because the Irish despite their poverty subscribed to small "hedgerow" classes where literacy was taught chiefly to master the catechism. But entrance into the professions was barred. Irish civil and property rights and ability to protect those rights in courts or participate in juries or hold judgeships – all this was lacking and handicapped *economic* advance.

3. Burke, *Works,* 1910, 5:446, 453 (citation is from a confidential letter to C. J. Fox Oct. 1777).

4. Irish migratory labor brought to life in Britain the model of the "pre-industrial society with unlimited supplies of labor." Some 58,000 men were enumerated in the British 1841 Census as seasonal migrants working on the harvest. By 1845 these migrants made up half the British harvest labor force (Landes 1969, 116; Clapham 1926–1938, 1:57, 61, 405; Thompson 1966, 429; Almquist 1979, 715).

5. The absentee landowner of Irish property was not subject to certain taxes normally paid by landowners or their tenants on English estates (land tax or poor rates). Hence the widespread sentiment in England for a special tax on the Irish holdings of "absentee proprietors," advocated by Adam Smith and opposed by Edmund Burke. The large scale of absentee ownership in Ireland – denied or denigrated by Mokyr – arose out of the mercantilist policy of paying for the subjection of Ireland by distribution of forfeited Irish estates to British investors willing to invest funds to support suppression of Irish

insurrection. The arrears of pay and supplies were financed by grant of lands at token prices (Bottigheimer 1971; Esson 1971, Chap. 7; Mokyr 1983, 202). The knowledgeable William Petty, who contributed to the founding of English economic theory, managed the surveying operations in 1653–1656 that placed thousands of British soldiers and gentlemen on their Irish estates. He himself built up a large estate in Ireland. He estimated in 1672 that one-quarter of the owners of Irish real and personal estates lived in England, causing the Irish currency to exchange at appreciable discount. Jonathan Swift who had little professional knowledge on the subject stepped up Petty's estimate to one-third in a pamphlet published in 1727. In later decades detailed lists of absentee rental transfers were published. The list of Arthur Young, the traveling English agricultural economist, ran to £732 thousand (1776–1779) out of an estimated total land rental of £6 million, a much smaller fraction than that pointed to by Petty. The difference may be due partly to the emergence of a class of relatively wealthy Irish intermediate "agents" or "tenants" who leased large tracts from landlords and subleased to smaller farmers or graziers who hired or subleased to "cottars" or laborers. The estimate of "rental" by Young was of rentals collected at the intermediate level. The listing of absentee "rentals" was on net transfers paid to English ownership interests. The interesting 1848 novel by Anthony Trollope illuminated precisely the complex relationships of landlords, agents, and tenants on Irish estates. In later decades an 1876 census enumeration on "absentee" Irish landlords enumerated 13.1 percent absentee; 15.7 percent "residence never or rarely in Ireland"; 6.8 percent "usually out but occasionally in"; 10 percent "not ascertained." But that survey (like one contrived by Mokyr with much inferior data) was for landlords per se. Since there were six to eight thousand landowners most of whom held relatively small tracts under 1,000 acres and since absentee landlords tended to hold relatively large tracts, a survey of all owners would significantly understate "absentee rentals" (Smith 1776/1937, 846; Burke 1910, 5:437; Steele 1974, 3; Petty 1899, 2:157; Petty 1751; Marx 1863–1878/1967, 1:700; Black 1960, 72 n. 4; Young 1776–1779/1892, 2:114, 226; Mokyr 1983, 201; Trollope 1848/1982).

6. This hypothesis of mutual involvement of Irish and British life with its effect on Irish nuptiality and birth rate was the subject of a study using evidence from the 1841 Census. Earlier marriage and fertility were apparently stimulated in districts where, granted available waste or bog land, cottage industry or seasonal labor in England could produce the necessary income supplement. Cottage industry in turn varied with distance from Belfast, the center of the linen trade employing altogether 573,200 women spinners in 1841 and 122,800 male weavers and 197,400 workers handling linen or woolen cloth (Almquist 1979; Booth 1886, 399).

7. Thus we differ from Clapham who sought to portray in his truly great economic history of modern Britain that modern "British" economic development includes Scotland and Wales with only "incidental" treatment of Ireland. Recent events, he writes, "justify this on the political side," having reference to the 1922 separation of the Irish Republic from Great Britain (Clapham 1926–1939, 1:viii). "Justify" in what sense? Even politically, the separation drew a line only between the *future* political history of the two regions. The past history was as politically entangled as it was economically intertwined.

8. See Williams 1964, Chap. 4, 92. "They bought votes and rotten boroughs and so got into Parliament." With their allies – sugar merchants,

sugar refiners, and slave traders – they made up a powerful interest.

9. By large landlords I mean owners of estate property calling for a resident manager or "bailiff" of which some 17,189 were enumerated in the 1891 British Census (Taylor 1919, 306). The detailed investigation into land ownership carried out in 1871 showed that 400 peers and peeresses held 5.7 million acres and an additional 1288 "great landowners" held some 8.5 million acres out of a total of 34.5 million (Bateman 1883/1970, 515). These results in turn are close to estimates derived from analysis of land tax returns from a 9 percent sample for 1832. Forty-five large landowners defined as paying £20 or more of tax held 64 percent of the land. Smaller nonoccupying landowners who presumably leased out the land for farming, held some 22.6 percent of the land. Some 132,000 small to medium occupying holders farmed 13.4 percent of the acreage (Carus-Wilson 1954–1966, 1:279). The 1871 Census counted 217,049 "small proprietors" holding 11.3 percent of the land and about 700,000 cottagers holding a fraction of an acre or less. Using this and other survey information Sir John Clapham, in his balanced and well-researched enquiry, estimated that at midcentury some 12 percent of British farmland was farmed by "smallholders" working the land yeoman style (Clapham 1926–1938, 1:33, 105, 450, 452, 2:252; see also Checkland 1964, 184). These results hold for England, Scotland, and Wales. Irish landlords were believed by F. Engels who carefully studied Irish economic materials to number between 8,000 and 9,000. Later authority has it that 6,500 proprietors with 500 acres or more owned 90 percent of Irish land (Steele 1974, 3; Marx and Engels 1845–1891/1972, 297).

10. Deane and Cole 1962, 247, 301, 323–28. The 1860–1869 rent income is down from the relatively high 20 percent level of 1800 partly because of the rise of industrial income and partly because of the abolition of the corn tariff in 1846.

11. The social character of these British capitalist farmers is illustrated by employment on their farms of 216,851 family members such as sons, daughters, nephews (Marx 1863–1879/1967, 1:677 n. 2).

12. Tension in part was due to deterioration during the period of the wars of the French Revolution in the standard of living of village laborers converted into paupers and paid partly on the poor rates. See the analysis classically laid out in Hammond, 1920 and Marx 1845–1891/1972, 1:673–96). I doubt if Marx could prove his claim that "poor Irish farmers" treated their laborers "incomparably" more humanely than rich British farmers (686 n. 3).

13. Capitalist farmers were by no means as emancipated from landlord control as Marx sometimes claimed (Gottlieb 1984, 73). Alfred Marshall (1890/1920, 650) was convinced that the bargaining power of an alert tenant even without fixity of tenure enabled him to settle terms with an intelligent landlord, though the law (1883) had earlier been amended to enable tenants to claim full reimbursement for the unexhausted value of their improvements put into the land.

14. The advent of the "master builder" as contractor for large landlords, manufacturers in factory towns, or as "speculative builders" developing whole districts on their own account has been variously dated from the middle of the eighteenth century to the first quarter of the nineteenth century (Clapham 1926–1938, 1:163; Marx 1863–1878/1968, 2:233; 3:774; Webb 1897, 1:340; Summerson 1962, 78, 191; Clapham 1941–1978, 7:134; Thompson 1966, 258). A turning point in the development of what Marx called "capitalist building" was reached by a London builder, T. Cubitt, who employed building craftsmen

on a permanent basis in the 1820s, keeping one building project going after another. Except for fancy homes specially built for owners, British housing was typically built as rental property in flats or tenements (as in Scottish cities) or in row housing or cottages by landlords, manufacturers (in factory towns), or real estate developer-builders. See the perceptive comments by Frederick Engels in his 1845 study of the English working class (Marx and Engels 1845–1895/1970, 59, 68, 92, 217). The small builder-craftsman survived especially in rural areas or suburbs doing maintenance and repair work on his own or building a few houses a year (See Dyos 1961, 125; Clapham 1926–1938, 1:163, 166, 2:129).

15. Gayer 1953, 1:421; Clapham 1926–1938, 2:24. Since 144,000 seamen was the censal count in 1851, seamen serving on vessels abroad were not enumerated and these for adjoining censal years run around 100,000 (Booth 1886, 431).

16. Gayer et al. 1953, 1:414, 417; Ward 1974; Clapham 1926–1938, 1:75.

17. Gayer et al. 1953, 1:434; Deane and Cole 1962, 229.

18. Gayer et al. 1953, 1:436; Clapham 1926–1938, 1:381.

19. Marx and Engels 1841–1870/1974–1986, 10:491.

20. See Marx 1863–1878/1967, 1:253, 455, 628, 2:163, 173. Only in his more incidental writings did Marx reckon more fully with the tremendous role of rail investment in the British business-cycle expansion of the 1840s, the peculiar fate of "management" of railways as a "common enterprise" conspicuous for "glaring frauds, swindles and total neglect of safety precautions" or the role of railway development as a necessary "forerunner of modern industry" (Marx and Engels 1841–1870/1974–1986, 12:219, 14:209; Marx 1973, 43).

21. Hence in making up a new stock price index it was found difficult to obtain viable mining corporations with active stock price history, 1830–1850 (Gayer et al. 1953, 1:432).

22. The major investigator of British business organization in the nineteenth century found that corporate development in the 1850–1870 period in mining involved investors who were "small local men . . . taking shares in mines they knew well." The famous Oldham cotton textile corporations involved shareholders "chiefly of machine makers, small business men and traders of Oldham and neighboring towns. . . ." In the shipping industry shareholders "were often all members of one family or drawn from a limited group of wealthy merchants." Limited companies in the coal, iron, and engineering industries were in the majority of cases "conversions of private mines, furnaces and works among the original owners, local men of some standing and a few town investors" (Carus-Wilson 1954–1966, 1:354). Hence Landes (1969, 222), Cairncross (1953, 84, 95), and Clapham (1926–1938, 2:134), though using cautious language concur that the quasi-public corporation had very limited use in midcentury British industry though it began to come on in later decades.

23. The default, bankruptcy, and loss of experience of newly formed industrial corporations with limited liability indicated to a recent investigator that grant of the privilege was "no unmixed blessing" (Carus-Wilson 1954–1966, 1:372, 405).

24. Davis 1966, 236; Mantoux 1906/1961, 111; Clapham 1926–1938, 1:221. "Much of the retail trade of the large towns was done by hawkers" (Ashton 1955a, 69).

25. Clapham 1926–1938, 1:224; Mayhew 1861–1862, vol. 1.

26. Mayhew 1861–1862, 1:6, 63, 98, 125, 132, 211.

27. Thus British occupational census data under such headings as "drapers," hosiers, silk mercers, grocers, and fishmongers hopelessly mix retail and wholesale levels together. For U.S. data see Barger 1960, 327.

28. Thus among the "building trades" from the 1891 Census, Booth enumerates 2,032 architects, 2,329 civil engineers, 127 surveyors. Booth 1902–03, 1:45.

29. American investigators found that in 1929 some 3 million Americans were in the professions or 6 percent of the occupied labor force but that only one-fifth of the professionals of all types – though 78 percent of all physicians, 82 percent of all dentists, and 68 percent of all lawyers – were practicing professionals, making up 1 percent of the labor force (Friedman and Kuznets 1954, 5, 390). The rise in professional service as a fraction of the labor force is largely attributed to the rise of the employed professional. Lawyers, doctors, and dentists were as common and accepted in Great Britain in the mid–nineteenth century as in the United States. An American distribution of "gainful workers" derived from census records shows that for 1870 and 1880, a time when most professionals except educators and ministers were in independent practice on a fee basis, professionals were 1.08 and 1.09 percent of the occupied labor force.

30. Marx 1863–1878/1967 1:697; Marx and Engels 1972, 138; Steele 1974, 5.

31. For the tragic story of death and emigration, see pp. 155–60.

32. See the interesting presentation of "old principles" which characterized local government in England prior to the mid–nineteenth century, before liberal reforms of that era. (Webb 1903–1929, 4:350–96).

33. Apart from the standing army the Royal Irish Constabulary in the 1820s ranged around 20,000. Sir Robert Peel believed they kept order in Ireland (Halévy 1912–1934/1951, 4:296; Broeker 1970, 225).

34. On the London Metropolitan police, launched as it happens by the creator of the Irish constabulary, Sir Robert Peel (whence the short title "Bobbies"), see Mather 1967; Ascoli 1979.

35. On this legislation of the 1830s, see Mather 1969, 130. By 1840 it was estimated that the paid police force in England and Wales outside London numbered 18,640 (Howard 1953, 150). By 1848, 138 cities and half of the counties had installed a "new-style" police force (Mather 1969, 113).

36. For a comprehensive review of elementary education in Great Britain, see Halévy 1912–1934/1937, Book 3:152; Hammond 1947, Chap. 9. Scotch law since 1696 – following Presbyterian injunctions laid down by John Knox – required parish authorities to provide elementary schooling, resulting in correspondingly lower rates of illiteracy. English law left education up to Sunday or charity schools where evangelical teachers taught the 3 R's with a heavy dose of catechism. Adam Smith boasted that in Scotland "the establishment of such parish schools has taught almost the whole common people to read and a very great proportion to write and account." In England, Smith goes on to observe, the establishment of charity schools has promoted literacy "though not so universally because the establishment is not so universal." Smith observes with unsubtle sarcasm that if the textbooks used in English schools were "a little more instructive" it would help. Smith was perhaps correct in his comparative judgments of English and Scotch education. Regarding quality of schooling, his own experience as a lad in the Kirkcaldy parish school

was instructive. Their faculty standards must have been high; Thomas Carlyle in his early years served there as teacher, many decades after Smith. By 1819 when the first official statistics of schooling were compiled in Great Britain, the number of children attending on a per capita basis was only one-third of the Scotch number attending, leaving out of account Sunday schools. And a recent debate in *Past and Present* regarding relative schooling and literacy in Scotland confirmed Smith's judgment that many Scotch students taught to read could not write. Thompson believed that English workingmen in the early 1800s had strong drives for self-education and learned to read "after some fashion." Thompson 1966, 713; Smith 1776/1937, 737; Checkland 1964, 252; Knox 1559–1571/1982, 251; Houston 1982; Smout 1982, 114–28.

37. Both Engels and Marx gave informative accounts of the lace-making industry (Marx 1863–1878/1967, 1:466; Marx and Engels 1845–1895/1970, 224). The 1851 Census enumerated 64,000 lace workers (Clapham 1926–1938, 2:24).

38. Marx 1863–1878/1967, 1:472; Clapham 1926–1938, 1:13, 92.

39. Dobb 1963, 263; Marx and Engels 1845–1895/1970, 232, 235. See also and more authoritatively, Clapham 1926–1938, 1:176, 2:97, 128; Checkland 1964, 148.

40. "English factory labor provided [linen] yarn for the cheap domestic laborer of Ireland and Scotland" (Dean and Cole 1962, 205).

41. Collated from Booth 1886, App. A; Marx 1863–1878/1967, 1:446. For English domestic indoor service as quasi-feudal, see an appreciation by Hobsbawm 1979, 263.

42. Our presently available summary income data in 1851 for domestic service in Great Britain shows annual earnings per domestic annually at £21.1. The comparable earnings for manufacturing, mining, and building when spread over the wage and salary income paid in those fields amounts to £22.5. Our count of domestic servants includes a considerable number of personal or extra service employees nondomestic. Clapham (1926–1938, 2:464) quite properly cautions of the difficulty of measuring the value of board and room commonly furnished house servants. Booth's research indicates that quite definite standards for holidays, time off, and salary pervaded the London market and that servants changed positions frequently "to better themselves" with an annual earning of £9 yearly in the lower grades and some £18 for the upper grades or older staff (Booth 1886, 222). Servants expect tips "for the slightest personal service" (Checkland 1964, 220). Marx conceded that "regular servants received the good treatment usual for their class" (Marx, 1863–1878/1967, 1:683).

43. U.S. Bureau of Census, *Historical Statistics,* 74.

44. I draw from a survey of occupational statistics put together by the Woytinskys. They happened to group together countries (1935–1940) at quite dissimilar levels of income and economic development which have similar proportions of the labor force engaged in personal and domestic service: Great Britain and Chile (12.6 percent, 11.9 percent), Switzerland and Portugal (10.3 percent, 10.3 percent), Austria, Brazil, Germany, India (7.2 percent, 7.3 percent, 7.0 percent, 7.3 percent) Woytinsky and Woytinsky 1953, 359. Irish employment of indoor domestic servants was unusually heavy, 8.7 percent of the occupied labor force though very little industry was available.

45. Parish assistance to the poor was in Malthus's judgment an unmitigated evil. He found it "difficult to conceive" that workmen "would not save

part of their wages for the future support of their families, instead of spending it in drunkenness and dissipation, if they did not rely on parish assistance for support in case of accidents." Extensive giving of relief tends to bid up the price of food yielding very little real relief. "Hard as it may appear . . . dependent poverty ought to be held disgraceful." Giving of relief regularly contributes "powerfully" to generate that "carelessness and want of frugality observable among the poor" who seem "always to live from hand to mouth" (Malthus 1799/1914, 2:49, 38, 49).

46. Malthus advocated elimination of general public relief. He also urged that wealthy persons should be careful not to indulge in "indiscriminate charity." He believed that "no man should look to charity as a fund on which he may confidently depend." Landlords were cautioned about encouraging population growth among their laborers by furnishing them with their cottages an allotment of land sufficient for a cow, a potato patch, and garden land, as required by ancient statutes. Laborers' cottages should not be "so large as to allow of two families settling in them" (Malthus 1799/1914, 2:220, 228, 246, 250).

47. The occupier of land was given "an inalienable right to destroy hares and rabbits on his land" (Clark 1962, 249) and tithes were commuted and scaled down.

48. Bagehot (1873, 51–55) gave a detailed account of how a bold policy of lending on any and all securities broke the force of panic in 1825, though the cash reserves of the Bank of England sank to a low ebb.

49. Marx had occasion frequently both in his contemporary newspaper articles of the 1850s and his *Capital* written largely in the 1860s to criticize the credit policies of the Bank of England and even more the statute that imposed upon the Bank of England, beyond a set £14 million issue of currency, a pound for pound gold reserve requirement for additional currency notes issued. It very much annoyed Marx, a severe critic of the regulating statute of the Bank of England (Peel Act 1844), that instead of finding "the periodical violation of the law" to relieve the Bank of England from its reserve requirements was wrong, or that the law was right "and the Government ought to be interdicted from arbitrarily tampering with it," a responsible committee of Parliament "contrived to simultaneously vindicate the perpetuity of the law and the periodical recurrence of its infraction" (Marx and Engels 1841–1870/1974–1986, 16:2; Marx 1857–1858/1973, 184; Marx 1863–1878/1967, 3:546). In much of this criticism of the Peel Act Marx was echoing the views of the so-called Banking School whose leading theorists were Tooke and Fullarton (Gottlieb 1984, 298).

50. The bill was sponsored chiefly by Sir Robert Peel the son of a famous textile manufacturer who employed large numbers of pauper apprentices. Sir Robert sought later in 1816, partly with the aid of Robert Owen, to improve the bill. Enforcement of the bill was entrusted to local inspectors appointed by county quarter sessions of justices (Pike 1966, 93, 96–110; Ward 1962, 19; Clapham 1926–1938, 1:372).

51. Though five acts altogether were passed between 1802 and 1833, the "concessions conquered by the workpeople were purely nominal" because no funding for enforcement was provided (Marx 1863–1878/1967, 1:278; Clapham 1926–1938, 1:374).

52. Marx 1863–1878/1967, 1:9. In his interesting article, Marvel (1977) argues that the driving force behind the restrictive regulation was the larger textile mills using steam power and hence capable of operating more steadily

as compared to waterpowered mills subject to shutdowns with power failure and hence more needful of the ability to enforce a longer workday when power was available. The evidence for this in enforcement actions is slim especially since enforcement records are only available on a consolidated parish basis. A change was in progress toward greater use of steam power and lesser reliance upon children as compared to young juvenile workers. In search for an interpretation as to why the Reform Parliament with its dominant Whig majority should have gone ahead with factory control legislation, is it so difficult to envisage that even hard-nosed defenders of capitalist property rights could cherish some concern for women, children, and juveniles hardly capable of protecting their own interests in the labor market?

53. Marx's account of factory control legislation is pungent and penetrating but the account later provided by such historians as J. T. Ward (1972) provides a fuller view (Marx 1863–1878/1967, 1:256, 278–97). Though the final enactment of 1850 was called a "Ten Hour Bill," it stipulated a ten and one-half hour workday on weekdays and a seven and one-half workday on Saturday, a compromise reluctantly accepted by advocates of the legislation.

54. Marx 1863–1878/1967, 1:295, 492; Clapham 1926–1938, 2:412.

55. Clapham 1926–1938, 2:419; Marx 1967, 1:494.

56. Altogether about one-quarter of the House of Commons came from so-called nomination boroughs or tiny constituencies where owners of landed property or purchasers thereof, such as David Ricardo, bought their way into Parliament (Checkland 1964, 339).

57. Marx in his journalistic writings often pilloried corrupt electoral proceedings. John Stuart Mill deplored the "slavish deference" of capitalist farm tenants to their landlord, believing that "their vote goes with the rent" (Marx and Engels 1841–1870/1974, 11:533, 12:147, 16:526). Mill 1831–1870/1963, 275. Hence the worker demand for the secret ballot was a major item on their program for effective political representation. Mill later came to believe that the power to coerce voters had declined and that the open ballot would make for a more responsible exercise of a public trust (Mill 1910, 299).

58. The final vote on the threat by the king to create new peers, with many Tory peers headed by Wellington abstaining and after two dismissals of the Commons and new elections solely on the issue of the Reform Bill, was 184–175 (Halévy [1912–1939] 1951, 3:54).

59. Borough voters under the 1832 Reform Act had to own or rent a house rated at 10s. or more; and in the counties only freeholders of 40s. or over or leaseholders on properties over 50s. voted.

60. The 1867 reform extended the borough suffrage requirement to counties. The more radical suffrage reform of 1884 resulted in a voting roster for members of Parliament 40 percent greater than before and made up 60 percent of wage earners (Checkland 1964, 375).

61. Both Smith (1776/1937, 871) and Marx (1863–1878/1967, 1:755) believed that the public debt securities were readily saleable, made excellent collateral and hence served as business current assets.

62. Mitchell 1962, 401. The table commences with 1691 but Adam Smith asserted that "the foundation of the present enormous debt of Great Britain" was laid in the war that began in 1688 and was concluded by the Treaty of Ryswick in 1697 (Smith [1776]/1937, 874). Of course British kings and their treasury officers had borrowed before and on a large scale from bankers domestic and foreign.

63. The old gold parity was reestablished with convertibility as usual in

1821. "Indexes of non-agricultural prices reveal, uniformly, a secular decline from about 1815 to the middle of the century." For all imported commodities this averaged per year 2.8 percent; for coal, 4.5 percent; for raw cotton, 4.7 percent; and even the Gazette price of wheat, 1.4 percent (Gayer et al. 1953, 2:623, 625).

64. Clapham 1926–1938, 1:318; Gottlieb 1953, 36.

65. Hence a powerful school of thought in England headed up after the Napoleonic wars by David Ricardo advocated a capital levy (see Gottlieb 1953).

66. Mitchell 1962. In estimating national income an allowance of under-stated income reported from trades and professions was put at 50 percent for the period 1842–1861 (Deane and Cole 1962, 167).

67. Marx 1863–1878/1967, 1:750. See Thompson (1966, 304) for an itemization of taxes paid in 1834 by an average British worker, totalling £11.7s. 7d. or one-half of his income. See also Clapham (1926–1938, 1:319).

68. This was copiously related and criticized by Adam Smith (1776/1937, 490). Though aiming at steadying grain prices, allowing imports with duties when prices were high but subsidizing exports with bounties when prices were low, the system had the wasteful effect, as Marshall (1919, 749) pointed out, in a good year of encouraging exportation (thus reducing the carryover that would have served a bad year following), and wasting "the cost of carriage."

69. Oddly enough Marx (1841–1870/1974–1986, 6:455) noted these injuries to farmers in his 1848 address on the adoption of free trade in corn in England. The reduction of rent must, he noted, cause a decline in grain cultivation and this "must inevitably ruin a number of the tenant farmers."

70. The campaign for repeal of the corn laws was organized on a massive scale with the distribution of 9 million tracts, incessant meetings, and demonstrations partly arranged with the Chartists (Hammond 1947, 189); Marx and Engels (1845–1895/1970, 265, 302).

71. On that doctrinaire premise Marx in 1848 charged that the repeal of the grain tariff would result in reduced wages since competition reduces price "to the minimum cost of production." This was alleged to harm workingmen since with higher grain prices and wages "a small saving in the consumption of bread sufficed to procure him other enjoyments" (Marx and Engels 1841–1870/1974–1986, 6:457). See also Engels in 1845 (Marx and Engels 1845–1895/1970, 314). Presumably by the time of *Capital* that harsh doctrine was softened but no extended analysis of the corn tariff repeal is found in the *Capital.*

72. Mitchell 1962, 411; Deane and Cole 1962, 282.

73. In his chapter on the "Poor Rates" David Ricardo was able to show that poor rates, assessed as a fraction of the annual produce of the land, were not shifted back to the landlord but were in part shifted to the consumer at least in a progressive state (Ricardo 1817/1911, Chap. 18).

74. Marx, 1863–1878/1967, 1:674; Webb 1903–1929, 7:180. Karl Polanyi (1944, 86, 98) claimed the Speemhamland "shaped the fate of the whole civilization" and "precipitated a social catastrophe." His analysis, greatly exaggerated, played up a short-term episode whose effects were substantially eradicated by the Poor Law Reform Act of 1834.

75. If relief expenditure is measured not in terms of current money but in quarters of wheat that could be purchased at current prices with that money,

relief in thousand quarters was as follows for successive five-year periods, annual average: 1813–1815, 1540; 1816–1820, 1828; 1821–1825, 2263; 1826–1830, 2102; 1831–1835, 2509; 1836–1840, 1461; 1841–1845, 1840; 1846–1850, 2199 (Mitchell 1962, 412; Rostow 1948, 124).

76. These were districts gathered in unions of parishes under special municipal legislation (Clapham 1926–1938, 1:352; Webb and Webb 1903–1929, 7:170).

77. For choice details, see Webb and Webb 1903–1929, 8:132; Hammond and Hammond 1947, 110; Thompson 1966, 267.

78. This shows up in the cyclical analysis patterns of poor relief expenditure 1816–1848 (Gayer et al. 1953, 2:Fig. 147e, 968, especially in nonagricultural counties; Marx 1863–1878/1967, 1:653, 654, 670).

79. See data for censal years 1861–1881, Booth 1886, App. D. See also Clapham 1926–1938, 1:585; 2:436.

80. Without citing cases Marx declared in 1867 that the "frightful increase of 'deaths by starvation' in London during the last ten years proves beyond doubt the growing horror in which the working people hold the slavery of the workhouse, that place of punishment for misery" (Marx 1863–1878/1967, 1:654). Marx's alter ego in his 1845 book did not pull any punches and declared he had on hand "reports of five cases in which persons actually starving, when the guardians refused them outdoor relief, went back to their miserable homes and died of starvation rather than enter these hells" (Marx and Engels 1845–1895/1970, 327).

81. Philip Curtin, the acknowledged authority on the subject, estimates that by 1810 the total imports of slaves into the New World were some 7.7 million. Though reproduction of this population was inadequate due to sexual imbalance of slaves imported and harsh treatment in slavery, probably one-third to one-half of the number remained by 1810. Bear in mind that 85 percent of the slaves imported were in the eighteenth century itself. The British Caribbean by 1810 imported perhaps 1.2 million Africans and in 1833–1838 barely some 625,000 were on hand for emancipation (Curtin, 1969, Tables 77, 34, 40; Mathieson 1932, 13, 59).

82. Already in the seventeenth century the older British Caribbean colonies – Jamaica, Barbados, and Leeward Islands – had acquired 263,700 African slaves. In the eighteenth century Jamaica and Barbados alone acquired another 588,000, enough so that Jamaica itself was a center of slave re-export (Mathieson 1932, 119, 136).

83. The prospect of production of tropical staples in the East Indies, once well established in British hands, hangs over the entire British anti-slavery movement (Williams 1964, 123, 146, 137, 164).

84. Mathieson 1926, 9; Williams 1964, 149.

85. The zeal and dedication of these crusaders is well known. They emphasized the toll of the slave trade on British seamen, estimated by Curtin from a wealth of data to have a mean value of 17 percent, as high or higher than the slaves (Curtin 1969, 282).

86. Great Britain expended an estimated £10 million to enforce the ban on the slave trade and it is known that Britain paid the Portuguese £2.9 million cash subsidies to this end (Mathieson 1926, 24; David 1970, 255).

87. The total number of recaptured Africans rescued from slaver ships in the period 1810–1870 is estimated by Curtin at 160,000 over 90 percent by British warships, and mostly returned to Sierra Leone (Curtin 1969, 249). The

British warships intercepted only a small amount of the trade.

88. Williams 1964, 85; Burn 1951, 53; Mathieson 1926, 56, 61.

89. See especially Williams 1964, 145; Burn 1951, 108.

90. In the 1840s with duty protection of West Indian sugar, English sugar prices were substantially higher than on the Continent, one-fifth of the purchase price going "in tribute to the West Indian planter." Merivale estimated that £3½ million of British exports to the West Indies in 1838 purchased "less than half as much sugar and coffee as they would have purchased if carried to Cuba and Brazil" (Williams 1964, 138).

91. Williams 1964, 197; Mathieson 1926, 122.

92. "In most of the colonies the slaves were allotted tracts of waste land for raising provisions such as plantains, yams, bananas. . . . They were also permitted to keep hogs, rabbits, fowls and small stock" (Ragatz 1928, 27).

93. The struggle by West Indian blacks for garden plots and homesteads, reluctance by planters to sell, and the struggle over the back land provision grounds stands out in the various accounts. In 1840 some 7848 freeholders in Jamaica were recorded, called a "mountain peasantry." Squatting was widespread in Trinidad where vacant crown lands abounded, not for sale however except in tracts of 100 acres. Blacks paid fantastically high prices for small tracts near work opportunities (Mathieson 1932, 52, 66, 92, 131, 135, 69, 92).

94. The record of sugarcane output by annual averages in million hundredweights is as follows: 1829–1833, 3.92; 1834–1838, 3.53; 1842–1845, 2.58; 1853–1855, 3.42 (Burn 1951, 127, 134; Mathieson 1926, 233; Williams 1964, 153).

95. Mathieson 1932, 118, 226; Burn 1951, 130, 134. In 1883 Trinidad had 48,000 coolies in a population of 153,000. British Guyana had 65,000 in a population of 250,000. Jamaica experienced greater difficulties in arranging for importation. For an extended review, see Engerman 1983, 635–59.

96. The fungus appeared suddenly in 1842 in the New World and then again Europe and noteworthily in Ireland in 1845 and has been with us ever since. The blight is now treated by applying a copper compound in potato fields when climatic conditions are ripe for activity of the fungus (Woodham-Smith 1962, 94).

97. Central Statistical Office 1978, 61. The potato acreage enumerated for 1851 was a little over 600,000 acres.

98. The evidence is convincing. The knowledgeable William Petty (1899, 1:156) in 1672 coupled milk with potatoes as making up the Irish diet and in 1776–1779 Arthur Young (1776–1779/1892, 2:35) set out typical pasture rentals charged Irish cottars for supporting one or two cows. Mokyr (1983, 225) does not list milk or even buttermilk or skimmed milk in the typical Irish diet but he alludes to a terrible deterioration in that diet during the 1800s. Costigan (1969, 174) flatly asserts milk substantially disappeared from the diet. See also Salaman 1949/1985, 217–229.

99. K. H. Connell (1968, 27, 49) has done an exhaustive study that strongly suggests that illicit distillation was one of the major household rural sidelines in the Irish countryside useful for the "payment of rent" or "to prevent eviction." Seizures of illicit stills discovered by revenue officers averaged some two to three thousand a year during the 1840s, 1850s, and 1860s, and in two years alone, 1833–1834, some 16,000 stills were seized.

100. Smith 1776/1937, 608; Clapham 1926–1938, 1:341; Young 1776–1779/1892, 2:196.

101. Weaving was highly correlated with young male nuptiality while spinning as well as more abundant wasteland was highly correlated with earlier marriage of young females (Almquist 1979, 713). Mokyr (1983, 63) does not concur.

102. "England factory labour provided yarn for cheap domestic labour of Ireland and Scotland" (Deane and Cole 1962, 205).

103. Booth 1886, 346; Almquist 1979, 705.

104. Marx and Engels 1845–1891/1972, 39. Mokyr's work (1983, Chaps. 2, 5, 6, 7, 10) is devoted to an explanation of Irish poverty, which he attributes largely to low productivity in agriculture due to poor crop rotation schemes, inadequate fertilizer, unenterprising landlords, little drainage, and endemic social conflict.

105. A recent analysis of the composition of 1982 gross agricultural output of the Free State of Ireland shows that poultry, dairy, and livestock output comprised 84.2 percent (O'Hagen 1983, 301).

106. Modernization of Irish agriculture was the heart and soul of an extended address in 1849 on Irish policy by Sir Robert Peel; it was strongly advocated by Lord John Russell and by the great liberal economist J. S. Mill. See Halévy 1912–1934/1951, 4:296; Williams, 1956, 180; Costigan 1969, 183; Marx and Engels 1845–1891/1972, 67, 147, 296. We can accept the thoughtful commentary of Steele (1974, 13) that "For all its horror, the Famine appeared in Britain to present the opportunity of reconstructing Irish landholding with unhoped-for speed and thoroughness." The land was not only to be cleared of tenants. Expedited and fully extraordinary mortgage procedures were adopted in 1849. They were designed to enforce bankruptcy proceedings against Irish landlords who were delinquent on their debts or tax assessments. Altogether in the fifteen years following the Famine some one-fifth of Irish landholdings were put through the wringer. Mokyr (1983, 126, 146) has shown that before 1845 pasturage had become more profitable but that land clearing operations were impeded by tenant resistance.

107. The story of the November decision to purchase corn for £100,000 and the detailed way it was finally stockpiled in Irish port towns, milled and dribbled out for sale under the auspices of a relief commission is told in Williams (1956, 212) and in Woodham-Smith (1962, 54, 73, 167). Some 73 percent of all grain purchases, freight and distribution costs were recovered on sale.

108. Woodham-Smith 1962, 118–19. Since the British government undertook to pay all shipping, freight, and distribution expenses of grain purchased by English or foreign private relief societies, much of the private relief was handled for distribution by British government agencies, except for a Quaker relief committee running an independent program (ibid., 157, 170, 292, 309; for U.S. aid, see 241).

109. An Irish deputation of the "highest respectability" met with the lord lieutenant in Dublin and urged him to adopt summary measures in October 1845 "to avert calamity." The measures called for immediate stoppage of the export of grain and provisions, prohibition of distilling and brewing from grain, ports to be thrown open for import of food (rice and maize) from the colonies free of duty; relief committees to be set up in every county; stores of food to be established and employment provided on works of public utility. Relief was to be financed by a tax of 10 percent on rental incomes of resident landlords and from 20 to 50 percent on absentee landlords. A loan of £1.5 million would be raised on the security of the proceeds of Irish woods and forests. The British government showed no interest (Woodham-Smith 1962,

48). In the three months from the date the potato failure was established up to 5 February 1846, 258,000 quarters of wheat and 701,000 hundredweight of barley worth about £1 million left Ireland along with 1 million quarters of oats and oatmeal (ibid., 75, 125). Irish butter had regularly gone to Liverpool and West Country butter to London along with swine, pork, bacon, and ham. "At the height of the famine butter in its thousands of tons was arriving on the London market" (Clapham 1926–1938, 1:22, 499). Irish grain exports to Great Britain between 1839 and 1842, the last four years for which data is available, averaged 213,000 quarters (Mitchell 1962, 95). Yet it can be shown that in prior times of distress, as recently as 1803, the British government had as one of its actions put an embargo on grain exports from Ireland.

110. A well-considered plan for railway construction in Ireland as public works was turned down (Woodham-Smith 1962, 180; Williams 1956, 231).

111. The original March 1845 half-and-half financing was later shifted to 100 percent local financing. That was so obviously unworkable that it was relinquished. Much later the local 50 percent was forgiven.

112. The stimulus to eviction was probably greatest when the full cost of the public works relief program was chargeable to poor rates and government leaders in England declared that not until property taxes for relief would go up to 25 percent of assessed value would they contemplate giving further public funds. The decline of rental income caused many landlords to evict for self-preservation; others evicted out of policy. During the Famine resistance to evictions, normally very quick to assert itself in Ireland, was at low ebb. Many landlords offered a choice of eviction or emigration.

• 113. The eviction provision of the public works act, debarring occupiers of more than one-quarter acre from relief until they surrendered their rights to the land, was knowingly adopted on the premise that "small holdings were the bane of Ireland" (Steele 1974, 319 n. 35; Halévy 1912–1934/1951, 4:163). In 1847–1848 this clause was a "convenient aid in clearance" (Williams 1956, 162, 253).

114. The difficulties of estimating famine population loss are indicated by Mokyr (1983, 261–68), who comes up with a carefully crafted understatement of the loss for which he has an upper-bound and lower-bound estimate of 1–1.5 million "excess deaths," caused partially because the Irish poor were "unable to shed their habit of eating potatoes."

115. Pestilence on some scale was expected from the outset. The government late in 1845 while arranging for the purchase of American corn to hold down price profiteering circularized Irish local authorities to construct "fever hospitals" to abate the spread of contagious disease. In 1847 special legislation was enacted and the British government finally assumed the cost of pestilential control. Medical attention at fever hospitals was minimal, and they were regarded by the Irish as death traps.

116. In April 1847 the death rate in poorhouses reached an annual rate of 50 percent and recorded workhouse deaths during the entire famine period added up to 283,765 (Williams 1956, 294, 309).

117. The dread story of disease and pestilence pursuing its victims as they were fleeing the stricken land whether to Liverpool, Glasgow, Boston, New York City, or Quebec and Montreal is well told by Woodham-Smith (1962, 206, 217, 220, 254, 270). Mortality in passage is estimated at 20 percent. Mokyr (1985, 287) characterizes much of this as "horror stories."

118. Both in 1840 and in 1850 the capacity of installed steam engines in

the United Sates was ahead of those installed in Great Britain by 42 percent in 1860 (Landes 1969, 221, Table 7).

Chapter 6

1. (Slichter 1961, 166). Werner Sombart in a famous chapter in his third volume of *Der Moderne Kapitalismus* treated *Spätkapitalismus* and presciently gave a foretaste of coming developments then indicated in the twenties. This view was further elaborated in his essay on "Capitalism" (*Encyclopedia of Social Sciences* 3:206). For general commentary on labels for the epoch, see Eliot 1977, 351; Gruchy 1977, 31.

2. The concept of "state-monopoly capitalism" was coined by Lenin after 1914 to place his version of the "imperialist" phase of "monopoly-capital" into the epoch of state regulation sprung up during the war by war-control measures of rationing, allocations, price control (Afanasyev 1974, Chap. 9). For critical Marxist versions see Varga 1968, 51–75; Mandel 1978, 513. For a less happy French Marxist reworking, see Fairley 1980, 305.

3. OECD countries were originally the Marshall Plan countries but now include: Austria, Belgium, Canada, Denmark, Finland, France, West Germany, Greece, Spain, Sweden, Switzerland, Japan, Netherlands, Norway, Portugal. The credo of OECD, set forth in all their publications, involves the promotion of policies to "(1) achieve the highest sustainable economic growth and employment and a rising standard of living in Member countries, while maintaining financial stability; (2) contribute to sound economic expansion in Member countries in the process of economic development; (3) contribute to the expansion of world trade on a multilateral non-discriminatory basis in accordance with international obligations." The credo is an interesting formulation of the ultimate objectives of the mixed economy.

4. My review of the mixed economy closes substantially with the collapse of the Bretton Woods gold standard in 1971–1978, not because the mixed economy terminated then but because a complex macroeconomic process commenced then, taking off from the explosion of oil prices, the emergence of OPEC as a world power with gross imbalance in the economic balance of the Western world economy, and the rise of conservative economic policy in Great Britain and the United States. My analysis of the mixed economy thus differs considerably from that of Moses Abramovitz in his insightful AER Presidential address of September 1980, "Welfare Quandaries and Productivity Concerns." Abramovitz put the spotlight on the economic performance of the seventies especially in the United States. My interest is in a broader theater for a longer time period. However, I will take note in the appropriate context of the tendency, emphasized by Abramovitz, for the welfare and the regulatory state and of progressive income and wealth taxation to impair incentives for economic performance. Though my analysis recognizes impairment here and there of incentives, it does not do so on a scale accounting for the difficulties of the American economy noted by Abramovitz. As the concluding paragraphs of this chapter indicate, these difficulties have been traced to other factors. See also the analysis of the dominant and accelerating process of innovation and of biased measure of productivity and output change associated with it.

5. Real GNP per capita in 1970 and 1980 calculated in dollars at the exchange rate prevailing in 1976 and 1980 are the following percentages of the American GNP per capita in 1970 and 1980 at $7,029 and $12,661 expressed in 1976 and 1980 prices, respectively. Use of 1976 exchange rates corrects for the marked overvaluation of the dollar in 1970.

Country	1970 (%)	1980 (%)
France	75.7	84.0
Canada	95.5	87.0
West Germany	90.1	88.0
United Kingdom	50.8	76.7
Japan	54.9	74.0
Sweden	115.3	106.9

Source: U.S. Bureau of Census, *Statistical Abstract*, 1979, 895; 1985, 846.

6. The predominant tendency for anticolonial movements among the Arab, Chinese, Asiatic, African, and Latino societies of the New World to have a bourgeois-democratic character was emphasized by Lenin in the debates of the Second Congress of the Communist International and partly reflected in its resolutions on the nationalist-colonial movements (Varga 1968, 85; Lenin 1971, 3:465). In his bitter but insightful protest against what he termed the "national bourgeoisie" of the ex-colonial countries, Fritz Fanon (1967, 122) castigates them for stepping "into the shoes of the former European settlers: doctors, barristers, traders, commercial travelers, general agents and transport agents."

7. A vivid account of the crisis in British-Indian relationships during World War II is provided in the later chapters written in 1944 in a British prison in India by Nehru (1944/1961, 416).

8. Hence the tendency to a double revolutionary pattern in ex-colonial countries, a second revolution sometimes coming shortly (as in Viet Nam) after expulsion of the colonial power, sometimes long after (as in Cuba, Mexico, Egypt, Iraq). Hence also the general pattern of political instability characteristic of the Third World shown at length by Huntington (1968, Chaps. 2, 3, 5, 6, 7). See also Geertz 1973, 234–55.

9. Fanon 1967, 122.

10. Thus a stratum of an advanced African Bantu agricultural people given to trade and private property, the Kenyan Kikuyu, evolved into a position of agricultural estate-operators of capitalist farms and developed a kind of solidarity with their English confreres who before liberation completely excluded African ownership of the "White Highlands" (Leys 1974).

11. Technological revolution liquidated the landlord-tenant farming mode of the American South. Soil preparation, planting, cultivation, and harvesting of cotton were mechanized in large capitalist farms. The number of cotton farms enumerated at 609,000 in 1950 shrunk to 242,000 in 1959 and to 41,000 in 1969. Cultivated acreage fell in half and work hours used per bale of cotton shrunk from a 1945–1949 level of 209 to 25 in 1968–1972. Yet the cotton harvest for a recent crop year (1973) is over a quarter greater than in 1950 (U.S. Bureau of Census, *Statistical Abstract*, 1974, 600, 614, 615).

12. As late as 1900, still effectively in the heyday of the capitalist economy though in the early phases of evolution into the mixed economy, the Marxist E. Varga (1961) notes that "remnants of feudalism were still strong."

Landed aristocrats in Prussia and the upper bourgeoisie through a scheme of multiple voting controlled the Prussian Landtag that was the controlling body of the German state. "In Germany, Austria-Hungary and Russia emperors could depose prime ministers, . . . could issue decrees . . . . The administration, the army and the diplomatic service were headed exclusively by aristocrats." The right to vote was restricted by domiciliary, property, and literacy qualification so that in Japan only 2 percent, in Italy 7 percent, in Sweden in 1909 only 19 percent of the population was enfranchised (Brems 1970, 14).

13. Radical land reform in Japan acquired 80 percent of all rented land and divided the same among small farmers (Woytinsky and Woytinsky 1953, 505). For an interesting appreciation of the reform streak in the Douglas MacArthur reign in Japan see Lattimore 1949, 105; Ladejinsky 1977, 67–214.

14. Lenin 1917/1965, 32; Bukharin 1917/1929, 71; Gruchy 1977, 102, 141.

15. Lenin 1917/1965, 32, 42, 49; Pickersgil and Pickersgil 1974, 134; Shonfield 1965, 248.

16. Montias 1976, 268; U.S. Tariff Commission 1973, 849.

17. U.S. Tariff Commission 1973, 838; Klein 1973, 89.

18. Gruchy 1977, 234. United States in 1972 originated 60 percent of all Western multinational corporations. The United States originated only 37.8 percent of OECD GNP (as of 1975). U.S. Bureau of Census, *Statistical Abstract,* 1978, 910.

19. On the potent role of nationalization, arising in part out of wartime adjustments but in part due to the rise to power of socialist-oriented governments, see Crosland 1974, 37, 28, 37; Gruchy 1977, 77.

20. Gruchy 1977, 140, 251, 200; Shonfield 1965, 179, 186 n. 27, 185, 247, 241. The public sector is on a scale that gives the federal government in Germany control of 60 percent of the nation's building and construction activity. Italian public enterprise like the German chiefly arose by nationalization of distressed enterprises in the Great Depression and now accounts for the three biggest banks, airlines, 89 percent shipbuilding, steel production 59 percent, etc. (Klein 1973, 49)

21. Klein 1973, 83; Clapham 1941–1978, 7:Part 1, 220.

22. Kuznets 1966, 243; Varga 1961, 119.

23. Clapham 1941–1978, 7:Part 1, 220; Arzumanyan 1966, 77. The responsible socialist minister in the British labor government felt on balance the mergers had a "beneficial" influence by "leading to better management or genuine economies of scale without eliminating workable competition" (Crosland 1974, 233).

24. Gruchy 1977, 252; Klein 1973, 133.

25. Corporate farming so-called in the United States mostly reduces to capitalist farming. In 1974 there were 29,000 corporate farms enumerated holding some 11 percent of the land in farms with only some 8 percent of its improved value in land and buildings but marketing 18 percent of farm products. Three-quarters of these corporations, chiefly livestock ranches or orchards, were family corporations with 51 percent or more of the stock held by persons related by marriage or blood and only 3.6 percent of the corporations had 11 or more stockholders (U.S. Bureau of Census 1979, 684, 703). Of the U.S. farm population in the labor force in 1970, 83 percent were farm operators or their family helpers and only some 400,000 were hired laborers resident on the farm. Counting part-time and migratory workers, the total count in

1970 of hired laborers was 2.5 million but of these 40 percent worked 25 days or less and another 25 percent for roughly a season (between 1 to 3.5 months). I set out these controlling facts because many generally responsible observers grossly overstate the development of capitalist farming in the United States. See Harrington 1976, 225, who orates about "gigantic agribusiness" because larger farms with more than $20,000 of sales rose since 1960 to 1974 by 80 percent while the one-fifth of farms that were largest received 89 percent of cash receipts from earnings. Harrington disregards the 88 percent rise in farm prices between 1960 and 1974; nearly a third of farm operators conduct only part-time farm operations and hence have small gross marketings but substantial nonfarm incomes. Hence the large amount of agricultural income received from nonfarming operations. See U.S. Bureau of Census, *Statistical Abstract,* 1979, 682, 687, 696. Capitalist farms employing wage labor chiefly migratory, have characterized California agriculture since the late nineteenth century (McWilliams 1939).

26. Lenin (1899/1956, 291, 277, 305, 313, 317) gave a vivid picture of the way commercial agriculture gives birth to a supporting network of processing and fabricating operations such as dairy enterprises, cheese making, distilling, starch manufacture, oil extraction from vegetable seed.

27. Commercial enterprises with 4 or fewer persons active in them employed in 1965 nearly 3.5 million persons or some 35 percent of the Japanese workforce in commerce and trade; but 350 corporations in the same field show a net profit which is 13.3 percent of all national income originating in commerce and trade (Japan, Office of Prime Minister, *Bureau of Statistics,* 1972, 103–7).

28. The line between what has been called "managed" or "matured" capitalism and the "democratic-socialist economies" is an unclear one especially for the United Kingdom where social-democratic and conservative governments have alternated. Gruchy for example in one chapter classifies the British economy under Conservative guidance as "matured capitalism" and in another chapter under Labor control as matured "socialist economy" (Gruchy 1977, Chaps. 4, 11). Yet the greater role of overt social-democratic parties espousing "socialism" to varying degrees, the greater role for nationalization in Europe, the readier willingness to utilize state action, the penchant noteworthy in France for central economic planning, and the lesser role for the industrial-military complex so central to American experience – all seem to suggest a dichotomization in the mixed economy between a social-democratic and an American model.

29. De Tocqueville called attention to the neglect in America for the "higher sciences" but the great attention given to the "practical part of science . . . immediately requisite to application." (Rosenberg 1972, 33). Marx (1863–1878/1967, 1:387) put it more acidly: "Dr. Ure himself deplores the gross ignorance of mechanical science existing among his dear machinery-exploiting manufacturers and Liebig can a tale unfold about the astounding ignorance of chemistry displayed by English chemical manufacturers." Commodore Vanderbilt dismissed Westinghouse and his new air brakes with the remark that "he had no time to waste on fools" (Stern 1937, 42). See also Cameron 1961, 43; Solo 1967, 127; Mumford 1934, 215; Lilley in his essay in Cipolla 1972–1976, 3:187–255, especially 190, 194, 226; Braverman 1974, 155.

30. Hidy and Hidy 1955, 155–63. The experience of General Motors, formed a quarter century or so after Standard Oil, is different. In 1916 the

young motor combination acquired the Dayton Engineering Laboratories with a talented and inventive engineer, C. F. Kettering, who headed up a General Motors research division. After its initial preoccupation with the design of a copper air-cooled engine, that division went on to design and research many of the revolutionary changes in the modern automobile (Sloan 1965, 71, 343, 222, 249, 260).

31. Gilfillan 1964, 19. Warner (1962, 43) asserts that "the first research laboratory started by private industry" dates from 1900.

32. The Balfour Committee (1927, 319) reports expenditures of $75 million in the early 1920s while the list of laboratories in the United States published in 1920 by the National Research Council enumerated 526 laboratories maintained by firms or associations. Perhaps more significant than the dollar outlays reported are the research personnel reported by the 1921 survey conducted by the National Research Council. This identified 482 companies reporting the employment in R and D of 9350 research personnel (Perazich and Field 1940, 64).

33. The war was fought by Germany largely with the use of synthetic rubber and gasoline derived from laboratory research.

34. A huge literature on these problems has arisen drawn together for us by two masterly survey articles (Frankel 1962; Nadiri 1970). The inability to devise an adequate measure of the movement of output when the character of output is changing and the resulting gross underestimation of output in a period of dynamic technical change put under question many of the implications drawn by Moses Abramovitz (1981). Yet the accelerated pace of technical change, especially with the onset of so-called automation in the 1950s and 1960s is well-attested to by independent studies (Landes 1969, 519; Mandel 1978, Chaps. 6, 7, 8; Lynn 1966; Berri 1977, 1:203). Keynes (1936, 38) excluded the volume of output from the units of analysis usable for macroeconomic theory because two "incommensurable collections of miscellaneous objects," which make up the volume of output in two time periods, "cannot in themselves provide the material for a quantitative analysis. . . ."

35. Even after the repeal of the Combinations Acts in 1825, "barbarous laws" as Marx (1863–1878/1967, 1:740) called them, repealed "before the threatening bearing of the proletariat," significant restrictions hampered unions: requiring the giving of notice, limiting tactics usable in strikes, and making union treasuries liable for the payment of damages assessed by hostile courts because of strike actions. These restrictions remained on the statute books through most of the nineteenth century. In France the basic prohibition enacted during the French revolution of labor combination to raise wages or bargain collectively was relaxed only partially in 1864 and more fully in 1884. Not until the antisocialist laws were repealed in 1890 could unions act openly. In the United States trade unions were constantly suspect under the common law ban of conspiracy in restraint of trade. Strikes were subject to judicial control by injunction with drastic penalties at the instant control of local courts. Not until the Clayton Act of 1914 was a positive legal charter for unions obtained; the real *magna carta* of labor came only in the Roosevelt New Deal. See Commons and Andrews 1916, 91–124.

36. See Marx and Engels 1953, 246, 275; Marx and Engels 1845–1895/ 1970, 6:206; 2:71, 82; 3:448; Marx 1973, 28, 141, 391, 451.

37. See Slichter 1954; Slichter 1951, 75; Throop 1968, 79.

38. The process of maturation is excellently presented in the Webbs

two-volume treatise (1897) on the more matured state of British unionism. For a more recent commentary on American unionism, see Barbash 1968, 45.

39. The main features of this transformation of macroeconomics were developed in literature dealing with "cost-push" going back in part to the work of Keynes (1930). For more recent writing see Galbraith 1972, Chap. 22; Slichter 1951, 126; U.S. Congress, Senate, Committee on Judiciary 1957, Part 1; U.S. Congress, Joint Economic Committee Jan. 1968; U.S. Government, Executive, see especially *Economic Reports of the President* 1964 (112–21), 1966 (63–93), 1981 (57–68); see also Weintraub 1978.

40. See especially the paper prepared by Marx for reading at the London Council of the First International, "Wages, Price, and Profit." Marx sought to demolish the untutored views of an old English Owenite worker, a carpenter, on the relations of wages and prices and the ability of organized labor to effect a general rise in wage rates. He argued that price levels of commodities are determined or regulated by wage levels, a premise that Marx labored to destroy. See Marx and Engels (1970, 2:31–76, 45, 73). The pamphlet should be interpreted in the light of Marx's letters to Engels on the debate (Marx 1973, 391).

41. Though 87 percent of wage-earning families in New York carried some insurance, the "money invariably goes to meet the expenses of the funeral or of the last illness" (Seager 1910, 4).

42. Ibid., 65, 129; Commons and Andrews 1916, 363, 387, 400.

43. Ibid., 411; Seager 1910, 98.

44. Thus in 1960 general government revenues provided 74, 66.9, and 59.2 percent of social security outlays in Denmark, Sweden, and the United Kingdom, respectively. The United States began to contribute from general revenues in a formally designated social security program in the mid-1960s with supplementary medical care providing physician services to retired persons. The original 50 percent share for government has been raised on this program costing in 1978 some $7.3 billion to nearly 70 percent. Moreover, old-age pensions to beneficiaries qualifying under a loosely drawn means test administered by states financed pensions from federal and state funds under a program (originally called "old-age assistance" but recently included in "supplementary security income") and now runs at some $2.5 billion yearly. U.S. Bureau of Census, *Statistical Abstract,* 1979, 331, 352; Klein 1973, 118.

45. The American pattern of equal sharing by employee and employer is adopted in principle by the Netherlands and by the United Kingdom. But in France, West Germany, Austria, and Italy, the employer share is the following ratio of the employee share: 4:0, 1:65, 2:1, 5:0. The converse pattern holds in Sweden, Denmark, and Norway (Klein 1973, 118).

46. That is the prevailing assumption embodied in the national income accounts, treating both the employer and employee contribution to social security as forms of "employee compensation" before tax (Smith 1975, 46). The assumption of backward shifting of the employer's contribution to wages is stronger in European social security systems like the French that levy extremely high employer contributions for social security purposes, 30.65 percent of a substantial annual ceiling of earnings at 60,120 francs (in 1980) and 4.5 percent of earnings above the ceiling plus additional contributions for industrial accident insurance (see French Embassy 1980).

47. Noteworthily the earliest old-age pension plans not financed from a payroll levy – such as that of Denmark in 1891 and the United Kingdom 1908 –

involved a flat pension on a means-test basis (Seager 1910, 134, 138). By 1934 in the United States some twenty-eight states had adopted similar schemes of an old-age pension that in 1934 gave benefits to some 231,000 recipients, invariably based on a means test and usually requiring that "children and other immediate relatives of the aged persons must be unable to support them" (Douglas 1936, 6).

48. There is an intricate relationship between the earning power of husbands and wives, the decision of the female spouse to go to work, the influence of the husband's earning power on the wife's decision to work. See informed comments by Budd 1967, 102; Mincer 1970, 22; Smith 1975, 213. These factors and their reciprocal effects have changed in recent decades.

49. From 1950 to 1965 the benefit formulas were determined as follows from the average monthly wage (Derthick 1979, 275): 1950, 50 percent of the first $100 plus 15 percent of the next $200; 1952, 55 percent of the first $100 plus 15 percent of the next $200; 1954, 55 percent of the first $110 plus 20 percent of the next $240; 1958, 58.85 percent of the first $110 plus 21.4 percent of the next $290; 1965, 62.9 percent of the first $110 plus 22.9 percent of the next $290 plus 21.4 percent of the next $150.

50. For the exact procedure of benefit computation as of 1982, see U.S. Department of Health, Education and Welfare 1974, Chap. 7. For changes in German social security "in favor of workers with relatively low wages," see Shonfield 1965, 92.

51. The U.S. Constitution required "all duties, imposts and excises" to be "uniform throughout the United States" and that capitation or other direct taxes shall be apportioned the states in proportion to population (Article I, Section 8, 9, number 4). Except when strained by the fiscal needs of war, the young republic was thus constitutionally confined to indirect taxation, chiefly excises and customs, though the judiciary tolerated the use of a corporate income tax, construed as an excise in 1911 (Corwin 1963, 27, 280). Moreover, many state constitutions in the nineteenth century developed a fiscal clause stipulating for taxation a "rule of uniformity" ruling out an income tax unless authorized by specific constitutional amendment. The Wisconsin constitution was amended for this purpose in 1905 at the heyday of the La Follette Progressive revolt (Wisconsin 1977, 220, 239).

52. Thus in 1793 the revolutionary French government enacted an income tax and eight years later the British government followed suit. With victory in 1815 the income tax was repealed with such jubilation that Parliament decreed that all taxpayer records of the tax were to be destroyed. So also in the American civil war an income tax was enacted and allowed to lapse in 1872 (Hope-Jones 1939, 1–3).

53. Executive salaries reported by smaller (nonpublic) business corporations have always in the United States exhibited considerably higher levels of salary taking than the larger public corporations. As of 1959 the corporate income tax rate was 30 percent for the first $25,000 of corporate net income and 22 percent thereafter. The base rate in 1981 was 17 percent and by $25,000 brackets the tax was stepped up to a top rate of 46 percent on corporate net income over $100,000.

54. In the United States corporate profits taxes have exceeded dividends paid to stockholders *every year since 1941* and for eight of the years by more than twice. Between 1946 and 1979 dividends were only 57.1 percent of corporate taxes. Japanese corporate dividends for the years 1960, 1965, and 1970

were only 36 percent of corporate profits taxes paid. United Kingdom corporate dividends for 1951–1953 were only 27 percent of corporate profits taxes (U.S. Government, Executive, *Economic Report of the President* 1980, Table B-79; Japan 1972, Table 58, 59; Kaldor 1955, 153).

55. O'Connor (1973, 206) treads on thin ice when he contends that "business leaders have favored taxing their corporate rather than personal income because monopoly sector corporations control price and thus can shift the corporate income tax rate to consumers."

56. See Mieskowski 1969, 1115; Shoup 1972, 18; Goode 1951, 44; Due 1959, 219; Kaldor 1955, 141.

57. The uneven profit position of many market suppliers has been a constant theme of empirical studies of industrial and commercial price making. See Stigler 1963; Due 1959, 225.

58. Musgrave et al. 1951, 1–53; Musgrave 1964 and other publications.

59. The income returns are statistically questionable on their face. Thus the average business partnership for the years 1960, 1970, and 1976 reported an average income per partnership of $9,055, $12,487, and $11,370. Net rental incomes from rented properties—farms, business premises, and 26.5 million nonfarm dwellings are so low that for purposes of estimating the share of real estate rents in national income, the U.S. Department of Commerce chose not to use the tax returns for unincorporated enterprises as "tax data may be assumed to be too low because of the incentive to understate income for tax purposes." Similarly, the highly competent analysts in the Bureau of Agricultural Economics prepare estimates of farm operator incomes in total abstraction from the tax return information piled up in the Bureau of Internal Revenue. U.S. Bureau of Census, *Statistical Abstract,* 1979, 265, 443; U.S. Department of Commerce 1951, 70, 77, 79. A thorough investigation of landlord tax returns of residential urban properties in one Wisconsin city disclosed understatement of net income reported for taxation of around one half (Groves 1958).

60. Bureau of Internal Revenue examiners give only a superficial scrutiny to returns that on their face exhibit some marked anomaly. A sample of 50,000 tax returns covered in a 1963 special audit study resulted in an increase of taxable income by $6.5 billion mostly in business, partnership, and rental returns (Smith 1975, 468; Farioletti 1952).

61. The percent reported by IRS in their annually reported Statistics of Income for wages and salaries of Adjusted Gross Incomes of individual tax returns rose from 80.5 in 1965 to 83.8 in 1970 at which level it fluctuated during the 1970s. U.S. Bureau of Census, *Statistical Abstract,* 1985, 316.

62. A regressive twist is sometimes indicated for the lowest income group on tax studies tracing payment of taxes by records of expenditures made in sample years by various income classes. This regressive twist at the lowest layer of the income scale arises because many families in that scale position have temporarily low incomes because of illness, unemployment, bad business conditions, or poor crops, but maintain expenditures at more normal levels financed by savings or borrowings. Other retired families with low current incomes are drawing upon capital or annuities funded out of past incomes. One of Milton Friedman's (1957, 39, 209) few services to economic theory was pointing out the unreliability of an annual time period for determining "normal" income. "Negative savings at low measured incomes reflect precisely that measured income is not a valid index of wealth; that many people have low

incomes in any one year because of transitory factors and can be expected to have higher incomes in other years." Correspondingly, at the upper end of the income scale consumption expenditures will appear low because they are compared to incomes swollen by transitory factors. This biases many tax studies where incidence of indirect taxes are traced by expenditure studies based upon measured behavior over a single year. It also biases studies, as Friedman pointed out, showing the distribution of incomes from measurements of income received in a single year.

63. Since only one-third of the heat produced in an electric power plant is utilized for energy purposes, much heat needs to be vented, usually achieved by using local cooling waters drawn from a nearby lake or stream. This heats the ambient waters, speeds up biochemical processes, tends to deplete oxygen, and may cause fish kills or compel fish migration from the area. To avoid this, most electric power plants are now required in new plant construction or, where feasible, in existing plants to erect cooling towers where heat is released into the atmosphere by circulating the heated waters. Such a tower for a large plant may be as large as a 30-story building one block in diameter and may increase the cost of power by some 10 percent. Between 1977–1987 estimated expenditure for avoidance of "thermal pollution" was projected at $894 million raising costs per Kwh between 3 to 13 percent. Correction for thermal pollution has been estimated at $6 per kilowatt (in 1975 prices) for a plant to begin operations in 1983. In addition, a forced-draft cooling tower can use up to 3 percent of the plant's electrical output. A New York City power executive once wistfully suggested that it seemed almost insane in that great city where so many people suffered from summer heat to provide cooling for the marine life in the adjacent waters at the cost of several hundred million dollars (Freeman 1974, 78, 300; U.S. Council on Environmental Quality 1976, 160 and 1978, 439; Mills 1978, 110, 118.

64. This involves the famous Tellico Dam (under the auspices of TVA) in Tennessee, which at the cost of several hundred million dollars was nearing completion when work was halted by a court order to enforce compliance with an environmental law requiring the conservation of endangered species. In this instance it was found that the river was the last remaining habitat of the Snail Darter, a small fresh water fish. After extended debate in Congress – with a celebrated exchange between two liberal senators – completion of the dam was finally authorized. See U.S. Council on Environmental Quality 1978, 334.

65. It took an act of Congress in late 1973, spurred on by presidential requests for action, to provide for an adequate right-of-way, to settle on the all-Alaskan route to Valdez, and to remove environmental objections from court scrutiny. The pipeline project expenditures were boosted to relieve environmental concerns for wildlife, possible injury to the tundra, and possible earthquake damage. Cost estimates projected at $1.6 billion in 1970 were raised to $6.0 billion in 1974 and reached $7.7 billion upon completion of construction in 1977 (Mead 1977, 87; Senate, Committee on the Interior 1973, 17, 35, 73; Mancke 1974, 60).

66. Mead 1977, 41; House Committee on Interior and Insular Affairs 1977, 54, 92, 82, 127, 270. Canadian authorities were responsive to Indian opposition to any pipeline without prior settlement of their land claims. The U.S. State Department made no effort to intercede with Canadian authorities to promote a Mackenzie River route and the prime movers in the whole affair were the multinational oil companies with special interests of their own.

67. Federal legislation has encouraged workfare programs under which welfare recipients are required to work at minimum wages in return for welfare support (2 October 1981, *Congressional Record,* H6894; 22 October 1981, H7625). By the end of the Reagan years, workfare programs will prevail in most American cities.

68. Thus the United States has gone farther than Labor in Britain by promoting home ownership chiefly by making mortgage interest deductible from income for purposes of computing taxable income and by exempting from taxation housing services in kind received by the owner-occupant of a dwelling. See Crosland 1974, 126. Before 1936 home loans "were handled entirely by private money lenders" who charged "high interest, required large down payments, and required rapid repayment typically in 7 or 10 years." The Federal Housing Administration was created in 1935 to support home ownership by underwriting mortgage loans for eligible moderate-income borrowers specifying low interest rates and long-term periods of repayment (U.S. National Commission on Urban Problems, 1969, 94). The VA (Veterans Administration) performed a similar service for veterans. For a review of the influence of federal aids to mortgage finance in the first twenty years, see Grebler et al. 1956, 238, 286. The authors conclude that federal aids acted to reduce interest rates and liberalized terms of lending by setting new standards for long-term loans and low down payments.

69. U.S. National Commission on Urban Problems, 1969, 108, 143; U.S. Bureau of Census, *Statistical Abstract,* 1979, 784.

70. See Bowley 1945; Lewis 1965, 223; Crosland 1974, 130.

71. Elasticity measures for consumer demand for red and poultry meats, fruits, and vegetables and many other particular foodstuffs are high enough that low prices for a particular class of food product will draw expenditure away from competing food products. For broad classes of agricultural output such as bread grains or cereals, meats, poultry and fish and fruits and vegetables, elasticity measures are lower and for foodstuffs as a whole or for cotton or tobacco lower still. The supply function for overall farm output appears to have zero elasticity in response to change of price or to be "backward sloping." See the authoritative treatment by Heady 1962, 151, 215, 223.

72. The processing and marketing margin – the gap between the price at the farm gate of farm produce and the charge for the retail product – has risen from 52.4 percent in 1913 to 68 percent in 1964. See U.S. National Commission on Food Marketing, June 1966, 11.

73. Henry Schultz's pioneer studies (1938, 400) of price elasticity for major farm staples (sugar, cotton, corn, wheat) for 1875–1895, 1896–1914, and 1915–1929 exhibited falling price elasticities. See also Heady 1962, 217.

74. "The theory of short-period prices has been so much neglected that this simple equation, which helps to explain the violence of the fluctuation of the relative prices of staple commodities, is . . . unfamiliar." The equation was $pq = xy$ in which x = the total cost per annum of carrying stocks measured as a proportion of the normal price; y = the proportion of the redundant stocks to a year's consumption; p = the proportionate fall of prices below the normal at its maximum; and q = the proportionate fall of new production below its normal (Keynes 1930, 2:140).

75. Keynes 1938, 449. This paper, which continued the discussion of price instability for agricultural and raw products from the *Treatise on Money* (1930), was itself an outgrowth of extended investigations by Keynes into

price instability in raw material markets during the 1920s.

76. The variance and coefficient of variation for annual average prices of six major farm products for 1910–1949 and for 1950–1971 have been calculated in constant dollars. The coefficients varied for the early period from 79 percent for beef cattle to 92.9 percent for cotton (U.S. Government, Executive Economic Report of the President, 1975, 175).

77. Thus the index of wholesale prices for foods available for 11 cycles from 1891–1938 (excluding the war period) shows an average rise of 7.2 percent in reference expansion periods and a fall of −7.4 percent in contraction periods even though agricultural output had no detectable cyclical resonance. Mitchell 1951, Ser. 41, Chart 1 (18). See also his graphed cycle patterns for farm and retail prices of foods and cotton. Fig. 20, 22. Though Mitchell's investigation only covered U.S. statistical measures, the same patterns are found internationally.

78. That was the lapidary phrase of W. W. Cochrane, brilliant agricultural economist at the University of Minnesota (U.S. Congress, Joint Committee, *Hearings* Dec. 1957, 330).

79. Keynes (1930, 2:141) drew attention to the price stabilization and valorization programs operative in the 1920s for rubber, wool, and coffee. Stabilization programs for wheat, cotton, and sugar came later.

80. Seventeen states had legislation authorizing price regulation in milksheds and fifteen states authorized regulation for other products. See U.S. Congress, Joint Committee, *Hearings* 1962, 439.

81. These were evolved from strict production control arrangements commenced in the mid-1930s and have come to center upon an alienable permit to grow or market tobacco or peanuts that in two-thirds of the cases is sold or leased to other farmers in the county. There are 59,000 peanut allotments in six states and some 276,000 tobacco allotments usually of only a few acres, worth about $5000 per acre. The congressional debate on agricultural price controls in Sept.–Oct. 1981, when a four-year authorization of the 1977 act was up for revision, strained the control system, which was weakened for peanut growers but upheld for tobacco growers in the U.S. Senate. See 16 September 1981, *Congressional Record,* S9699, S9735; 17 September 1981, S9861. See also Heady 1962, 437.

82. The famous "soil bank" program launched in 1956, tactfully labelled "conservation," by 1960 involved 6.2 percent of cropland nationally but more in western states where land was more easily taken out of cultivation (Heady 1962, 554; Committee for Economic Development [CED] 1956).

83. This system was developed in 1977 farm legislation authorizing a farmer-owned wheat and rice reserve, on which farmers may borrow at set "local rates," held in farmer-owned storage facilities. Farmers may not redeem loans or sell reserve stocks within a contract period (generally three years) without penalty unless market prices reach a certain fraction of loan value. This combination of "call price and . . . loan rate establishes a known corridor of market prices" and the Reagan administration made its peace with this system (U.S. Government, Executive, *Economic Report of the President,* 1980, 150).

84. Ibid., 1975, 169. Some of this reserve was "illusory" since when restrictions were released only some 37 million acres by 1974 bounded back into cultivation. Cropland used for crops expanded by 28 million acres between 1969 and 1974 (U.S. Bureau of Census, *Statistical Abstract,* 1979, 686,

692). In the 1977 Senate debate on the food and agriculture bill, a knowledgeable senator noted that up to 1972 U.S. farm programs had kept 51 million acres from cultivation (23 May 1977, *Congressional Record,* S8273).

85. See U.S. Congress, Joint Committee on the Economic Report of the President, *Compendium* Dec. 1957, 271, 269; Heady 1962, 630. From 1949 to 1960 the percent of farm exports wholly or largely subsidized was at its lowest 18.9 percent and at its highest 65.9 percent. By 1964 concessional exports included two-thirds of wheat exports, two-fifths of milled rice exports, and one-fifth of cotton and edible oil exports (U.S. Government. Executive, *Economic Report of the President,* 1966, 136). Most cotton, wheat, and soybeans in this period moved abroad with export subsidies, which contravened the pristine principles of multilateral free trade ideology.

86. The anatomy of agricultural depression and crisis is carefully spelled out in Melichar 1984, 1–13.

87. Since the CAP was negotiated when France was under De Gaulle's leadership, his programmatic statements indicate the importance of CAP to France, providing the main grounds for the French veto of the British application to enter the Common Market (Gen. Charles De Gaulle 1964, 214, 254). The provisions of the Rome Treaty are conveniently for American readers set forth in Committee for European Development (CED) 1959, 95.

88. See description in Klein 1973, 133; French Embassy, Press and Information Division 1973.

89. Thus the levy raised the 1981 American price for wheat delivered to Rotterdam by 38.7 percent (11 September 1981, *Congressional Record,* S9440).

90. Thus the valuable license or allotment to grow regulated products, which raises the value of farmland several thousand dollars per acre, was only in the later 1970s abolished for rice and is in process of being phased out for peanut growers but is apparently well buttressed for tobacco growers. See the intensive debate on this subject as the Congress worked over the 1981 Food and Agriculture Bill (16 September 1981, *Congressional Record,* S9699; 19 September 1981, S9846; 21 October 1918, H7550).

91. Though the Common Market was a wheat-deficit area, still wheat surpluses accumulate there and are shipped out under subsidy. A wheat-growing U.S. senator in the 1981 debate on the food and agriculture bill complained that the French had sold 50,000 tons of wheat to Brazil at $140 per ton or $8.50 less than the lowest U.S. price with their export subsidy. A similar complaint was made about French wheat exports to Poland, Finland. . . . (31 August 1981, *Congressional Record,* S9440). U.S. "concessional" farm exports or subsidized commercial exports were opposed by other leading grain exporting nations.

92. U.S. Congress, Joint Committee, *Hearings* and *Compendium,* Dec. 1957, 193.

93. More or less in these terms see Hansen 1951, 26; Mathews 1959, Chap. 12.

94. See Hansen 1951, Chap. 3; Mathews 1959, Chap. 6; Gottlieb 1976; and bibliography references to the work of A. Burns, M. Abramovitz, A. Cairncross, C. D. Long, and others. The "long-swing" building depressions of the nineteenth century have been casually denigrated as "relatively stable . . . growth interrupted by two monetary episodes from which the system rebounded to approximately its initial path" (Friedman and Schwartz 1963, 187).

95. " . . . the classical masters have paid but incidental attention to the

rhythmical oscillation of trade" (Mitchell 1927, 4). A form of the "tinkering" hypothesis has been revived in the 1960s by Friedman and Schwartz (1963, 104, 113) by explanation of the major depressions of the 1890s as due to uncertainty caused by threatened or impending legislation on currency or the "policies of silver." In their latest joint work on Monetary Trends, a long chapter seeks to back up their earlier claim that long swings are attributable primarily to episode disturbances of the money supply.

96. See my account of that remarkable institution, the Ohio office of Commissioner of Statistics, established in 1858, from which issued eleven memorable reports and a half-century of annual statistical data (Gottlieb 1976, 285).

97. Mitchell 1927, 10; Schumpeter 1939, 1:162.

98. The outstanding figures were Tugan-Baranovsky (1894), Spiethoff (1902), and Schumpeter (1910). Hansen 1951, 277.

99. Only the third part of the Mitchell treatise of 1913 has been republished (1950).

100. The National Bureau of Economic Research (NBER) whose publications have so frequently been cited in this work was established as a scientific institute in 1920 as the focal center of applied economic research into national income and business cycles by a group of forward-looking businessmen and academics.

101. " . . . Econometrics combines economic theory with economic statistics and tries by mathematical and statistical methods to give concrete quantitative methods to the general schematic laws established by economic theory" (Lange 1959, 13). Lange is noteworthy for forming a link between modern and Marxian economic theory. The first serious use of large-scale quarterly econometric models of the American economy began only in the 1960s with the development in 1967 of the quarterly Wharton model (see Evans 1969, 416) and the publication in 1965 of the Brookings model, the composite work of a group of investigators (Dusenberry et al. 1965). Quite remarkable is use of Western Keynesian-type econometric models in a recent Soviet theoretical work on postwar (1946–   ) U.S. business cycles with quite interesting results (Menshikov 1975, 270–303).

102. See U.S. Congress, Joint Committee, *Hearings,* May 1980 for the record of testimony of prominent econometric model builders and model users debating the suitability of models for analyzing the "supply side."

103. The method of achieving devaluation by slow daily bidding up of the market price of gold (using appropriated dollar public funds for that purpose) extending over several months was psychologically unstabilizing and upsetting in other financial markets. As J. M. Keynes (1933) wrote to President Roosevelt, it looked less like a proper management of currency than a gold standard on the booze." But however it looked, the devaluation was a bold action which put the American economy on a sound financial footing with leeway for expansion in our foreign trade without balance of trade deficits.

104. That was embodied in legislation for most Western countries in the postwar era, noteworthily in Great Britain with the issuance of famous White Papers, the development of the French "indicative" national economic planning, and the United States adoption in 1946 of the Full Employment Act. The latter stated plainly the continuing responsibility of the federal government to create and maintain "conditions under which there will be afforded useful employment opportunities, including self-employment, for those able, willing

and seeking to work." This moral commitment to full employment has been reaffirmed time and again by successive presidents of both political parties. Even so conservative an economist as Arthur F. Burns (1969, 175, 221), economic advisor to two Republican presidents and chief executive for many years of the Federal Reserve Board, states that "it expresses faithfully the prevailing sentiment of the American people" and its organized groupings. On this entire development of public policy in the Western world, see Hansen 1951, 524.

105. The strength of "automatic stabilizers" in various Western economies has even been quantified (see Klein 1973, 181). The importance of the stabilizers is recognized by Menshikov (1975, 151) who notes that "the state budget acts as a double-acting pump, which helps to provide additional demand during crises and curtails effective demand during advances."

106. On "incomes policy" in Western economies, see the brief review in Klein (1973, 206); for a kind of doctrinaire opposition to "incomes policy" see Burns (1969, 232).

107. In only three of Japan's postwar recessions and one of West Germany's did a monthly index of industrial production, our best concurrent measure of cyclical behavior, show recessional decline prior to 1973–1975.

108. Gottlieb 1957, 347–58.

109. See Abramovitz 1968. In my own work (1976, 33), analysis of long building cycles was generally excluded from the post-1946 world because of my stated conviction that the central mechanisms of these long swings had altered since they were working in a dramatically changed economic and demographic environment with substantial inputs from government policy.

110. Hence the international conference called to consider the question whether the business cycle had become obsolete (Bronfrenbrenner 1969).

111. Friedman and Schwartz 1963, 434; Friedman 1968, 75.

112. IMF 1979, 47; 1980, 59. A full analysis of the dollar capital flight of 1971–1973, which broke the Bretton Woods system and resulted after prolonged negotiation in the demonetization of gold, is attempted in Gottlieb (1984, 310–28).

Chapter 7

1. This was true even in Nazi Germany where as German defeat in war loomed closer a strong Left resistance with a core of worker-Communists and their fellow-travelers stepped forward in most of the principal German cities to carry on emergency functions of government, to ferret out Nazis, and to offer assistance to military government. See Gottlieb 1960, 5, 7; Brzezinski 1967, 3, 22.

2. For East Germany the earlier forms of coalition government, which only began to disintegrate as the Cold War heightened in 1947–1948, allowed scope not only for a relatively strong social-democratic party but two bourgeois-democratic parties. See my account and references in Gottlieb (1960, Chap. 3). The problematics of the "People's Democracy" phase of coalition governments is well explored by Brzezinski (1967, 41).

3. Richman 1969, Chap. 12, especially 895, 906; Schurmann 1968, 221.

4. Schurmann 1968, Table 12-1. Soviet publications of sinological re-

search, understandably influenced by a strong partisan viewpoint but often well-informed, have treated the role of private enterprise and the so-called "national bourgeoisie" or "red capitalist" fully. See e.g., Progress Publishers 1975, 101.

5. Mao 1961–1977, 5:113. State partnership was achieved because of state investments and control over raw materials and orders. See Xue Muqiao 1981, 27.

6. Mao 1961–1977, 5:357. Interest payments were set at 5 percent of negotiated or scaled down capital values which according to Soviet critics amounted to 2.2 billion yuan or to annual interest payments of from 110 to 120 million yuan plus of course executive salaries which apparently sometimes ran beyond the scale set for state employees of comparable rank. See Krivtsov et al. 1972, 193.

7. Informed sources differ as to whether the "national bourgeoisie," whose members while financially well treated were worked over with psychological "remoulding" exercises, survived the revolutionary upsurge of the Cultural Revolution or whether this class was gradually submerged or wiped out. See Eckstein 1977, 84; Lane 1976, 162; Schurmann 1968, 94. A knowledgeable Chinese authority asserts that interest payments stopped in 1967 (Xue Muqiao 1982, 268). For indications of a lessened role for the "national bourgeoisie" see interesting reportage by Joan Robinson (1969, 124), with a detailed account of four factories visited in 1966–1967. A well-informed Soviet analyst writing in 1969 found the "national bourgeoisie" still active and holding its positions and income standing, with the period of interest payments (on the 5 percent), originally set to terminate in 1962, extended for another ten-year period to 1976 (Krivtsov et al. 1972, 131). After publication in 1979 of a statute on "joint ventures" as a "new economic sector of a semi-socialist nature" coming into being, this sector involves not only foreign Western investment involving especially compatriots from Hong Kong or Macao but also joint ventures of these with domestic mainland capitalists still active at least in Shanghai where a Shanghai Federation of Industry and Commerce (an organization of former industrialists and businessmen) set up a corporation with a capital of 50–60 million yuan "to build houses" for sale to the overseas Chinese (*Beijing Review* 8 Sept. 1981, 20). At the commemoration proceedings on the anniversary of the 1911 Revolution various bourgeois-democratic notables were trotted out to celebrate the occasion and to express their hope for closer relations with Taiwan compatriots (*Beijing Review* 19 Oct. 1981, 22).

8. For two outstanding Western appraisals of the Communist party, see the sweeping though apologetic account of Webb and Webb 1944, 262–323. See also the insightful and well-researched account of the Chinese Communist party by Schurmann (1968, 105–72). With his usual light but perceptive touch J. M. Keynes after a visit to Russia in 1925 described Russian Communists "as though the early Christians [were] led by Attila . . . using the equipment of the Holy Inquisition and the Jesuit Missions" (Keynes 1931, 298). Even knowledgeable foreign observers have not fully appreciated that diversity of makeup of communist organization enables it to take advantage of "experience, the observations, the opinions of all its members placed at the various rungs of the ladder of economic administration," including machinists, clerks, accountants, engineers, both blue collar and white collar. L. D. Trotsky, who wrote those lines in a pamphlet published in the USSR in 1923, went on to emphasize that this many-sided communist cell, thus collecting the "experiences of these mu-

tually complementary workers, draws conclusions from them and thus determines its line for directing economy in general and each enterprise in particular" (Trotsky 1923/1943, 25).

9. Still memorable is Lenin's brochure of 1902, *What is to be Done* which was only the first of a long series of essays, letters, speeches on the topic of party building.

10. Schurmann 1968, 29; China, People's Republic, 1973, 80; *Beijing Review*, 13 July 1981, 22.

11. The startling Khrushchev message came in an address to a closed session of the 1956 Congress of the CPSU. The address was later read as a secret communiqué to closed sessions of all Communist party units in the Soviet Union. Public disclosure came only much later, noteworthily in the Khrushchev reports to the Twenty-second Party Congress of the CPSU. It took the Chinese leadership as long to link up the rule of the "gang of four" (who held the reigns of power under Mao) with Mao, although the devastation over which the "gang of four" presided was an outgrowth of the Cultural Revolution led and instigated by Mao himself. See the amazing "Resolution on Certain Questions in the History of Our Party" (*Beijing Review*, 6 July 1981, 6–39). Characteristically, both parties denounced the "cult of leadership" with the same unanimity with which they applauded it and indulged in what the Chinese leadership now terms a "steady weakening and even undermining of the principle of collective leadership," castigating itself indirectly for complicity in a kind of "feudal autocracy."

12. Beatrice Webb (1944, xxiii) admitted she stumbled a bit upon reading that article of the Soviet 1936 Constitution which she had applauded for its democratic character in the earlier edition of her work. The article is now found in Section I of the USSR *Constitution* and reads as follows: "The leading and guiding force of Soviet society and the nucleus of its political system, of all state organizations and public organizations is the Communist Party of the Soviet Union" (USSR, Soviet Union 1978, 21).

13. The 1982 Constitution for the People's Republic of China was adopted by a national legislative assembly on the basis of an extended eight-month discussion of a draft constitution, which itself was in preparation by a national commission for over a year. The constitution formalizes the policy of a broad "national front" inclusive of noncommunist groups accepting the principles of a socialist worker's and peasant's state under the leadership of the Communist party. These ideas are copiously recited in the extended preamble to the constitution. The long text of that document, enshrined as the supreme law of the land binding on all individuals and tribunals, makes no reference to the "leading position" of the Communist party, establishes clear-cut political and civil rights of all citizens in an extended chapter of the document (Chap. 2, "The Fundamental Rights and Duties of Citizens"), establishes a state structure based on elected officers and an appointed judiciary, and establishes the principles of a socialist state based on socialized and collective property. At the session of the congress which adopted the constitution, it was pointed out that the 1954 Constitution was also "quite good" but that it was simply disregarded in the ten-year "confusion and turmoil" of the "Cultural Revolution." To prevent such "disregard," a clause was added to Article 5, dealing with the "uniformity and dignity of the socialist legal system": "All acts in violation of the Constitution and the law must be looked into." See *Beijing Review*: text of the Constitution 27 Dec. 1982, 10–29; news article on the adopting session of the People's

Congress, ibid., 30; P. Zhen, Vice-Chairman of the Committee for the Revision of the Constitution, ibid., 10 May 1982, 18–47. Probably the state constitution should be interpreted in conjunction with the constitution of the Communist party (CP), which was adopted by the Twelfth National Congress of the CP meeting a few months before. The CP Constitution boldly declares that the CP is the "vanguard of the Chinese working class, the faithful representative of the interests of the people of all nationalities in China and the force at the core of leading China's cause of socialism." Party members are free to make suggestions and to participate in discussions but are obligated "to execute the Party's decisions perseveringly . . . , to uphold the Party's solidarity and unity to firmly oppose factionalism and all factional organizations and small-group activities." See full text of the Party Constitution (*Beijing Review,* 20 Sept. 1982, 8).

14. "Standing in line, waiting years for cars and apartments, searching the shops, bribing the butcher and the repairman, are still a way of life," U.S. Congress, Joint Economic Committee, *Compendium* 1977, 27.

15. In the early phases of revolutionary struggle and through the early years of the young republic, concern with the "population problem" was regarded as reactionary and as ideologically suspect. See Mao 1961–1977, 4:453 for a typical example. A Chinese student of Chinese population policy under the republic could assert "the direct cause of the blind increase in China's population growth was the one-sidedness of the population theories and policies that prevailed in the past" (Liu Zheng et al. 1981, 52). For a few years in the mid-fifties government leaders considered the need for population control and Mao in the fall of 1957 spoke warmly of the need for family planning (Mao 1961–1977, 5:488, 512). For a few years government bans on sterilization and induced abortion were lifted (Liu et al. 1981, 58, 60, 131, 136, 150, 155, 159, 53). In the leftward binge of 1958–1962 and through the Cultural Revolution, expression of opinion and research on the subject was checked though in certain communities family planning facilities were active. Government allocation and rationing policy (housing and living subsidies for urban families, food grain, private plots and housing land in rural communities) all were on a per capita basis and thus rewarded additional children. For Western commentary, see Eckstein 1977, 49; Prybyla 1978, 14.

16. This was vividly set forth in Khrushchev's memoirs (1974, 56): "We'd come a long way from the time when Stalin was terrified we would be attacked by our imperialist enemies at any moment. No longer were we contaminated by Stalin's fear; no longer did we look at the world through his eyes. Now it was our enemies who trembled in their boots. Thanks to our missiles we could deliver a nuclear bomb to any target any place in the world."

17. The "transition period" between capitalism and socialism "must combine the features and properties of both these forms of economy," that of "dying capitalism and nascent socialism," a regime in which we forge a link between "the new economy that we have begun to create (very badly and very clumsily . . .) and the peasant economy." I cite variously from writings of 1919 to 1922 (Lenin 1971, 3:189, 440, 618, 680).

18. Expressing himself ambiguously, he spoke of the regime he himself had introduced as a "special kind of state capitalism" that functioned under a proletarian state and was subordinated to and controlled by a socialist state (Lenin 1971, 592, 602, 687, 725). Perusal of a volume recently published of Lenin's informal writings, letters, and notes 1920–1923 indicates that the label

"state capitalism" was designed partly to startle "inert communists" satisfied with traditional party doctrines, partly to make them realize that the new policy "is moving forward in earnest," and partly to make these Communists learn *business methods* (Lenin 1971, 443). Stalin (1928, 387, 435) and Trotsky (1937, 245) both thought the label inappropriate.

19. As a faithful Marxian socialist Trotsky (1937, 3) adhered throughout his adult life to this Marxian concept of socialism as suited only to an advanced state of society with well developed productive forces.

20. For recent Soviet arrangements, see Berri 1977, 1:231, 242. The basic statute governing the industrial enterprise adopted in 1965 allowed a part of the profit or bonus earned by exceeding plan requirements to be available for use by the enterprise to "better the cultural and living conditions of its workers and improving technique" (Novosti Press Agency Publishing 1965, 155; Koval and Miroshnichenko 1972, 180).

21. The Premier of the Chinese State Council, in his report on the sixth Five-Year Plan, noted a current shortage of funds for central investment, whereas "funds in the hands of localities and enterprises have increased by a big margin." The plan therefore included measures to mobilize funds from enterprises, localities, and collectives; to prohibit or curtail capital outlay projects initiated locally; and to call for more comprehensive centralized investment planning (*Beijing Review*, 20 Dec. 1982, 25). The same call for "concentrating funds on key development projects" was stressed in the report of the party Central Committee to the Twelfth CP Congress (*Beijing Review*, 13 Sept. 1982, 17).

22. U.S. Congress, Joint Committee, *Compendium*, 1976, 457; Novosti Press 1965, 35. A well informed Soviet economist later notes a four- to five-year "gestation" period (Kushnirsky 1982, 33).

23. See Hansen 1951, 319, 350; Schumpeter 1939, 1:132. The research work of the National Bureau of Economic Research demonstrated that factual records of large numbers of business cycles did not fit this hypothesis.

24. The annual rate of growth of the stock of fixed productive assets in the Soviet economy in the 1951–1970 period was 8.2 percent, which involves doubling of the stock of assets in less than a decade. Berri 1977, 1:129.

25. The Webbs provided a faithful account of the liveliness of this national debate. Webb 1944, 510; Berri 1977, 1:22, 880.

26. The Hungarian economist Kornai emphasized this "expansion drive" and the somewhat pejorative Hungarian term "investment hunger." By inference this "hunger" results in many unwise and irrational investment expenditures including scrapping of allegedly "outdated equipment," a desire to "show off" a "new" machine or workshop, and the like (Kornai 1980, 191). He hardly takes account of the screening role played by the higher level of industrial organization – a combine or ministry – whose staff is presumably familiar from visits, inspections, and the like with the technology and industrial plant concerned and who are mindful of the need to make effective use of such investment funds as the plan may put at their disposal.

27. This goal was highlighted in Stalin's industrialization campaign throughout the early five-year plans.

28. See Kornai 1980, Chaps. 9, 10, and pp. 194, 55 . He emphasizes that "investment drive" is "not just limited by fear of loss or failure since bankruptcy is impossible" and financial loss "can always be compensated by state subsidies, price adjustment or other means." Any general state policy of this

kind with loose resort to subsidies would soon exhaust state funds and could then be financed only by reckless inflation. He overlooks that enterprise or combine directors who build up financial records of this type would soon be earmarked for replacement and possibly, after investigation, to demotion or some kind of penalty. Kornai even claims it is exceptional for a producer to withhold expanding production just because a product is "unsaleable." While socialist enterprise managers or combine directors cannot under ordinary circumstances go "bankrupt," they surely can be demoted or removed from their positions and suffer permanent injury to their career. It is odd that Kornai who is so experienced in Hungarian economic affairs has paid no attention to job stability among management and combine directors, to their hope for upward promotion and the criteria for this, and their fear of demotion or other sanctions.

29. Examples are found in the recent reports of Communist party leaders at a recent party congress. Brezhnev asserted that economic policy was "coming to hinge on a matter that would seem simple and quite routine – a thrifty attitude to social property and an ability to make full and rational use of everything we have, arguing that 'an economy must be economical.'" Tikhonov more concretely filed a bill of particulars: many enterprise directors "hoard equipment . . . and materials and devote all their energies to getting lower plan targets and higher allocations of resources" (Communist Party Soviet Union 1981, 54, 144).

30. Misuse of state property has bordered on "stealing" (though not for personal benefit) according to a young Soviet economist who has recently moved to the United States. Brezhnev is cited as alleging that such property loss amounts to 25 billion rubles (Kushnirsky 1982, 138). Property loss from peculation, carelessness, and personal malfeasance appears in nearly all modes of production where economic assets are handled by those who do not own them or have direct responsibility for them. Even in small shops and retail stores merchandise can be stolen by employees who may withhold cash from collections or who may cooperate with customer thievings. In Western large-scale organization so-called white-collar crime is a major source of asset shrinkage. Quantification of such shrinkage for an entire economy would be difficult to establish except as a range of estimates and comparison of such shrinkage between economies is almost a hopeless matter.

31. It is quite amusing to read top CIA projections of Soviet oil output declining. In June 1977 Admiral S. Turner, one of the ablest CIA directors, asserted in a congressional hearing "we still expect that oil output is going to fall to between 9 to 10 million barrels daily by 1985" (in 1976 the output statistic was 10.4 million). U.S. Congress, Joint Committee, *Hearings*, 1977, 5.

32. It was thus a capital error of J. K. Galbraith (1972, 33) to build an analysis of the modern Western mode of production on the premise that it and the "modern apparatus of socialist planning are variant accommodations to the same need."

33. Soviet pricing policy prescribes "uniform national retail prices for basic manufactured goods" and "uniform zonal prices for the overwhelming proportion of foodstuffs" (Koval, 1972, 303). That pricing policy would obscure cost differentials of location and thus probably foster uneconomic location of new investments.

34. Franck and Quint 1947, Chap. 3.

35. Kornai 1980, 355, 360. In the Hungarian economic reform of 1968,

central price control was dropped on a great many products of the "construction and engineering industries." In 1985 the Chinese leadership dropped central price controls for a wide range of industrial products, though that policy may be subject to some modification since during the year the national price index rose by 9 percent.

36. In his classic 1917 *The State and Revolution,* Lenin spoke of the need "to convert the functions of public service into such simple operations of control and accounting as are within the reach of the vast majority of the population and ultimately of every single individual" (Lenin 1932, 65). Such was the utopian mood of the anticipatory days of the Revolution.

37. The Secretariat and Politbureau under Brezhnev met weekly but the general secretary and his assistant or deputy secretaries are in a continuous state of activity. The Politbureau functions informally between sessions since many of its members keep in close contract with each other. In contrast the Central Committee was convened only twice yearly (CPSU 1981, 90).

38. Trotsky 1937, 135–43. For a related analysis by Western Marxists see Sweezy 1980; Sweezy and Bettelheim 1971. These authors go beyond Trotsky and claim the ruling class function like a "state bourgeoisie."

39. Lane 1971, 63; Lane 1976, 99.

40. We reproduce here the array of decile ratios as compiled by Wiles (1974, 25), giving a capsule history of income stratification in the USSR for some forty-two years. The entries for 1972 and 1976 are extracted from an illuminating recent article by two Soviet economists, Rabkina and Rimashevskaia (1979, 40–58). The Soviet authors present a graph of decile coefficients from 1924 to 1976 and discuss the principal forces shaping the movement of the coefficient: rise in minimum wage rates, relative improvement in retirement and disability pensions, the distribution of skills in the labor force.

1928	3.84	1956	4.4	1968	2.7
1934	4.15	1964	3.7	1970	3.2
1946	7.24	1966	3.2	1972	3.10
				1976	3.35

41. A fellow Soviet expert has expressed a judgment that Wiles's characterization is "somewhat overdrawn" though it is widely recognized that income inequality since Stalin has been considerably scaled down by massive boosts in the lower wage scales and in building up kolkhoznik and pensioner incomes (U.S. Congress, Joint Economic Committee, *Compendium* 1976, 264, 624; ibid. 1973, 379).

42. Low subsidized cereal prices permitted bread and cereals to be used for cattle feed (Khrushchev 1956, 73). An attempt was made to prohibit this at least by urban workers with suburban plots (U.S. Congress, Joint Economic Committee, *Compendium* 1962, 113).

43. Bergson 1944, 27, 36, 207; Koval and Miroshnichenko 1972, 301; Bergson 1964.

44. U.S. Congress, Joint Committee, *Compendium* 1962, 235–68, especially 258, 273–303; ibid. 1973, 594–627.

45. Ibid. 1962, 289.

46. Lane 1976, 189. In 1970 some 4 percent of all admissions to institutions of higher learning were in this category. The fraction was much greater in the twenties and thirties (Bergson 1944, 109).

47. Tuition was imposed in 1940 and withdrawn in 1956 or thereabouts (Nove 1969, 346).

48. Lane's own data drawn from one province in the USSR shows that manual workers and collective farmers contribute in 1968 48 percent of enrollments at higher institutions of learning and a higher fraction at evening and correspondence courses. A similar fraction was found in Poland though for Hungary the fraction was less by half (Lane 1976, 186).

49. In speculating on the possibilities of a democratic evolution in the Soviet Union, Talcott Parsons (1971, 126) paid particular attention to the democratizing pressures arising from the Soviet development of mass education.

50. These are at any rate the reported social origins of party members though how "origin" is defined and measured is not indicated (Lane 1976, 99). As Shapiro (1964, 58) makes clear, "social composition is not easy to determine with certainty," especially when present occupation differs from social origin (Khrushchev 1961a, 156).

51. My information on social composition of party membership dates from 1956 to 1957 as published in Chinese in party documents associated with the Eighth National Congress of the CPC (Schurmann 1968, 132; Progress Publications 1975, 245). The much greater role now played by the urban population and urbanized working class and salariat must have influenced the social composition of the CPC but in ways we do not know. Soviet sources indicated that in the Cultural Revolution students and servicemen predominated in new enrollments but their judgments do not appear to be founded on reliable information. The Yugoslav Communist party in 1964 with a reported 1,030,041 members declared that 36.2 percent were workers, 7.9 percent farmers (League of Communists 1965, 320).

52. For this curious emphasis on the "making of revolution" and for Mao's doctrine of "permanent revolution," see Schram 1974, 94, 142, 243.

53. For these statistics of output and a detailed account of the catastrophe of Mao's "Great Leap Forward" see Xu Dixin et al. 1982, 59, 88, 153. For damage and decline in agriculture see the careful review of Eckstein 1968, 440, 624; U.S. Congress, Joint Economic Committee, *Compendium* 1967, 66; Schurmann 1968, 464, 474, 479. For Mao's own recognition of the catastrophic impact of his Leap Forward note his own recital of tonnage output advocated for steel in 1959 set first at 30 million tons at Peitaho, lowered to 20 million at Wuchang, and again in June 1959 to 13 million. The trouble, he alleged, was that coal and steel needed to be transported in vehicles and "this I did not foresee" (Schram 1974, 142; Mao Zedong 1977, 123). For cogent Soviet inspired criticism, see Krivtsov 1972, 150; Progress Publications 1975, 149.

54. See the documents collected in Robinson 1969, 85, 92.

55. "In essence, Mao's Cultural Revolution aims to go beyond the humbling of the existing bureaucratic and technocratic elite, and to extirpate the very roots of any stratification which might emerge in the future, by destroying respect for the special status of the Party member or the special knowledge of the expert" (Schram 1969, 109).

56. "[more] . . . a market economy with some anomalous features than . . . a planned economy with some decentralization" (Campbell 1974, 201) and "has more in common politically with Mexico than with Stalin's Russia" (Ward 1968, 571); "an unregenerate nineteenth century market economy" (U.S. Congress, Joint Committee, *Compendium* 1977, 247); "Yugoslav enterprises operate in a market economy similar to that of most Western countries" (Chase Manhattan Bank 1974, 37).

57. M. Djilas (1969, 220) contends that the idea of "self-management" was conceived in 1950 by him and Kardelj with "some help" from Kidric and

that Tito was persuaded later. The political and psychological pressures on Yugoslav leadership, arising from the Cominform – while they still were shut off by their Communist stance from obtaining assistance from the Western world, are described by Brzezinski (1967, 188). He is perhaps correct in postulating that "in large measure the changes in Yugoslav thinking were shaped by the political requirements of the unenviable international position of the Yugoslav regime."

58. On the biases of a "participatory economy" or of an economy made up to a significant degree of "labor-managed firms," see Horvat and Montias 1986; Vanek 1971, 8, 21, 25, 54. This labor-managed firm is substantially the "workers' cooperative" which I, somewhat prematurely, found a fading branch of the cooperative movement (Gottlieb 1984, 110). I had not then become aware of the flowering of interest in the industrial "workers' cooperative" that followed the writing of Vanek and earlier attempts to build up a general theory of the behavior of "labor-managed" firms. Very obviously this flowering is largely an outgrowth of the reshaping of the Yugoslav economy along worker cooperative lines and of an interesting growth of worker's cooperatives in Basque Spain. On this latter see Oakeshott 1982; Bradley and Gelb 1982, 153–72. A thoughtful evaluation of Yugoslav practice in the life of this newer self-management economic theory is found in Estrin (1983). I believe the conclusions I reached in 1984, especially for more advanced Western countries, are still sound but that the entire subject needs to be reworked in the light of Yugoslav experience for the effort to develop worker cooperation in economies that have already taken the socialist path.

59. Of 567 banks in 1960, 74 were left in 1968 and by 1971 the 22 largest banks did 98 percent of the banking business. See J. Dirlam, "Problem of Market Power and Public Policy in Yugoslavia," in Bornstein 1974, 215.

60. U.S. Congress, Joint Economic Committee, *Compendium,* 1977, 955.

61. Ibid., 945. Lane (1976, 151) reported that from 1953 to 1965 they paid only 30 percent.

62. U.S. Congress, Joint Economic Committee, *Compendium,* 1977, 497.

63. Ibid. 1974, 245.

64. Measured unemployment rose from 6.3 percent in 1964 to 11.3 percent in 1975 and industrial production had a marked cyclical decline between 1965 and 1967, and again in 1969, 1972, and 1975 (Gruchy 1977, 560).

65. The tendency of "worker self-management" to bias, use of investable funds, and retarding employment growth is laid out in a voluminous literature. Horvat and Montias (1986, 9–25) argue vigorously that the bias is negligible or is completely offset.

66. U.S. Congress, Joint Economic Committee, *Compendium* 1974, 242. One-fifth of the Yugoslav employed labor force worked in Western Europe in late 1971.

67. "The Yugoslav party has in fact become six parties each in control of a separate republic and the country is governed by continuing negotiation. . . ." Ibid., 464; see also Lane 1976, 144. No matter how splintered, the party cannot accept or fully restore apostate Djilas who declares the party will change all institutions "provided the new owners do not threaten the Communists' property monopoly of government" (M. Djilas 1969, 193). Brzezinski (1967, 313) concurs.

68. The "Decree on Land" together with Lenin's accompanying report are celebrated documents in Soviet history and have been frequently reproduced (see Lenin 1965, 52, and 1971, 2:425, 447).

69. The decree on land cited above specifically exempted from local land allocation by peasant committees "lands on which high level scientific farming is practiced" (orchards, plantations, seed plots, nurseries, hothouses or stud farms, stock breeding, and poultry farms). This and other provisions of land reform had been worked out from a comprehensive collection of mandates from local Soviets of Peasant Deputies, under the leadership of the Social Revolutionary party or its Left Wing. Only some 2–3 million acres were withheld from local land allocation, chiefly it seems sugar beet farms (Dobb 1956, 81). Withholding land for state farm or other purposes in Eastern Europe was far more extensive, especially in Czechoslovakia, Poland, Romania, and East Germany (Woytinsky 1953, 497).

70. Robinson 1932, Chap. 11; Trotsky 1932, 1:46; Lewin 1968, 86; Carr and Davies 1974, 137.

71. The turn to "Poor Peasant Committees" was especially associated with requisitioning grain and was one of the causes contributing to the breakup of the coalition with the Left Social Revolutionary party in 1918. See Lenin 1965, 59–77; 1971, 3:194.

72. Speaking with authority because he had access to immense amounts of information filtered through the Soviet government and because he had a keen eye for evaluating information or data relating to class differentiation, Lenin (1971, 3:570) declared on 15 May 1921 that "the kulak's position has been undermined and he has been in considerable measure expropriated, in Russia more than in the Ukraine and less in Siberia." See also Woytinsky 1953, 498; Chayanov 1966, 253.

73. The activity and scope of the village communities in the 1922–1928 period is authoritatively treated in Carr and Davies 1974, 121. Some 95 percent of peasant farmland was under mir authority in 1928 (Lewin 1968, 128, 131).

74. Mao 1961–1977, 2:323; 3:248; 4:235; 5:29.

75. These statistical findings are drawn from a survey by Chinese investigators of over 16,000 peasant households in twenty-five provinces in 1954 (Nolan 1976, 203 and Table 9). See also Cheng-yuan 1963, 28.

76. The Lenin NEP strategy was developed in a series of addresses, articles, notes, and legislative drafts commencing with his basic address on the tax in kind (to the Tenth Congress of the Russian Communist Party on 15 March 1921). The pamphlet, *The Tax in Kind,* written shortly thereafter, addresses to the Third and Fourth Congresses of the Communist International and addresses before the Eleventh Congress of the Russian Communist Party (March–April 1922). For the cited remarks on the "link" see Lenin 1971, 3:680. Recognition of the decisive importance of currency stabilization and termination of the currency inflation only came in 1922 (Lenin 1971, 3:721, 723). Also see Lenin 1970, 495, 539. For a rounded presentation that still misses many themes, see Bandera 1963.

77. On Lenin's enthusiastic support of GOELRO program of electrification and the need for central economic planning both before and after adoption of NEP, see Lenin 1971, 3:522, 555, 627, 744.

78. This NEP strategy was elucidated most carefully in Mao's pamphlets *On New Democracy* and *On Coalition Government* (Mao 1961–1977, 2:339; 3:205).

79. The statistical service in China, never of a high order, was only gradually reestablished after 1949 and measures of recovery of agricultural production from a prewar level, which goes back to 1933–1935, are apparently

very speculative. Hence judgments of recovery of agricultural production lack secure basis. Official Communist estimates claim an increase from 1949 to 1952 in agricultural output of some 50 percent (Eckstein 1968, 468). Our best Western students of Chinese national accounts put 1952 agricultural levels some 15 percent below 1933 (ibid., 76, 145). But that appears inconsistent with the known levels of popular feeding in China in 1933 and 1952 and the growth in population, which Eckstein believes was running at a rate between 0.5 percent to 1.0 percent per year (Eckstein 1977, 17).

80. Some 35 percent of Russian peasants were classified in 1929 as bednyaks and exempt on that account from all taxes because holding less than 2 dess. and no horse or cow (Lewin 1968, 30). As Chayanov calculated, such small farms could not afford to maintain a draft animal year around and feed both the cultivator and his family and the horse or ox (Chayanov 1966, 53). The phenomenon of impoverished horseless peasants, who must have supported themselves primarily from wage labor or craft work, was endemic in the countryside in prewar Russia. The fraction of Russian peasant horseless households was reported in the early 1890s as 27.3 percent; for 1893–1894, 31.9 percent; and for 1896–1900, 20.2 percent. See Lenin 1956, 137, 140.

81. This was the major conclusion in Lenin 1956, and in his later monograph (1930s, n.d., 11:139–217).

82. Mao 1961–1977, 1:26, 32, 87, 137; 2:323, 353. The way rich peasants were handled was found to be crucial for the development of stable workable "base areas."

83. The complexities of measuring differentiation in a dynamic rural world where households are continually being fissioned, augmented, and disintegrated or simply terminated by migration or accidental death is shown to the non-Russian reader by the fascinating work of Shanin (1972).

84. "The spontaneous force of capitalism has been steadily increasing in the countryside in recent years [1955] with new rich peasants springing up everywhere and many well-to-do peasants striving to become rich . . ." (Mao 1961–1977, 5:202).

85. The gist of the argument in 1925 of the brilliant oppositionist economist, Preobrazhensky (1965, 95, 106), is that by raising state taxes on agriculture or raising charges for transport services for shipping peasant grain and by other charges and fees on industrial products furnished by state industry to rural households that income can be deflected to state coffers thereby financing a kind of "primitive socialist accumulation." I must stress here the significance of the renunciation of the farm tax in kind enacted in 1921 scheduled for that year at 200 million poods but reduced because of famine. The tax was shifted to a money form with the stabilization of the currency and issuance of what was believed to be a strong (gold) currency. In later NEP years 1926–1928 the tax raised between 350 and 450 million rubles, between 6 and 7 percent of peasant current money income and payable in part out of cash incomes obtained from other sources (outside work, craft products). That permitted grain producers to pay moderate taxes and still withhold supplies and build up livestock herds (Carr and Davies 1974, 805, 1031). Campbell (1971, 71) contends that Soviet farm procurement prices in 1927–1928 made it advantageous to feed grain to livestock and withhold current grain sales as meat prices were more favorable than grain prices.

86. This general Marxian position was set forth with special clarity in an 1894 essay of F. Engels "The Peasant Question in France and Germany," Marx

and Engels 1845–1895/1971, 3:457–76; see also Lenin 1971, 3:209, 440.

87. J. Stalin with heavy-handed humor referred to a "slight misunderstanding" between the Soviet government and collective farm women "about the cow," which he promised would be permitted each collective farm household with their private plot (Stalin 1933, 20). The decrees establishing the rights to private plots, personal livestock holdings, and bazaar markets with free pricing (but all subject to taxation) were issued in 1931–1932 (Bienstock et al. 1944, 141).

88. Nolan 1976, 193. The activities of the mutual-aid teams and their manner of functioning is interestingly revealed by Myrdal 1965, 128, 145, 159, 183, 190, 377.

89. An illuminating monograph treats major developments affecting the private plot in the strategy of cooperativization. Walker (1965, Table 5) has collected reports showing the size of private plots, their food output, and fraction of household income generated by them (from 18.6 percent in northwestern China to 37.6 percent in southern China).

90. Perkins and Yusuf 1984, 39. The number of pigs in Chinese farms fell 18 percent in 1954 and 32.4 percent in 1955 under impact of cooperativization. Pig supply built up again in the calmer years 1956 and 1957 only to fall drastically under communalization (Walker 1965, 82).

91. This rightward shift of agricultural policy is variously described. Walker 1965, 86; U.S. Congress, Joint Committee, *Compendium*, 1967, 1:221; Schurmann 1968, 490.

92. Deng 1984, 297–99; Perkins and Yusuf 1984, 80–83; *Beijing Review*, 11 May 1987, 14–20; 3 Nov. 1986, 26–27; Blitzstein 1987, 4–6; Yak-Yeow 1984, 353–75. Apparently lease deliveries are mainly of cotton and grain and they involve a somewhat lower level of price than open market sales. Since lease contracts are executed at the outset of the crop year the purchase prices stipulated in them both for lease deliveries and for other deliveries serve as a price umbrella for the leasing peasant. With a good harvest, market price may fall lower than the contract price. There are two state marketing agencies. One is a network of all state-owned commercial departments under the Ministry of Commerce; the other a vast network of nominally cooperative supply and marketing organizations now employing some 4 million workers and with 500,000 purchasing and selling establishments. I say nominally cooperative since they have mostly operated as government agencies between 1978 and 1982. Further field research into farm markets and agricultural price determination in China is obviously needed.

93. The Code Napoleon abolished serfdom during the period of French control in the early 1800s. The czarist regime later in 1846 and again in 1863 carried through an agrarian reform intended to dispossess Polish aristocrats, and bestowed undisputed property to the landed peasant (Weber 1950, 108; Shanin 1971, 293; Thomas and Zanaiecki 1958, 1:161–62; 2:1273).

94. "Personally I think Gomulka was absolutely right to oppose collectivization" (Khrushchev 1974, 208). Polish Marxists of Western background like the famous economist Oscar Lange (1962, 18, 36, 47, 148) quietly held that a socialist regime could function comfortably with private farming. The Polish state kept up indirect pressure on Polish farmers by refusing to make farm equipment suitable for small farms like 1-cylinder garden tractors usable for row-strip cultivation. Hence Polish peasants had to keep their horses on which they apparently lavished much care (U.S. Congress, Joint Committee,

Compendium, 1974, 67, 192). Polish reform sentiment in 1979–1980 had minimal complaints to target against official policy in agriculture and requested chiefly more opportunity for peasant self-management in associations, cooperatives, and local government. Later, a concern developed for retirement pensions or some extension of social security to peasants. See S. Obidzinski's recent research papers in Polish journals on issues of rural social security.

95. U.S. Congress, Joint Committee, *Compendium,* 1977, 335, 294.

96. Some 250,000 were sent to villages during the first decade of collective farming, 1928–1938 (Bienstock 1944, 179). Returning to old tricks Khrushchev (1956, 64) in 1954–1955 sent out 20,000 Communists "from the town to country," all "recommended as collective farm chairmen" (see also Bergson 1964, 218).

97. "Under ordinary circumstances, as most of the cases in the Archive bear witness, the members of the Kolkhoz had little to say about the choice of their chairman and it was customary for the authorities to designate a candidate who was more or less automatically approved by the Kolkhoz meeting" (Fainsod 1963, 236). The Archive is the repository of Soviet documents captured by invading German troops in 1941 and later turned over to the American army. The report is invaluable.

98. Fainsod (1963, 273) reports that the "difficulty of finding reliable and efficient kolkhoz chairmen is emphasized over and over again in the Archive."

99. Khrushchev (1964, 88) took note that many who are sent out are "reluctant to go" and such a one simply "sits it out, waiting of the moment to slip back to his old job." Nonetheless, he favored sending out cadres to convert "economically weak collective and state farms. . . . We should naturally start the work of getting the laggard collective farms on their feet by selecting well-trained, efficient men who know their business and recommending them for the post of chairmen in these collective farms." As if pay were the critical shortcoming, he thought of offering special financial assistance for outside specialists. The Soviet leaders never reflected that perhaps the source of the trouble in their lagging agriculture was the urbanized cadres sent out to run farms (and farmers) without farming background, without experience in farm management, and without knowledge of local conditions.

100. "The acreage quotas for compulsory deliveries are permanent" declares a Soviet economic text on one page but notes on the next page of the "incorrect practice" of boosting quotas for the more "advanced collective farms" (Institute of Economics 1957, 652, 653). Many years later Brezhnev again declares that procurement quotas are fixed and "no one has the right to change them" (Sherman 1969).

101. Central Statistical Board 1979, 136; Makhov and Frish 1969, 125.

102. A wide disparity has been disclosed in Soviet collective farm incomes, some of them so high to be spoken of as Soviet millionaires. A distribution of collective farm incomes in rubles per 100 ha for 1960 shows that 2.5 percent of the farms had incomes under 1000 rubles, another 6.2 percent had incomes between 1000 to 2000 rubles, and the remainder run as follows (Bergson 1964, 199):

Rubles	Percentage
2,000– 3,000	10.2
3,000– 5,000	10.2
5,000–10,000	23.9
10,000–20,000	17.9
over 20,0000	4.7

For a similar spiral of earnings in Chinese collective farm teams and brigades after 1979, see Xu Dixin et al. 1982, 128. Much rural income frequently owes to disparities between regions (Perkins and Yusuf 1984, 108).

103. Collective farms are not charged formal land rents though rentals are implicit in schedules for zonally differentiated procurement prices. See Bergson 1964, 192; USSR, Academy of Sciences, Institute of Economics 1957, 655. Zonal pricing can only pick up the smaller part of rent from natural and acquired advantages (see Nove 1968, 250; U.S. Congress, Joint Committee, *Compendium* 1976, 42). A land cadastre is in process and perhaps may serve as the basis for a more thorough mode of determining rents and siphoning them off for public budgets (Mikhasiuk 1979, 65).

104. U.S. Congress, Joint Economic Committee, *Compendium*, 1976, 387.

105. On the concept of command economy see Grossman 1963, 101–23. Benjamin Ward (1967, 102, 161), who made this concept the basis of this book, distinguishes between a command society and a command economy.

106. On consumer goods rationing in the Soviet Union see Bergson 1964, 52. Food rationing prevailed between 1928 and 1935 and 1940 to 1947. The Chinese leadership preferred to ration short supplies rather than to raise prices (U.S. Congress, Joint Economic Committee, *Compendium*, 1967, 337).

107. On the buyer's market for many kinds of consumer goods that began to show up in the Soviet economy in the 1960s, see U.S. Congress, Joint Committee, *Compendium*, 1976, 632. Using inventory-sales ratios as a crude measure of consumer goods in short, normal, or excessive supply – the latter class making possible selective consumer buying – Bergson (1964, 64) found that about one-third of Soviet retail sales were in the latter category. In 1975 massive nationwide price cuts were made on shopworn, slow-moving inventories.

108. Between 1919 and 1928 private residential construction in meters of useful floor space was 15 percent greater than public construction (USSR, Central Statistical Board 1979, 184). The 1922 civil law code permitted private cooperative housing with limitations (Xiao Liang and Qi Mingchen 1986, 79).

109. Schwartz 1954, 459; Sosnovy 1954; U.S. Congress, Joint Economic Committee, *Compendium*, 1974, 329.

110. Soviet citizens in the postwar period were authorized by local government to form housing cooperatives to build apartment houses for occupancy by cooperative shareholders, paying 30–40 percent of construction costs down and paying the balance over a 10–20 year period. In 1966–1970 cooperative housing made up 7 percent of total nonfarm residential construction (U.S. Congress, Joint Committee, *Compendium*, 1973, 412, 426).

111. U.S. Congress, Joint Committee, *Compendium*, 1973, 412; USSR, Central Statistical Board 1959, 187. According to a Soviet economist now living in the United States (Katsenelinbogen 1978, 179), subleasing of apartments and of suburban cottages is a thriving business tolerated on the grounds that relations are involved though of a remote degree.

112. Xiao Liang and Qi Mingchen 1986, 83; Daniel 1985, 395. In Hungary privately owned housing, making 75 percent of the housing stock, may be bought and sold on the market apart from "a few administrative restraints" (Daniel 1985, 392).

113. Lenin 1971, 3:523. Of the many secondary accounts one of the best is by Deutscher 1965, 2:491.

114. U.S. Congress, Joint Economic Committee, *Compendium*, 1973, 48, 486, 725.

115. A Soviet research institute examined more than 1,000 plans of individual enterprises and discovered that in not one case did the supply plan agree with the financial plan. (U.S. Congress, Joint Economic Committee, *Compendium,* 1966, 27)

116. On the reform in investment analysis and pricing and along with it the desirability of profits as an incentive measure of effective management, see Campbell 1974, 173, 213; Liberman 1974; Bornstein 1974, 327; Nove 1968, 219, 241, 261.

117. The basic move was embodied in a comprehensive "Statute of the Socialist Industrial Enterprise" enacted Oct. 1965, Novosti Press Agency 1965, 152–75.

118. U.S. Congress, Joint Economic Committee, *Compendium,* 1974, 164, 172, 176, 198.

119. See the interesting presentation in Fedorenko 1974, 126.

120. This program of reform has been most comprehensively analyzed and persuasively stated with full awareness for its tendencies to liberalize or at least open up the political regime and widen the scope for enterprise self-determination and hence worker's influence on management by Polish economists, reflecting the influence of Oscar Lange who returned to Poland after World War II as a patriotic Polish socialist and distinguished Western economist. See besides Lange's works, Brus 1972, 1973. The opinion of Kushnirsky that rationing interfirm commodity distribution improves control of assets and minimizes "stealing" or commodity peculation is not obvious and appears a bit odd (Kushnirsky 1982, xvi, 45, 139). These arrangements introduce additional personnel involved with commodity distribution beyond what is needed at producing enterprises. The arrangements reduce the direct contacts of enterprise management with *users* of the product or service and direct knowledge about their needs, interests, and capacities.

Bibliography

In the following instances, the full title or designation is replaced in textual references or Endnotes by an abbreviation:

Century	C
Communist Party of the Soviet Union	CPSU
International Monetary Fund	IMF
Special Drawing Rights	SDR
National Bureau of Economic Research	NBER
Government Printing Office	GPO
Joint Committee on the Economic Report of the President	JEC
Mode of Production	MP
New Economic Policy	NEP

The date of publication cited in Endnotes or in the text following designation of author is generally a single date. Where two dates separated by a hyphen are specified, the dates mark the set of years for the publication of a multivolumed set. Where a slash appears between two dates or sets of dates, the first date or set records generally the year of initial publication in the first edition; the second date always records the year of publication of the edition cited in this work. In a few instances the first date or set of dates behind a slash correspond to the period of composition where initial publication was long delayed or was posthumous.

Abel, W. 1935/1980. *Agricultural Fluctuations in Europe: From the Thirteenth to the Twentieth Centuries.* Translated from 3d German edition. London: Methuen.

Abramovitz, M. 1968. "The Passing of the Kuznets Cycle." *Economica,* Nov.

_____. 1981. "Welfare Quandaries and Productivity Concerns." *American Economic Review,* Mar. (Presidential Address, AER, Sept. 1980).

_____. 1986. "Catching Up, Forging Ahead and Falling Behind." *Journal of Economic History* 56:385–406.

Afanasyev, F. 1974. *The Political Economy of Capitalism.* Moscow: Progress.

Almquist, Eric L. 1979. "Pre-Famine Ireland and the Theory of European Proto-Industrialization: Evidence from the 1841 Census." *Journal of Economic History,* vol. 39.

Altschul, E. 1938. Review of *Agrarkrisen und Stockungsspannen: Frage zur Lange Wellen,* by S. Ciriacy-Wantrup. *Journal of Farm Economics* May 519–22.

_____. 1939. "Agricultural Depression." Manuscript of study prepared for

351

NBER. Of five outlined chapters only fragments are available, about 100 typewritten pages dated variously in 1939.

Altschul, E., and F. Strauss. 1937. *Technical Progress and Agricultural Depression*. NBER Bull. 67, Nov.

Amin, Samir. 1976. *Unequal Development: An Essay on the Special Formations of Peripheral Capitalism*. New York: Monthly Review Press.

Anderson, B. L., J. E. Inikori, and D. Richardson. 1983. "Market Structure and Profits of the British African Trade in the Late Eighteenth Century" and "Rejoinder." *Journal of Economic History* 43:713–29.

Anderson, P. 1974a. *Passages from Antiquity to Feudalism*. London: Verso.

———. 1974b. *Lineages of the Absolutist State*. London: Verso.

Appleby, A. B. 1979. "Grain Prices and Subsistence Crises in England and France 1590–1740." *Journal of Economic History* 39:(Dec).

Arnal, O. L. 1980–1981. "Luther and the Peasants: A Lutheran Reassessment." *Science and Society* 44 (Winter):443–65.

Arzumanyan, A. 1966. *Crisis of World Capitalism*. Moscow: Progress.

Ascoli, D. 1979. *The Queen's Peace, Origin and Development of the Metro Police*. London: H. Hamilton.

Ashton, T. S. 1955a. *Economic Fluctuations in England 1700–1800*. Oxford: Oxford Univ. Press.

———. 1955b. *An Economic History of England: The Eighteenth Century*. London: Methuen.

Aston, T., ed. 1965. *Crisis in Europe 1560–1660*. New York: Basic Books.

Bacon, Francis. 1625/1903. *The Essays or Counsels Civil and Moral*. London: Methuen.

Bagehot, Walter. 1873. *Lombard Street*. London: J. Murray.

Bailey, A. M., and J. R. Llobera. 1981. *The Asiatic Mode of Production: Science and Politics*. London: Routledge and Kegan Paul.

Balazs, E. 1964. *Chinese Civilization and Bureaucracy: Variation on a Theme*. (Collected Papers.) New Haven: Yale Univ. Press.

Bandera, V. N. 1963. "The New Economic Policy (NEP) as an Economic System." *Journal of Political Economy* (June):265–79.

Barbash, Jack. 1968. "American Unionism: From Protest to Going Concerns." *Journal of Social Issues* 2:(Mar.).

Barger, Harold. 1960. "Income Originating in Trade, 1869–1929." In *Trends in the American Economy in the Nineteenth Century*. Vol. 24, *Studies in Income and Wealth*. New York: NBER.

Barkin, Solomon. 1969. "Trade Unions Face a New Western Capitalist Society." *Journal of Social Issues* 3:(Mar.).

Bateman, J. 1883/1970. *The Great Landowners of Great Britain and Ireland*. 4th ed. Reprint. New York: Kelly.

Bautier, Robert-Henri. 1971. *The Economic Development of Medieval Europe*. London: Harcourt Brace.

Bean, I. M. W. 1968. *The Decline of English Feudalism*. Manchester: Manchester Univ. Press.

Becker, Gary S. 1975. *Human Capital*. 2d ed. New York: NBER.

Bede. 731/1955. *A History of the English Church and People*. Harmondsworth: Penguin.

Beijing Review (formerly *Peking Review*). *A Chinese Weekly of News and Views*.

Bendix, R. 1956/1974. *Work and Authority in Industry: Ideologies of Management in the Course of Industrialization*. 2d ed. Berkeley: Univ. of California Press.

Benton, J. F. 1968. *Town Origins: The Evidence from Medieval England.* Lexington: Heath.

Bergson, Abram. 1944. *The Structure of Soviet Wages: A Study in Socialist Economics.* Cambridge: Harvard Univ. Press.

———. 1964. *The Economics of Soviet Economic Planning.* New Haven: Yale Univ. Press.

Berliner, J. S. 1976. *The Innovation Decision in Soviet Industry.* Cambridge: MIT Press.

———. 1984. "Income Inequality under Soviet Socialism." *Journal of Economic Literature* 22(Sept.):1052–99.

Berri, L. Y., ed. 1977. *Planning a Socialist Economy.* 2 vols. Moscow: Progress.

Best, G. 1979. *Mid-Victorian Britain, 1851–1870.* Glasgow: Fortana.

Bettleheim, C. 1976–1978. *Class Struggles in the USSR.* 2 vols. Vol. 1, *1917–1923.* Vol. 2, *1923–1930.* New York: Monthly Review Press.

Bienstock, G., S. M. Schwartz, and A. Yugow. 1944. *Management in Russian Industry and Agriculture.* Oxford: Oxford Univ. Press.

Black, R. D. C. 1960 *Economic Thought and the Irish Question, 1817–1870.* Cambridge: Cambridge Univ. Press.

Blitzstein, A. "Industrialization on Chinese and Israeli Collectives: Case Studies." 1987. Paper presented at Sixty-second Annual Conference of Western Economic Association 10 July 1987 at Vancouver, Canada.

Bloch, M. 1931/1966. *French Rural History: An Essay on Its Basic Characteristics.* Berkeley: Univ. of California Press.

———. 1939–1940/1961. 2 vols. *Feudal Society.* Chicago: Univ. of Chicago Press.

———. 1969. *Land and Work in Medieval Europe: A Collection of Essays.* Berkeley: Univ. of California Press.

Blum, J. 1961. *Lord and Peasant in Russia: From the Ninth to the Nineteenth Century.* Princeton: Princeton Univ. Press.

———. 1978. *The End of the Old Order in Rural Europe.* Princeton: Princeton Univ. Press.

Bois, Guy. 1984. *The Crisis of Feudalism: Economy and Society in Eastern Normandy, 1300–1550.* Cambridge: Cambridge Univ. Press.

Bolin, S. 1958. *State and Currency in the Roman Empire to 300 A.D.* Stockholm: Almquist and Wiksell.

Booth, Charles. 1886. "Occupations of the People of the United Kingdom, 1801–1881." *Journal of the Royal Statistical Society* 47(June):314–444.

———. 1902–1903. *Life and Labour of the People of London.* 17 vols. 3d ed. London: Macmillan.

Bornstein, B., ed. 1974. *Comparative Economic Systems: Models and Cases.* 3d ed. Homewood, Ill.: Irwin.

Bottigheimer, K. S. 1971. *English Money and Irish Land: The Adventurers in the Cromwellian Settlement of Ireland.* Oxford: Clarendon Press.

Boussard, J. 1969. *The Civilization of Charlemagne.* Harmondsworth: Penguin.

Bowley, Marion. 1945. *Housing and the State, 1919–1944.* London: Allen and Unwin.

Boxer, C. R. 1962. *The Golden Age of Brazil.* Berkeley: Univ. of California Press.

Boyd, Catherine. 1952. *Tithes and Parishes in Medieval Italy: The Historical Roots of a Modern Problem.* Ithaca: Cornell Univ. Press.

Bozan, J., S. Xunzheng, and H. Hua. 1981. *A Concise History of China.* 2d ed. Beijing: Foreign Language Press.

Bradley, K., and A. Gelb. 1982. "The Mondragon Cooperative: Guidelines for a Cooperative Economy." In *Participatory and Self-Managed Firms: Evaluating Economic Performance,* ed. D. Jones and J. Svejnar. Lexington: Heath.

Brady, Conor. 1974. *Guardians of the Peace.* Dublin: Gill and Macmillan.

Braudel, F. 1973. *The Mediterranean and the Mediterranean World in the Age of Phillip II.* 2 vols. New York: Harper and Row.

_____. 1982–1984. *Civilization and Capitalism: Fifteenth-Eighteenth Centuries.* 3 vols. Vol. 1, *The Structures of Everyday Life.* Vol. 2, *The Wheels of Commerce.* Vol. 3, *The Perspective of the World.* New York: Harper and Row.

Braudel, F., and E. Labrousse, eds. 1970–1977. *Histoire Économique et Sociale de la France, 1450–1789.* 2 vols. Paris: Presses Universitaires de France.

Braverman, H. 1974. *Labor and Monopoly Capital: The Degradation of Work in the Twentieth Century.* New York: Monthly Review Press.

Brems, Hans. 1970. "Sweden: From Great Power to Welfare State." *Journal of Economic Issues* 4:(June–Sept.).

Brenner, Robert, et al. 1976–1982. "Agrarian Class Structure and Economic Development in Preindustrial Europe." *Past and Present* 70(Feb. 1976):30–75; followed by commentaries in later issues by M. M. Postan and J. Hatcher, P. Croot and D. Parker, H. Wunder, E. Le Roy Ladurie, G. Bois, R. H. Hilton, J. Cooper, A. Klima, and followed by a reply article by R. Brenner, "The Agrarian Roots of European Capitalism" 97(1982):16–113.

Briffault, R. 1927. *The Mothers: A Study of the Origin of Sentiments and Institutions.* 3 vols. London: Allen and Unwin.

Broeker, Galen. 1970. *Rural Disorder and Police Reform in Ireland, 1812–1836.* London: Routledge and Kegan Paul.

Bronfrenbrenner, Martin, ed. 1969. *Is the Business Cycle Obsolete?* New York: Wiley.

Brucker, G. A. 1962. *Florentine Politics and Society, 1343–1378.* Princeton: Princeton Univ. Press.

Brunt, P. A. 1971. *Social Conflicts in the Roman Republic.* London: Chatto and Windus.

Brus, W. 1964/1972. *The Market in a Socialist Economy.* London: Routledge and Kegan Paul.

_____. 1973. *The Economics and Politics of Socialism: Collected Essays.* London: Routledge and Kegan Paul.

Brzezinski, Z. 1967. *The Soviet Bloc: Unity and Conflict.* 2d ed. Cambridge: Harvard Univ. Press.

Buchanan, B. J. 1986. "The Evolution of the English Turnpike Trusts: Lessons from a Case Study." *Economic History Review* 2d ser. 39:223–43.

Buck, J. L. 1937. *Land Utilization in China.* Chicago: Univ. of Chicago Press.

Budd, E. C., ed. 1967. *Inequality and Poverty.* New York: Norton.

Bukharin, N. 1917/1929. *Imperialism and World Economy.* New York: International Publishers.

Burckhardt, Jacob. 1860/1958. *The Civilization of the Renaissance in Italy.* 2 vols. New York: Harper.

Burke, Edmund. 1910. *The Works of Edmund Burke.* 5 vols. London: G. Bell.

Burn, W. L. 1951. *The British West Indies.* London: McGraw-Hill.

Burns, A. F. 1969. *The Business Cycle in a Changing World.* New York: NBER.

Bury, J. B. 1925/1958. *History of the Later Roman Empire: From the Death of*

Theodosius I to the Death of Justinian. 2 vols. New York: Dover.

Bury, J. B., et al., eds. 1929–1936. *The Cambridge Medieval History.* Vols. 5, 6. Cambridge: Cambridge Univ. Press.

Cairncross, Alexander K. 1953. *Home and Foreign Investment, 1870–1914.* Cambridge: Cambridge Univ. Press.

Cameron, R. E. 1956. "Some French Contributions to the Industrial Development of Germany, 1840–1870." *Journal of Economic History,* Vol. 16.

_____. 1961. *France and the Economic Development of Europe, 1800–1914.* Princeton: Princeton Univ. Press.

Campbell, Robert C. 1974. *The Soviet-Type Economies.* 3d ed. Boston: Houghton-Mifflin.

Carr, E. H., and R. W. Davies. 1974. *Foundations of a Planned Economy, 1926–1929.* Harmondsworth: Penguin.

Carr-Saunders, A. M., and P. A. Wilson. 1933. *The Professions.* Oxford: Clarendon Press.

Carus-Wilson, E. ed. 1954–1966. *Essays in Economic History.* 3 vols. London: St. Martin.

_____. 1967. *Medieval Merchant Venturers: Collected Studies.* 2d ed. London: Methuen.

Central Statistical Office, Ireland. 1978. *Statistical Abstract of Ireland, 1976.* Dublin: Stationery Office.

Chambers, J. D. 1957. "The Vale of Trent, 1670–1800." *Economic History Review,* suppl., no. 3. Cambridge: Cambridge Univ. Press.

Chang, Chung-Li. 1962. *The Income of the Chinese Gentry.* Seattle: Univ. of Washington Press.

Chart, D. A. 1920. *An Economic History of Ireland.* Dublin: Talbot.

Chase Manhattan Bank. 1974. *Yugoslavia: An Introduction to the Yugoslav Economy for Foreign Businessman.* New York: Chase Manhattan Bank, Oct.

Chayanov, A. V. 1925/1966. *The Theory of Peasant Economy.* Homewood, Ill.: Irwin.

Checkland, S. G. 1964. *The Rise of Industrial Society in England, 1815–1885.* New York: St. Martin.

Cheng Shih. 1974. *A Glance at China's Economy.* Peking: Foreign Language Press.

Cheng-Yuan. 1963. *Communist China's Economy, 1949–1962.* South Orange, N.J.: Seaton Hall Univ. Press.

Chien, Szuma. 93 B.C./1979. *Selections from Records of the Historian.* Beijing: Foreign Language Press.

China, People's Republic. 1973. *The Tenth National Congress of the Communist Party China.* Beijing: Foreign Language Press.

Chomsky, N. 1985. *Turning the Tide: U.S. Intervention in Central America and the Struggle for Peace.* Boston: South End Press.

Cipolla, C. M. 1965. *Guns, Sails and Empires: Technological Innovation and the Early Phases of European Expansion, 1400–1700.* New York: Funk and Wagnalls, Minerva Press.

_____, ed. 1972–1976. *The Fontana Economic History of Europe.* 6 vols. Vol. 1, *The Middle Ages.* Vol. 2, *The Sixteenth and Seventeenth Centuries.* Vol. 3, *The Industrial Revolution.* Vol. 4, *The Emergence of Industrial Societies.* Vol. 5, *The Twentieth Century.* Vol. 6, *Contemporary Economics.* Glasgow: Fontana Collins.

————. 1978. "Economic Fluctuations and Economic Policies in Italy XVI-XVII Centuries." In *Proceedings of the Seventh International Economic Congress,* ed. M. Flynn. Edinburgh: University Press.

————. 1980. *Before the Industrial Revolution: European Society and Economy, 1000–1750.* 2d ed. New York: Norton.

Clapham, J. H. 1926–1938. *An Economic History of Modern Britain.* 3 vols. Cambridge: Cambridge Univ. Press.

————. 1928. *The Economic Development of France and Germany, 1815–1914.* Cambridge: Cambridge Univ. Press.

Clapham, J. H., and E. Power, eds. 1941–1978. *Cambridge Economic History of Europe.* 7 vols. (Projected under their editorship through vol. 2 but with succeeding vols. published under different eds. the first vol. subtitled *From the Decline of the Roman Empire.* Cambridge: Cambridge Univ. Press).

Clark, Colin. 1967. *Population Growth and Land Use.* New York: Macmillan.

Clark, G. K. T. 1962. *The Making of Victorian England.* Cambridge: Harvard Univ. Press.

Cobbett, W. 1835/1947. *Legacy to Parsons.* London: Watts.

Cole, C. W. 1939. *Colbert and a Century of French Mercantilism.* 2 vols. New York: Columbia Univ. Press.

Coleman, D. C. 1977. *Economy of England, 1450–1750.* Oxford: Oxford Univ. Press.

Collins, W. F. 1922. *Mineral Enterprise in China.* Rev. ed. Tienstin: Tienstin Press.

Colm, Gerhard. 1955. *Essays in Public Finance and Fiscal Policy.* New York: Oxford Univ. Press.

Committee for Economic Development (CED). 1956. *Economic Policy for American Agriculture.* New York: CED.

————. 1959. *The European Common Market: Its Meaning to the United States.* New York: CED.

Commons, John R. 1924. *Legal Foundations of Capitalism.* Madison: Univ. of Wisconsin Press.

Commons, John R., and J. B. Andrews. 1916. *Principles of Labour Legislation.* 3d ed. New York: Harper.

Communist Party Soviet Union (CPSU) 1981. *Documents and Resolutions of the 26th Congress CPSU, Feb.–Mar., 1981.* Moscow: Novosti Press.

Comte, Auguste. 1830–1842/1896. 3 vols. *The Positive Philosophy.* Translated and edited by H. Martineau. London: G. Bell.

Connell, K. H. 1968. *Irish Peasant Society: Four Historical Essays.* Oxford: Clarendon Press.

Conrad, T. 1909. "Agrarkrisen." *Handwörterbuch der Staatswissenschaften.* 3d ed. 1:205–21.

Corwin, E. S. 1963. *The Constitution and What It Means Today.* 12th ed. Princeton: Princeton Univ. Press.

Costigan, G. 1969. *A History of Modern Ireland: With a Sketch of Earlier Times.* Indianapolis: Bobbs-Merrill.

Coulton, G. G. 1923–1950. *Five Centuries of Religion.* 4 vols. Cambridge: Cambridge Univ. Press.

————. 1926. *The Medieval Village.* Cambridge: Cambridge Univ. Press.

Crankshaw, F. 1959. *Khrushchev's Russia.* Harmondsworth: Penguin.

Crosland, A. 1974. *Socialism Now and Other Essays.* London: J. Cape.

Curtin, P. 1969. *The Atlantic Slave Trade: A Census.* Madison: Univ. of Wisconsin Press.

_____. 1984. *Cross-Cultural Trade in World History.* Cambridge: Cambridge Univ. Press.

Daggett, Stuart. 1955. *Principles of Inland Transportation.* 4th ed. New York: Harper.

Daniel, Z. 1985. "The Effect of Housing Allocation on Social Inequality in Hungary." *Journal of Comparative Economics* 9(Dec.):391–410.

Davis, David B. 1970. *The Problem of Slavery in Western Culture.* Harmondsworth: Penguin.

Davis, Dorothy. 1966. *Fairs, Shops and Supermarkets.* Toronto: Univ. of Toronto Press.

Deane, P., and W. A. Cole. 1962. *British Economic Growth, 1688–1959: Trends and Structure.* Cambridge: Cambridge Univ. Press.

De Foe, Daniel. 1724–1726/1928. *A Tour Through England and Wales.* 2 vols. London: Everyman.

De Gaulle, Gen. Charles. 1964. *Major Addresses, Statements and Press Conferences, May 1958–Jan. 31, 1964.* New York: French Embassy.

Deng Xiaoping. 1975–1982/1984. *Selected Works.* Beijing: Foreign Language Press.

De Roover, Raymond. 1948. *Money, Banking and Credit in Medieval Bruges. Italian Merchant Bankers, Lombards and Money-Changers: A Study in the Origins of Banking.* Cambridge: Medieval Academy of America.

_____. 1966. *The Rise and Decline of the Medici Bank, 1397–1494.* New York: Norton.

Derthick, M. 1979. *Policymaking for Social Security.* Washington, D.C.: Brookings.

Deutscher, I. 1965. *The Prophet Armed: Trotsky.* Vol. 1, *1897–1921.* New York: Random House.

De Vries, T. 1976. *Economy of Europe in an Age of Crisis, 1600–1750.* Cambridge: Cambridge Univ. Press.

Djilas, M. 1969. *The Unperfect Society: Beyond the New Class.* New York: Harcourt-Brace.

Dobb, M. 1947/1963. *Studies in the Development of Capitalism.* Rev. ed. New York: International Publishers.

_____. 1956. *Soviet Economic Development Since 1917.* New York: International Publishers.

Douglas, Paul. 1936. *Social Security in the United States.* New York: Whittlesey.

Downs, N., ed. 1959 *Basic Documents in Medieval History.* Princeton: Van Nostrand.

Driver, G. R., and J. C. Miles. 1904–1923/1952. *The Babylonian Laws.* Vol. 1, *Legal Commentary.* Oxford: Oxford Univ. Press.

Duby, G. 1968. *Rural Economy and Country Life in the Medieval West.* New York: Columbia Univ. Press.

_____. 1974. *The Early Growth of the European Economy: Warriors and Peasants from the Seventh to the Twelfth Century.* Ithaca: Cornell Univ. Press.

Dudley, D. R. 1960. *The Civilization of Rome.* New York: New American Library.

Due, John. 1959. *Government Finance.* Rev. ed. Homewood, Ill.: Irwin.

Duesenberry, J. S., et al. 1965. *The Brookings Quarterly Model of the United States Economy.* Chicago: Rand McNally.

Dyos, H. J. 1961. *Suburb: A Study of the Growth of Camberwell.* Leicester: Leicester Univ. Press.

Eberhard, Wolfram. 1977. *A History of China.* 4th ed. Berkeley: Univ. of California Press.

Eckstein, A. 1977. *China's Economic Revolution.* Cambridge: Cambridge Univ. Press.

———, ed. 1968. *Economic Trends in Communist China.* Chicago: Aldine.

———, ed. 1973. *Comparison of Economic Systems: Theoretical and Methodological Approaches.* Berkeley: Univ. of California Press.

Eggertsson, T. 1986. Review. Gottlieb, *Theory of Economic Systems, Journal of Economic Literature* 24(Mar.):95–97.

Ehrenberg, R. 1896. *Das Zeitalter der Fugger.* 2 vols. Stuttgart: G. Fischer.

Eliot, J. 1977. *Comparative Economic Systems.* 2d ed. Englewood Cliffs, N.J.: Prentice-Hall.

Ellis, P. B. 1975. *Hell or Connaught! The Cromwellian Colonisation of Ireland, 1652–1660.* New York: St. Martin's Press.

Elvin, M. 1973. *The Pattern of the Chinese Past: A Social and Economic Interpretation.* Stanford: Stanford Univ. Press.

Elvin, M., ed. 1980. "Symposium on Joseph Needham," *Science and Civilization in China* [relating to scientific philosophy, mathematics, and astronomy]. *Past and Present* 87:19–53.

Emanuel, D. 1981. "The Growth of Speculative Building in Greece: Modes of Housing Production and Socio-Economic Change, 1950–1974." Ph.D. diss., London School of Economics.

Emerson, Ralph W. 1856/1940. *English Traits.* In *The Complete Essays and Other Writings of Ralph Waldo Emerson.* New York: Modern Library.

Encyclopedia of Social Sciences (ESS). 1930–1934. 15 vols. E. R. A. Seligman et al. New York: Macmillan.

Engels, Frederick. 1850/1926. *Peasant War in Germany.* New York: International Publishers.

———. [1877–1878]. n.d. *Anti-Dühring: Herr Dühring's Revolution in Science.* New York: International Publishers.

———. 1884/1978. *Origin of the Early Family, Private Property, and the State in Connection with the Researches of Lewis H. Morgan.* Peking: Foreign Language Press.

Engerman, S. L. 1983. "Contract Labor, Sugar and Technology in the Nineteenth Century." *Journal of Economic History* 43(Sept.): 635–59.

Ernle, Lord. 1912/1961. *English Farming Past and Present.* 6th ed. London: Heinemann.

Esson, D. M. R. 1971. *The Curse of Cromwell: A History of the Ironside Conquest of Ireland, 1649–1653.* London: Leo Cooper.

Estrin, S. 1983. *Self-Management Economic Theory and Yugoslav Practice.* Cambridge: Cambridge University Press.

Evans, E. J. 1976. *The Contentious Tithe: The Tithe Problem and English Agriculture, 1750–1850.* London: Routledge and Kegan Paul.

Evans, Michael K. 1969. *Macroeconomic Activity: Theory, Forecasting and Control.* New York: Harper and Row.

Experience and Future Group. 1981 *Poland Today: The State of the Republic.*

Translated from Polish and edited by J. Bielasiak. White Plains, N.Y.: Sharpe.

Fainsod, Merle, 1963. *Smolensk under Soviet Rule.* New York: Random House.

Fairley, J. 1980. "French Developments in the Theory of State Monopoly Capital." *Science and Society,* vol. 44 (Fall).

Fanfani, Amitore. 1935. *The Origin of the Capitalist Spirit in Italy.* London: Sheed and Ward.

Fanon, Fritz. 1967. *The Wretched of the Earth.* Harmondsworth: Penguin.

Farioletti, M. 1952. "Some Results of the First Year's Audit Control Program of the Bureau of Internal Revenue." *National Tax Journal* (Mar.).

Fedorenko, N. P. 1974. *Optimal Functioning for a Socialist Economy.* Moscow: Progress.

Fei, Hsiao-Tung. 1939. *Peasant Life in China: A Field Study of Country Life in the Yangtze Valley.* New York: Dutton.

———. 1953. *China's Gentry: Essays in Rural-Urban Relations.* Translated, revised, and edited by M. P. Redfield. Chicago: Univ. of Chicago Press.

Felix, D. 1956. "Profit Inflation and Industrial Growth: The Historic Record and Contemporary Analogies." *Quarterly Journal of Economics* 70:441–63.

Fellner, W. 1956. *Trends and Cycles in Economic Activity: An Introduction to Problems of Economic Growth.* New York: Holt.

Finlay, R., and A. Sharin. 1981. "Debate: Natural Decrease in Early Modern Cities." *Past and Present* 92(Aug.):168–80.

Finley, M. I. 1973. *Ancient Economy.* Berkeley: Univ. of California Press.

Fitzgerald, C. P. 1942. *China: A Short Cultural History.* London: Quaker City.

Flinn, M., ed. 1978. *Proceedings of the Seventh International Economic History Congress.* Edinburgh: Edinburgh Univ. Press.

Foreign Language Press, ed. 1974. *China: A Geographical Sketch.* Beijing: Foreign Language Press.

Franck, P. G., and M. Quint., eds. 1947. *Problems in Price Control: Pricing Techniques.* Office of Temporary Controls, OPA, Historical Reports on War Administration. Washington, D.C.: GPO.

Frankel, M. 1962. "The Production Function in Allocation and Growth: A Synthesis." *American Economic Review* 52(Dec.):995–1021.

Frêche, G. 1974. *Toulouse et la Region Midi-Pyrénées au Siecle des Lumieres (vers 1670–1789).* Paris: Centre National de la Recherche Scientifique.

Freeman, S. D. 1974. *Energy: The New Era.* New York: Random House.

French Embassy, Press and Information Division. 1979. *France's Position on the Common Agricultural Policy of the European Community.* Washington, D.C.: French Embassy.

———. 1980. *Social Security and National Health Insurance in France.* Washington, D.C.: French Embassy.

Friedman, Milton. 1957. *A Theory of the Consumption Function.* New York: NBER.

———. 1968. *Dollars and Deficits.* Englewood Cliffs, N.J.: Prentice-Hall.

Friedman, Milton, and A. S. Schwartz. 1963. *A Monetary History of the United States.* New York: NBER.

Friedman, Milton, and Simon Kuznets. 1954. *Income from Independent Practice.* New York: NBER.

Furubotn, E. G., and S. Pejovich. 1973. "Property Rights, Economic Decentralization and Evolution of the Jugoslav Firms." *Journal of Law and Economics* (Oct.).

Galbraith, K. 1972. *The New Industrial State.* 2d ed. Boston: Houghton-Miflin.

Gardner, B. B., and D. G. Moore. 1952. *Human Relations in Industry.* Homewood, Ill.: Irwin.

Garvey, G. 1935. "Kondratieff's Theory of Long Cycles." *Review of Economics and Statistics* (Nov.):104–25.

Gates, P. W. *The Farmers Age: Agriculture, 1815–1860.* 1960. New York: Harper and Row.

Gayer, A. D., W. W. Rostow, and A. S. Schwartz. 1953. *The Growth and Fluctuation of the British Economy, 1790–1850.* 2 vols. Oxford: Oxford Univ. Press.

Geertz, C. 1973. *The Interpretation of Cultures: Selected Essays.* New York: Basic Books.

Gehman, H. S., ed. 1970. *The Westminster Dictionary of the Bible.* Philadelphia: Westminster Press.

Genovese, E. D., and E. Fox-Genovese. 1983. *Fruits of Merchant Capital: Slavery and Bourgeois Property in the Rise and Expansion of Capitalism.* Oxford: Oxford Univ. Press.

Georgescu-Roegen, N. 1976. *Energy and Economic Myths, Institutional and Analytical Economic Essays.* New York: Pergamon.

Gerschenkron, A. 1952. *Economic Backwardness in Historical Perspective.* Cambridge: Harvard Univ. Press.

Gibbon, Edward. 1776–1788/1932. *The Decline and Fall of the Roman Empire.* 3 vols. New York: Modern Library.

Gilfillan, S. C. 1964. *Invention and the Patent System.* (A study originally prepared for the U.S. Senate, Judiciary Committee, and reproduced by the Joint Economic Committee, U.S. Congress, Committee Print.) Washington, D.C.: GPO.

Gilmore, H. W. 1953. *Transportation and the Growth of Cities.* Glencoe: Free Press.

Gimpel, J. 1977. *The Medieval Machine: The Industrial Revolution of the Middle Ages.* Harmondsworth: Penguin.

Golas, P. F. 1980. "Rural China in the Song." *Journal of Asian Studies* 39(Feb.).

Goldsmith, Raymond W. 1979. *Financial Structure and Development.* New Haven: Yale Univ. Press.

Goode, Richard, 1951. *The Corporate Income Tax.* New York: Wiley.

Goodrich, L. C. 1969. *A Short History of the Chinese People.* 4th ed. New York: Harper and Row.

Gosplan USSR [Presidium of the State Planning Commission]. 1929. *The Soviet Union Looks Ahead: The Five-Year Plan for Economic Construction.* New York: Horace Liveright.

Gottlieb, Manuel. 1953. "The Capital Levy and Deadweight Debt in England, 1815–1840," *Journal of Finance* 8(Mar.):34–46.

———. 1957. "Stability Characteristics of World Trading Systems." *Economia Internazionale* 10:(Nov.):3–13.

———. 1958. "On Reform of the Capital Gains Tax." *Public Finance,* 13:338–50.

———. 1960. *The German Peace Settlement and the Berlin Crisis.* New York: Paine-Whitman.

———. 1972. "Pluralistic or Unitary Economic Systems." *African Review* 1(Apr.):77–92.

_____. 1976. *Long Swings in Urban Development.* New York: NBER.

_____. 1984. *A Theory of Economic Systems.* New York: Academic Press.

Goubert, P. 1986. *The French Peasantry in the Seventeenth Century.* Cambridge: Cambridge Univ. Press.

Gould, J. D. 1962. "Agricultural Fluctuations and the English Economy in the Eighteenth Century." *Journal of Economic History,* vol. 22.

Goy, J., and E. Le Roy Ladurie, eds. 1972. *Les Fluctuations du Produit de la Dîme. Conjuncture décimale et domaniale de la fin du Moyen Age au XVIII siecles.* Paris: Mouton.

_____. 1982. *Prestations Paysannes dîmes, rent fonciere et mouvement de la production agricole a l'epoche preindustrielle.* 2 vols. Paris: L'école des hautes Études en Science Sociales.

Great Britain, Committee on Industry and Trade. 1927. *Factors in Industrial and Commercial Efficiency.* London: His Majesty's Stationery Office.

Grebler, Leo, et al. 1956. *Capital Formation in Residential Real Estate: Trends and Prospects.* New York: NBER.

Gregory of Tours. 1974. *The History of the Franks.* Harmondsworth: Penguin.

Grossman, G. 1963. "Notes of a Theory of a Command Economy." *Soviet Studies* (Oct.).

Groves, Harold. 1958. "Empirical Studies of Income Tax Compliance." *National Tax Journal* (Dec.).

Gruchy, A. C. 1977. *Comparative Economic Systems.* 2d ed. Boston: Houghton Miflin.

Hajnal, J. 1965. "European Patterns in Perspective." In *Population in History,* ed. D. V. Glass and D. E. Eversley, 101–48. Chicago: Aldine.

Halévy, Élie. 1912/1937. *A History of the English People in 1815.* Vol. I. Harmondsworth: Penguin.

_____. 1912–1934/1951. *A History of the English People in the Nineteenth Century.* Vols. 2–6. 2d ed. rev. New York: Harcourt-Brace.

Hamilton, Earl J. 1934. *American Treasure and the Price Revolution in Spain.* Cambridge: Harvard Univ. Press.

_____. 1947. *War and Prices in Spain, 1651–1800.* Cambridge: Harvard Univ. Press.

_____. 1967. "John Law of Lavriston: Banker, Gamester, Merchant, Thief?" *American Economic Review Proceedings* (May).

Hamilton, Walton. 1940. *The Pattern of Competition.* New York: Columbia Univ. Press.

Hamilton, Walton, and I. Hill. 1940. *Anti-Trust in Action.* TNEC Monograph 16. Washington, D.C.: GPO.

Hammond, John L. and Barbara Hammond. 1920. *The Village Laborer, 1760–1832.* 2d ed. London: Longman Green.

_____. 1947. *The Bleak Age.* Rev. ed. Harmondsworth: Penguin.

Hansen, Alvin. 1951. *Business Cycles and National Income.* New York: Norton.

Harrington, Michael. 1976. *The Twilight of Capitalism.* New York: Simon and Schuster.

Harriss, G. L. 1975. *King, Parliament and Public Finance in Medieval England to 1369.* Oxford: Oxford Univ. Press.

Haskins, C. H. 1923/1957. *The Rise of Universities.* Ithaca: Cornell Univ. Press.

Hawkes, J. 1973. *The First Great Civilizations.* New York: Knopf.

Hay, D., ed. 1961. *The Renaissance, 1493–1520.* Vol. 1 of *The New Cambridge*

Modern History. Cambridge: Cambridge Univ. Press.

Heady, Earl O. 1962. *Agricultural Policy Under Economic Development.* Ames: Iowa State Univ. Press.

Heckscher, E. F. 1935/1955. *Mercantilism.* 2 vols. London: G. Allen and Unwin. Reprint, revised, with new materials.

Herlihy, D., et al., eds, 1969. *Economy, Society and Government in Medieval Italy.* Kent: Kent State Univ. Press.

_____. 1970. *History of Feudalism.* New York: Walker.

_____. 1978. *The Social History of Italy and Western Europe, 700–1500: Collected Studies.* London: Variorum Reprints.

Hidy, Ralph W., and M. F. Hidy. 1955. *Pioneering in Big Business, 1882–1916: History of Standard Oil Company of New Jersey.* 2 vols. New York: Harper and Row.

Hill, C. 1956. *Economic Problems of the Church: From Archbishop Whitgift to Long Parliament.* Oxford: Clarendon Press.

Hillerbrand, H. J., ed. 1968. *The Protestant Reformation.* New York: Harper and Row.

Hilton, R. H., ed. 1976. *The Transition from Feudalism to Capitalism.* Norfolk: Left Book.

Hobbes, T. [1651]/1914. *Leviathan.* London: Everyman.

Hobsbawm, E. J. 1960. "The General Crisis of the Seventeenth Century." *Science and Society* 24(Spring).

_____. 1979. *The Age of Capital, 1848–1875.* New York: New American Library.

Hoffman, P. 1986. "Taxes and Agrarian Lands in Early Modern France: Land Sales, 1550–1730." *Journal of Economic History* 46(Mar.).

Holland, D. M. 1962. *Dividends Under the Income Tax.* New York: NBER.

Homans, George C. 1941/1975. *English Villagers of the Thirteenth Century.* New York: Norton.

Hope-Jones, Arthur. 1939. *Income Tax in the Napoleonic Wars.* Cambridge: Cambridge Univ. Press.

Hopkins, A. G. 1973. *An Economic History of West Africa.* New York: Columbia Univ. Press.

Horvat, B. 1976. *The Yugoslav Economic System: The First Labor-Managed Economy in the Making.* White Plains, N.Y.: IASP.

Horvat, B., and J. M. Montias, ed. 1986. "Colloquium on Participatory Economics and Politics," a special issue of *Journal of Comparative Economics* 10 (Mar.):1–88.

Houston, Rab. 1982. "The Literacy Myth: Illiteracy in Scotland, 1630–1760." *Past and Present* 96(Aug.):81–103.

Howard, George. 1953. *Guardians of the Queen's Peace.* London: Adams Press.

Hsiao, Kung-Chuan. 1960. *Rural China: Imperial Control in the Nineteenth Century.* Seattle: Univ. of Washington Press.

Hsiao, L. 1975. "Reflections on the 'Discourses on the State Control of Salt and Iron.'" In *Selected Articles Criticizing Lin Piao and Confucius.* Beijing: Foreign Language Press, 115–41.

Hume, David. 1955. *Writings on Economics.* Edited by E. Rotwein. Madison: Univ. of Wisconsin Press.

Huntington, Samuel P. 1968. *Political Order in Changing Societies.* New Haven: Yale Univ. Press.

Ibn Khaldun. 1377/1968. *The Muqaddimah: An Introduction to History.*

Abridged. Princeton: Princeton Univ. Press.

International Monetary Fund (IMF). *Annual Report of the Executive Directors.* Washington, D.C.: IMF (appearing since 1947).

Jackson, T. A. 1970. *Ireland Her Own: An Outline History of the Irish Struggle for National Freedom and Independence.* Rev. ed. New York: International Publishers.

Japan. Office of the Prime Minister. 1972. *Statistical Handbook of Japan, 1972.* Tokyo: Japanese Statistical Association.

Jensen, J. J. 1931. *Property Taxation in the United States.* Chicago: Univ. of Chicago Press.

Johr, W. A. 1952. *Die Konjunkturschwankungen.* Tübingen: Mohr.

Jolowicz, H. F., and B. Nichols. 1932/1972. *Historical Introduction to the Study of Roman Law.* 3d ed. Cambridge: Cambridge Univ. Press.

Jones, A. H. M. 1966. *The Later Roman Empire: 284–602. A Social, Economic and Administrative Survey.* 2 vols. Norman: Univ. of Oklahoma Press.

———. 1974. *The Roman Economy: Studies in Ancient Economic and Administrative History.* Totowa, N.J.: Rowman and Littlefield.

Jones, D. C., and J. Svejnar. 1982. *Participatory and Self-Managed Firms: Evaluating Economic Performance.* Lexington: Heath.

Juglar, Clement. 1862/1916. *Brief History of Panics and Their Periodical Occurrence in the United States.* Partial translation of 2d 1889 ed. New York: Putnam.

Kaldor, N. 1955. *An Expenditure Tax.* London: Allen and Unwin.

Katsenelinbogen, Aaron. 1978. *Studies in Soviet Economic Planning.* White Plains, N.Y.: Sharpe.

Keynes, J. M. 1930. *Treatise on Money.* 2 vols. London: Macmillan.

———. 1931. *Essays in Persuasion.* London: Rupert Hart-Davis.

———. 1933. "Open Letter" (to President Roosevelt). *New York Times,* 31 Dec.

———. 1936. *General Theory of Employment Interest and Money.* New York: Harcourt-Brace.

———. 1938. "The Policy of Government Storage of Foodstuffs and Raw Materials." *Economic Journal* (Sept.).

Khrushchev. N. S. 1956. *Report of the Central Committee to the Twentieth Congress of the CPSU.* Moscow: Foreign Language Publications.

———. 1961a. *Report on the Program of the CPSU.* (Twenty-second Congress of the CPSU, Oct., 1961, authorized translations.) New York: Crosscurrents Press.

———. 1961b. *Report of the Central Committee to the Twenty-Second Congress.* New York: Crosscurrents Press.

———. 1964 *Boosting the Chemical Industry for Economic Progress and Prosperity. Report and Concluding Speech to a Plenary Session of the CC, CPSU.* Moscow: Progress.

———. 1974. *Khrushchev Remembers: The Last Testament.* Boston: Little Brown.

Kindelberger, C. P. 1973. *The World in Depression 1929–1939.* Berkeley: Univ. of California Press.

———. 1978. *Manias, Panics and Crashes: A History of Financial Crises.* New York: Harper and Row.

Klein, Philip. 1973. *The Management of Market-Oriented Economies: Comparative Perspective.* Belmont: Wadsworth.

Knox, John. 1982. *The History of the Reformation within the Realm of Scotland, 1559–1571.* (Selections) Edinburgh: Banner Truth Trust.

Kolb, A. 1963/1971. *East Asia: China, Japan, Korea, Viet Nam. Geography of a Cultural Region.* London: Methuen.

Kondratieff, N. 1935. "The Long Waves in Economic Life." *Review of Economics and Statistics* (Nov).

Kornai, J. 1980. *Economics of Shortage.* 2 vols. Amsterdam: North-Holland.

Koval, N., and B. Miroshnichenko. 1972. *Fundamentals of Soviet Planning.* Moscow: Novosti Press Agency.

Krader, L. 1975. *The Asiatic Modes of Production: Source, Development and Critique in the Writings of Karl Marx.* Assen: Van Gorcum.

Krivtsov, V. A. et al. 1972. *A Critique of Mao Tse Tung's Theoretical Conceptions.* Moscow: Progress.

Krivtsov, V. A. et al., eds. 1972. *Maoism Unmasked: Collection of Soviet Press Articles.* Moscow: Progress.

Kushnirsky, F. I. 1982. *Soviet Economic Planning, 1965–1980.* Boulder, Colo.: Westview Press.

Kuznets, Simon. 1966. *Modern Economic Growth: Rate, Structure, and Spread.* New Haven: Yale Univ. Press.

Ladejinsky, W. 1977. *Agrarian Reform as Unfinished Business: Selected Papers.* Edited by L. J. Walinsky. Washington, D.C.: World Bank.

Landes, D. 1969. *The Unbound Prometheus: Technological Change and Industrial Development in Western Europe from 1750 to the Present.* Cambridge: Cambridge Univ. Press.

Lane, David. 1971. *The End of Inequality: Stratification under State Socialism.* Harmondsworth: Penguin.

———. 1976. *The Socialist Industrial State: Toward a Political Sociology of State Socialism.* London: Allen and Unwin.

Lane, F. C. 1966. *Venice and History: Collected Papers of Frederick C. Lane.* Baltimore: Johns Hopkins Univ. Press.

———. 1973. *Venice: A Maritime Republic.* Baltimore: Johns Hopkins Univ. Press.

Lane, F. C., ed. 1953. *Enterprise and Secular Change: Readings in Economic History.* Philadelphia: Blakiston.

Lange, Oscar. 1959. *Introduction to Econometrics.* London: Pergamon Press.

Lange, Oscar, ed. 1962. *Problems of Political Economy of Socialism.* Delhi: Peoples.

Larsen, M. R. 1967. "China's Agriculture under Communism." In *An Economic Profile of Mainland China.* Studies prepared for the Joint Economic Committee of the Congress. Washington, D.C.: GPO, Feb.

Latourette, K. S. 1953. *A History of Christianity.* New York: Harper and Row.

Lattimore, O. 1940. *Inner Asian Frontiers of China.* American Geographical Society Research Series 21. New York: Oxford Univ. Press.

———. 1949. *The Situation in Asia.* Boston: Little, Brown.

League of Communists of Jugoslavia [Communist Party]. 1965. *Practice and Theory of Socialist Development in Jugoslavia.* 8th Congress. Beograd: Medunarodna Politika.

Lefebvre, G. 1967. *The Coming of the French Revolution, 1789.* Princeton: Princeton Univ. Press.

LeGoff, T. J. A., and D. M. G. Sutherland. 1983. "The Social Origins of Counter-Revolution in Western France." *Past and Present* 99(May):65–87.

Lenin, V. I. 1917/1932. *The State and Revolution: The Marxist Theory of the State and the Tasks of the Proletariat in the Revolution.* New York: International Publishers.

————. 1930s (n.d.). *Selected Works* [earlier ed.]. 12 vols. New York: International Publishers.

————. 1899/1956. *Development of Capitalism in Russia.* Translated from 2d Russian edition. Moscow: Foreign Language Publications.

————. 1917/1965. *Imperialism: The Highest State of Capitalism. A Popular Outline.* Peking: Foreign Language Press.

————. 1917–1922/1965. *The Land Questions and the Fight for Freedom: Articles and Speeches.* Moscow: Progress.

————.1920–1923/1970. *Collected Works.* Vol. 43. Moscow: Foreign Language Publications.

————. 1971. *Selected Works* [later ed.] 3 vols. Moscow: Progress.

Le Roy Ladurie, E. 1971. *Times of Feast, Times of Famine: A History of Climate since the Year 1000.* New York: Doubleday.

————. 1966/1974. *The Peasants of Languedoc.* Urbana: Univ. of Illinois Press.

————. 1979a. *The Territory of the Historian.* (Collected Papers.) Sussex: Harvester Press.

————. 1979b. *Carnival in Romans.* New York: Braziller.

————. 1979c. *Montai llou.* New York: Vintage.

————. 1981. *The Mind and Method of the Historian.* (Collected Papers.) Brighton: Harvester Press.

Ladurie, Le Roy, and J. Goy. 1982. *Tithe and Agrarian History from the Fourteenth to the Nineteenth Centuries: An Essay in Comparative History.* Cambridge: Cambridge Univ. Press.

Lewin, M. 1968. *Russian Peasants and Soviet Power.* London: Allen and Unwin.

Lewis, B., ed. 1974. *Islam from the Prophet Muhammed to the Capture of Constantinople.* New York: Harper and Row.

Lewis, J. P. 1965. *Building Cycles and Britain's Growth.* New York: Macmillan.

Leys, Colin. 1974. *Underdevelopment in Kenya: The Political Economy of Neo-Colonialism.* Berkeley: Univ. of California Press.

Liberman, F. G. 1973. *Economic Methods and the Effectiveness of Production.* New York: Doubleday.

Liu Zheng et al., eds. 1981. *China's Population: Problems and Prospects.* Beijing: New World Press.

Locke, John R. [1690–1691]/n.d. *Some Thoughts on Education and an Essay on the Consequences of the Lowering of Interest and Raising the Value of Money.* Included in a series of volumes. *The Works of John Locke.* London: Ward, Lock.

Longfield, Montifort. 1835/1938. "Three Lectures on Commerce and One on Absenteeism." Reprinted. London: Univ. of London Press.

Lopez, R. S., and I. W. Raymond, eds. 1967. *Medieval Trade in the Medieval World.* New York: Norton.

Lord Ernle [R. E. Prothero] 1912/1971. *English Farming: Past and Present.* 6th ed. London: Heinemann.

Luther, Martin. 1520/1947. "Open Letter to the Christian Nobility of the German Nation Concerning the Reform of the Christian Estate." In *Three Treatises.* Philadelphia: Muhlenberg Press.

Luxemburg, Rosa. 1913/1968. *The Accumulation of Capital.* New York: Monthly Review Press.

Lydall, H. 1968. *The Structure of Earnings.* Oxford: Oxford Univ. Press.

Lynn, F. 1966. "An Investigation of the Rate of Development of and Diffusion of Technology in Our Modern Industrial Society." National Commission on Technology, Automation and Economic Progress. In *Technology and the American Economy*, App. 7, "Employment Impact Technological Change." Washington, D.C.: GPO.

Lyons, T. P. 1986. "Explaining Economic Fragmentation in China: A Systems Approach." *Journal of Comparative Economics* 10:209–36.

Lyuboshits, S. L. I. 1949. *Problems of Marxist-Leninist Theory of Agrarian Crises*. (in Russian) Moscow: Gospolitizad.

McManners, J. 1985. "Tithe in Eighteenth Century France: A Focus of Rural Anti-clericalism." In *History, Society and the Churches*, edited by D. Beales and G. Best. Cambridge: Cambridge Univ. Press.

McWilliams, Carey. 1939. *Factories in the Field: The Story of Migratory Farm Labor in California*. Boston: Little, Brown.

Machiavelli, N. 1513–1521/1950. *The Prince and the Discourses*. New York: Modern Library.

———. 1525/1909. *Florentine History*. London: Everyman Library.

Makhov, A. S., and A. S. Frish. 1969. *Society and Economic Relations*. Moscow: Progress.

Malthus, T. R. 1798/1914. *An Essay on the Principles of Population, as It Affects the Future Improvement of Society. With Remarks on the Speculations of Mr. Godwin, M. Condorcet and Other Writers*. (title altered somewhat in later editions) 2 vols. Rev. 7th ed. London: Everyman.

Mancke, R. B. 1974. *The Failure of U.S. Energy Policy*. New York: Columbia Univ. Press.

Mandel, E. 1972/1978. *Late Capitalism*. London: Verso.

Mann, M. A. 1986. *History of Power from the Beginning to A.D. 1760*. (forthcoming trilogy.). Vol. 1, *The Sources of Social Power*. Cambridge: Cambridge Univ. Press.

Mantoux, Paul. 1906/1961. *The Industrial Revolution in the Eighteenth Century*. Rev. ed. London: J. Cape.

Mao Tse Tung (translated also as Mao Zedong). 1961–1977. *Selected Works of Mao Tse Tung*. (contents initially published between 1926–1957). 5 vols. Beijing: Foreign Language Press.

———. 1958–1960/1977. *A Critique of Soviet Economics*. Monthly Review Press.

Marrese, M., and J. L. Mitchell. 1984. Review of Kornai, *Economics of Shortage*. *Journal of Comparative Economics* 8:74–84.

Marshall, Alfred. 1919. *Industry and Trade*. London: Macmillan.

———. 1890–1920. *Principles of Economics*. 8th ed. London: Macmillan.

Marx, Karl. 1862–1863/1963–1971. *Theories of Surplus Value*. 3 vols. Moscow: Progress.

———. 1863–1878/1967. *Capital: A Critique of Political Economy*. 3 vols. (Years of original publication in German noted in brackets.) Vol. 1 *The Process of Capitalist Production* [1867]. Vol. 2, *The Circulation Process of Capital* [1885]. Vol. 3, *The Process of Capitalist Production as Whole* [1894]. New York: International Publishers.

———. 1858/1971. *Contribution to the Critique of Political Economy*. New York: International Publishers.

———. 1857–1858/1973. *Grundrisse: Foundations to the Critique of Political Economy*. New York: Random House.

_____. 1973. *Karl Marx on the First International.* Edited by S. Padover. New York: McGraw-Hill.

Marx, Karl, and Frederick Engels. 1845–1895/1970. *On Britain.* Moscow: Foreign Language Press.

_____. 1841–1870/1974–1986. *Collected Works* (in process). 21 vols. New York: International Publishers.

_____. 1850–1894/n.d. *On Colonialism.* Moscow: Foreign Language Press.

_____. 1845–1846/1964. *The German Ideology.* Moscow: Progress.

_____. 1845–1891/1972. *Ireland and the Irish Question.* New York: International Publishers.

_____. 1845–1895/1970. *Selected Works.* 3 vols. Moscow: Progress.

Marvel, H. P. 1977. "Factory Regulation: A Reinterpretation of Early English Experience." *Journal of Law and Economics,* vol. 20.

Mather, F. C. 1967. *Public Order in the Age of the Chartists.* New York: Kelly.

Mathews, R. C. O. 1959. *The Business Cycle.* Chicago: Univ. of Chicago Press.

Mathieson, W. L. 1926. *British Slavery and Its Abolition, 1823-1838.* London: Longman Green.

_____. 1932. *British Slave Emancipation, 1838-1849.* London: Longman Green.

Mayhew, Mathew. 1861–1862. *London Labour and the London Poor: Cyclopedia of the Condition and Earnings of Those That Will Work, That Cannot Work and Those That Will Not Work.* 4 vols. London: Griffin Bohn.

Mead, W. J. 1977. *Transporting Natural Gas from the Artic: The Alternative Systems.* Washington, D.C.: American Enterprise Institute.

Melichar, E. 1984. "A Financial Perspective on Agriculture." *Federal Reserve Bulletin* (Jan.):1–13.

Menshikov, S. 1975. *The Economic Cycle: Postwar Developments.* Moscow: Progress.

Mieskowski, Peter. 1969. "The Incidence Theory: The Effect of Taxes on the Distribution of Income." *Journal of Economic Literature* 7 (Dec.).

Mikhasuik, I. 1979. "The Economic Evaluation of Land and the Improvement of Rental Relationships in the USSR." *Problems of Economics* (Feb.).

Mill, John Stuart. 1831–1870/1963. *Essays on Politics and Culture.* New York: Doubleday.

_____. 1859–1861/1910. *Utilitarianism, Liberty and Representative Government.* London: Everyman.

Mills, Edwin S. 1978. *The Economics of Environmental Quality.* New York: Norton.

Mincer, Jacob. 1970. "The Distribution of Labor Incomes: A Survey with Special Reference to the Human Capital Approach." *Journal of Economic Literature.* 8 (Mar.).

Mingay, C. L. 1956. "The Agricultural Depression, 1730–1750." *Economic History Review* 8, 2d ser. (Apr.):323–38.

Miskimin, Harry A. 1975. *The Economy of Early Renaissance Europe, 1300-1460.* Cambridge: Cambridge Univ. Press.

_____. 1977. *The Economy of Later Renaissance Europe, 1460-1600.* Cambridge: Cambridge Univ. Press.

Mitchell, B. R. 1962. *Abstract of British Historical Statistics.* Cambridge: Cambridge Univ. Press.

Mitchell, W. C. 1927. *Business Cycles: The Problem and Its Setting.* New York: NBER.

_____. 1913/1950. *Business Cycles and Their Causes* [Part III of original 1913 Monograph]. Berkeley: Univ. of California Press.

_____. 1951. *What Happens during Business Cycles.* New York: NBER.

Mitchell, R. J., and M. D. R. Leys. 1963. *A History of London Life.* Harmondsworth: Penguin.

Mokyr, J. 1983. *Why Ireland Starved: A Quantitative and Analytical History of the Irish Economy, 1800-1850.* London: G. Allen and Unwin.

Montesquieu, Baron de. 1748/1899. *The Spirit of Laws.* 2 vols. New York: Colonial Press.

Montias, J. M. 1976. *The Structure of Economic Systems.* New Haven: Yale Univ. Press.

Moore, B., Jr. 1967. *Social Origins of Dictatorship and Democracy.* Harmondsworth: Penguin.

Mousnier, R. 1970. *Peasant Uprisings in the Seventeenth Century: France, Russia, and China.* New York: Harper and Row.

Moynihan, D. P. 1973. *The Politics of a Guaranteed Income.* New York: Random House.

Mumford, Lewis. 1934. *Technics and Civilization.* New York: Harcourt, Brace.

_____. 1961. *City in History: Its Origins, Its Transformations, and Its Prospects.* New York: Harcourt, Brace.

Mundy, J. H., and P. Riesenberg, eds. 1958. *The Medieval Town.* Princeton, N.J.: Van Nostrand.

Musgrave, R. A. 1951. "Distribution of Tax Payments by Income Groups: A Case Study for 1948." *National Tax Journal.* Vol 6.

_____. 1964. "Estimating the Distribution of the Tax Burden." *Income and Wealth* 8:186-219.

Myers, R. H. 1970. *Peasant Economy: Agricultural Development in Hopei and Shantung, 1890-1919.* Cambridge: Harvard Univ. Press.

Myrdal, Jan. 1965. *Report from a Chinese Village.* New York: New American Library.

Nadiri, M. I. 1970. "Some Approaches to the Theory and Measurement of Total Factor Productivity: A Survey." *Journal of Economic Literature* 8 (Dec.):1137-77.

Needham, Joseph. 1954–1978. *Science and Civilization in China.* 5 vols. Cambridge: Cambridge Univ. Press.

_____. 1964. *The Development of Iron and Steel Technology in China.* Cambridge: Newcomen Society.

Nef, John U. 1932. *The Rise of the British Coal Industry.* 2 vols. London: Cass.

_____. 1943. "The Industrial Revolution Reconsidered." *Journal of Economic History* 3 (May).

_____. 1940/1961. *Industry and Government in France and England, 1540-1650.* Ithaca: Cornell Univ. Press.

Nehru, J. 1944/1961. *The Discovery of India.* Bombay: Asia Publishing House.

Neveaux, Hugue. 1980. *Vie et Déclin d'une Structure Économique: Les Grains du Cambresis* (fin du XIVᵉ debut du XVIIᵉ siecle). Paris: École des Hautes Études en Sciences Sociales.

Newhouse, W. J. 1959. *Constitutional Uniformity and Equality in State Taxation.* Ann Arbor: Legal Publications, Univ. of Michigan Law School.

Nolan, P. 1976. "Collectivization in China: Some Comparisons with the USSR." *Journal of Peasant Studies* 3 (Jan.):192-217.

Nove, Alex. 1968. *The Soviet Economy.* 3d ed. rev. London: Allen and Unwin.

_____. 1969. *An Economic History of the USSR.* Harmondsworth: Penguin.

Novosti Press Agency Publishing House, ed. 1965. *Soviet Economic Reform: Main Features and Aims.* Moscow: Novosti.

Oakshott, K. 1982. "Spain: The Mondragon Performance." In *Performance of Labour-Managed Firms,* edited by F. H. Stephen. London: Macmillan.

O'Connor, James. 1973. *The Fiscal Crisis of the State.* New York: St. Martins.

O'Dell, A. C., and P. S. Richards. 1956/1971. *Railways and Geography.* London: Hutchinson Univ. Library.

O'Hagen, J. W., ed. 1984. *The Economy of Ireland: Policy and Performance.* 4th ed. Dublin: Irish National Institute.

Oliver, R., and I. D. Fage. 1966. *A Short History of Africa.* 2d ed. Harmondsworth: Penguin.

Oman, Sir Charles. 1937. *A History of the Art of War in the Sixteenth Century.* London: Methuen.

Origo, I. 1957. *The Merchant of Prato, 1335–1410: F. Di Marco Datini.* New York: Knopf.

Outhwaite, R. B. 1986. "The Progress and Backwardness in English Agriculture, 1500–1650." *Economic History Review* 39, 2d ser. 1:1–18.

PACCA (Borbach, Roger, et al.). 1984. *Changing Course: Blueprint for Peace in Central America and the Caribbean.* Washington, D.C.: Institute for Policy Studies.

Pan, Ku. 1950. *Food and Money in Ancient China: The Earliest Economic History of China to 25 A.D..* Edited and translated by N. L. Swann. Princeton: Princeton Univ. Press.

Parsons, T. 1971. *The System of Modern Societies.* Englewood Cliffs, N.J.: Prentice-Hall.

Perazich, B., and P. M. Field. 1940. *Industrial Research and Changing Technology.* Philadelphia: Works Progress Administration.

Perkins, D., and S. Yusuf. 1984. *Rural Development in China.* Baltimore: Johns Hopkins Univ. Press.

Perlman, R. 1969. *Labor Theory.* New York: Wiley.

Perlman, Selig. 1928. *A Theory of the Labor Movement.* New York: Kelley.

Petit, P. 1976. *Pax Romana.* Berkeley: Univ. of California Press.

Petty, Sir William. 1655–1656/1751. *The History of the Survey of Ireland: The Down Survey.* Edited by T. A. Larcon. Dublin: Irish Archaeological Society.

_____. 1662–1687/1899. *The Economic Writings of Sir William Petty.* 2 vols. Edited by C. H. Hull. Cambridge: Cambridge Univ. Press.

Pickersgil, G. M., and J. E. Pickersgil. 1974. *Contemporary Economic Systems.* Englewood Cliffs, N.J.: Prentice-Hall.

Pike, E. R., 1966. ed. *Human Documents of the Industrial Revolution in Britain.* London: Allen and Unwin.

Pirenne, H. 1936. *Economic and Social History of Medieval Europe.* London: Routledge and Kegan Paul.

Pliny (Younger). 1963. *Letters of the Younger Pliny.* Harmondsworth: Penguin.

Plutarch. [1864.] *The Lives of the Noble Grecians and Romans.* Reprint. New York: Modern Library.

Polanyi, K. 1944. *The Great Transformation.* New York: Rinehart.

Postan, M. M. 1973. *Essays on Medieval Agriculture and General Problems of the Medieval Economy.* Cambridge: Cambridge Univ. Press.

_____. 1975. *Medieval Economy and Society.* Harmondsworth: Penguin.

Power, Eileen. 1924. *Medieval People*. London: Methuen.

Preobrazhensky, E. 1925/1965. *The New Economics*. Oxford: Clarendon Press.

Progress Publications., ed. 1975. *Present-day China: Socio-Economic Problems*. Moscow: Progress.

Prybyla, J. S. 1978. *The Chinese Economy*. Columbia: Univ. of South Carolina Press.

Rabkena, N. E., and N. M. Rimashevskaia. 1979. "Distribution Relations and Social Development." *Problems of Economics* 7 (July).

Radin, Max. 1917. *Handbook of Roman Law*. St. Paul: St. Paul Publishing.

Ragatz, L. J. 1928. *The Fall of Planter Class in the British Caribbean, 1763–1833*. New York: Century.

Randall, James E. 1987. "Household Production in an Industrialized Society." Ph.D. diss., Department of Geography, University of Washington.

Reddaway, T. F. 1940. *The Rebuilding of London*. London: J. Cape.

Reischauer, E. O. 1955. *Ennin's Travels in T'ang China*. New York: Ronald.

Resnick, S. 1986. Review of Gottlieb, *A Theory of Economic Systems*. *Journal of Economic History* 46 (Mar.):305–6.

Ricardo, David. 1817/1911. *The Principles of Political Economy and Taxation*. London: Everyman.

Richman, Barry. 1969. *Industrial Society in Communist China*. New York: Random House.

Rives, J. 1976. *Dime et sociète dans l'Archveche d'Auch au XVIII^c siecle*. Paris: Bibliotheque National.

Robinson, G. T. 1932. *Rural Russia under the Old Regime: A History of the Landlord-Peasant World: A Prologue to the Peasant Revolution of 1917*. New York: Longman Green.

Robinson, Joan. 1969. *The Cultural Revolution in China*. Harmondsworth: Penguin.

Rodney, Walter. 1970. *A History of the Upper Guinea Coast, 1545–1800*. Oxford: Oxford Univ. Press.

Rogers, J. E. T. 1883. *Six Centuries of Work and Wages*. New York: Putnam.

Rörig, Fritz. 1967. *The Medieval Town*. Berkeley: Univ. of California Press.

Rosenberg, Nathan. 1972. *Technology and American Economic Growth*. New York: Harper and Row.

Rostow, W. W. 1948. *British Economy of the Nineteenth Century*. Oxford: Oxford Univ. Press.

Roundell, Earl Selborne. 1888. *Ancient Facts and Fictions Concerning Churches and Tithes*. London: Macmillan.

Ste. Croix, G. E. M. d.e. 1981. *The Class Struggle in the Ancient Greek World from the Archaeological World to the Arab Conquest*. London: Duckworth.

Salaman, R. 1949/1985. *The History and Social Influence of the Potato*. Edited by J. G. Hawkes. Cambridge: Cambridge Univ. Press.

Schmoller, Gustav. 1884/1967. *The Mercantile System and Its Historical Significance*. Reprint. New York: Kelley.

Schram, Stuart. 1969. *The Political Thought of Mao-Tse-Tung*. 2d ed. Harmondsworth: Penguin.

———, ed. 1974. *Chairman Mao Talks to the People: Talks and Letters, 1956–1971*. New York: Random House.

Schultz, Henry. 1938. *The Theory and Measurement of Demand*. Chicago: Univ. of Chicago Press.

Schumpeter, J. 1939. *Business Cycles: A Theoretical Historical and Statistical*

Analysis of the Capitalistic Process. 2 vols. New York: McGraw-Hill.

———. 1954. *History of Economic Analysis.* New York: Oxford Univ. Press.

Schurmann, Franz. 1968. *Ideology and Organization in Communist China.* 2d ed. Berkeley: Univ. of California Press.

Schwartz, Solomon. 1954. *Russia's Soviet Economy.* 2d. ed. Englewood Cliffs, N.J.: Prentice-Hall.

Scoville, W. C. 1960. *The Persecution of Huguenots and French Economic Development, 1680–1720.* Berkeley: Univ. of California Press.

———. 1967. "Government Regulation and Growth in the French Paper Industry during the Eighteenth Century." *American Economic Review Proceedings* (May):283–93.

Seager, Henry R. 1910. *Social Insurance: A Program for Social Reform.* New York: Macmillan.

Seé, H. 1927. *Economic and Social Conditions in France during the Eighteenth Century.* New York: Knopf.

Seligman, E. R. A. 1892. "The Taxation of Corporations." *Political Science Quarterly* 5, no. 2:269–308, no. 3:438–67, no. 4:636–76.

———. 1908. *Progressive Taxation in Theory and Practice.* 2d ed. Princeton: American Economic Association.

Sering, M. 1925. *Agarkrise und Agrarzoelle.* Berlin: Gruyter.

Selzer, L. H. 1955. *Interest As a Source of Personal Income and Tax Revenue.* Occasional Paper 51. New York: NBER.

Shanin, Teodor, ed. 1971. *Peasants and Peasant Societies.* Harmondsworth: Penguin.

———. 1972. *The Awkward Class. Political Sociology of the Peasantry in a Developing Society: Russia 1910–1925.* Oxford: Clarendon Press.

Shapiro, Leonard. 1964. *The Government and Politics of the Soviet Union.* Rev. ed. New York: Random House.

Sherman, Howard. 1969. *The Soviet Economy.* Boston: Little, Brown.

Shinohara, M. 1962. *Growth and Cycles in the Japanese Economy.* Tokyo: Kinokuniya.

Shmelv, G. 1979. "The Private Household Plot in CMEA Countries." *Problems of Economics* (May).

Shonfield, Andrew. 1965. *Modern Capitalism. The Changing Balance of Public and Private Power.* Oxford: Oxford Univ. Press.

Shoup, Carl S. 1972. "Quantitative Research in Taxation and Government Expenditures." *Public Expenditures and Taxation.* 50th Anniversary Colloquium. New York: NBER.

Simiand, F. 1932. *Le Salaire, l'evolution sociale et la monnaie.* 3 vols. Paris: Alcan.

Slicher van Bath, B. H. 1959/1963. *The Agrarian History of Western Europe,* A.D. *500–1850.* London: Arnold.

———. 1967. "The Yields of Different Crops (Mainly Cereals) in Relation to the Seed. c. 500–1820." *Acta Historiae Neerlandica* 2:26–106.

———. 1978. "Agriculture in the Vital Revolution." In *Cambridge Economic History of Europe,* edited by J. H. Clapham and E. Power, 5:42–132.

Slichter, Sumner. 1951. *What's Ahead for American Business.* Boston: Little, Brown.

———. 1954. "Do Wage-Fixing Arrangements in the American Labor Market Have an Inflationary Bias?" *American Economic Review Proceedings* (May):322–46.

_____. 1961. *Economic Growth in the United States.* New York: Macmillan.

Sloan, Alfred P., Jr. 1965. *My Years with General Motors.* New York: Macfadden-Bartell.

Smith, Adam. 1776/1937. *An Enquiry into the Nature and Causes of the Wealth of Nations.* Edited by E. Cannan from 5th ed. New York: Modern Library.

Smith, James D., ed. 1975. *The Personal Distribution of Income and Wealth.* New York: NBER.

Smout, T. C. 1982. "Born Again at Cambusland: New Evidence on Popular Religion and Literacy in Eighteenth-Century Scotland." *Past and Present* 97(Nov.):114–28.

Solo, R. A. 1967. *Economic Organizations and Social Systems.* Indianapolis: Bobbs-Merrill.

Solow, B. L. 1971. *The Land Question and the Irish Economy, 1870–1903.* Cambridge: Harvard Univ. Press.

Soltow, Lee, ed. 1969. *Six Papers on the Size Distribution of Wealth and Income.* New York: NBER.

Sombart, Werner. 1902. *Der Moderne Kapitalismus.* 2 vols. Leipzig: Duncker and Humblot.

_____. 1928. *Der Moderne Kapitalismus.* 2d. ed., vol. 3, pt. 2. Munich: Duncker and Humblot.

Sorokin, P. 1937. *Social and Cultural Dynamics.* Vol. 3, *Fluctuation of Social Relationships: War and Revolution.* New York: American Books.

Sosnovy, L. 1954. *The Housing Problem in the Soviet Union.* New York: Research Program on the USSR.

Spectator, M. (pseudonym for M. I. Nachimson, in Russian). *Theory of Agricultural Crisis.* Moscow: International Agrarian Institute.

Spence, J. 1975. *Emperor of China: Self-Portrait of K'ang-Hsi.* New York: Random House.

Spykman, N. J. 1942. *American Strategy in World Politics.* New York: Random House.

Stalin, Joseph. 1928. *Leninism.* New York: International Publishers.

_____. 1933. *Speech at the First All-Union Congress of Collective Farm Shock Brigade Workers, February 1933.* Moscow: Cooperative Publishing House.

Steele, E. D. 1974. *Irish Land and British Politics.* Cambridge: Cambridge Univ. Press.

Stephen, F. H., ed. 1982. *The Performance of Labour-Managed Firms.* London: Macmillan.

Stern, B. J. 1937. "Resistance to the Adoption of Technological Trends." In *Technological Trends and National Policy: Including the Social Implications of New Inventions.* Edited by National Resources Committee. Washington, D.C.: GPO.

Stigler, G. C. 1952. *Theory of Price.* 2d ed. New York: Macmillan.

_____. 1963. *Capital and Rates of Return in Manufacturing Industries.* New York: NBER.

Summerson, J. 1962. *Georgian London.* Rev. ed. Harmondsworth: Penguin.

Sutherland, N. M. 1980, *The Huguenot Struggle for Recognition.* New Haven: Yale Univ. Press.

Sung Ying-Hsing. 1966. *Chinese Technology in the Seventeenth Century.* Philadelphia: Pennsylvania Univ. Press.

Sweezy, Paul. 1980. *Post-Revolutionary Society.* New York: Monthly Review Press.

Sweezy, Paul, and Charles Bettleheim. 1971. *On the Transition to Socialism.* New York: Monthly Review Press.

Swift, Jonathan. 1727/1850. "A Short View of the State of Ireland." In *The Works of Jonathan Swift,* Vol. 12. London: Bohn.

Tawney, R. H. 1926/1947. *Religion and the Rise of Capitalism: A Historical Study.* New York: New American Library.

Taylor, H. C. 1919. *Agricultural Economics.* New York: Macmillan.

Teggart, F. J. 1939. *Rome and China: A Study of Correlations in Historical Events.* Berkeley: Univ. of California Press.

Thierry, Augustin. 1825/1907. *The Norman Conquest of England. 2 vols.* London: Everyman.

Thirsk, Joan, ed. 1984–1985. *The Agrarian History of England and Wales.* Vol. 5. *1640–1750.* Cambridge: Cambridge Univ. Press.

Thomas, R., and R. Bean. 1974. "The Fishers of Men: The Profits of the Slave Trade." *Journal of Economic History* (Dec.).

Thomas, W. I., and F. Znaniecki. 1918/1958. *The Polish Peasant in Europe and America.* 2 vols. New York: Dover.

Thompson, E. P. 1966. *The Making of the English Working Class.* New York: Random House.

Throop, A. W. 1968. "The Union-Nonunion Wage Differential and Cost-Push Inflation." *American Economic Review* 58(Mar.).

Tierney, B. 1964. *The Crisis of Church and State, 1050–1300.* Englewood-Cliffs, N.J.: Prentice-Hall.

Tigar, M. E., and M. R. Levy. 1977. *Law and the Rise of Capitalism.* New York: Monthly Review Press.

Tilly, C. 1964. *The Vendée.* Cambridge: Harvard Univ. Press.

Timoshenko, V. 1935. *World Agriculture and the Depression, 1929–1933.* Ann Arbor, Mich.: Univ. of Michigan Business School.

Tobin, James. 1981. "Reaganomics and Economics." *New York Review of Books.* Republished in *Congressional Record, 24 Nov.,* S14070–72.

Tone, Wolfe. 1973. *Freedom the Wolfe Tone Way.* Edited by J. Bennett. Tralee: Anvil Books.

Treasure, G. R. R. 1972. *Cardinal Richelieu and the Development of Absolutism.* New York: St. Martin's.

Trollope, Anthony. 1848/1982. *The Kelly and the O'Kelleys or Landlords and Tenants.* Oxford: Oxford Univ. Press.

Trotsky, Leon D. 1932. *History of the Russian Revolution.* Vol. 1. New York: Simon and Schuster.

_____. 1937. *The Revolution Betrayed: What Is the Soviet Union and Where Is It Going?* New York: Doubleday.

_____. 1923/1943. *The New Course.* New York: New International.

T'ung Tsu Ch'u. 1961. *Law and Society in Traditional China.* Paris: La Have.

_____. 1962. *Local Government in China under the Ching.* Cambridge: Harvard Univ. Press.

Turnbull, J. G., C. A. Williams, and E. F. Cheit. 1967. *Economic and Social Security.* 3d ed. New York: Ronald.

Twitchett, D. C. 1953/1970. *Financial Administration under the T'ang Dynasty.* 2d ed. Cambridge: Cambridge Univ. Press.

_____. 1969. "Merchant, Trade and Government in Late T'ang." *Asia Minor* 14:63–95.

Twitchett, D. C., and J. K. Fairbanks. 1979. *The Cambridge History of China.*

Vol. 3. *Sui and T'ang China, 589–906.* Cambridge: Cambridge Univ. Press.

USSR. Academy of Sciences. Institute of Economics. 1957. *Political Economy: A Text Book.* London: Laurence and Wishart.

USSR. Central Statistical Board. 1980, 1981. *The USSR in Figures: Statistical Handbook.* Moscow: Statistika.

USSR. Soviet Union. 1978. *Constitution: Adopted at the Seventh Special Session of Supreme Soviet of the USSR, October 1977.* Moscow: Novosti.

U.S. Congress. *Congressional Record. Proceedings and Debates.* Published each day a house of Congress is in session.

_____. Senate. 1957. Committee on Judiciary. *Hearings. Administered Prices.* 85th Cong., 1st sess. Washington, D.C.: GPO.

_____. Senate. 1973. Committee on Interior. Print. *Presidential Energy Statements.* 92d Cong., 1st sess. Washington, D.C.: GPO.

_____. House. 1977. Committee on Interior and Insular Affairs. *Hearings. Transportation of Alaskan Natural Gas.* 94th Cong., 1st sess. Washington D.C.: GPO.

_____. JEC. Annual *Report.* Washington, D.C.: GPO.

_____. *JEC. Hearings and Compendium of Papers.* Dec. 1957. *Policy for Commercial Agriculture: Its Relations to Economic Growth and Stability.* 85th Cong., 1st sess. Washington, D.C.: GPO.

_____. *Hearings.* Jan. 1968. *JEC. The Wage Price Issue.* 90th Cong., 2d sess. Washington, D.C.: GPO.

_____. *Hearings.* 1977. *JEC. Allocation of Resources in the Soviet Union and China.* 94th Cong., 1st sess. Washington, D.C.: GPO.

_____. *Hearings.* May 1980. *JEC. Forecasting the Supply Side of the Economy.* 95th Cong., 2d sess. Washington, D.C.: GPO.

_____. Print. May 1980. *JEC. A Comparison of Econometric Models.* 95th Cong., 2d sess. Washington, D.C.: GPO.

_____. *JEC. Compendium of Papers and Studies.* 1962. *Dimensions of Soviet Economy* (published as annex to hearings of same title). 87th Cong., 2d sess. Washington, D.C.: GPO.

_____. *JEC. Compendium of Papers and Studies.* 1966. *New Directions in the Soviet Economy.* 89th Cong., 2d sess. Washington, D.C.: GPO.

_____. 1967. *JEC. Compendium of Papers and Studies. An Economic Profile of Mainland China.* 90th Cong., 1st sess. Washington, D.C.: GPO.

_____. 1973. *JEC. Compendium of Papers and Studies. Soviet Economic Prospects for the Seventies.* 92d Cong., 1st sess. Washington, D.C.: GPO.

_____. 1974. *JEC. Compendium of Papers and Studies. Reorientation and Commercial Relations of the Economies of Eastern Europe.* 92d Cong., 2d sess. Washington, D.C.: GPO.

_____. 1976. *JEC. Compendium of Papers and Studies. Soviet Economy in a New Perspective.* 93d Cong., 2d sess. Washington, D.C.: GPO.

_____. 1977. *JEC. Compendium of Papers and Studies. East European Economies Post-Helsinki.* 94th Cong., 1st sess. Washington, D.C.: GPO.

U.S. Government. Council on Environmental Quality. Annual *Reports* (since 1970). Washington, D.C.: GPO.

_____. June 1966. National Commission of Food Marketing. *From Farmer to Consumer.* Washington, D.C.: GPO.

_____. 1969. National Commission of Urban Problems (chaired by Paul Douglas). *Building the American City.* Washington, D.C.: GPO.

_____. Annual. Executive. *Economic Report of the President.* Washington, D.C.: GPO.

_____. Internal Revenue Service (Supplement to Statistics of Income). 1973. *Personal Wealth.* Estimated from Estate Tax Returns, No. 482. Washington, D.C.: GPO.

U.S. Department of Commerce. 1951. *National Income and Product of the United States, 1929-1950.* (As Supplement to the *Survey of Current Business.*) Washington, D.C.: GPO.

_____. Office of Price Administration. 1947. Historical Reports No. 8. *Problems in Price Control: Pricing Techniques.* Edited by H. C. Mansfield. Washington, D.C.: GPO.

U.S. Bureau of Census. Annual. *Statistical Abstract of the United States.* Washington, D.C.: GPO.

_____. 1960. *Historical Statistics of the United States Since Colonial Times to 1957.* Washington, D.C.: GPO.

U.S. Department of Health, Education, and Welfare. 1982. *Social Security Handbook.* 7th ed. Washington, D.C.: GPO.

U.S. Tariff Commission. Feb. 1973. *Implications of Multinational Firms for World Trade and Investment and for U.S. Trade and Labor.* (Report to Senate Finance Committee.) Washington, D.C.: GPO.

Unger, R. W. 1980. "Dutch Herring, Technology and International Trade in the Seventeenth Century." *Journal of Economic History* (June).

Usher, A. P. 1943. *The Early History of Deposit Banking in Mediterranean Europe.* Cambridge: Harvard Univ. Press.

Vakhrshev, Vasilu. 1973. *Neocolonialism: Methos and Manoeuvers.* Moscow: Progress.

Vance, W. R., ed. 1916. *Cases on the Law of Property.* St. Paul: West.

Vanek, J. 1971. *The Participatory Economy: An Evolutionary Hypothesis of a Strategy for Development.* Ithaca: Cornell Univ. Press.

Varga, Y. 1961. *Twentieth Century Capitalism.* Moscow: Foreign Language Press.

_____. 1968. *Politico-Economic Problems of Capitalism.* Moscow: Progress.

Vucinich, A. 1952. *Soviet Economic Institutions.* Stanford: Stanford Univ. Press.

Waley, D. *The Italian City Republics.* New York: McGraw Hill for World Hutchinson Library.

Walker, K. R. 1965. *Planning in Chinese Agriculture: Socialization and the Private Sector, 1956-1962.* London: Cass.

Wallace, S. 1938. *Taxation in Egypt from Augustus to Diocletian.* Princeton: Princeton Univ. Press.

Wallerstein, I. 1979. *The Capitalist World Economy: Essays.* Cambridge: Cambridge Univ. Press.

_____. 1974/1980. *The Modern World System.* New York: Academic Press. (A projected history of the capitalist world economy from the sixteenth century onward.) Vol. 1, *Capitalist Agriculture and the Origins of the European World Economy in the Sixteenth Century.* Vol. 2, *Mercantilism and the Consolidation of the European World Economy, 1600-1750.*

Ward, Benjamin. 1967. *The Socialist Economy: A Study of Organizational Alternatives.* New York: Random House.

_____. 1968. "Political Power and Economic Change in Yugoslavia." *American Economic Review Proceedings* (May).

———. 1969. "What Is Distinctive About Contemporary Capitalism?" *Journal of Economic Issues* 3(Mar.).

Ward, J. R. 1974. *The Finance of Canal Building in the Eighteenth Century England.* Oxford: Oxford Univ. Press.

Ward, J. T. 1962. *The Factory Movement.* London: Macmillan.

Warmington, E. H. 1928. *The Commerce between the Roman Empire and India.* Cambridge: Cambridge Univ. Press.

Warner, W. L. 1962. *The Corporation in Emergent American Society.* New York: Harper.

Watson, A. 1982. translator and editor. *China's Search for Economic Growth.* Beijing: New World Press.

Webb, Sidney, and Beatrice Webb. 1897. *Industrial Democracy.* 2 vols. London: Longman Green.

———. 1903–1929. *English Local Government from the Revolution to the Municipal Incorporation Act, 1689–1835.* (Individual volumes deal with a wide range of topics: liquor licensing, highway administration, town, borough, and manor, poor law administration.) 11 vols. London: Longman Green.

———. 1944. *Soviet Communism: A New Civilization?* 3d ed. London: Longman Green.

Weber, Max. 1924. *Gesammelte Aufsätze zur Sozial- und Wirtschaftsgeschichte.* Tübingen: Mohr.

———. 1923/1950. *General Economic History.* Glencoe: Macmillan.

———. 1916/1964. *The Religion of China: Confucianism and Taoism.* New York: Macmillan.

———. 1921/1968. *Economy and Society: An Outline of Interpretive Sociology.* 2 vols. Berkeley: Univ. of California Press.

———. 1909/1976. *The Agrarian Sociology of Ancient Civilizations.* London: Schocken.

Weintraub, S. 1978. *Capitalism's Inflation and Unemployment: Beyond Monetarism and Keynesianism.* Reading: Addison-Wesley.

White, Lynn, Jr. 1962. *Medieval Technology and Social Change.* London: Oxford Univ. Press.

Wilbur, C. M. 1943. "Industrial Slavery in China." *Journal of Economic History* (May).

Wiles, Peter. 1974. *Distribution of Income: East and West.* Amsterdam: North-Holland.

Williams, E. 1964. *Capitalism and Slavery.* London: Deutsch.

Williams, T. D., and R. T. Dudley, eds. 1956. *The Great Famine: Studies in Irish History, 1845–1852.* Dublin: Brown and Nolan.

Wilson, C. H. 1969. *Economic History and the Historian: Collected Essays.* New York: Praeger.

Wilson, T. *A Discourse on Usury.* 1925. Edited with Introduction by R. H. Tawney. London: Bell.

Wisconsin, State of. 1978. *Blue Book 1977.* Madison: Univ. of Wisconsin Extension.

Wittfogel, K. A. 1931. *Wirtschaft und Gesellschaft Chinas: Versuch der wissenschaftliche analyse einer grosser Asiatischen agrargesellschaft.* 1st Part. *Produktions-und Zirkulationsprozess.* Leipzig: Hirschfeld.

Woodham-Smith, Cecil. 1962. *The Great Hunger: Ireland, 1845–1849.* New York: Harper and Row.

Woods, R. 1977. "Technology and Society: The Impact of Gold Mining on the Institution of Slavery in Portuguese America." *Journal of Economic History* (Mar.).

Woytinsky, W., and E. S. Woytinsky. 1953. *World Population and Production.* New York: Twentieth Century Fund.

Wright, A. F., and D. Twitchett, eds. 1973. *Perspectives on the T'ang.* New Haven: Yale Univ. Press.

Wyclif, John. 1929. *Select English Writings.* Edited by H. E. Winn. Oxford: Oxford Univ. Press.

Xiao Liang, and Qi Mingchen. 1986. "Commercialization of Dwellings and Socialist Practice." *Social Sciences in China* 7(June):77–92.

Xu Dixin et al. 1982. *China's Search for Economic Growth: The Chinese Economy Since 1949.* Beijing: New World Press.

Xue Muqiao. 1981. *China's Socialist Economy.* Beijing: Foreign Language Press.

Yang, Lien-Sheng. 1952. *Money and Credit in China: A Short History.* Cambridge: Harvard Univ. Press.

Yak-Yeow Kueh. 1984. "China's New Agricultural Policy Program: Major Economic Consequences, 1979–1983." *Journal of Comparative Economics* 8:353–75.

Young, Arthur. 1892. *Tour in Ireland, 1776–1779.* 2 vols. Edited by B. A. Wollaston Hutton. London: G. Bell.

Yoshinobu, S. 1970. *Commerce and Society in Sung China.* Ann Arbor: Univ. of Michigan Press.

Yu-Tang, Lin, ed. 1963. *The Wisdom of China.* New York: Four Square Books.

Zheng, Liu, ed. 1981. *China's Population: Problems and Prospects.* Beijing: New World Press.

Zimbalist, A. 1986. Review of Gottlieb, *A Theory of Economic Systems. Journal of Comparative Economics* 10:188–90.

Zukin, S. 1975. *Beyond Marx and Tito: Theory and Practice in Yugoslav Socialism.* Cambridge: Cambridge Univ. Press.

Index

Absentee proprietor, Ireland, 125, 310
  n.5
Africa, imperial partition, 163–64
Agrarian controls, 208
  administration of, United States, 211
  background for, 208–9
  and farm income, 209
  and farm staples, national price
    schedules of, 211–12, 334 n.85
Agrarian revolution
  China, 1930–1952, 259
  Russia and East Europe, 1917–1920,
    1944–1948, 259
Agricultural depressions, 96–97
Agriculture, modes of production
  capitalist, 126
  medieval Europe, 65–67
Anderson, Perry
  on Roman Catholic church, 54–55, 88
Avowson, right of, 58

Banking, commercial
  and expansion of trade, 112
  and Industrial Revolution, 112
  and Italian bourgeois, 64
  and role of English, 113
Bank of England, and panics and
  cyclical instability, 141–42
Bishop, and church tithes, 59
Bloc, Marc, on periods of feudalism, 87
Burckhardt, Jacob, on Roman church,
  High Renaissance, 60
Bureaucratic hierarchies, 38
Business cycles, mercantilist Europe,
  95, 96

Capitalism, use of term, xii, xiii

Capitalist economic system, 122–23
  and new regulatory interests, 143
Capitalist mode of production (CMP)
  beginnings in trade, agriculture, and
    industry, 11–12
  instability of, 214–15
  six behavioral laws of, 13
  in United Kingdom, mid-19th C, main
    branches of, 127–28
Catholic church, Roman. *See also* Tithes
  and celibacy, 56
  and income current, 57–59
  and ministry to the poor, 56
  and preservation of learning, 56
  and secular authority, 60–61
Central banks, 222
Charlemagne, 63–64
China
  civilization, early phase of, 31–32
  collectivization in, 266–68
  Cultural Revolution, 253–54
  land reform in, 261
Chinese-Roman ancient imperial
  economies, 33–34
Church and state, copartnership,
  medieval Europe, 52–53, 57, 59f,
  60
Collectivization
  and acceptance of, reasons, 172–73
  causes, 264
  and Eastern Europe, 269–71
Commodity producer
  and China, 36
  defined, 6
Common Agricultural Policy (CAP)
  Western Europe, Common Market,
  213–14
Communist party
  class and party relationships, 232

Communist party (*continued*)
dictatorship of, 232–34
Lenin's theory of, 229
membership, countries and social
strata, 230
socialist constitutional formula, USSR
and China, 231, 338 n.13
Cooperative mode of production, 15–16
Corporate mode of production
mercantilist, 109, 110–12, 305 n.89
modern, 13–15, 174
United Kingdom, mid-19th C, 128–30
Corporate profits tax, mixed economy,
198–99

Decolonization, mixed economies
authenticity of, 172
and Central America and southern
Africa, present struggles in, 171
and Latin America, 169
and nature of nationalist movements,
169–72
Demand growth, 116
Devaluation of dollar (1972–1973), 212
Domestic mode of production, 4–5, 281
n.2

Edict of Nantes (1598), 104
Education, mass, USSR, 251–52
Emmanuel, D., on home building in
Athens, 5
European Common Market, 168

Famine, Irish (1845–1848)
and causes of, 155–57
and effects of, 158, 321 n.105
and emigrants, 160
and landlord-tenant mode, 123–24,
132–33
Farm output (1685–1720), 102–3
Feudal mode of production
exploitative aspects of, 7–9
and manorial serfdom, description of,
65, 107
Friedmanism, and mixed economy, xii,
224–25
Functional priority patterns
Roman and Chinese, 43–45
United Kingdom, mid-19th C, 238

Gold mining, China, 46
Grain tariffs, United Kingdom
and income redistribution, 146–48,
157

during Irish famine, 157
Growth planning for socialist economy,
240–42

Income inequality, 250–51
Industrial Revolution, mercantilist era
coal output, United Kingdom, 94, 299
n.25
mineral output and metallurgy, 109
skills and processes fostered by, 94–
109
Inflation, 117
effect on farm markets, 98–99
Inheritance, rights of property, 40
Inheritance taxation, 197
Institutions essential to economic
systems, 22–23
International Monetary Fund (IMF), 27
Ireland and 19th C British capitalist
economy, 123–25
Irish diet and milk, 156, 320 n.98

Keynes, John Maynard
creator of macroeconomics, 116, 218–
19
on equation for analysis of price
instability, 208
on gold standard, 220
on price causation, characteristics of,
218–19
Kondratieff, N., Russian agricultural
economist, 99–100
on theory of "long waves," 99–100,
301 n.41
Kornai, J.
on price control, 247
on socialist growth planning, 243

Landis, David, on labor force and social
product dynamics, 138–39
Landlord-tenant mode of production,
10, 35
in Ireland, mid-19th C, 132–33
Law, John, 111–12, 113
Lenin, V. I. *See* Africa, imperial partition; Communist party; Luxemberg,
Rosa
as founder/leader, Russian
Communist party, 230
and Marxian theory, 232
and theory of imperialism (1917),
163–64
Locke, John, 307–8 nn.114, 116
Luxemberg, Rosa, 164

Manchester, 85
Manor, local church control by, 58–59
Mao Zedong (also Mao Tse Tung), 230
  and Cultural Revolution, 254
  and principle of permanent
    revolution, 253
Market, USSR
  and consumer goods, 273–74
  and housing, 274
Marx, Karl
  on "monetarist" mercantilism's shift to
    "commercial" mercantilism, 119
  on skilled artisan and capitalism, 110
  on trade unions, 188
Medieval economies
  Byzantine and Muslim, 54–55
  European, 54–56
Mercantilism
  commercial, 119–20
  and European economic model, 89
  and European overseas expansion, 90
  and factories, 108–9
  regulatory structure dismantled,
    United Kingdom, 142–43
Merchandizing in mercantilist
  commerce, 81, 91
Mixed economy
  and applied science, 184–85
  and Cold War setting, 179–80
  and corporate mode, 175
  and democratization by unions, 187–
    88
  and direct commodity producers,
    176–77
  labeling of, 166
  and laboratory research, 182–83
  and labor force, technical schooling
    of, 185–86
  and modal shifts of, 177–81
  and 1970s, end of, 123, 323 n.4
  and older models, 172–73
  and public mode, 178–79
  and stability, 216–17
  and U.S. hegemonic role, 167
Modes of production, eleven types
  defined and detailed, 3–17
Monetary form, mercantilist system,
  117–19
Money
  as basic institution, 23–27
  Chinese, 41–42
  European, medieval, 61–62, 64
  and inflation, 117
  Roman, 40–41
MOP. See individual modes of
  production
Multinational capitalism, late 19th C,
  161–63

Multiple modes, economic system, 19–
  20

National Bureau of Economic Research
  (NBER), 217
Newcastle, England, charter of, 85
New Economic Policy (NEP)
  advanced by Lenin, 227, 262–63
  and Chinese form of, 263
  and European satellites, 263
  and "market socialism," 263–64
  and termination of, 266
Northern Ireland, 125
North Sea, energy discoveries, 168

Offsets, USSR, measure income
  inequality of, 251
Organization for Economic Cooperation
  and Development (OECD), 167
Overseas expansion, European, 91

Parsons, Talcott, on Catholic church, 55
Peasant farms, land reform and, 261
Peasant proprietor
  China, 35, 36 n.20
  Roman Empire, 35
Peasant revolts, France, 101
Peon mode, 9–10
Petty, W., mercantilist economist, 116
Pinnacle, ruling classes, 52, 249
Poor Law, 148–49, 152
Portuguese, 90
Potato fungus, 155. See Famine
Po Valley, 90
Precious metals, New World, 91–92
Price control, socialist economy, 246–47
Price declines, farm markets, 97
Private property in land, 39
Productive forces, mercantilist period,
  93, 298 nn.16, 17
Progressive income and wealth taxation,
  195–96
Progressive income taxation, 200–201
Property, principles of
  bourgeois, 85–86
  feudal, 81–84
  summary of, 28–29
Provisionment, mercantilist system, 93–
  94
Public economy
  medieval, 78–81
  mercantilist, 114–15
Public mode of production
  Roman Empire, 36–37
  Sui-T'ang, 37

Public mode of production (*continued*)
summary of, 16, 17
Put-out manufacturing, 108

Rationalization of Irish agriculture,
157–58. *See also* Famine, Irish
Rationing, USSR
in goods and equipment, 277–79
in job markets, 275–76
Redistribution of national income
and capitalist United Kingdom, 145–
46
and mercantile system, 115
and mixed economy, 191–95, 195–202
Regulation extended
mercantilist economy, 115–16
mixed economy, 207
Roman society and state, 31–32

Sales taxation, 114, 130–32, 202, 312
n.9
Slavery
Chinese form, 35 n.14
as household drudgery and
concubinage, 7
late Roman Empire, 35 n.2
mode of production, 6
Small-holder farming, and land reform,
265
Socialist, label as, 235–37
Socialist economy "takeover," 227–28
Socialist growth planning, 237
Social Security
and income equalization, 194–95
in mixed economy, 192
Special Drawing Rights (SDR), 27
Stabilization programs, 222–23
Stalin, Joseph
and Communist party, USSR, 230
and proclaims economy socialist, 235
State, role of, 20–22
State capitalism, 235, 262–63
State control of collective farms, 270–
71, 348 nn.96, 97
Steady state norm, ix, x, 25

Stolypin reforms, 260
Systems, economic, defined, 29

Tax administration
Roman and Chinese empires, 48–49
Taxation
Roman and Chinese empires, 50–53
Third World, ix, 89–91, 123–25, 152–
55, 155–60, 169–72
Tithe collections, resistance to, 103–4
Town, bourgeois
craft and mercantile activities, 72–73
protection and specialization, 72–74
Trade unions, 189–90
Trotsky, L. D., 243

United Kingdom economy, bounds of,
123
Urban medieval growth, 68–70
U.S. hegemony, mixed economy, 167–69

Victorianism, mid-19th C, 122–23
Village community, mode of production,
5–6
Village production, reorganization of,
265

Wage earners and income tax, 200
Wage earnings, distributional
characteristics of, 193–94
Wage labor, 38
Wallerstein, E., xii, xiii
Webb, Sidney and Beatrice, 85
Welfare state, mixed economy, 203–5
West Indies, slavery in, 153–55
White, Lynn, Jr., and shift in medieval
social structure, 77–78

Yugoslavia
breaks from socialist bloc, 255, 259
worker self-management in, 256–58